Victor Pemberton' s
THE SLIDE
And Other Radio Dramas

Victor Pemberton's

THE SLIDE

And Other Radio Dramas

The Gold Watch
The Slide
Kill The Pharaoh!
The Fall of Mr Humpty
Dark

fantom publishing

First published in 2010 by Fantom Films
fantomfilms.co.uk

A catalogue record for this book is available from the British Library.

ISBN: 978-1-906263-46-1

Typeset by Phil Reynolds Media Services, Leamington Spa
Printed in Great Britain by the MPG Books Group, Bodmin and King's Lynn

Cover design by Iain Robertson

Contents

Foreword

Difficult though it is to talk or write about a close friend, there is one quality in Victor's work about which I have no reservations: he is a born storyteller. Within writers of that 'once upon a time' tradition there are those inner murmurs of a thousand and one stories, the oral narration of fables, tales and fantasies from centuries before told by firelight in jungle villages. There is an important part of Victor's writing that belongs to that tradition.

Many times, in tube trains or buses, I have noticed him observing another passenger and then something in his expression changes and one knows that he has begun to tell himself a story which he has also begun to enjoy; and why shouldn't storytellers enjoy their own stories? Often at the end of a journey he may have forgotten what it was about, but these half-glimpsed tales may later return as a solution to a commissioned story he is working on. So it is not surprising that among his dramatisations are *A Thousand and One Nights*, a brilliant adaptation using 'chroma key' for BBC Television; Edgar Wallace's *Case of the Frightened Lady*; and an adaptation for radio of Rider Haggard's *She*, a favourite of mine as I was allowed to direct it.

There is another quality in Victor's work that I particularly like and can relate to, and which is also connected with a storyteller's craft, and that is the clear contrast between the Goodies and the Baddies. At the end of all his stories Goodness triumphs and Wickedness fails. Even when dealing with characters and ideas with which he is not particularly in sympathy, he manages to understand something more about them when he has entered their worlds as a writer. It is this warm sympathy that moves so many readers of his novels.

A born storyteller? Oh yes. His Mother told me that when Victor was a boy, she and his dad bought him for his birthday a wooden desk from Woolworth's that he had wanted. She showed me where, in the scullery of their home in Islington, he would sit scribbling school essays and stories in pencil in an ordinary exercise book; and it was at that schoolboy's desk that he wrote his first plays. I remember seeing one of these masterpieces, called I believe *The Cellar*, laid out in a very professional manner. At that time, of course, it never occurred to him that he might become a writer – certainly not a playwright.

His inspiration does not come from books; he is not a great reader, though when he does get caught up in one he rattles through it like an express train. His real inspiration comes wholly from the cinema. In his books his love of films shines through. During the horrifying days of the London blitz it was the power of the screen that helped families to survive the nightmares around them. For Victor, films opened his inner creativity.

There is an example of this that I look back on with personal affection: Victor was interviewed on local radio after the publication of one of his books, and for his choice of music he chose the Tara theme from *Gone With the Wind*. When I was interviewed about being a child actor my choice was the beginning of a

Ravel Piano Concerto; on the publication of Vic's next book he chose music from *E.T.*, and I believe that illustrates perfectly the source of his inspiration.

But what came as a great surprise to me was his extraordinary professionalism. When we first met (and it is no secret that it was some time ago), I had no idea that he ever wanted to be a writer. I suspect that at that time such a thought had never seriously entered his head. So, I have often wondered, where did such a professional attitude come from? He has always insisted, regardless of personal cost, on meeting a deadline; and one of my favourite memories is of splashing around in the warm Mediterranean and watching Victor, sitting on the beach, surrounded by sheets of paper held from blowing away in the wind by large pebbles, a pencil held between his teeth, and knowing that some new bits from the play he was working on would be read to me before dinner. The ability to discuss ideas, in however embryonic a form, is a powerful force in any relationship, and I am not ashamed to admit pleasure at the ease with which trust was established between us. Consequently I became the recipient of some marvellous parts written specially for me: a school teacher escaped from East Germany, a poor South American fisherman claiming an island which had just burst out of the sea, a rather sinister Egyptian, a Tibetan soldier loyal to the Dalai Lama, a doctor in a Kentish new town, and (very much based on parts of my own life) a character returning to Sri Lanka seeking for his father.

In the wide variety of settings of Victor's plays, there is one constant quality: his instinct for good dialogue. I never heard an actor complain about that; in fact in many cases Victor was congratulated on his talent for writing speakable, naturalistic lines. Whether this came from his never-ending love affair with the cinema, or his ability to pick up the rhythms and emotional cadences of his different characters, or his admirable ability to listen and to imitate, or probably all of them, he certainly repaid the encouragement he received from BBC Radio Drama.

During his early frustrating attempts to be allowed to contribute to television he constantly came up against the comment: 'Oh, but you're a radio writer.' It took a long time for some Editors to realise that a skilled writer could function in more than one medium. There was a time when actors and actresses suffered from the same inane prejudice: that they were only 'radio actors'.

If I were asked which of Victor's radio plays were special to me, I would reply without hesitation, his trilogy of 90-minute plays based on his parents under the umbrella title *Our Family*, later turned into a successful and very moving novel. I was allowed to direct the last two plays and when it came to the death of Victor's father, and the song *Amazing Grace*, I could not see the studio for tears. From our first meeting, Mum and Dad Pemberton were like loving parents to me.

I have to add with a touch of personal pride and gratitude that Victor and I have remained close friends over the years and that our friendship has survived the many different ways we have worked together, and that any arguments that developed during those times were always solved in laughter.

David Spenser
February 2010

A note on the scripts

Dramas written for radio – just like those for television and the stage – invariably go through numerous rewrites and revisions. The scripts published in this book have been transcribed from original typescripts held by Victor Pemberton. These are mostly final drafts made just prior to recording. It is not uncommon, however, for further revisions to be made during the recording process – and of course even after recording the programme may be edited before transmission. So the scripts as they appear here may not always correspond precisely with what was actually recorded and broadcast.

A few of the typescripts – those for *Dark* and the first and last episodes of *Kill the Pharaoh!* – show handwritten alterations. These give an interesting insight into the revision process and so, to preserve as much of this information as possible, they have been included in the scripts presented here using the following notational conventions: lines that have been cut are shown struck through ~~like this~~; and lines that have been added are enclosed in square brackets [like this].

The cover sheet of each typescript includes production details such as the recording and transmission dates, cast and studio personnel involved and so on. These have been presented here in their original form. A brief glossary may be helpful in understanding these notes:

- TX – Transmission. The date on which the play or serial episode was scheduled to be first broadcast.
- RPT – Repeat. The date of the first scheduled repeat.
- R.P. No – The unique production code used internally at the BBC to identify each recording.
- S.M.s – Studio Managers. The technical personnel involved at the recording.

The original scripts have been transcribed for this book by Phil Reynolds, Robbie Dunlop and Dexter O'Neill.

3

Introduction

This book is not a full-blown autobiography, but it does contain autobiographical details about aspects of my life in relation to the career that I never expected to follow. What I am going to attempt to do is to tell you about what I was up to at the time I wrote my early radio plays that you will read here.

For me it was a very exciting time, and if I occasionally sound a bit naïve or innocent please try to understand that I did not come from a writer's background, so it was quite obvious that I was an amateur who was merely trying to learn his job. In many respects, I am still an amateur; I have always admired and been impressed by what other people can do – authors, playwrights, screenwriters – and I always will. I still stare in awe when I meet famous names in person, and it takes me a long time to take in that I am actually working with them. And I'm proud to say that I have been lucky enough to have worked with some of the most well-known names in our profession.

This book deals primarily with the first half of my career, the early years of my time as a radio script writer. As I consistently tell so many young people, in my opinion, if you want to learn how to write, radio is the perfect medium – especially for character dialogue. Here, the spoken word is what counts. You have no scenery or beautiful images to help you out, no wide screen or visual effects; it's just you – you and your pen or typewriter, or computer keyboard. Radio is where you invite the listener to build their own picture of what the characters in the play look like, and whatever setting you have given them, it is up to them to sketch it in their mind.

And remember, radio can take your mind anywhere it wants. You can set your action in the kitchen or sitting room, or at a bus stop, on a train, a ship, in any town or country, or even on any planet in the universe. *You* are the storyteller, and your listener controls what *they* want to see.

At this moment I can't actually remember how many radio plays I wrote; all I know is that there were an awful lot of them, and there are plenty more where they came from! When you read the selection made here, you will, of course, realise that writing styles have changed somewhat over the years. Many characters are not what you would expect to find today, nor indeed the way they talk.

But what the selection will do is to give you an insight into what a certain type of radio drama used to be like, whether it was transmitted on the Home Service, as Radio 4 used to be known, or the Light Programme, better known today as Radio 2. And don't forget that experimental drama was regularly broadcast on the Third Programme, which eventually became Radio 3. They were indeed the Golden Days of radio for listeners – and for writers too.

So, just for a while, sit back, turn off your PCs, MP3s, mobiles and smartphones, read the scripts, then close your eyes and cast your mind back with me to a bygone age, an age where writing styles and dialogue were somewhat different to today!

I do hope you will enjoy this short selection of plays, the first of them written only a couple of years before the creation on television of a certain Time Traveller and his companions. What you are about to read is my own contribution to radio drama, a medium I shall always cherish.

Victor Pemberton
February 2010

The Gold Watch

As the years pass by, and you start the inevitable process of looking back, you begin to wonder how and why things happened. These days I find it hard to believe that my journey through the maze of what is called 'show business' began with a simple half-hour radio play that seemed destined to shape what I clearly wanted to do with the rest of my life.

But if it hadn't been for my friendship with David Spenser, *The Gold Watch* would have remained in the dark cavity of my mind. It is no coincidence that during the course of this book, David's name will appear many times. But more of that as we go along. First of all, I want to tell you how that radio play saw the light of day, how David made it happen, and how the extraordinary circumstances surrounding the live transmission transformed not only my life, but also that of my parents, Oliver and Letty.

When David and I first met in the early 1960s, we decided to share a flat together with one of David's friends, the now well-known actor, Charles Kay. At the time, David was an actor member of the BBC Radio Drama Repertory Company, and the three of us shared what can only be described as a very warm but hilarious relationship, endlessly swapping tales of some of the plays and programmes we had criticised in the theatre, on television, and even on radio.

David and Charlie talked shop most of the time, a lot of their exchanges going above my head, for, at that period in my life, I had taken no part in 'the business' as it was called. I was a counter clerk in a travel agency, and that was all I was expected to know about. Therefore, imagine the indignant reaction I incurred when I dared to express an opinion about the play my two flatmates were discussing which we had all listened to on the radio the previous evening.

'Well if you know so much,' they snapped indignantly, 'then write something yourself.'

It was a challenge I could hardly refuse. After toiling in the early hours of every morning before work at the travel office, and in the evenings when I got home, a week later I handed David my first ever radio script. To my astonishment, he seemed genuinely impressed with it – so much so that he secretly took it to show to one of the radio drama producers he was working with at that time at the BBC.

The story of *The Gold Watch* was not only a simple statement about injustice, but it also told how ordinary people can overcome bureaucracy by just being themselves. In many ways the play was easy to write, for, as you will read in the script itself, I was spurred on by the anger and frustration I felt about what had happened to my dad, who had been badly injured in the First World War, which had resulted in the amputation of his left leg. Like many soldiers coming back from that horrifying trench war, he was desperate to find a job; and when the chance came along for him to work as a ticket collector on the London Underground, he was elated and grateful. By then he had married Letty Edginton who had come from a fairly well-to-do middle-class family in north west London, defying the protests of both their families. It wasn't easy for them, for my dad's lot were pretty rough, hard-working brickies and labourers.

When you read this play, you will understand the title. *The Gold Watch* was actually a wristwatch, which I still have to this day. After the poor old chap had to retire, he was denied a pension; his reward after 47 loyal years working on a cold ticket barrier in a North London underground station was that cheap watch, inscribed on the back: *For O.J. Pemberton – For services rendered.*

However, my parents took it all in their stride. They had struggled to survive all their married life together, and they were prepared to do the same for whatever time they had left. One thing you will notice from reading the script is that the old man's job was changed to a rather mundane clerk in a business company, because I knew it would upset him if I identified the situation too closely.

So then came the long wait whilst David, Charlie, and I waited for the reaction to my first masterpiece. David had given it to Audrey Cameron, who during that time was practically a household name in Broadcasting House. She was quite a robust, plain talking, butch lady, who never failed to remind you that once, during the blackout in World War 2, she had accidentally bumped into the Prime Minister, Winston Churchill. But she had a heart of gold, and had a high reputation for her busy schedule as a radio drama producer. Eventually, David told me what he had done, and from that moment on it was pure agony. I waited all of three weeks – three whole weeks – before I heard even a word about my poor little play. And whilst I waited, I cursed everyone I came into contact with. David was cursed (for stringing me along!), so was Charlie (for clearly knowing what rubbish I had written), and so were all the clients who turned up at the travel office counter for such boring things as airline and railway tickets and information on Butlin's Holiday Camps.

But most of all I cursed Audrey Cameron herself. Who did she think she was, I asked myself, tossing and turning in my sleep night after night? Who did she think she was in her nice, comfortable little job at Broadcasting House, with my little gem of a script at her side, unread, unloved, and above all... ignored? I remember it well – oh *so* well. When David came back to the flat after acting in a radio play, he gave me the script, and I immediately knew what the answer was going to be. Before he had said a word, in my rage I wanted to blurt out that that woman was a demon with horns on her head. Nothing more than a demon!

'She loves it,' David said, containing a smirk.

'Oh yes!' said I, not taking in what he had said. 'Well, she's a stupid old...' I stopped dead, and did a double take. 'She what?' I croaked.

'She loves it,' repeated David, with a wicked grin. 'Furthermore, she wants to do it as an Afternoon Theatre. She's already asked the Contracts Department to offer you a fee.'

I slumped back onto the sofa. For one moment I thought the steak and kidney pudding I'd had for lunch was going to throw up on me. But then my face gradually lit up. Bells were ringing in my ears. I was so elated, I could hear the London Symphony Orchestra playing a triumphant symphony inside me, a fanfare of trumpets proclaiming that I was a genius. I had done it, I had written a play that had been accepted for broadcasting. *My* play, *my* masterpiece! And then, in those few split seconds, all I could see was that face, the face of the demon.

But suddenly it wasn't a demon any more. It was a beautiful face, more beautiful than any film star I had ever seen on the screen. Audrey! That delightful, clever, intelligent, shrewd lady producer. Audrey Cameron! *Saint* Audrey!

'But –,' said David, briefly interrupting my moment of ecstasy.

I slumped back again. Oh God, I thought, why does there always have to be a 'but'? Since then I have learnt how writers, musicians, artists and even travel office clerks always have to cope with that nightmare word of the English language.

'But,' continued David, 'you have to change the ending.'

Suddenly, in my mind, the saint's halo had disintegrated; suddenly, that lady producer's face was not looking so lovely again.

'Why?' I asked haughtily. 'Why do I have to change it?'

'Because she wants a happy ending,' replied David. 'Everyone wants a happy ending. Audrey says it would be wrong to end the play on a down note.'

After I had taken it in, I took a deep breath and replied, 'A down note?' I spluttered uncomprehendingly. 'That's stupid – really stupid! Typical BBC! Typical the way producers think!'

'Typical or not,' warned David, 'if that's what they want, that's what they want.'

'That's show-biz,' added Charlie, with a shrug. He had just come home from his own acting job in a new movie.

By the end of the evening, an evening in which it was my turn to wash up after dinner, I locked myself in the tiny kitchen and started cursing everyone all over again. It's a miracle that any of the dishes survived, but they did; and as I bid goodnight to the two *professionals*, I knew exactly the kind of ending I was going to write, the kind of ending that would make everyone squirm with embarrassment.

A couple of months later, *The Gold Watch* went into rehearsal at Broadcasting House. It seemed to me that meeting Audrey Cameron face to face to discuss my work would be a debilitating experience, and on my way to the studio on that first day I really did think my knees would give way beneath me. But by the end of the morning's rehearsal, mixing with the cast and control room crew, for the first time I felt like a professional. In that studio with all those lights flicking on and off, and the sound-effects girl creating all sorts of strange noises such as creaking doors and knives and forks being used to suggest supper time, I suddenly felt as though I had arrived. There was I, in that studio, mixing with what I imagined to be all kinds of important people, the actress and actor playing my mum and dad, and all those names that I had typed onto paper for weeks on end, their fictional character names all coming to life. I felt my chest expand to bursting.

And Audrey was the essence of kindness itself. She made me laugh, I made her laugh, and despite the fact that she had forced me into writing the silliest ending in the history of drama, in those two days we became bosom pals. Yes, she loved my new ending. She just *loved* the way my hero wins a huge amount on the football pools – £75,000 – with my father getting his own back on his wicked company boss. How about that for a *happy* ending? 'They walk off into the sunset, their pockets full of money, the sound of retribution ringing in their ears.'

Yuk! But… hold on… here comes that word again… *but*… wait until you hear what happened on the day of the live transmission.

It's hard to believe that in those days plays were transmitted live on air. It wasn't until some time later that the process of rehearse/record gradually took over from the nerve-wracking ordeal of actors having to perform to millions of people – LIVE. For those two days, I had sat in the small studio at Broadcasting House, watching, listening, learning everything I could from the professionals, constantly watching that terrible bulb on the wall above the studio exit, imagining what it would be like when the green light turned to red for a live transmission. I sat there, chewing my nails down to my elbows, in my mind watching and waiting for that light to turn from green to red; and the whole thing made me feel quite ill, so much so that I told Audrey that there was no way I would be able to undergo the strain of sitting in the control room during the live transmission. In any case, I wanted to go home and listen to my masterpiece on our own radio, just like all the other listeners around the country would be doing at exactly the same time.

Saturday afternoon came, and back at the flat David, Charlie and I waited for the big moment. '*Afternoon Theatre*,' purred the announcer's voice from the loudspeaker. '*The Gold Watch* – by Victor Pemberton.' I covered my face with embarrassment. And in another part of London, I knew that my dear old mum and dad were listening proudly with the volume full up, mainly because the old chap couldn't hear too well. The play seemed to go down very well indeed, or so everyone said, and quite suddenly I felt like William Shakespeare. But I was also glad it was all over, for whilst I was listening to the end credits, it somehow felt like a bit of an anti-climax. So what, I asked myself? All that work, and it's over in a flash. But the congratulations that were showered upon me by David and Charlie made up for that void; and when my old mum and dad telephoned to say how proud they were, I felt it was all worth the effort. *But* – that word again – I still hated that ending. It was so cringe-making, so – so comfortable – so… unreal.

But at 5.45pm that Saturday afternoon the telephone rang. It was my mother to tell me that my dad had just checked his football coupons, and found that he had won that week's football pools draw. Although he discovered later that the amount he would receive was not exactly the fortune won by the character in the play – £1,500 – it was still more money than the old chap had ever seen in his entire life. To him it was indeed a huge fortune.

The national publicity this astonishing coincidence attracted nearly killed off my poor old dad. He had always been a shy, retiring and inarticulate man, and the sight of newspaper photographers outside the family's rented terraced house in Islington, waiting for him to appear in his tube uniform as he made his way to open up the underground station in the early hours of the morning, was a terrifying ordeal. But £1,500 was a lot of money in those days, and the coincidence of his winning it at the same time as the live transmission of my half-hour radio play was a story no newspaper was prepared to ignore. There was even a huge cut-out photograph of the old man at that year's *Daily Mail* Ideal Home Exhibition at Olympia in London. Yes, for him it was a huge ordeal, but for me, the start of something that would never have been possible if it hadn't been for David Spenser giving my script to that demon producer at Broadcasting House.

When I think about that first extraordinary period in my writing career, I have often wondered why a very simple little thirty-minute radio play about two very ordinary people should have appealed to listeners in all walks of life. Over the next few years, *The Gold Watch* was repeated five times on both the BBC Home Service (latterly Radio 4) and the Light Programme (now Radio 2). It then went on to be translated into different languages, and was transmitted around the world in places as far apart as South Africa to the Falkland Islands, Canada to Australia, and Italy to Lithuania.

There is, of course, a very simple answer. Anyone who spends their life working in a job that is their only means of survival can identify with those two old people. They are a mirror image of their own lives: they share their fears, and horrors of what could happen to them if, after years of dedicated service, they should lose their job, and for no fault of their own. I could never claim that *The Gold Watch* was a great piece of writing – far from it, after all it was a first attempt – but I do like to think that it is honest and truthful; my tribute to old people everywhere who never expect anything from life other than to bring up their family, and to survive whatever hardship comes their way, something that is as relevant today as it was all those years ago.

The play also gave me the chance to show my disdain for the injustice my father had to endure, a subject that had just been waiting there for me to use, to help get the anger out of my system. You can probably tell that I still have a great deal of affection for that first play, mainly because I never for one moment expected it to achieve anything more than entertain the listeners who regularly tuned into the BBC Home Service on a Saturday afternoon.

When you read *The Gold Watch*, you will be left wondering what the real characters in the play did with that £1,500. Well, after helping out all the members of their family with their inevitable generosity, they bought something they had wanted all their lives: a caravan in the English countryside.

As for me: well, I went on with my job as a counter clerk in that travel office, relishing the attention I had attracted from my colleagues there. But the lure of more writing soon became a bug, and it wasn't long before I was back at my old Everest typewriter again (which, ironically, my father bought me for my sixteenth birthday, and which I still have today).

And guess what? That demon lady producer asked me for another play! And so another thirty-minute script followed. It was called *The Beano*, about a pub outing to the sea; but the real test came when I was commissioned to write full-length plays such as, amongst others, *Ziggie*, *The Flag Wavers*, *Eyes of the Buddha*, *Dark*, *Escape to Lhasa* and, much later, my trilogy of full-length autobiographical radio plays, *Our Family*, which eventually were published as the start of a whole series of London saga novels.

Of course, television was already well in its stride, but it would be some years before I would climb aboard the Tardis to join the Doctor and his companions for six episodes of *Fury from the Deep*. Before that, there was an awful lot of writing to cope with before I even attempted to learn my craft, and a seemingly endless number of rejections with which to plaster the walls. But *The Gold Watch* gave me the unexpected kick that I needed; and that inscription on the back of my dad's wristwatch is always there to remind me that if you feel strongly enough about something, you must say so:

For O.J. Pemberton
For services rendered

The Gold Watch

A play for radio
by Victor Pemberton

Produced by Audrey Cameron

REHEARSALS:	Friday 21 July 1961	1030–1800
	Saturday 22 July 1961	1030 onwards
STUDIO:	8 B.H.	
TRANSMISSION (LIVE):	Saturday 22 July 1961	1410–1440 HOME SERVICE
R.P. No.	TLO 59815	

CAST:

Mr Skinner	Godfrey Kenton
Gladys Davis	Meg Wynn Davies
Stan Parks	James Thomason
Pam	Angela Munnion
George Moffatt	Frank Duncan
Vera	Beverley Dunn
Mollie Parks	Mary O'Farrell
Mr Dudley	Wilfred Babbage
Paul	Nigel Anthony
Voices	John Bryning, Keith Buckley,
	Anthony Hall, Andrew Irvine,
	Philip Morant, Tom Watson

Announcer This is the BBC Home Service. "Afternoon Theatre."

Music up full, fade down and hold behind

We present James Thomason as Stan Parks, Mary O'Farrell as Mollie Parks and Godfrey Kenton as Mr Skinner, in "The Gold Watch" – a new play for radio by Victor Pemberton. "The Gold Watch".

Music up full: fade out

Fade in: inter-office telephone

Skinner Yes Miss Davis?

Miss Davis It's Mr Parks from the Accounts Department to see you sir.

Skinner Who?

Miss Davis Mr Parks, sir.

Skinner Parks? Parks…? Oh, yes. What's he want?

Miss Davis He says it's private sir.

Skinner Oh – all right. Show him in.

Replaces receiver

Another increase I suppose.

Knock on door

    Come in!

Stan Good morning Mr Skinner.

Skinner Good morning.

Stan Sorry to trouble you sir.

Skinner That's all right. What's the trouble?

Stan Well sir – it's a bit of a problem. I have to give a week's notice.

Skinner Oh dear, I'm sorry to hear that. What's gone wrong?

Stan Oh, there's nothing wrong with the job sir. It's just that – well, I have to retire – on Doctor's orders.

Skinner Indeed. That is unfortunate.

Stan Believe me sir, it's nothing to do with the job.

Skinner Good. I'm glad to hear that. What appears to be the trouble?

Stan It's my leg sir. An old wound I got in the war – the First War that is. It's been playing me up something terrible these last few weeks.

Skinner Oh dear, I am sorry.

Stan I think it'll be all right after a time, but the Doctor seems to think it won't improve until I give up my job.

Skinner Well Mr Parks, all I can say is, we shall be sorry to lose you, and I'm sure your colleagues in Accounts will miss you very much.

Stan Thank you sir.

Skinner I presume you'll want to go next Friday?

Stan If that's convenient sir?

Skinner Of course. Just make certain you hand over your work to somebody else in the Department, and come and see me before you leave.

Stan Thank you sir. Er – there was something else I wanted to discuss with you Mr Skinner – if I may.

Skinner Yes?

Stan It's about the Company's low-rent houses for retired staff. I want to apply for one.

Skinner For you? How long have you been here Parks?

Stan Just coming up to 38 years sir.

Skinner (*surprised*) 38 years? My word! I didn't know that. Have you always been in the Accounts Department?

Stan Oh no sir. I worked in the Sales Department until 1940 – or was it '41…?

Skinner D'you mean to tell me you've been here all those years?

Stan Er – yes sir.

Skinner How extraordinary! Ah well you can't expect to know all the staff I suppose. Now then, let's have a look at your file.

Picks up receiver

Miss Davis (*at other end of telephone*) Yes sir?

Skinner Will you bring in Mr Parks' personal file please.

Miss Davis Yes sir.

Replaces receiver

Skinner Mr – er – Parks, I must of course warn you that these houses the Company offer, are usually only available to employees who have completed at least 40 years' unbroken employment.

Stan Well Mr Skinner sir. As you know, I haven't been here for quite 40 years, but I have given practically my whole life to the firm. I've had hardly any other job since I left school. I've seen people come and go. As a matter of fact I remember your father well sir. A fine man he was. He once presented me with a bottle of champagne in the Christmas Raffle. Told me to take it home to the wife, and tell her I bought it for her.

Skinner Ha! Just like Father.

Door opens

Thank you Miss Davis. Now, let's have a look.

Door closes

Hm. I see you were exempt from the Army in the last war.

Stan Yes sir. It was this wound.

Skinner Ah yes, what a pity. Well, it certainly appears to be an excellent record. Time-keeping has been very good…

Stan I think I've only ever been late twice…

Skinner Very few absences…

Stan I had the 'flu a couple of times…

Skinner No, it all seems very good, very good indeed.

Stan Thank you sir. D'you think I have a chance of getting a house then sir?

Skinner I'm afraid not Mr – er – Parks. As I've already mentioned, the Company rule does insist on an employment of at least 40 years. I know your record of service is exemplary – there's no question of that – but you must see that if we make an exception with one person, we shall have to do it time and time again, and we just cannot give these houses to any Tom, Dick or Harry.

Stan But surely Mr Skinner – I'm hardly any Tom, Dick or Harry? After all, I'm less than two years short of the requirement. Don't you see sir, the wife and I have been banking on this. It's not as though the firm were giving us the house, and it's only what we're entitled…

Skinner (*abruptly*) You're entitled to nothing Mr Parks! You are an employee who has given long and loyal service to this organisation, but you have also been well paid for that service, and when you terminate it…

Stan But I can't help being ill…

Skinner …and when you terminate it, you must find other means of supporting yourself. Use a little common sense man. You'll be eligible for a pension in a few years.

Stan Pension. A fat lot of good that'll do us! Then I'm to take it that nobody gets one of these houses we've been promised?

Skinner If you have completed 40 years with this company…

Stan I've worked my life for this company!

Skinner Mr Dudley has worked his life for this company, and that is considerably more than 40 years. *He* is entitled to, and is receiving, one of the Company's houses.

Stan But Mr Dudley is a Director of the firm. He can afford to buy his own house…

Skinner It's no good Mr Parks, I cannot discuss this matter with you. I fully understand how difficult the situation must be, but the only compromise I can make is to put your application before the Board of Directors at the meeting on Monday morning. Until then, I can make no further comment. Be good enough to hand your resignation in writing to Miss Davis this evening. Good morning Mr Parks.

Stan Er – good morning sir.

Door opens and closes as Stan exits

Miss Davis (*whispers*) What did he say Stan?

Stan No good I'm afraid.

Miss Davis What d'you mean?

Stan He says I haven't been here for 40 years.

Miss Davis What! That's ridiculous! D'you mean to tell me he's turned you down because of two years? I don't believe it.

Stan Afraid it's true. Anyway, he's going to ask the Board on Monday.

Miss Davis Ooh! I've never heard such a thing. Pompous old ass! After all the years you've given this firm. I call it downright disgusting. Just you wait 'til everyone hears about this!

Stan No – don't Gladys. I suppose in a way, he's right. Rules *aren't* made to be broken you know. I've worked long enough to know that.

Miss Davis You're out of your mind Stan! Surely you're not going to let him get away with this?

Stan It's not a question of…

Miss Davis The whole trouble Stan Parks, is that you aren't a Director. Now if your name were Dudley…

Stan Mr Dudley is a Director of the firm Gladys, *and* he's been here for over 40 years. He's entitled to…

Miss Davis Oh, don't Stan! You sound just like him in there! Now you listen to me. It you let him get away with this, you're a bigger fool than I've ever taken you for.

Stan That's enough now Gladys! I don't want any more of this!

Miss Davis Oh…!

Stan Anyway, let's wait and see what happens on Monday. I must go…

Miss Davis Oh Stan – before you go, there is just one thing.

Stan Yes?

Miss Davis I suppose George Moffatt will be taking over your job?

Stan Yes, I suppose he will.

Miss Davis That means there'll be a vacancy in Accounts?

Stan That's right. Why?

Miss Davis Well, my young man – you know, you met him at the staff dance last Christmas…

Stan Oh yes.

Miss Davis …well, he's been trying to get a job with this firm for ages – though heaven knows why. I was wondering, Stan – well – seeing as how you…

Stan I'll speak to the old man about him.

Miss Davis Would you really Stan? Oh, thanks a lot. You are a sport. And – don't forget now, you jolly well fight for your rights. For goodness' sake don't take this lying down, or they'll walk right over you!

Stan All right Gladys, all right…

Fade out

Fade in. Typists in background

Pam Here's your tea Mr Moffatt.

George Thank you Marilyn.

Pam Get away with you…

George Well you are, aren't you? Look at that trim little figure. Put Marilyn at the side of you, and she wouldn't stand a chance.

Pam Oh, do stop it!

George I mean it gorgeous! (*whispers*) Incidentally, what you doing tonight?

Pam Depends.

George On what?

Pam On the best offer. Mr Robins in Sales wants me to go to the Palais with him tonight.

George Robins? Him! He's only a twopenny-halfpenny clerk…

Pam Ha! – and what d'you suppose you are then –Vice-President?

George Maybe not my pretty one, but at least I hold the best position in this Department.

Pam I'm sure I don't know what you mean. Mr Parks is in charge here.

George Ha! That's all you know!

Pam Oh, stop talking in riddles!

George I merely mean that Mr Parks will be terminating his employment with this company, as from Friday next.

Pam What? Stan Parks? After all these years? I don't believe it!

George Well, you will my little one, you will. Just imagine it… George Moffatt – senior member of the Accounts Department.

Pam Coo, you don't 'alf fancy yourself. Wait 'til I tell the girls.

George Well, what about tonight then? Are you still otherwise engaged?

Pam What? – Oh well, I suppose I could put Mr Robins off.

George That's my girl! See you outside the Odeon at seven. OK?

Pam OK.

George And by the way…

Pam Yes?

George Don't forget to bring along those cute little legs – Marilyn!

Pam (*giggling*) Oh Mr Moffatt, you are a fool!

Door opens

George Oh, hallo Stan.

Door closes

How d'you get on old boy?

Stan Not so good. Says he's got to see the Board on Monday.

George And what does that mean?

Stan It means they'll turn me down.

George Go on, you're joking.

Stan I wish I was.

George Well, did he give you any reason?

Stan Not really. Just that I haven't been with the Company for 40 years, so I don't qualify.

George I don't believe it. I just don't believe it!

Stan I know. I'm not sure I do either.

George Well, what you going to do about it old son? You're going to appeal, aren't you?

Stan Appeal? There's no point really…

George No point? Now you listen to me Stan Parks. It's every man's right as a human being to appeal against anything he considers unjust…

Stan All right now, don't go on…

George I will go on. You wait 'til the lads in the factory hear about this…

Stan That's enough now George. I don't want anybody to hear about this before they have to. It's my own business…

George It's all our business! Listen Stan. You know as well as I do, that when anybody joins this firm, they're given to understand that they get a cheap rent house on retirement.

Stan After 40 years…

George After 40 years, you're too old to appreciate the bloomin' house! You've spent 38 years of your ruddy life working for the likes of them upstairs, and this is all the thanks you get for it! I tell you Stan Parks, this is going to cause the biggest strike amongst the boys this firm has ever known. They'll all be out in 24 hours.

Stan You'll do no such thing!

George The management have violated our contracts…

Stan Don't talk such bosh George! All right, so I'm disappointed. But this isn't the end of the world you know. I've got a bit saved in the bank, and I'm pretty sure my daughter and her husband will give us a room for the time being. If needs be I could always stay on here a couple more years.

George What? – Now – now look here Stan, don't be such a fool. You've got your health to consider. Besides, they won't think any more of you for it.

Stan Then let's forget about a strike, shall we?

George Huh? – Well – er – whatever you say Stan. But I still think we should call 'em out, and teach this lot a lesson.

Stan "Call 'em out"! Yes, that's about the only solution you blokes have. You've only got to be ticked off by a manager, and it's "call 'em out". I don't know: times have changed.

George It's a case of standing up for your rights…

Stan Oh don't, George. You sound like one of those long-playing records. Anyway, you've no need to worry. I've no intention of staying on here any longer. My Doctor's put paid to that.

George Well, we're going to miss you old son. You've been like the Rock of Gibraltar here. I just don't see how the Department can keep going without you.

Stan It will George. It will.

Fade out. Typists in background

Fade in. Door slams

Vera (*calls*) That you Dad?

Stan Yes. What you doing here Vera? Where's your mother?

Vera She's just gone round the Dairy. She said she won't be long – but you know Mum!

Stan Ha! Yes.

Vera I'm not meeting Fred 'til six, so Mum said I could stay and have a cup of tea.

Stan Of course.

Vera Everything all right at the office Dad?

Stan Hm? Oh – er – yes. Fine.

Vera Is it next Friday you leave?

Stan Yes.

Vera Good job too. Bet you'll be pleased to get away from the place after all those years?

Stan I suppose so.

Vera By the way, where's your new house going to be? Mum said something about outside London. Do you the world of good. All that country air – blow the cobwebs away.

Stan Wish we were dear. I'm afraid we can't get the house. I'm not entitled to it for another two years.

Vera Oh Dad! What a shame! Mum will be upset. She doesn't know yet does she?

Stan No, not yet.

Vera Never mind love, I'm sure you'll find a furnished room somewhere. Get rid of all this old furniture, and start again.

Stan That's what I wanted to speak to you about Vera.

Vera Oh?

Stan Is there any chance of your letting us have a room – just for the time being?

Vera Dad…

Stan It wouldn't be for very long, just until we find a cheaper place to live in.

Vera Oh Dad, I'd really like to – really I would, but… well, we just haven't got the room…

Stan But you've got two spare rooms Vera.

Vera Yes I know but…

Stan Don't you want us?

Vera Dad! Don't say that! It's just that – well, we need one of the rooms for baby. She's nearly two now, and she'll have to have her own room any time now. As for the other room, you know it's full of muck.

Stan Yes of course – I was forgetting.

Vera Besides, you must admit Dad, your furniture is a bit outdated. Nearly everything we've got is modern. Oh, but I do wish we could help, but you *can* see how it is, can't you Dad?

Stan Hm? Oh – oh yes, of course I can. Don't worry dear.

Street door opens and slams

Mollie (*calls*) Are you in Stan?

Stan (*calls*) Yes, in here dear.

Mollie Brr. It's quite nippy out. Forgot the bloomin' butter. Hallo dear. D'you know, the more I see of that Mrs Fielding, the more I detest her.

Vera Here we go again…

Mollie No, it's true. Every time I see her, all I get is how her Michael is such a big noise in America. Got his own office now. Nasty little weed he was. Couldn't keep a civil tongue in his head when I knew him. D'you know…

Vera Mum…

Mollie Hm? Oh, all right. I haven't been gossiping you know. I never get the chance. All I ever do with our neighbours is pass the time of day…

Stan That's why it's taken you nearly an hour to buy eight ounces of butter… (*laughs*)

Mollie Oh, you two clever cats. Make a fine pair don't you!

Stan Come and sit down dear.

Mollie Just for a minute then.

Vera I'll go and put the kettle on. Bet you could do with a cuppa, eh Dad?

Stan I'll say.

Mollie Well, don't forget your poor old Mum's been working hard as well.

Vera Shan't be a jiffy.

Door opens and closes

Stan Good girl that.

Mollie You've always spoilt her.

Stan She's worth it. Mollie dear –

Mollie Before you go any further Stan, I already know.

Stan What d'you mean?

Mollie News soon gets around. George Moffat 'phoned Mrs Fielding. He lodges there…

Stan (*laughing*) Oh, I see… but you never get a chance to gossip…

Mollie I merely met Mrs Fielding as I was coming out the Dairy…

Stan That's where you've been for the last half-hour!

Mollie Oh… well? What's going to happen then?

Stan I don't know love, I just don't know.

Mollie Did you say anything to old Skinner?

Stan No, not exactly. He's going to ask the Board on Monday morning.

Mollie I can guess what that means. We don't stand a chance. Oh Stan my love, what are we going to do with you? Didn't you even argue with him?

Stan Of course I did…

Mollie Well then…?

Stan It's no good Mollie, we're not entitled to a place…

Mollie After all these years? Stan, it's *always* been the same with you. You've always been too scared to open your mouth. Oh well, who cares about Skinner and Co. Nobody buys their stuff any more.

Stan That's not true. They produce just about the best textiles in the business, and well you know it!

Mollie And still you defend them! Well Stan, I suppose you know what this means? We shall have to go and live with Vera and Fred.

Stan I'm afraid we can't do that either.

Mollie What's that?

Stan I've already asked Vera. She says they need the extra room for baby.

Mollie For baby? She's not old enough.

Stan I know love, I know. But it's not for us to say. They have a right to do what they want. Their place is their own.

Mollie I'm going to have a word with that girl…

Stan Now you stop that Mollie. Leave the girl alone.

Mollie (*very annoyed*) The selfish little…

Stan It's no good love. We'll just have to think of something else. Perhaps I can get a part-time job or something.

Mollie You'll do no such thing. If the Doctor says you're to retire, retire you will, whatever happens. – But that flippin' girl. After all you've done for her, and that snipey little squirt of a husband of hers…

Stan Oh please don't Mollie! I've had quite enough for one day. It's not the end of the world you know.

Mollie (*a little ashamed*) I – I'm sorry love. It's just that – after all these years, struggling to bring up a kid on your nine pound ten a week – it's not been easy.

Stan Don't you think I know it. It's a bloomin' awful wage when you come to think of it, especially when you think I'm the senior one there.

Mollie I wouldn't mind so much if she didn't just turn her back on us now, just when we need her most…

Stan Leave the girl alone, love.

Mollie We shall have to take in a lodger. That's it. We'll advertise on the board around the corner.

Stan I was wondering about that…

Mollie He could have Vera's old room. Wonder how much we'd get? I must ask old mother Fielding. It's going to be strange though. Our home Stan – no longer ours.

Stan Of course it is dear.

Mollie No. Once a stranger sets foot inside, it's no longer just ours. Still, what's the use of worrying. We can't afford to keep this place on unless we do let a room, so that's all there is to it.

Stan I'm sorry Mollie, I really am.

Mollie Look Stan. When we got married, we made a vow about staying together, "in sickness, and in health". We made a start in that one-roomed flat in Islington, brought Vera up there, and we've had a good home ever since. Who cares what happens now. Let the future take care of itself. Let me have my occasional moan by all means – it's a woman's privilege you know. But above everything else Stan, we've got each other. That's all I care about.

Stan What would I do without you?

Mollie That's enough now. It's about time we cheered up.

Fade out

Fade in

Miss Davis Good morning Stan.

Stan Hallo Gladys. Is he in?

Miss Davis Yes, he's expecting you. Oh, by the way Stan, thanks ever so much for speaking up for Paul.

Stan Huh?

Miss Davis You know, my young man.

Stan Oh yes. That's all right. Did he get the job?

Miss Davis Yes. He starts next Monday, thanks to you. Oh, I do hope old misery gives you some good news. We've all got our fingers crossed for you.

Stan Thanks Gladys.

Miss Davis Oh, I suppose you know there's been a collection for you?

Stan Collection?

Miss Davis Yes, amongst the boys upstairs. It's a sort of going-away present. Of course you'll know what it is.

Stan A wristwatch?

Miss Davis How *did* you guess?

Stan "A wristwatch for the gentlemen, a handbag for the ladies." Isn't that in the Company Regulations?

Miss Davis Wouldn't be at all surprised. Wish they'd think of something new. It's always the same old things.

Stan It's been like that ever since I can remember. Anyway, I'd better go in now.

Miss Davis Oh yes – and Stan...

Stan Huh?

Miss Davis Good luck.

Stan Thank you Gladys.

Knocks on door

Skinner (*calls*) Come in!

Door opens

Stan Good morning Mr Skinner.

Skinner Ah, there you are Parks. Er – do come in.

Door closes

I think you know Mr Dudley?

Stan Oh yes. How d'you do sir.

Dudley Good morning Parks.

Skinner Well now, I've just received the minutes of yesterday's Board Meeting, so I think we might get right down to brass tacks.

Stan Yes sir.

Skinner Mr Dudley, would you take it from there please.

Dudley Yes. Parks, one of the items on the Agenda was your application for one of the Company's cheap-rent houses. Mr Skinner tells me you're leaving this week.

Stan That's right sir.

Dudley I'm sorry to hear that, I'm sure you're going to be a great loss to us all. Now then, this application. The Board were most impressed with your record of long and faithful service within our organisation. Your conduct appears to have been exemplary.

Stan Thank you sir.

Dudley There is always room for a good man within this organisation, and I only hope, Parks, that your replacement will set as fine an example as you have, during these many years.

Stan Thank you Mr Dudley.

Dudley However, the Board have reviewed your application most carefully Parks, particularly with regard to your outstanding service with us. But – I'm sorry to say that they were not able to consider your request. If you could have remained with us for a further two years, I'm sure there would have been no doubt about our granting this, but the Company rules clearly state…

Stan I know sir. Mr Skinner has already told me.

Skinner I'm sorry Parks, I really am.

Dudley Yes. It is most unfortunate. But I'm sure you'll manage. Isn't that so Parks?

Skinner Parks?

Stan (*in a daze*) Hm? – er – pardon?

Dudley I said I'm sure you'll manage somehow.

Stan Oh – oh yes. I'll be quite all right sir. As a matter of fact, we're going to live with my daughter and her husband. They've been pestering us to go and stay with them for a long time. Reckon this is a good opportunity to go.

Skinner I am pleased to hear that Parks. I'm sure you'll be made very welcome.

Dudley Good for you Parks.

Stan Oh yes sir, I shall be quite all right. – Er, well, I'd better not take up any more of your time gentlemen. If you'll excuse me…

Skinner Of course. Oh, Parks, there is just one thing.

Stan Yes sir?

Skinner As is customary, the members of the staff have contributed towards a retirement gift for you, and, with your permission, l shall make a formal presentation, in the staff canteen, on Friday evening.

Stan That's very kind of you sir.

Skinner Not at all. You will of course know that we normally present a wristwatch to staff on their retirement, but in view of your rather exceptional length of service, I have personally added a little extra to ensure a solid gold watch.

Stan (*to himself*) Gold?

Skinner I hope you'll like it?

Stan Pardon? – Oh – er – yes. That really is a wonderful thing for you to have done sir. Thank you very much indeed.

Skinner Not at all. Not at all, my good man. That is the very least I can do. We don't have a Mr Parks joining us every day of the week you know!

Stan No, I suppose not. Well, thank you again sir. Oh – I believe you are retiring soon yourself, Mr Dudley?

Dudley Yes, as a matter of fact I am, Parks.

Stan I'd like to wish you the best of luck sir.

Dudley That's very kind of you, thank you. Must say, I'm going to miss this place when I go. Somehow I can't imagine myself pottering around a garden all day.

Stan You have a garden in your new house sir?

Dudley Yes, quite a big one really. Not many flowers but a nice lawn, and a couple of apple trees.

Stan Fancy. That would just suit my wife. Real green fingers she's got, even though it's only in a window-box! Pity we never had a garden. I think she'd have done wonders with it.

Skinner Yes, indeed. Er – well Parks. If you'll excuse me, I have a few things to discuss with Mr Dudley.

Stan Oh, I beg your pardon sir. Anyway, thank you very much indeed. You too Mr Dudley.

Dudley Not at all. I'm very sorry that…

Stan Oh that's all right sir. It's not so bad really.

Dudley The best of luck to you – Mr Parks.

Stan And to you sir.

Skinner See you on Friday evening Parks.

Stan Right you are sir. Good morning.

Skinner Good morning.

Dudley Good morning Parks.

Door opens and closes

Nice chap that.

Skinner Yes. Good worker too.

Dudley He'll be a big loss to the Company.

Skinner So will you.

Dudley Hm? Ha! I wonder. But *he* will. His type always are.

Fade out

Fade in – staff canteen

George I bet you never knew you had so many friends, eh Stan?

Stan You're right. Looks like the whole building's here. It's very good of them.

George Get away with you. They're all very fond of you. Your husband is going to be missed around here Mrs Parks. You must be very proud of him?

Mollie Oh yes Mr Moffatt, I am.

George Bet you can't wait to get away from the place eh Stan, old boy? No more getting up early in the morning, nice cup of tea in bed – oh boy! What a life! Now why can't I retire.

Mollie You will Mr Moffatt – one day.

George Huh? – oh – yes, yes I suppose so. Well, I must say Mrs Parks, you certainly don't look your age.

Mollie Thank you very much Mr Moffatt, but I can assure you looks are always different to the way you feel!

George Get away with you. You and Stan are going to outlive the lot of us! I bet you any money you like… oh, hallo gorgeous.

Pam Good evening Mr Parks, Mrs Parks. Good evening Mr Moffatt.

George And where are *you* going to my pretty maid?

Pam I'm just going over to have a drink with Monica.

George Oh? – and what has Monica got that I haven't?

Pam I'm sure I don't know what you mean…

George Come along now, my little Rose of Picardy. Let your Uncle George be the one to introduce you to the evils of alcohol. Excuse me will you Stan – Mrs Parks?

Stan & Mollie (*laughing*) Of course.

George See you later.

Exits

Mollie He's a real live wire that one.

Stan Yes, he always has been.

Mollie How are you feeling love?

Stan Oh, all right I suppose. A bit nervous I think. Be glad when it's all over.

Mollie I bet you will. The thing to do is to take the watch, tell 'em what you think of them, and get out. I've got no time for any of this crowd.

Stan Now don't you start that again love. It's bad enough as it is. You know I never lose my temper.

Mollie I know, but I wish you would – just once.

Stan Watch out, here comes the old man.

Skinner (*calls across the crowd*) Ah, there you are, Mr Parks. I've been looking all over for you. There's someone on the telephone for you – it's personal I think.

Stan Oh, thank you sir.

Skinner And is this Mrs Parks?

Stan (*nervously*) Er – yes sir. Mollie? This is Mr Skinner.

Mollie How do you do Mr Skinner.

Skinner It's a great pleasure to meet you.

Stan If you'll excuse me a minute…

Skinner Of course; take the call in my office.

Stan (*calling*) Thank you sir…

Exits

Skinner You must be very proud of your husband tonight?

Mollie It doesn't take just tonight to make me proud of him, Mr Skinner. To me, he's always been a man with a fine sense of duty, with only one ambition in life – to give me and my daughter a good home – and that he's always done.

Skinner I'm quite sure he has. He's a great home-loving man.

Mollie That he is… and he's a very contented man, Mr Skinner, very contented. He's not selfish, he always gives more than he takes. There's a lot to be said for that these days, don't you agree?

Skinner (*nervously*) Er – yes. Yes indeed.

Mollie I mean you must meet all sorts of selfish people in business firms, don't you find that so?

Skinner Why – er – yes, of course. It's very difficult – er – if you'll excuse me now, I think I'd better start the proceedings.

Mollie Of course.

Skinner So nice to have met you Mrs Parks.

Mollie Likewise Mr Skinner. (*to herself*) Old croak! Oh Stan, I wish you'd lose your temper – just once.

Stan (*approaching*) All right love?

Mollie Hm? Oh – yes. I had a nice little chat with Mr Skinner. Who was it on the 'phone… Are you all right love?

Stan (*a little breathless*) Yes, yes, I'm all right. I'll tell you about it later.

Miss Davis (*calling*) Hallo Stan.

Stan Hallo there Gladys. Mollie, this is Gladys Davis, Mr Skinner's secretary.

Mollie Oh yes, how d'you do.

Miss Davis How d'you do Mrs Parks. Oh, and I'd like you to meet my young man. Paul, this is Mr and Mrs Parks.

Paul Pleased to meet you.

Stan Likewise.

Paul Mr Parks, I would like to thank you very much for speaking up for me. I think it'll be a good job, don't you?

Stan I'm sure it will son. Just play the game right. How old are you?

Paul I'll be 21 next month.

Stan 21. Yes, that's a nice age. Try and keep it at 21 as long as you can.

Paul I will Mr Parks. Thanks again.

Exit

Mollie Stan, I think Mr Skinner's waiting for us.

Stan Oh yes. See you Gladys. You've get a nice boy there.

Miss Davis Thanks Stan. (*whispers*) Good luck.

Skinner (*bangs on table*)

Crowd noise fades

Ladies and gentlemen. May I have your attention please. (*clears throat*) We are gathered here this evening, to pay tribute to a man who has long held a place of undenied respect and affection within this organisation.

Voices Hear! Hear!

Skinner Mr – er – Parks, joined Skinner and Co. 38 years ago, when we were just beginning to build up the fine business we have today.

Voices (*a few subdued jeers*)

Skinner Somehow I feel, it is always with a sense of deep regret that one says *au revoir* to an old friend, and particularly one of the calibre and quality of Mr – er – Parks.

Voice (*whisper*) Lying old so-and-so!

Skinner I have always noticed Mr Parks to be an intelligent, well-mannered, and completely unselfish member of our staff, and cannot for one moment imagine the Accounts Department without him. As you know, Skinner and Co. are forever on the look-out for young people who are able to fill the gap left by old friends such as Mr Parks. But believe me, it is not easy and this is a great pity, for in a mighty organisation such as this, the rewards are unlimited...

Voice (*whisper*) Who's he kidding!

Skinner Mr Parks, in presenting you with this little token of our undying appreciation, may I add the thanks, not only of the Board of Directors and myself, but also of all your colleagues and friends whom you have worked alongside for so many years. Please accept this, Mr Parks, with our thanks, regards, and love, for a most happy retirement.

There are loud cheers. All sing "For He's a Jolly Good Fellow". They call "Speech! Speech!"

Stan Er – Mr Skinner, (*nervously*) ladies and gentlemen. I really don't know what to say. This speech lark isn't my cup of tea.

George (*in half-whisper*) Poor old Stan. Looks quite overcome.

Stan I would like to thank you all for coming down here this evening. It's very good of you. I can hardly believe this is my last time here. 38 years I've been coming in and out of this canteen, and now – oh well, that's life. In fact I've had a pretty good life. A good home, loving family, and a good job. What more can a man ask for? You know, this is a marvellous watch – and a gold one too. D'you know, I've never had a watch in my life. Not that I couldn't afford one, just that I never got around to it. And now I have one; after all these years... What's it say here: (*reads*) "To Stan Parks, from your friends. Skinner & Co., 1961"... From my friends. I'm a very lucky man to have so many friends. Friends who'd buy me a gold watch. D'you know, I never knew I had so many friends – that is, not until this week. My friends, this is the first and last chance I shall have to talk to you like this, so please listen to me. This week, you all know I've been done what I think an injustice...

Crowd Hear! Hear! (*There is a lot of rumbling amongst them*)

Stan ...At least, I thought it was an injustice, but now I'm not so sure.

George (*shouts*) Don't let 'em get away with it Stan!

Stan (*shouting back*) What's that George?

George (*shouts*) Don't let 'em get away with it!

Crowd mumble their agreement

Stan What are you so worried about George? (*His voice is getting stronger*) It's not your house. Besides you've got my job now! That's what you've been waiting for isn't it? Of course it is. (*getting a little angry*) And you were going to call the men out on strike – for me! Ha! Oh George, you don't fool anyone. There are George Moffatts in every firm in the country, and there always will be. The big shots, just waiting to press the button! The troublemakers! That's what they are – troublemakers! "CALL 'EM OUT!" (*voice now almost shouting*) Where have I heard that before? (*voice calming down*) You make me sick George. In fact my friends, a lot of you make me sick. Sick of your endless moans about Mr So-and-So, or Miss Whatsit. Sick of hearing how much better you could do at another firm, but never have the courage to pack up and go! For Heaven's sake – what's wrong with you lot? You're all eating well, aren't you? – And drinking, and going to the pictures, and the pub. But still that's not enough! When I think of all the people in this world who have to fight for a piece of bread, or struggle to keep their kids alive, then I become more sick; I just don't know what's wrong with this day and age.

Skinner Well said Mr Parks! Well said!

Stan Thank you Mr Skinner. I'm glad you agree, 'cause there's something I want to say to you as well.

Mumbles from crowd

Mr Skinner, in all your years as Chairman of this company, have you ever once thought about getting to know your staff? You talk about the "great respect" you've always held for me? But until I walked into your office last week, you hadn't even heard of me – after 38 years! How the hell do you and your Board expect this lot to have any confidence in your firm, when they don't even know you. In Heaven's name talk to them, come and ask them about their problems. Make them feel they're working for a man – not his office!

Crowd Hear! Hear!

Stan And as far as your reduced-rent houses are concerned Mr Skinner, I suggest you get the Company's regulations clarified as soon as possible. (*calms down*) I – I hope you'll all forgive this outburst. It's – it's not really like me. But I hope you'll remember what I said. Mr Skinner, I'd like you to know I hold no grudge against you, or the firm. Up until yesterday, and even until tonight, I've been worrying myself sick about finding accommodation for me and my wife. But thanks to that telephone call, I can now buy my own house, so I won't have need of yours.

Crowd gets excited

Skinner What's that?

Mollie What d'you mean Stan?

Stan I'm glad to say my little weekly investment on the Australian Football Pools has reaped me a harvest of – 72 thousand dollars!

Crowd very excited

Mollie Stan! Oh Stan!

Stan (*to Mollie*) Nothing to worry about now love. (*calls to crowd for order*) My friends! Thank you for listening to me, and thank you for my watch. I promise you I shall always treasure it. Goodbye, and good luck to you all.

Crowd, very excited, discuss amongst themselves

Skinner My dear Mr Parks, this is splendid news. I can't tell you how delighted I am for you.

Stan Thank you sir.

Skinner And may I say how very much I agree with your speech. You make me feel most ashamed.

Stan Not at all. I just said what I felt.

Mollie You were marvellous dear. I was so proud of you.

Stan Thank you love. Mr Skinner, I want to put some money into this firm.

Skinner Into – this firm?

Stan That's right.

Skinner You mean – er – shares?

Stan That's right.

Skinner Well, that's most generous of you. Er – how much were you thinking of?

Stan Five thousand pounds.

Mollie Stan!

Skinner Five thousand pounds! That really is most generous. Are you sure you...

Stan I've been happy working here, and this is one way to keep in contact.

Skinner How very nice of you. It'll take about a month to draw the papers up...

Stan Don't worry about that. I'll have my solicitor take care of things.

Mollie We don't have a solicitor Stan.

Stan We will have now.

Skinner Just as you say Mr Parks.

Stan Well. Goodbye Mr Skinner, and thanks again.

Skinner Goodbye Mr Parks, Mrs Parks. I'll look forward to seeing you in a few weeks' time.

Stan A few months' time.

Mollie What d'you mean love?

Stan (*to Mollie*) Because we're going to look at the world first my love. Are you ready?

Mollie I'm ready.

Stan Then let's go.

Music up full, fade down and hold behind

Announcer That was James Thomason as Stan Parks, Mary O'Farrell as Mollie Parks and Godfrey Kenton as Mr Skinner in "The Gold Watch", by Victor Pemberton. The rest of the cast was as follows: Gladys Davis – Meg Wynn Davies; Pam – Angela Munnion; George Moffatt – Frank Duncan; Vera – Beverley Dunn; Mr Dudley – Wilfred Babbage; Paul – Nigel Anthony. Other parts played by members of the BBC Drama Repertory Company. Production by Audrey Cameron.

Music up full to end

THE END

The Slide

1 966 was quite a year. In the Far East, the US and its Allies were still engaged in a bloody war against rebels in Vietnam; Britain and France agreed plans to build a tunnel beneath the English Channel; in New York they were starting on groundwork for the erection of a new skyscraper building eventually to be known as the World Trade Center, whilst on Broadway in that same city, the musical *Cabaret* was having its world stage premiere. 1966 was also a good year for new pop songs in which the Beatles had two great hits with *Eleanor Rigby* and *Yellow Submarine*, whilst on television in the US a new science fiction series called *Star Trek* was drawing record viewing figures, a worthy competitor to the comparatively new British television series about a certain Time Traveller named *Doctor Who*. In Britain itself, Harold Wilson was re-elected as Prime Minister after the Labour Party won the General Election.

But in October of that year, there was a tragic human disaster of such magnitude that it shocked the entire nation. It happened at 9.15am on the morning of Friday 21 October in the tiny South Wales mining village of Aberfan, where a towering coal slag heap collapsed and engulfed the village school, killing 116 children and 28 adults.

It's strange to recall that, during the summer of the previous year, I had been sitting at my typewriter in the house in Islington I had recently moved into with David Spenser, nervously launching into the opening of a six-part serial which BBC Radio had commissioned me to write. It was my first attempt at writing any kind of science fiction, so it was a bit of a risk for both them and me. But my interest in science fiction had always been confined to more realistic earth-based stories, such as H.G. Wells' *The War of the Worlds*, Nigel Kneale's *Quatermass* and John Wyndham's *The Day of the Triffids*. Therefore it seemed perfectly natural to me that something like an earthquake in England, which I thought at the time to be a totally unlikely possibility, would be rich material for the type of story I wanted to write. Little did I know that an earthquake, something I had feared being in all my life, was not as unlikely as I had thought. In fact, official records show that ever since our planet was formed, there have been minor earthquakes and tremors in various parts of the United Kingdom.

But what I also didn't know was how prophetic the first scene of my radio serial, which I now called *The Slide*, was going to be: for how was I to know that, not long after the broadcast, science fiction would become science fact. In the opening scene of Episode 1, I had written that the first setting was to be a school classroom in an English village in the south of England, and that severe earth tremors were causing the school building to collapse. I still have that first rewritten scene on file. During the early morning classroom lesson, there is a sudden, eerie silence, until gradually we hear the sound of objects rattling – a cup and saucer on the teacher's desk; a window slams, a dog barks from beyond the school gates. Then out of the blue, a small child yells to her teacher: 'Miss! Everything's moving!' Chaos and confusion, terror, screaming. In panic, the children rush for the doors. The ground is shaking. No one can understand what is happening. Just over a year later in the real world came Aberfan. For me it was a horrifying, frightening experience to know that in some strange way, only one year before, I had predicted it. Fortunately everyone decided that my opening scene was a bit too unnerving and realistic, so I was persuaded to rewrite it. Just as well when you consider what would happen in October of the following year.

During the writing of the serial, I worked a great deal with John Tydeman, a senior producer at BBC Radio, who not only produced the majority of my radio plays, but also became a firm long-time friend. His ebullient personality helped to guide me through the mechanics of writing a serial as opposed to a single play, something you can only really learn by experience. My God, poor John had a lot to put up with. No wonder he was awarded an OBE! Quite seriously though, both he and David Spenser taught me a great deal about radio; and when I came to write *The Slide*, I was lucky to have John to produce the serial, and David to play a leading part in it. By this time, of course, I had already written several plays produced by John, having abandoned my job in the travel agency some four or five years before. But when the serial was finally broadcast, after what happened at the end of *The Gold Watch* and then that prophetic rewritten opening to *The Slide*, I had a nasty feeling that I was becoming some kind of a psychic!

With constant headlines in the media about the awful tragedy in the small Welsh village, having written a science fiction serial that had started in such similar circumstances really distressed me. The sight of children being pulled from the slime and slush of the coal heap was, for me and for everyone, a dreadful experience, particularly as my story about mud oozing from a fissure in the road in a fictional part of southern England was about to be broadcast. Also, it should be remembered that this was the middle of the so-called 'Swinging Sixties': the time of Flower Power, hippies, heavy rock, flared jeans, Carnaby Street, Batman, Hammer horror films, James Bond, and pirate radio stations; a time when television was now becoming a real threat to radio ratings – so a science fiction serial on radio had more of a struggle to find an audience than *Star Trek* or *Thunderbirds*. In fact BBC Radio hadn't really done a science fiction serial since their immensely successful *Journey Into Space* back in 1963, which ran to a phenomenal 60 episodes. Therefore I had a lot to live up to. I had to cope with comments such as: 'You'll have a job to compete with *Journey Into Space*. That was one of the best sci-fi serials of all time.' My word didn't I know it! But then, I wasn't writing a space epic. *The Slide* was my way of commenting on how vulnerable Planet Earth was, and still is. You see, I was an amateur environmentalist even in those days! Nonetheless, I lost a lot of sleep at night when I realised just what I was up against, dabbling in an area of drama that I knew very little about. However, after meeting the cast John had assembled, my apprehensions soon disappeared.

It would be pointless for me to describe each and every one of the actors and actresses, but I'll give you a few snapshots of some of them. For instance, the late and much loved character actor, Maurice Denham, who plays the impossible MP Hugh Deverill, was someone I had only ever heard in radio situation comedies. His 'silly chap' chuckle in *Much Binding in the Marsh*, set on an RAF station after the war, was for many years a cherished memory for listeners of that period.

But when I saw him in the flesh for the first time, with that bald head and almost cherubic face, I realised at once what a clever, versatile actor he must be. And I was so right. His dramatic outbursts at his constituents in *The Slide* were so real and believable. And then there was the late Roger Delgado, who became so well known during the 1970s for his chilling performance as The Master in *Doctor Who*. He was perfect casting as the South American seismologist, Professor Gomez; an actor at the height of his powers. It was ironic that he and David Spenser were cast in the same show, for it turned out that Roger was married to one of David's distant cousins in Sri Lanka. And what can I say about Miriam Margolyes? Not only is she a wonderful, first-rate actress in everything she does, but away from the camera and microphones she is highly intelligent, vastly amusing, thoroughly liberal-minded, and just great fun to be with. I loved watching her in the studio, playing her Kentish farmer's wife character with a broad 'Mummerzet' accent! No wonder Hollywood beckoned. Miriam is now a greatly sought-after film actress.

As for David Spenser, well his career goes back to when, at the age of 12, he played 'Just William', specially chosen by the author, Richmal Crompton. Having played everything from Shakespeare to the classics, David tells me that he had been totally intrigued to play the romantic hero in *The Slide*, Ken Richards. Much of the rest of the cast were, of course, drawn from the multi-talented BBC Radio Drama Repertory Company, with voices so incredibly versatile that one sometimes forgot that in real life they looked nothing like the character they were playing. Amongst them was the veteran broadcaster Rolf Lefebvre, whose voice had the uncanny knack of projecting anything from a crotchety old professor of sciences in *The Slide* to a rather sinister dwarf in *The Hobbit*. That was talent. That was professionalism.

The first episode of *The Slide* was scheduled for transmission on the BBC Light Programme on the evening of Sunday 13 February 1966 at 7.30pm. During the course of the day several brief regular 'news' flashes were made before and after other programmes warning listeners that earth tremors had been felt in the south of England, and that if they wanted to know more they should tune in to *The Slide* that evening. It was, of course, a bit of an attempt to emulate the dramatic news flashes that were used in the US years before, to prepare listeners for the airing of Orson Welles' famous sound version of H.G. Wells' *The War of the Worlds*. At the time this device sent waves of panic across the United States, for the tone of the announcements was one of chaos and mayhem as the space invaders appeared over populated areas. *The Slide* didn't quite have that same effect before its own broadcast, but I was told that one or two rather crusty listeners did telephone the BBC to complain about mixing fact with fiction!

At 7.30pm that creepy opening title music boomed out through radio sets around the country. But after the opening announcements, all I could think about was that prophetic opening I had written over a year before which, to my great relief, I had rewritten. It was a strange feeling to hear it all come to life, hearing all the fears that I had suffered most of my life. As we all know, an earthquake is one of Nature's most angry phenomena. I had spent months reading about the earth's crust and fault lines. I had mulled over newspaper and magazine photographs of the most terrible disasters over hundreds of years, the scenes of death and destruction stretching right across our planet. My research had turned up some really extraordinary discoveries. I had no idea that small earth tremors appear frequently on the sea bed off the east coast of England, or that during the middle ages there were serious tremors beneath central London, or that a serious earth tremor had terrified the people of Colchester in Essex nearly two hundred years before. Nor did I expect to hear of tremors causing minor damage in Kent just a few weeks prior to the broadcast of the first episode of *The Slide*. All my old fears, all my nightmares about earthquakes were being realised in this serial. I had once been in an area in southern Italy where the ground quite literally shook beneath me, and I was terrified. I never forgot it. And so as I listened to that tranquil opening scene, and the odd silence that pervaded it, I was terrified again. Even though I had watched the whole thing being played out in a studio in Broadcasting House, I was still uneasy. The friends we had invited to listen to the episode with us insisted we turn off the lights, and that was worse still. The dark was something else that did little to comfort me – as you will read and hear in one of the other scripts in this book.

The response to *The Slide* was very encouraging. Listeners were suitably scared, and fascinated by the experience. Needless to say there was a huge postbag after each and every episode. Amongst them was one from a young chap in Hampshire who wrote that, 'In some parts I thought it was very spooky... I'm glad I don't live in Holly Mill Lane!' But the most poignant was from a young girl who attended a school for the blind in Birmingham. She wrote: 'One night [*whilst listening to one of the episodes*] I screamed as I walked into the bedroom, because my sister was sitting by her wardrobe, zipping up her handbag. That was the kind of effect *The Slide* had on me.' One often forgets that radio is a natural choice for the blind. As I listened in the dark to the last episode of the serial some weeks later, I thought of her words.

Professional reaction to *The Slide* was also favourable – and encouraging. Those newspapers critics who had heard it compared it to *Quatermass* or *The Day of the Triffids*. What was exciting, however, was a phone call to my then agent from the Hollywood producer George Pal, who made the first screen version of *The War of the Worlds*, and who said he would be interested in buying an option on the story, provided he could reset the action in the US. Needless to say, we heard no more! The same thing happened with the small-budget British horror film director, Milton Subotsky. He was interested too, and not because I had copied one of his films which I had never seen. Ah well – that's showbiz!

However, during this time I was approached by various TV companies to suggest ideas for other science fiction stories, mainly for use in existing series. *The Slide* had clearly whetted a few appetites, and it was a good opportunity to show what I could come up with. However, I had little experience with television other than contributing a half-hour script for Thames Television's junior reporter series for children called *Send Foster*. At that time, I was also doing my best to pay my share of the relentless household bills that refused to go away!

Which brings me to how I managed to give up my job at the travel agency and earn money. I blame my dear, sorely missed friend Cedric Messina for that. After I had written my first two radio plays for the BBC, sitting up night after night trying to finish them, he said to me over dinner one night, 'If you want to learn about television I'll give you a job. You can come and be an extra for me. You'll get £5 a day, and you'll have plenty of free time to think of plots for radio or television plays – and what's more, you'll learn a lot more than selling travel tickets every day!' I have to say that Cedric proved to be a godsend. As one of the BBC's leading television producers, with such credits as *Play of the Month*, and the man responsible for getting the entire collection of Shakespeare's plays adapted for television, he kept to his word and helped secure me a whole series of jobs as an extra in his many productions.

The strange thing during this period, however, is that one of my early jobs in the studio was being cast in a tiny bit part in *Doctor Who and the Moonbase*. Unlike most performers, however, I never *ever* wanted to act, and always did everything in my power to melt into the background. After doing *The Slide* I only wanted to write! Nevertheless, I did the job, working with dear old Morris Barry, and of course 'the gang', namely Patrick Troughton, Deborah Watling and Frazer Hines. Little did I know that we would team up again later for a struggle against nasty creatures beneath the deep... The only reason I mention all this now is that some people have suggested that I wrote *The Slide* for television, and when it was turned down I offered it to radio. However, nothing was further from the truth. I wrote the idea for *The Slide* early in 1965, and gave it to Keith Williams, who at that time was Head of the Script Unit at BBC Radio. He liked it very much; and when he left to join BBC Television, he gave it to Peter Bryant to read, who also liked it. It was not until after the radio serial had been broadcast that I did a synopsis for David Whittaker who was Script Editor for *Doctor Who*, but he decided that it wasn't for him and that was that. But, although there are similarities in the story with my later six-part *Who* serial, *Fury from the Deep*, I certainly did not try to get *The Slide* into television by the back door!

And so I did my stint as an extra – probably one of the worst extras ever – whilst all the time learning about how people talk, walk, run, behave. And I continued to write radio scripts, usually in a notebook on my knee dressed as a Cavalier or an Italian soldier waiting to be called to the other end of the studio, or in the canteen, or on a darkened set that wasn't being used. Ideas and synopses were pouring out of me, most of them added to the list of rejections. But some of them were accepted and broadcast on the radio: such as *Ziggie*, the story of an East German schoolteacher at a London comprehensive school, who strikes one of his pupils over the head with a book and is charged with malicious assault – a story of post-Second World War prejudice; and my first jab at a satire, *The Flag Wavers*, which was about someone quite unlikely claiming a tiny island which suddenly appeared out of the middle of the Pacific Ocean – another absurd prediction of mine which manifested itself a couple of weeks later when a new island emerged from the sea off the coast of Iceland!

And then came the next serial to be published in this book, *Kill the Pharaoh!* And you should just hear what happened whilst we were rehearsing *that...!*

The Slide

by Victor Pemberton

Episode 1: Moments of Silence

TRANSMISSION:	Sunday 13 February 1966	1900–1930 LIGHT
REHEARSALS:	Monday 31 January 1966	1030–1830
	Tuesday 1 February 1966	1030–1700
RECORD:	Tuesday 1 February	1700–1800 (to H.11)
STUDIO:	B.11	
R.P. No.	TLO 605/551	
EDIT:	Friday 11 February	0930–1245 (H.54)
PLAYBACK:	Friday 11 February	1500–1530 (5108)

CAST:	Gomez.....................................Roger Delgado
	Deverill ....Maurice Denham
	Landers.................................Rolf Lefebvre
	Lippert..................................Allan McClelland
	Ken Richards.........................David Spenser
	Anna......................................Marion Mathie
	Baxter...................................Geoffrey Matthews
	'Tug' Wilson...........................Stephen Jack
	Mrs Wilson ....Miriam Margolyes
	Janet ....Elizabeth Proud
	Police Sergeant ....Wilfred Babbage
	Constable ....Anthony Jackson
	Newscaster.............................Nigel Graham
	Farmer..................................Nigel Graham
	Woman ....Elizabeth Proud
	Tannoy Announcer.................Anthony Graham

S.M.s:	Panel: Amna Smith; Grams: David Cain; Spot: Margaret Rushton
SECRETARY:	Helene Grygar, PABX 2168

All announcements to be recorded 1700–1800 31 January

The action is set in Redlow New Town, a highly modern development somewhere between Maidstone and the south coast of Kent

Although a freak March heatwave has sent temperatures soaring into the eighties, there is a gentle breeze blowing on the hillside overlooking the town. Birds chirp merrily from the trees as two young people struggle to climb the hill. It is Sunday morning

Janet (*calls*) Come on Ken! There's a much better view from up here. (*reaches top*) You can see the whole town.

Ken (*out of breath, irritable*) I know you can see the town! (*reaches her*) Really Janet! We've climbed this hill hundreds of times. The way you carry on you'd think we were the first to reach the summit.

Janet Stop being so grumpy – enjoy the view! (*inhales freely*) Oh! I haven't breathed air like this for a week. I feel as though I've been let out of a cage.

Ken We don't get heatwaves in March every year you know. You should be grateful for small mercies.

Janet Well you want to be locked up in that classroom some time. I thought I was going to suffocate the other day. The heat was unbearable.

Ken (*teasingly*) There's nothing I'd like better than being locked up in a classroom with my schoolteacher. (*close and intimate*) Especially… this schoolteacher…

Janet (*calls out*) Look! There *is* the school! Doesn't it look an odd shape from up here?

Ken (*bored*) Yes – very odd.

Janet Rather beautiful though. All that glass and concrete. Very futuristic. (*pause*) But then, I suppose all the buildings are.

Ken grunts uncompromisingly

You really hate Redlow, don't you Ken?

Ken No. I just don't like New Towns. They're too impersonal.

Janet That's because they *are* new. You have to give them time.

Ken D'you mean the buildings – or the people?

Janet You're just a miserable old-fashioned Londoner who resents progress. I happen to think we owe Hugh Deverill an awful lot. All of us.

Ken Really?

Janet Any man who starts life by sweeping floors in a factory and ends up building a town with his own money deserves every bit of admiration he can get.

Ken I distrust the self-made man.

Janet Well, there are plenty of those who don't. That's why they put him into Parliament.

Ken (*affectionately*) Well, let me tell you this, my darling. If our marriage is going to work, we're going to have to make one or two radical changes in your political direction.

Janet laughs

We are unaware that the background breeze and birds chirping has disappeared. Pause

Janet What d'you think they're all doing down there?

Ken Who?

Janet All of them. Sitting in their homes.

Ken Well, the civilised ones will have their feet up on the mantelpiece reading the Sunday newspapers. Which is what *I* should be doing right now.

Janet (*slightly trance-like*) Yes. Life mustn't change for them, must it? It has to go on the way it always has done.

Ken (*puzzled*) What an extraordinary thing to say!

Janet Not really. (*her attention diverted away from him*) Just think what they'd all do if suddenly their days were made to be different. (*pause*) I wonder what they'd do?

Ken I hope they never get the chance to find out, and anyway darling I do wish you wouldn't...

Janet Ssh.

Ken Huh?

Janet Listen.

Complete stillness in the air

Ken I can't hear a thing.

Janet Precisely. Haven't you noticed how quiet it is? (*pause*) You can almost hear the silence.

Another moment of stillness

Ken (*off mic*) Imagination.

Janet Look at the grass. It's absolutely still. When we came up, there was a cool breeze. (*pause*) And I can't even hear the birds any more. Not one single bird.

Ken (*looking out*) At least you can see the English Channel. It's as clear as a bell...

Janet Ken. Let's go. I hate this place.

Ken (*returns to her*) Hate it? But it's one of your favourite...

Janet It's the weather. I don't like it being like this. It scares me. I've had a headache all the week.

Ken (*comforting*) Janet. Why didn't you tell me darling? Getting yourself all worked up like this.

Janet (*with effort*) I'll be all right if I can – just get away from this place. The... sun... it's so bright. It hurts my eyes.

Ken You really *are* under the weather, aren't you? Well I tell you this. If you're not out of it by tonight, you're not going to any meeting at the Town Hall. Especially with the reception Hugh Deverill's going to get!

A sharp cut takes us into the middle of the rowdy Town Hall meeting. Deverill struggles to restore some kind of order

Deverill (*calls*) Ladies and gentlemen... please!

The deafening shouts continue

My friends. I appeal to you. (*pause*) How can I ask you to believe me if you won't listen?

Farmer (*jumps up, shouts angrily*) Believe! D'you expect us to believe *you* after all the lies you've given *us* over the years?

Shouts of "hear, hear!" and general agreement

Give the farmer back his land Mr Deverill! That's all we ask of you.

More boisterous general agreement which gradually subsides as Deverill speaks

Deverill (*struggling to hide his conceit*) My friends. I'm not talking to you now as a politician. I'm one of you. I always have been. I don't rely on Westminster for my decisions. And if I have to answer to anyone for my mistakes it's to myself. I *know* when I'm wrong.

A few mumbles from the audience

Ken (*whispers*) That'll be the first time.

Janet Give him his due, it takes guts to take on this lot.

Deverill You tell me I took the farmer's land away from him. Yes, that's true. But what did I give the farmer in return? I gave him a home. A place he could be proud to live in with his wife and children – for the rest of his days. (*a long pause*) When I came to Redlow ten years ago, it was a swamp in the middle of a Kentish marshland. A haven of flies and fieldmice. You couldn't walk more than five yards without being knee-deep in mud. (*pause*) Today, my friends, I have given you a standard of living unparalleled in the history of this nation. And Redlow New Town has become a giant in our new society. We have stepped well into the future before it has begun!

More mixed feelings from the audience

(*shouting above the noise*) Do you condemn me for this!

Ken (*to Janet*) Darling. Are you all right? You look ghastly.

Janet (*a little breathless*) I'm all right. It's just so hot in here.

Ken Then for Heaven's sake let's go.

Janet I'm all right.

'Tug' Wilson, a local farmer, stands up

Tug D'you mind if *I* ask you a question Mr Deverill?

Deverill Go right ahead please, Mr Wilson.

Tug Most of us in this hall tonight are farmers. We don't live in any of the fancy flats you've been puttin' up. Our job is to dig up the soil to give people food – includin' you Mr Deverill.

More agreement from the audience

Most of the money that's gone into the development of this town has come out of your own pocket. Now we reckon a man must have a reason to want to do that.

Deverill Does one need a reason to help his fellow man?

Tug Depends what that reason is Mr Deverill. We didn't ask you for a 'space-age' town as you call it. Some of us prefer the country the way it was.

More shouts of "Hear! Hear!" from the audience

Janet (*breathless*) I wish they'd open the doors or something… I can hardly breathe… it's stifling…

Ken Darling! Your hands! They're like ice. Come on. Let's get out of here.

Deverill's wife Anna stands up

Anna (*calmly indignant*) Mr Wilson. Perhaps I can ask you a question, if you'll allow me to?

Mumbled speculation from the audience

Tug It's a free country Mrs Deverill.

Mumbling subsides

Anna You don't have any children of your own, do you?

Tug I don't see what that's got to do with…

Anna It's quite all right. Neither do I and my husband. That's one of the reasons why we think about children more than most people who have them. Somebody has to plan their future Mr Wilson. Somebody has to guarantee their security. Even if they're not our children.

Tug And one man can do all that, can he?

Anna He can try, Mr Wilson. He can try. (*to everybody*) The creation of Redlow, ladies and gentlemen, is no lust for power. It is the one dream of a man that came true. A dream of progress – not of stagnation.

Quite unexpectedly, Anna is greeted with a gale of tumultuous applause. In the middle of this, however, the audience are shocked to hear the sound of a loud, stifled scream from Janet, who has collapsed at the back of the hall. She is quickly surrounded by anxious onlookers

Deverill (*shouting*) What is it! What's going on at the back there!

Ken (*close to Janet*) Janet… darling… come on now… lift your head…

Janet is fighting for breath

Janet I… can't breathe. Please…! I… can't…

Tug What is it Doctor? Has she fainted?

Woman It's this heat! They should have opened these doors. It's like a greenhouse in here.

Ken Now take it easy darling… just take it easy.

Tug Shall I get an ambulance…

Deverill makes his way through the crowd

Deverill Make way please… please. (*reaches Ken*) What is it? What's happened here?

Ken I'm sorry about this, sir. It's my fiancée. She's a bit under the weather.

Janet is fighting to control her breathing

Deverill Yes. I should think she is. We'd better get a doctor.

Ken It's all right, sir. I am a doctor. I'll take her straight home.

Deverill You can use my car if you…

Ken I have my own thank you Mr Deverill. If I can just get her out of the heat. (*calls*) Would you mind moving back please, ladies and gentlemen. We must have a little more air…

The crowd move back a little

Tug (*shouts out suddenly*) Listen!

The crowd stop moving

Everybody stand still for a minute!

Complete silence but for Janet's breathing

Woman What is it, Tug?

Tug (*looking around him*) There's something! Can't you hear it?

Complete silence

Woman I can't hear nothin'.

Janet (*breathlessly, half-whispering to Ken*) No Ken! It's too late… too late…!

The glass of a chandelier tinkling above

Woman (*cries out*) What is it?

Tug The chandelier! Look out for the chandelier.

Amidst screams and shouts the chandelier comes crashing to the floor. This is followed by the first sounds of rumbling beneath the floor of the hall. People begin to shout out in panic

Deverill (*shouts*) Get out! Everybody get out… as quick as you can!

Shouts of panicking crowds

Anna The walls! Get back from the walls… they're going to come down!

We hear a terrifying crack in the plasterwork as the rumblings become even more violent. People scream as debris begins to fall

Ken (*shouts out*) Tug! Tug Wilson! Come over here! Help me with Janet…!

Tug (*shouts back*) I can't Doctor! I can't! The whole lot's gonna cave in…! (*shouts hysterically*) Watch out…!

A very loud scream from a woman. Shouts from the crowd as they make their way panic-stricken through every available exit. Falling masonry everywhere

After a moment of listening to this, we mix into the sound of a telephone ringing and being answered at the County Constabulary, which has itself just been shaken by the rumblings

Police Sergeant (*picks up receiver*) County Constabulary. (*pause*) I'm sorry Madam – I have no idea. (*pause*) No, we're in just the same state here. (*briskly*) Right you are Madam, thank you. Goodbye. (*slams down receiver, immediately answers the telephone*) County Constabulary. (*pause*) I'm sorry, sir. We can't promise anything until we know what's happened. (*pause*) Yes, we're doing all we can, but as I say, we can't do anythin' until… (*stops*) Hallo? (*taps phone*) Hallo? (*slams down receiver*) Aw well!

A door opens. Inspector Baxter approaches briskly

Baxter How we doin', Sarge?

Sergeant Most of 'em think it's the Gas Works.

Baxter Well, is it?

Sergeant No sir. Not as far as I can see. But it's almost the only place that isn't?

Baxter What's the score so far?

Sergeant Seems to be mainly broken windows, roofs, walls – that sort of thing. Vicar says he's got a crack in the wall of the vestry, but it's not dangerous.

Baxter Anywhere else?

Sergeant (*sorting through papers*) Redlow Bus Station. Roof caved in on one of the double-deckers.

Baxter Anybody hurt?

Sergeant Not too bad. Few cuts and bruises, that's all. Looks as though Holly Mill's the worst hit. They've had a couple of fires at the filling stations on the London Road. The Fire Brigade boys are down there now. Apart from that it seems to be the Town Hall.

Baxter Town Hall?

Sergeant Hugh Deverill had a meeting…

Baxter Oh god! Was that tonight?

Sergeant They were lucky the whole lot didn't cave in on them. They took about thirty people off to Redlow General.

Baxter Serious?

Sergeant Mainly shock I think. Mind your back please, Inspector.

Somebody is sweeping glass on the floor

That was our window that was!

Baxter What about the Power Station? Did anyone check if it was there?

Sergeant Not yet sir.

Baxter Better do as quick as you can please, Sarge.

Sergeant Right, sir.

More telephone ringing

Baxter And somebody do something about these telephones! They're drivin' me mad!

He groans as yet another telephone rings

Sergeant (*picks up receiver*) County Constabulary. (*pause*) Oh yes, Doctor? (*pause. Shocked*) Do what, sir? (*pause*) Are you sure?

Baxter What is it?

Sergeant Just a moment please, Doctor. (*to Baxter*) It's Doc Richards, sir. He says they've found a crack in the road on Holly Mill Lane. Back of Tug Wilson's farmhouse.

Baxter Give us that! (*grabs telephone*) Hallo, Doc. Baxter. What's all this then? (*pause*) Are you sure? (*pause*) A fissure? Come off it, Doc! The next thing you'll be tellin' me… (*pause. Dismissingly*) Haven't you heard Doc? We don't have such things as earthquakes in… (*stops, obviously shaken*) A what? (*a long pause*) Yeah, yeah, heard you. I'll get some blokes down there as soon as I can. (*pause*) Huh! You're tellin' *me*. (*pause*) Right. Ten minutes then. (*replaces receiver*)

Sergeant Earthquakes in England? It's impossible.

Baxter Yeah? Then why is there a crack in Holly Mill Lane – a hundred yards long?

A sharp cut. Pause

In Holly Mill Lane, Dr Richards is doing his best to comfort a sobbing Mrs Wilson, wife of 'Tug'. In the background, a crowd have gathered. Fire engines, ambulances, race back and forth

Ken Come on Mrs Wilson. All over now.

Mrs Wilson (*sobbing*) Oh what a terrible thing! I thought the whole house was goin' to come down on top of me. My best china dinner set my dear mother left me – all gone. Smashed to smithereens! It's heart-breakin'… (*sobs*)

Tug If somebody had told me yesterday I'd live to see an earthquake in England, I wouldn't've believed 'em.

Ken I'd say it's much more likely to be earth tremors than an actual 'quake. Except for that road being torn open like that.

Tug Well, I don't know what it was. But it scared the livin' daylights out of me.

Ken You're not the only one.

Tug I thought doctors were supposed to have stomachs of iron?

Ken Earthquakes are the one thing in my life I can well do without. I've always had a dread of being near one. Even when I was a kid I used to have nightmares about buildings falling in on me, streets opening up in great chasms. It's not easy to wake up for the first time and realise you can't run away any more.

Tug What beat me was that girl of yours. Screamin' out in the middle of the hall like that. (*puzzled*) I can't make it out. She wasn't hit by anythin'.

Ken She has a concussion.

Tug But how? She went down long before any of us noticed the place shakin'.

Ken (*disquietingly*) I know. (*pause*) Anyway, it's up to the Hospital now. There's nothing I can do 'til I get their report…

Tug shouts out as a tree begins to topple over

Tug Watch out, Doc!

The tree comes thundering down. The crowd panic

Tug (*comes to his aid*) Doc! Are you all right?

Ken (*recovering*) Yes… (*struggles to get up*) I'm okay. Though I'm not so sure – if many of those trees start coming down…

Baxter pushes his way through the crowd

Baxter (*shouting*) Get these people out of the way!

Constable (*calls to crowd*) Come on now! Back… right back!

Baxter (*brusque and efficient*) You all right Doc?

Ken Just about.

Baxter (*horrified at what he sees*) Take a look at that will you!

Ken I shouldn't go too near the edge of that gap. It's rather a long way down.

Baxter (*stunned*) Holly Mill Lane! What happened to all those young elms along there?

Tug You tell us! They've been ripped out of the earth like a lot of weeds.

Baxter moves to the edge of the fissure and looks down. His voice is slightly off mic as it echoes

Baxter How deep is this thing? Does anyone know?

Ken Impossible to tell. But it's a good three feet across.

Loose soil is falling away

Baxter Soil's pretty loose.

Ken That's the trouble. It's as dry as a bone all the way along. For quite a way down too.

Baxter Is that bad?

Tug Try diggin' up a field some time. Soil's always damp – even an inch or so down.

Ken Which makes it all the more extraordinary when you think of the amount of rain we had before this heatwave.

Mrs Wilson It's heart-breakin'. Redlow's one and only beauty spot.

Baxter (*back on mic*) That's the least of our problems Mrs Wilson.

Tug (*angrily*) Not for us it isn't! (*shouts of agreement from the crowd*) Nobody cares a damn about the farmers! (*more shouts*) But if it was their precious New Town... (*more agreement*)

Baxter That's being just a bit stupid isn't it, Mr Wilson? Especially when there's hardly a building in the Town that isn't littered with glass and fallen ceilings. You'll all get compensation. You know that.

Tug Oh? And who can we rely on for that? Hugh Deverill – our celebrated benefactor?

Jeers from the crowd

Baxter We don't get earthquakes every day of the week you know, Mr Wilson.

Tug This is England Inspector. Hasn't anyone told you we don't get such things as earthquakes?

Baxter There's always a first time.

Tug Only when certain people start experimentin' with the things they know nothin' about!

More crowd agreement

Baxter (*irritated*) They've had tremors all the way along the South Coast – from Plymouth right the way up as far as Margate.

Ken Good Lord! Is that a fact Inspector?

Baxter Nothin' as bad as us, but they've had a twenty-foot tidal wave in the Isle of Wight. Quite a bit of flooding.

Tug There you are, you see!

Crowd apprehension

Baxter (*addressing the crowd*) You people will do yourselves far more good if you just go back to your homes and relax. We shall be doin' all we can, but in the meantime please keep well clear of this area. From now on it's strictly prohibited.

Constable (*calls out*) Come on now!

Moans from the crowd as they move off

Ken I know how they feel.

Baxter (*sighs*) So do I. But what can you do? You don't expect something like this to happen – do you?

Ken I'm not so sure about that...

Baxter What d'you mean?

Ken It was something Janet noticed up on that hill this morning. The air became so thick and dull. With that silence, something was bound to happen.

Baxter Silence?

Ken If you lived out East you'd know the meaning of that. There's always a moment of silence before an earthquake. It seems to be about the only warning Mother Nature's prepared to give. In some places they hang little wind-chimes outside the house. If they begin to flutter and there's no breeze – that's the time to run!

Baxter Yes. But in England –

Ken It'll teach us not to be so smug.

Pause

Baxter Oh well. It's up to the scientists now. Mr Deverill's got a couple of them on the way down from London. Let them sort it out I say… come on.

Ken No. Wait a minute Inspector. (*pause*) Is there a stream near here?

Baxter Stream? No. Not to my knowledge. Nearest is the Holly Mill River. But that's on the other side of town. Why?

Ken Just I thought I heard water, that's all. (*pause*) Perhaps not.

Baxter More like a broken water main.

Ken No. (*strangely puzzled*) In fact – I'm not even sure it was… water.

Baxter I'll get it checked.

Ken Yes. We want to be prepared next time.

Baxter (*sharply surprised*) Next time?

A fire engine races past and straight into the background of the next scene. Workmen are clearing up the debris in the damaged hall where the meeting was so hastily dispersed. Deverill and Anna talk to the two scientists, Professors Landers and Lippert

Deverill Well – here it is gentlemen. Not a very pretty sight, but I suppose we can think ourselves lucky we weren't killed.

Landers (*looking around*) I should say – very lucky sir. In fact I don't think there's any doubt that the force of these tremors was degree six.

Anna Degree six, Professor Landers? What does that mean?

Lippert It means, Mrs Deverill, that even by international standards, the tremors were extremely powerful. They could be the start of a series of shocks.

Anna Oh no!

Landers (*hastily*) Mind you this is not a proven fact. Professor Lippert merely suggests we must be prepared for the possibility.

Anna But I thought we weren't in an earthquake zone?

Landers Under normal circumstances we're not. The most the British Isles ever feel are a few shock waves. But there's no doubt on this occasion the seismographs show quite clearly degree six.

Deverill Don't seismographs ever go wrong?

Lippert Well –

Landers (*snaps in quickly*) No, Mr Deverill – never. They may haggle a little, but they do not go wrong.

Lippert (*looking around*) The extent of the damage in this hall alone is the sort of thing you'd normally expect to find in a severe 'quake area. Like South America, or the one at Skopje in Yugoslavia. I mean – look at the cracks in those walls. They're a perfect example of this degree.

Landers Plus the fact that an actual crevasse has occurred in the earth's crust. The whole thing's quite unique.

Anna Unique? I find it terrifying.

Baxter has entered the hall, and approaches

Deverill Ah – there you are Inspector! What news?

Baxter I think it's calming down a bit now sir. People seem to be shocked more than anything else.

Deverill Damage?

Baxter It's pretty extensive. Mainly broken windows, ceilings, plaster off the walls – that sort of thing. Quite a few gas and electrical fires too. And burst water mains.

Landers When the earth begins to move, everything moves with it.

Deverill (*brusquely*) Inspector. This is Professor Landers and Professor Lippert. (*They exchange greetings*) First thing in the morning they'll want to inspect the crack in Holly Mill Lane. I leave it to you to see they are offered every facility.

Baxter Very good, sir. (*turns to leave*)

Deverill And Inspector.

Baxter (*stops*) Sir?

Deverill I also leave it to you to see that the town is back in working order as quickly as possible.

Baxter (*puzzled*) Me sir? Isn't that up to the Chief Constable?

Deverill Get as many working parties together as you can. I don't care how. If necessary call on the Commanding Officer at RAF Redlow.

Baxter Won't he need authority from Whitehall sir…?

Deverill (*scoldingly*) Let me worry about authority, Inspector. Not you. (*pause. Dismissingly*) Good night.

Pause

Baxter (*continued indignation*) Good night, sir. (*walks off*)

Anna (*voice lowered*) Hugh! That was most unnecessary. You know very well it's not Baxter's job to…

Deverill Baxter has only me to thank for the job he holds today. If he doesn't like the way I do things he knows very well he can go back to the beat where I found him. (*briskly*) Right gentlemen! What next?

Landers We suggest you advise Whitehall immediately, sir.

Deverill Whitehall? What on earth for? Redlow is my responsibility.

Landers Mr Deverill. I think you and your colleagues should know that these tremors down here were not entirely unexpected.

Deverill (*shocked*) What!

Anna Professor! You mean – you knew this was going to happen? And you didn't tell us?

Landers We knew sooner or later there was going to be a seismological disturbance somewhere in southern England. The thing we didn't know was where and when.

Lippert But one man did. Or at least he had a rough idea.

Deverill What man?

Landers A young seismologist from Chile in South America. He's done quite a lot of research in his own country's 'quake areas. He worked with Lippert here for a time. In Geology at London University. Brilliant mind.

Anna But what made him forecast these tremors?

Lippert I don't know if you remember some years ago, people in Dover and Folkestone getting all worked up about a series of explosions they were hearing out at sea, in the English Channel? Usually in the middle of the night.

Anna Oh yes. I remember vaguely. Didn't they think they were unexploded mines or something?

Lippert That's right. But nobody could find anything. Not even the Royal Navy. That's when they called on us blokes. We sent down a team, and so did the French. But still nothing. At the time, we took very little notice. After all, there've been disturbances on the sea-bed of the Channel for years.

Anna I didn't know that.

Landers We've taken quite a few readings in the Observatory at Kew Gardens. Nothing much, but enough to register on the seismographs. After all, turbulence *is* mentioned in manuscripts dating back as far as the twelfth century.

Anna How fantastic! I hadn't realised.

Lippert However, this Chilean bloke decided to go and have a look for himself. He made his first dive to the sea-bed about three miles out from Dover. It took him quite a few days, but what he eventually found out there shattered me I can tell you. And quite a few others too. So much so that nobody believed him. They didn't want to. Not the Royal Institute, nor even Professor Landers here.

Deverill Is this true Professor?

Landers (*sadly*) Yes. I'm afraid so.

Deverill But for Heaven's sake, what was it he found?

Landers Something to convince him that one day seismological disturbances would no longer be confined to the English Channel.

Anna Then he was right?

Lippert In this country Mrs Deverill, you have to prove a theory before people believe it. Especially if it's one they haven't already thought of themselves.

Deverill If this man can help us, let's get him here – right away!

Landers I'm sorry, Mr Deverill. You won't get him as easily as that. His memories of England are none too pleasant.

Deverill That could be rectified. His visit will be made worthwhile.

Lippert (*amused*) Only science will get Gomez here, Mr Deverill. Not money.

Deverill Who? Who did you say? Gomez?

Landers Professor Gomez. Yes.

Pause

Deverill Then it's out of the question. Is there anyone else?

Lippert (*puzzled*) No. What's wrong with Gomez?

Landers He's the only one…

Deverill Josef Gomez has a long record of dubious political activity. It would be unwise to expose him to public scrutiny – particularly in Redlow.

Lippert That's nonsense! Josef's nothing more than a pacifist. He's no more politically minded than me.

Deverill (*adamantly*) I'm sorry. I cannot take the risk.

Anna Darling – you've got to. We have no choice. If the town's going to get another shaking like this, this man may at least be able to prepare us for it. (*to the others*) Gentlemen. Where is this Professor Gomez? How soon can we get hold of him?

Landers He's usually attached to the University of Santiago.

Lippert No. He's over in Zurich at the moment, attending a conference. We could probably get him over by the morning if he's interested enough.

Deverill No! I absolutely forbid it. I will not have Gomez in this town.

Landers (*calmly*) Very well, Mr Deverill.

The clearing-up operations are more prominent in the background. Broken glass and plaster being swept etc

But let me warn you this. Take a look around you. (*pause*) The whole nation is stunned by this appalling freak of Nature. By tomorrow morning there will be hardly a newspaper in the country that will not be buzzing with speculation of fear for the future. They *and* the people of this town have the right to know what they can expect. The chance to prepare for eventuality. (*pause*) Are you going to deny them that right? Because it's up to you Mr Deverill. It's up to you.

A quick, sharp cut to the sound of a jet liner landing. Mix in tannoy message in passenger arrivals lounge at London airport

Tannoy announcer British Continental Airways announce the arrival of their flight number 374 from Rome and Zurich. Passengers should proceed through Gate B for Customs and Immigration clearance. British Continental Airways flight number 374 from Rome and Zurich.

Airport lounge effects

Lippert (*off, calls*) Josef! (*approaches*) Josef, you old devil! There you are!

Gomez (*shaking hands, affectionately*) John! It's good to see you again. And Professor Landers. How are you, sir?

Landers (*affectionately*) Welcome back, Josef! (*pointedly*) Thank you for coming.

Gomez (*a wry smile*) Thank you for asking me.

Landers Josef. I want you to meet Mr Hugh Deverill. We shall be working quite closely with him.

Gomez (*politely*) How do you do sir.

Deverill (*very formal*) Professor Gomez. Thank you for coming. I've heard a lot about you.

Gomez And I've heard a lot about you, sir. I look forward to seeing your new town. I hear it is quite remarkable.

Deverill (*dismissingly*) Really? Well I hope we shan't have to detain you any longer than is absolutely necessary. I'm sure you'll be most eager to return to your own work.

Gomez (*accepting the tension*) My work is where science takes me Mr Deverill. There are no boundaries.

Deverill (*smiling*) Good. Follow me please. I have a car waiting.

They move off as we repeat the tannoy message

Tannoy announcer British and Continental Airways flight number 374 from Rome and Zurich. Passengers please report to Gate B…

Mix into this the sound of a TV newscaster

Newscaster …and it was announced early this morning that the Royal Institute's Department of Geology had recorded last night's tremors as force six degrees. A spokesman for the Royal Institute told our correspondent this was the highest ever recorded in British seismological disturbances. (*pause*) Meanwhile, in the stricken New Town of Redlow in Kent...

Mrs Wilson (*shouts*) Tug! Tug! They've got it on telly!

Newscaster ...the bewildered residents were still mopping up after a night of havoc and chaos...

Mrs Wilson (*shouts*) You're missin' it! (*a squeal of delight*)

Newscaster ...It was announced this evening that Mr Hugh Deverill MP, Chairman of the Deverill Foundation, will launch an immediate appeal to the Government for financial and other aid to compensate those distressed by damage and personal injury...

The television set is switched off abruptly

Mrs Wilson Oh Tug! What d'you do that for? I was watchin' the news.

Tug I don't wanna hear no more news. 'Specially about Deverill.

Mrs Wilson They had pictures of Redlow. I saw Mrs Luke.

Tug Huh! That must have been nice for you. We won't hear the last of that!

Mrs Wilson I recokon we'll get compensation you know. Everybody seems to think so.

Tug Well, I'm not paying for all those broken windows, that's for sure. And I want that lane repaired. I'm not trudgin' my livestock across those fields every Wednesday.

Outside a dog barks

What's up with *him* tonight?

Mrs Wilson Don't know. He's been goin' on like that all day. Can't be hungry. I only fed him at half-past seven.

Tug (*shouts out*) Shut up will yer! Blasted thing!

The dog begins to growl

Mrs Wilson Go and see what's wrong with him, Tug. He's givin' me an headache.

Tug He'll get my boot up him, that's what.

Mrs Wilson (*a monotonous voice*) No. We won't have to worry about him much longer. (*pause*)

Tug (*turns around, surprised*) Huh? What d'you say?

Mrs Wilson Well, he hasn't has he? He has to die sooner or later. We all do.

Tug (*staring at her*) He's still only a puppy.

Mrs Wilson (*hardly hearing him*) Hmm?

Tug Mickey. I say he's still only a puppy. (*pause*) You all right, love?

Mrs Wilson (*as though awakening*) Hmm? Oh yes. 'Course. Go out and see to him, Tug.

Tug (*irritably*) I'll see to him all right. Give us that torch.

He goes out and slams the door. Cut

Pause

Fade in: A man's deep and heavy breathing

Baxter Is it his heart, d'you think?

Ken I haven't the faintest idea. How long has he been like this?

Baxter Couldn't tell you. He'd have still been lying here if one of my blokes hadn't noticed the front door of the hut wide open.

Ken Does he live alone?

Baxter Who – old Ted? He hasn't moved out of these woods for years. He hates people. I think he's scared of 'em. That's why he locks himself away in this dump.

Ken In the left-hand pocket of my bag you'll find a syringe. Would you like to dig it out for me please.

Baxter Right. (*searches for the syringe*) Must be eighty if he's a day. Sad when they end up like this. Makes you dread old age, doesn't it? Is this the one?

Pause

Is he unconscious?

Ken Yes. It looks as though he's got a concussion. Probably fell down during the tremors last night. (*examining the old man*) Except I can't find any abrasions. Hold his arm for me will you please. I'm going to give him an injection. (*pause*) That's fine.

Baxter Will he come out of it d'you think?

Ken I don't know.

Baxter Better track down his relations, just in case. I know he has a cousin Winnie in Folkestone. Or he used to.

Ken If we can get him into my car, I'll run him straight up to Redlow Hospital.

Baxter Right!

Ken I'll take the weight of his head if you can just lift him up a little... (*struggling*) ...that's it!

Baxter Doc! Wait a minute. Look! He's opening his eyes!

The old man groans

Baxter Ted! Ted! Can you hear me ole mate?

Ken He can't do. I tell you he's out for a light!

Baxter (*unnerved*) Look at his eyes! He's... staring at me.

The old man groans. An unsuccessful attempt to speak

Baxter What's he tryin' to say? What is it Ted? Ted...?

The old man slumps back again into silence

He's closed his eyes again. (*pause*) Is he – ?

Ken No. Come on. Let's get him into the car.

Baxter I've never seen anythin' like that before. Those eyes... (*pause*) Will he make it to the hospital? I mean, if his heart gives...

Ken His heart is stronger than yours and mine, I can assure you.

Baxter (*bewildered and confused*) What? Are you sure Doc?

Ken Absolutely.

Pause

Baxter Then, if it's not his heart – what the heck is it?

A sharp cut

Pause

Tug Wilson is out in the dark whistling for his dog

Tug Damn you, where are you?

Mrs Wilson No signs?

Tug He's broken his leash.

Mrs Wilson Oh no.

Tug Probably gone after a rabbit. We'll find him sittin' on the doorstep first thing in the mornin'. Come on. I'm not chasin' around in the dark for him all night.

Mrs Wilson (*with a start*) Tug!

Tug What's the matter?

Mrs Wilson Let's find him. I don't want him out here on his own. Not tonight.

Tug Why not? He's been out plenty of times before…

Mrs Wilson Not tonight. Please. I – I don't want him goin' near that gap in the lane. (*pause*) Please.

Tug (*sighs irritably*) Come on then. We'll see if we can head him off. But I tell you this. If he doesn't show up pretty soon, he's out on his neck first thing in the mornin'. That I promise you.

Fade out

Pause

After dinner at the Deverill's home

Gomez The surface of the earth, Mr Deverill, is like the thin crust on the top of a pie. When the pressure beneath is too great, the crust will break open.

Deverill And that's what's happened here? A build-up of pressure in the bowels of the earth?

Gomez It's possible.

Anna But why has this happened Professor? All of a sudden like this?

Gomez That is something we have to find out Mrs Deverill.

Lippert I have a feeling it's the release of an extraneous gas. The intensity of that earth movement seems to point to it.

Deverill You mean volcanic?

Lippert Yes. Except this area has no record of a volcanic history. And in any case there's been no smoke from the fissure.

Landers Whatever it is, I think we can take it that it must be something extremely powerful that can produce tremors on this scale.

Deverill Which brings us back to this question of the English Channel. Professor Gomez. Do you believe the trouble originates there?

Gomez It is only a theory, Mr Deverill.

Deverill (*unconsciously*) Nevertheless, that is the reason you are here Professor. (*pause*) Now. Perhaps you'd be good enough to tell us what it was you found so alarming about your Channel survey.

Pause

Gomez (*unmoved dignity*) I found two enormous cracks.

Deverill Cracks? Where?

Gomez On the sea-bed. Both in different positions only a short way from the sea-shore. And both ridiculously out of proportion. About fifty yards long by three feet wide.

Anna Fifty yards!

Gomez Completely clean cuts, as though the rock had been forced open with a spade. (*intensely*) But the most extraordinary part of it all was that there was no sign of any marine life. Everything had gone within a radius of two or three miles of each fissure. The sea was dull and lifeless. Nothing lived – or perhaps... *could* live.

Anna How very strange.

Deverill Did you find any more of these cracks?

Gomez Yes, Mr Deverill. Many more. All following a perfect line at regular intervals along the coast. To the north and to the south-west. How far – I wouldn't like to guess. And remember, this was eight years ago.

Anna Which means this has been going on all this time, without our doing anything about it.

Deverill So these disturbances on the sea-bed of the Channel are now moving inland. Is that what you're suggesting?

Gomez What is your nearest point to the sea from here?

Deverill No more than eight or nine miles at the outside.

Anna The other side of Dover.

Gomez Close enough.

Deverill For what?

Gomez For us to find out what connection there is between the tremors you've had down here and the Channel fissures. (*suddenly urgent*) Robert. How long would it take you to get me a complete seismological record of this area?

Landers I could 'phone London first thing in the morning.

Gomez Please do. I want to know every seismograph reading – I don't care how far back or what degree.

Landers As far as I know the only thing they've ever had down here are a few shock waves. Three or four years ago.

Gomez (*to Lippert*) John. As soon as it's light in the morning, we'll take a look at that fracture in the surface of the road. Where is it?

Lippert A place called Holly Mill Lane.

Anna It runs along the back of a farmhouse – just near the main London Road.

Gomez We shall need to take some samples. Is there somewhere we can use as a laboratory?

Deverill Yes, we have a brand new school. Their laboratory is extremely well equipped. I'll speak to the headmaster.

Gomez Good!

Anna (*sceptically*) Professor Gomez. Be frank with me. Does this mean from now on we're going to have to live for the rest of our lives fearing earthquakes? Here – in England?

Gomez (*a wry smile*) You mustn't allow the prospect to concern you too much Mrs Deverill. In my country earthquakes are a part of our national heritage. My people have lived in their shadow all their lives. And died.

Deverill At least you know what to expect. You're prepared.

Gomez When the earth begins to tremble, Mr Deverill, you are never prepared. For those few terrifying seconds your complete world comes to a standstill. You can do nothing but put yourself in the hands of the Almighty. (*pause*) And when that devil beneath your feet opens up the ground like the jaws of a serpent, you stand there poised on the edge like a child – helpless. (*pause*) And when it is all over the child begins to wander around – too dazed to wake up. (*pause*) No, Mr Deverill… we are never prepared to meet this Devil. Whether it is in South America, Japan, Yugoslavia – or even Holly Mill Lane.

Sharp cut. Pause

Fade in: Inside Ken Richard's car. Passing traffic etc.

Ken How's the old chap? Can you see, Inspector?

Baxter (*leaning over seat*) All right, I think. At least he's still breathing.

Ken Few more minutes we'll be at the hospital.

Baxter (*sits back again*) Good job too, I say! Gave me the shudders when he opened his eyes like that. Like somebody who had already died.

Ken (*attention focused off*) That's funny.

Baxter What?

Ken Holly Mill Lane. There's someone moving around down there.

He pulls the car to a halt

Baxter Where? I can't see anybody…

Ken To the left. Can you see the torch?

Baxter (*straining to see*) Hey – yes! There's two of 'em. They must be out of their minds or somethin'. That whole lane's out of bounds. We gotta stop 'em goin' near that gap.

Ken (*opening the car door*) Come on!

Running steps as they dash off

Crossfade to Tug Wilson in Holly Mill Lane

Tug (*calling to the dog*) Mickey! (*whistling*) Mickey! You round here? (*silence*) It's no use. He's gone.

Mrs Wilson (*a dreary, but firm voice*) No. He's over there.

Tug (*looking*) Where?

Mrs Wilson In that bush – on the other side.

Tug (*disbelieving*) I can't see nothin'. It's much too dark.

Mrs Wilson He's there. I know he's there.

Tug Well, there he stays. I'm not gonna try and cross over that gap. The whole lot'll cave in – *me* with it!

Mrs Wilson You shouldn't be afraid, Tug. It's not like you.

Tug I tell you he's not over there. If he was he'd…

The dog barks from the other side of the fissure

Mickey! You stupid lookin'… (*sighs*) Here. Hold the torch then. Stand back. I'm gonna jump. (*pause*) One, two, three… and… (*He jumps*) Over!

The sound of falling earth down the fissure. The dog growls

Now – come here will yer! You tryin' make me break my neck or somethin'? (*He struggles to grab the dog*)

The sound of footsteps running towards them

Baxter (*shouts on his approach*) Tug! Tug Wilson! What the hell d'you think you're doin?

Ken (*angrily*) You'll get yourself killed doing things like that.

Tug I'm all right. Quite all right.

The dog growling

Shut up will yer!

Mrs Wilson (*faint suggestion of a smile*) He broke his leash. The dog.

Baxter That's not all he'll break if he doesn't get back here. D'you know how deep that thing is Mr Wilson?

Mrs Wilson Very deep.

Tug I'm comin' back!

Ken Don't be a fool man. You can't jump that gap holding the dog. Go the long way around.

Tug Oh no. Just keep out of the way. (*straining to see*) I'd be all right if it wasn't so dark.

Ken (*with urgency*) Inspector! Run up and put on my car headlights will you! He's going to go straight down this lot if he doesn't.

Baxter (*rushing off*) Right!

Ken (*calls*) Quick as you can!

Tug I'm all right I tell yer! I don't know what you're kickin' up all this fuss...

Ken (*snaps back*) Just stay where you are! Do as I say! (*turns back to Mrs Wilson*) Mrs Wilson. You'd be saving us an awful lot of trouble if you just go straight back to the house. It's extremely dangerous out here.

Mrs Wilson (*contentedly*) I'm not scared. Not a bit. (*looking up*) Why should *I* be scared of the night. It's the best time. I feel... wide awake.

Another fall of earth

Ken Keep back will you! The soil's falling all the time!

Mrs Wilson (*calls gently*) Tug.

Tug What?

Mrs Wilson Give me your hand.

Ken No! Don't be a fool!

Mrs Wilson (*strangely confident, quiet*) It's all right. He won't fall. *I* won't let him. (*pause*) Give me your hand Tug.

Ken No!

Mrs Wilson That's right love. Just a little further...

The dog begins to growl again, and then a more sudden fall of earth. Ken shouts out

Ken Tug!

Pause. The earth stops falling

Mrs Wilson (*smugly*) There! You see. I didn't let you fall, did I?

Tug The next time he goes over there – he stays!

Ken You fools!

Baxter comes running back, breathless and shocked

Baxter Doctor! Doctor... come quick... please!

Ken (*surprised and puzzled*) Inspector? What's the matter... what's happened?

Baxter Old Ted... the old boy. He's gone from the car.

Ken (*shocked*) What!

Baxter Disappeared. The car door was wide open. I can't find him anywhere.

Ken But he was unconscious. He can't have just walked off…
Baxter Well he has. And if we don't get hold of him pretty soon…

The dog begins to growl more furiously than ever

Tug (*irritably*) What's the matter with you now… Mickey!
Ken Shut up!
Tug Huh?
Ken All of you. Listen. (*pause*)
Baxter (*puzzled*) What?
Ken (*shaking with an expectant fright*) Listen. Can't you hear it?

For a moment there is complete silence. Gradually we hear the first sound of a faint bubbling movement – similar to volcanic lava. It is of a high pitch, and contains an uncanny resemblance to a human whining or screeching. The group are stunned into near disbelief

Baxter (*voice hushed with fear*) What the… what *is* it?
Ken Give me the torch! Somebody give me that torch!

Immediately the dog begins to whine, growl, and then bark. Suddenly and without warning he once again breaks his leash and dashes off

Tug (*calls*) Mickey! Come back here!
Ken The fissure! Look at the fissure. (*frozen horror*) It's mud! It's… coming out of the fissure…! Look at it!

The sound of the mud is beginning to swell up

Tug shouts in horror

Mrs Wilson (*shouts*) It's all right Tug! It's all right!
Baxter Oh my God! It's coming over the top! All the way along! It's coming over the top…!

Swell up and magnify the sound of the mud and then fade out

END OF EPISODE ONE

The Slide
by Victor Pemberton

Episode 2: Down Came A Blackbird

Produced by John Tydeman

TRANSMISSION:	Sunday 20 February 1966	1900–1930 LIGHT
REHEARSALS:	Wednesday 2 February 1966	1030–1830
RECORD:	Wednesday 2 February	1830–1930 (to H.11)
STUDIO:	B.11	
R.P. No.	TLO 605/552	
EDIT:	Friday 11 February	0930–1245 (H.54)
PLAYBACK:	Friday 11 February	1530–1600 (5108)

CAST:		
	Gomez	Roger Delgado
	Deverill	Maurice Denham
	Landers	Rolf Lefebvre
	Lippert	Allan McClelland
	Richards	David Spenser
	Anna	Marion Mathie
	Baxter	Geoffrey Matthews
	RAF Corporal	Anthony Hall
	'Tug' Wilson	Stephen Jack
	Mrs Luke	Noel Hood
	Nursing Sister	Eva Haddon
	Janet	Elizabeth Proud
	Sorensen	Fraser Kerr
	Barry	Glyn Dearman

S.M.s:	Panel: Amna Smith; Grams: David Cain; Spot: Margaret Rushton
SECRETARY:	Helene Grygar, PABX 2168

Announcer Redlow New Town has suffered a series of earth tremors. In nearby Holly Mill Lane, Doctor Richards and Inspector Baxter find mud seeping out of the vast fissure in the middle of the road. They immediately telephone the news to MP Hugh Deverill.

It is the early hours of the morning in Redlow New Town. Hugh Deverill and his wife Anna are asleep in their bed at home. As we open, the telephone is ringing continuously and it not for a moment or so that Deverill, tired and irritated at being disturbed, stretches out to answer it

Deverill (*hazy*) Redlow 306. Hallo. (*pause*) Yes. Deverill speaking. (*pause*) Who? (*pause*) Inspector. D'you know what time it is? It's four o'clock in the morning. (*pause*) Well of course I'm in bed – where d'you think I was... (*pause*) What? (*pause*) What has?

Anna begins to wake up

Anna (*half asleep*) What is it darling?

Deverill (*ignoring her*) Are you sure? (*pause*) Huh? (*pause*) Oh – don't be absurd man! Look at the wretched thing. Couldn't possibly... (*pause*) Are you sure? (*pause*) Well, is there danger of it – (*pause*) There is?

Anna What is it Hugh?

Deverill (*ignoring her*) Then I suppose we'd better get somebody down there...?

Anna (*insistent*) Darling! Tell me!

Deverill (*irritated*) Anna – will you please wait! (*returns to telephone*) Inspector. Have you notified Professor Gomez and the others? (*pause*) Then please do so – right away. (*pause*) No – I don't know his room number but you can ask Reception. (*pause*) Yes. I'll try and get down there right away. (*pause*) Oh I don't know. About fifteen minutes I should think. (*pause*) Right? (*pause. Brusque*) Yes. Yes. (*He replaces the receiver*) Damn!

Anna (*irritated*) What is it?

Deverill They've got some trouble at Holly Mill Lane. Mud overflowing from the crack in the road.

Anna Mud?

Deverill (*dismissing it*) Or something – I don't know. Four o'clock in the morning!

He gets out of bed and crosses the room

Anna Where's it coming from? It hasn't been raining, has it?

Deverill (*across the room*) Don't think so. (*slides open the wardrobe door*) Have you seen my sweater? The green one?

Anna Top shelf. (*pause*) How serious is it then?

Deverill (*getting dressed*) It's been gushing out all night apparently.

Anna What, all the way along?

Deverill Baxter exaggerates –

Anna (*concerned*) That fissure's about a hundred yards long. It'll take them days to get the mess cleared up.

Deverill The slide's going to reach the Wilson farmhouse. It backs onto the lane.

Anna Slide?

Deverill Down the hill.

Anna Hill?

Deverill (*irritated*) It's been sliding down the hill from the fissure.

Anna There isn't a hill.

Deverill Don't be stupid please.

Anna I tell you there isn't. Holly Mill Lane is as flat as a pancake. I've been down there dozens of times in the car.

Deverill Then you couldn't have noticed.

Anna You'll see. (*seductively*) Don't go Hugh.

Deverill I *have* to go.

Anna (*snaps sulkily*) Then go!

Deverill (*Deverill stops what he is doing, and comes close to her. Speaking intimately*) I *have* to go… *you* know that. (*pause*) You don't think I like going out in the middle of the night, do you? Not now – not leaving you here – like this?

Anna (*sulkily*) I don't know. (*pause*)

Deverill I'll show you… (*an intimate kiss*) Convinced?

Anna Don't be long. I hate being on my own.

Deverill (*crossing the room*) Half an hour. (*opens door*)

Anna (*calling*) Hugh.

Deverill (*stops*) Hmm?

Anna (*calls, haughtily*) I don't care what you say. Holly Mill Lane *isn't* a hill. It's as flat as a pancake!

Deverill (*calls back, smiling*) Of course it is my dear. (*pampering*) Of course it is. (*slams the door as he leaves*)

Sharp cut. Pause

Fade in: The sound of stone being chipped by a small chisel

Lippert (*stops chiselling*) It's no good. It's like chipping away at stone. It's a hell of a job even to get a few pieces. I can't believe this mud.

Gomez Inspector. Last night you told us this was a slide.

Baxter Last night it was, sir. Right up 'til just before you came. I went in to Mr Wilson's to 'phone you. When I came back – this is how it was.

Landers But it couldn't possibly have dried up in so short a time; look at it now – it's a solid mess.

Baxter All I'm tellin' you sir is that when we came up here last night, we got the shock of our lives. The mud pourin' out of that crack is like nothin' I've ever seen before. (*indicating*) Right up there – by that first group of trees.

Gomez Can you remember what it looked like Inspector? Was it the sort of mud you would expect to find after a downfall of rain?

Baxter No sir – it wasn't. (*a feeling of obvious concern*) It was filthy stuff. (*pause*) The sort of stuff you get out of a volcano.

Lippert Lava?

Baxter Yes sir. It was bubbling – moving. (*pause*) But what I hated most of all was that noise.

Landers Noise?

Baxter A sort of slithering… squeaking… Horrible!

Gomez What do you make of it John?

Lippert I'm dashed if I know really. The thing that gets me is this colour – this overall green.

Gomez It could be an iron content.

Lippert Yes it could – but I've never come across it so distinctly in this part of the country before. And certainly not down here. (*pause*) And look. (*indicating*) These long thin streaks – they're a different colour to the rest of the formation. You see at first glance it looks like a dried-out mud bank or something. But where the heck does it come from? Under normal conditions this sort of thing would take years to form.

Gomez The soil has obviously been swamped by a vast amount of water. Maybe an underground stream.

Lippert Well if it has, it's happened beneath the surface of the earth. It's as dry as a bone up here.

Gomez (*half to himself*) How can mud harden into stone almost instantaneously?

Baxter Incidentally sir, I checked with the Water Board at the Town Hall. It can't be a broken water main. There aren't any this side of the London Road.

Gomez Thank you Inspector. (*pause*) Robert. You remember the year I did my Channel survey?

Landers Of course.

Gomez Can you remember any seismograph readings at all for the British Isles around that time?

Landers Good lord old boy – you're asking something! I know there was something on the French side, but nothing very much. If you want, I could get London to send me down some photostats?

Gomez Could you do that?

Someone is heard approaching

Landers Of course.

Deverill (*approaches*) Good morning gentlemen.

Everyone greets him

How the devil are we going to get rid of all this stuff?

Baxter I've been in touch with RAF Redlow sir. The Station Commandant says he's quite willin' to let us have a few men, *if* we can get hold of some equipment.

Deverill What do you need?

Baxter Electric drills. We've got to try and break up the stuff. And anyway I'm all in favour of gettin' it sealed off before people start driftin' around.

Deverill Very well. Do what you can.

Baxter Yes sir.

Deverill And so Professor Gomez – what d'you make of all this?

Gomez At the present moment – (*sighs*) nothing.

Deverill Have you ever seen anything like this? Where has the mud come from?

Gomez Mr Deverill. This is the epicentre of the tremors felt in this area. One cannot expect a fracture of the earth's crust to go unnoticed. Geological disturbance of some description was inevitable.

Deverill Well I am quite aware of that Professor. I merely asked if you knew what was causing it?

Landers We have a feeling there's an underground river or stream. At this stage it's very difficult to tell. With your permission we should like to start a series of investigations.

Gomez Yes. I would prefer these investigations to be carried out with the maximum secrecy.

Deverill But isn't the real danger over now? Once we've sealed it back in the fissure…

Gomez Mr Deverill. We have no guarantee that such a thing will not happen again.

Deverill (*stops, startled*) You mean – this is possible?

Gomez Unfortunately Nature's ways are so unpredictable Mr Deverill, until proved otherwise. She is like a haughty child. We don't know how to treat her until we know what is wrong.

Lippert If you don't mind me saying Mr Deverill, I think Josef's right. The fewer people who know about this, the better. We don't want to start a panic.

Deverill The people of Redlow will *not* panic. That I promise you. (*pause*) Allow me to worry about that Professor. (*pause*) Inspector?

Baxter I'll do my best sir.

Pause

Deverill (*looking around*) It is flat – isn't it?

Landers (*puzzled*) I beg your pardon?

Deverill This lane. It's not on a hill – nor even an incline.

Landers (*looking*) Er – no. No, I suppose it's not. Hadn't really thought about it. Why?

Deverill I was just wondering how mud was capable of sliding upwards on a slope – that's all.

There is a silence from everyone

Gentlemen?

Pause

The sound of a 0.22 rifle being fired. In the background, a slight breeze

Ken Good shot Tug! Good shot!

The dog is panting

Tug (*to dog*) Go on boy! Go fetch him!

The dog barks out loud, then dashes off

Number of years I've been shootin' rabbits on this land – and still I can't seem to get rid of 'em. Not even with myxomatosis.

Ken (*looking around*) It's so quiet, isn't it?

Tug Huh? What is?

Ken Everything. The whole atmosphere. (*pause*) Don't you find the English countryside quite extraordinary? At times when the sun comes out even for five minutes, things take on a new meaning. The slightest dab of colour on the horizon stands out with such a pin-point clarity. (*pause*) Looking out there makes me feel very secure, you know.

Tug Secure? After an earthquake?

Ken Yes. Well, that's the escapist in me you see Tug. I'm just like the rest of us. I never believe it could really happen to me. It can happen to everybody else – but not to me. (*sighs*) Though mind you, when it does, it's a bit of a shock.

Tug That's the most terrifyin' thing I've ever seen in my life.

Ken What's that?

Tug Holly Mill Lane. The way the earth can just be ripped apart in a matter of seconds. It cut through that road like a tin-opener. And that mud – pourin' out of there like – like everythin' down below had just fallen away. (*returns to the practical*)

The dog is heard approaching

Ken Ah! Here he comes!

Tug (*calls*) Here boy! Here!

Ken What's he got in his mouth? That's not a rabbit.

The dog is panting

Tug Give it here boy… aw no! You dopey lookin'…

Ken It's a bird. A blackbird.Quite a big one.

Tug Has he killed it?

Ken (*looking at the bird*) No… I don't think so. There aren't any marks on him. It couldn't have been your bullet.

Tug That's funny. I didn't think it was the dog. He don't usually go after wild fowl. He's much too docile.

Ken Wait a minute, Tug. D'you remember a little while ago? Soon after we left your place? Didn't I tell you I thought I saw something drop from the sky…

Tug (*remembering*) Hey! That's right.

Ken I didn't hear a bullet shot, did you?

Tug No. Anyway, who wants to kill a blackbird?

Pause. Silence

Ken (*half-accusing*) Yes. Who? (*pause*) Which direction did it come from – can you see?

Tug (*indicating*) Somewhere over there. Near the Oak.

Ken (*dashing off*) Right! Take one side, I'll take the other.

Fade out

Pause

Fade in: The sound of a whistling kettle. After a moment it is taken off, and we hear the sound of hot water being poured into a teapot

Mrs Luke I'm glad you called Inspector. It's none of my business you understand, but I wouldn't be doing my duty if I didn't keep you fully informed.

Baxter I quite understand Mrs Luke, and I do appreciate it.

Mrs Luke Will you take one or two lumps?

Baxter (*unwilling politeness*) No sugar thank you very much.

Mrs Luke It was that terrible old man, you see. The one you're looking for – *and* I'm not surprised.

Baxter Old Ted – the farmworker?

Mrs Luke Yes. That's the fellow. What an unkempt person he is. I told him so, you know. Many a time.

Baxter You've seen him then? Madam?

Mrs Luke Of course.

Baxter When was this?

Mrs Luke First thing this morning. I was on my bicycle on the London Road. Tuesday is always my day to go into Redlow Market. It's about the only time I can leave my dear mother on her own – especially after all those awful earth-shake things…

59

Baxter (*exasperated*) Of course. So he was walking along the London Road was he?

Mrs Luke No, no, no. *I* was on the London Road. *He* was in Holly Mill Lane.

Baxter (*sharply surprised*) Holly Mill Lane? Are you sure?

Mrs Luke Absolutely! As I looked down, there he was – straggling along like the nasty old drunk he is. He was always a one for the bottle, you know. (*pours the tea*) Anyway, I was terrified he was going to walk right into that dreadful crater thing. It was straight ahead of him – he'd have fallen in…

Baxter What did you do?

Mrs Luke I called out.

Baxter Did he hear you?

Mrs Luke (*haughty*) Not at all. He didn't even look around to see who it was. Such an arrogant man. (*pause*) However, I buried my pride, got off my bicycle and ran after him.

Baxter And?

Mrs Luke I called, and I called, and I called – and *still* he wouldn't answer. Infuriating!

Baxter (*belligerently*) Of course.

Mrs Luke But I didn't give up. I ran up to him, and tapped on his shoulder.

Baxter And he stopped?

Mrs Luke (*a more serious tone*) Yes. He stopped. And it wasn't until that moment that I realised something was wrong.

Baxter Wrong?

Mrs Luke For a moment we just stood there, until gradually he turned around to face me. (*pause, with some effort*) His face – it was… yellow – so tired and drawn. He looked so old. (*pause*) But most of all it was his eyes.

Baxter Yes?

Mrs Luke They fascinated me – so pin-point sharp. And so very different from the rest of his face. I was very disturbed.

Baxter Did he say anything?

Mrs Luke Yes. (*with emotion*) He gave me a vicious look and said "Go away! Go away and mind your own business!" (*pause*) For one terrible moment I thought he was going to hit me.

Baxter But he didn't?

Mrs Luke No, he just turned his back on me and walked off. But thank goodness at least he went in a different direction – away from the Lane.

Baxter *Which* direction Mrs Luke? Can you remember?

Mrs Luke Across the fields at the back of Mr Wilson's farm. I tried to telephone your people, but by the time they got here it was too late. (*pause*) Inspector. What *is* wrong with that old man? Is he ill or something?

Baxter I don't know Mrs Luke, but thank you very much for your information. You've been most helpful… as soon as we know any more, we'll keep you advised…

Mrs Luke No, no Inspector – don't go. There's something more.

Baxter Yes?

Mrs Luke It was horrible. I noticed it as he was walking away. (*squirms. Pause*) A poor little thing. So cruel. So very cruel. (*pause*) Fancy wanting to go and kill a pigeon – a poor little...

A very sharp cut

Fade in: Slight breeze blowing through the branches of the oak tree

Tug A wood pigeon. Dead as a doornail. (*They look at the bird*)

Ken It's still warm. (*pause. Bitter*) Someone's been amusing themself, I'd like to know who.

Tug You mean, you think someone's been puttin' down the poison?

Ken I don't know, but I'm going to find out. Tug, have you got a handkerchief on you?

Tug Er – yes, I think so. What you gonna do?

Ken I'm going to take a couple back to have a look at them. If they find they've been poisoned, I'll inform the RSPCA.

Tug I can't imagine anyone wantin' to use poison. We haven't done that since the myxomatosis outbreak a few years back. And anyway, you can see everythin' that goes on here from Holly Mill Lane.

Pause

Ken (*slightly off mic*) Well, here's your rabbit. And that's no myxomatosis.

Tug (*looks at rabbit*) No – and it ain't no bullet neither.

Ken (*taken by surprise*) It's what? Let me see. (*looks at the rabbit*) Good Lord!

Tug The one I got – I got! And he's around here some place. But it ain't this one, I can tell you. He's as clean as a whistle...

Ken (*interrupts him abruptly, voice hushed*) Tug! Keep still! Stay where you are!

Tug Huh? Why – what's...?

Ken (*sudden urgency*) Get over here. Someone's coming – quick!

The sound of them dashing into the bushes

(*voice very low*) It'll be interesting to see what... keep down! Here they come...

The sound of someone treading softly through the thicket. Whoever it is suddenly comes to a halt

Tug (*a loud whisper, shocked*) Doc! D'you see who it is? Look – can you see!

Ken (*hushed voice*) Keep down!

The footsteps approach

Tug Hey! Can you see who it is? That's Mary. That's my wife Mary!

A sharp cut

Very slight pause

Schoolchildren very boisterous in their play-ground. Window is suddenly slammed closed, and the noisy sound is immediately cut into the background, where it is gradually faded out during the course of the scene

Gomez I'm very surprised. I had no idea the British were so capable of such radical planning.

Lippert Oh yes. They're pretty 'with it' down here, all right. Mind, you'll always find plenty of people ready to knock the idea of these New Town developments; but if there's one thing they do offer, it's a decent place to live in. And that's more than you can say for some parts of the country. You only have to look at this place. I'd give my right arm to send my kids to this kind of school. (*looking around*) In fact I could do with a laboratory like this for myself.

Gomez Think yourself lucky my friend. You should come out to Santiago some time. Everybody wants to know about earthquakes. Everybody wants to know when to expect them. (*smiles*) But mention the magic word 'money', and see how they shrink away.

Ken You've never really forgiven us, have you Josef?

Gomez Forgiven?

Lippert We have a pretty lousy deal – don't think I don't know. Oh, I'm not trying to say I was the blue-eyed boy who believed everything you said about that Channel survey, but…

Gomez (*smiles*) My dear john. I'm a South American. We Latins are noted for our excitable nature. I don't blame anyone for not believing me. What I knew – particularly at that time – must have taken some believing, I know that.

Lippert What *do* you believe Josef? (*pause*)

Gomez Believe? – (*pause*) I believe we are reaching a significant era in the history of the earth's surface. What it is – as yet I don't know. (*pause*) Maybe, if we have a look at that mud sample of yours, maybe we'll find out?

Landers enters in a very worked-up state. Behind him is Deverill

Landers Josef! My dear fellow – we've got to work fast.

Deverill Somebody had better do something – before the whole place blows to pieces.

Gomez Why? What's wrong?

Landers The same things happened. I've just been on the 'phone to London. They've had some earth tremors in the North.

Gomez/Lippert (*together, shocked*) What!

Lippert Where?

Landers The Lake District – *and* in Scotland. The water on Lake Belvedere was set in motion for nearly a minute. Apparently there's been absolute chaos.

Lippert Any fractures in the soil?

Landers We're just waiting to hear. The shocks were felt as far away as the Shetland Isles. Josef – what d'you think this means?

Gomez (*seriously*) I'm not sure.

Deverill (*very neurotic*) Not sure? What d'you mean… you're not sure?

Gomez I mean Mr Deverill, that at the moment it is too early to be sure about anything.

Landers It's all right Josef. Mr Deverill is very worried by all this.

Deverill Worried! What are we supposed to do? Sit patiently around and wait for you to work out your theories? Whilst the entire British Isles collapse all around us? You must have *some* idea?

Gomez All I can tell you is that this appears to be part of a pattern.

Deverill Pattern?

Gomez I don't have to tell you that the British Isles do not lie in what we usually refer to as 'an earthquake zone'. But the effects of the tremors you have felt down here sent a series of shock waves for quite an alarming distance. Is that right Professor?

Landers Indeed yes. As far as Bradford.

Deverill Bradford! In Yorkshire? But that must be three hundred miles away?

Gomez Precisely. That is why I think it is all part of this pattern. First of all the sea-bed in the English Channel, then the immediate south, and now the north.

Deverill Does that mean that we can expect more of these disturbances?

Gomez Mr Deverill, the first man who is able to foretell the exact position that the earth will shake will be a very rich man indeed.

Pause. Lippert, across the room, suddenly calls out

Lippert Josef! Come and have a look at this!

They all rush over to join him

The sample. It's burnt a hole in my briefcase.

Gomez Burnt?

Lippert Be careful – don't touch it! When I tried, it was like getting hold of dry ice.

Gomez Here – tip it out onto the table.

Lippert holds up his briefcase and tips the hard lump of mud formation onto the table. It falls with a thud

Gomez Now – let's have a look.

They are all bending over, inspecting the sample

Lippert It's bright green. Extraordinary.

Gomez It could be the fluorescent lighting in here.

Landers In a way, it's really rather beautiful to look at. Like a precious stone.

Lippert What I can't understand are those streaks running through…

Gomez Now I remember where I have seen this! We have a rocky beach just south of Valparaiso in Chile. I have seen this type of thing soon after the great earthquake of 1960.

Lippert But Josef – this isn't rock. It's a definite mud formation. (*indicating*) These streaks are usually part of stalactite. In fact I've seen this before myself – in various parts of the Pennines.

Deverill Well, couldn't this be the same thing?

Lippert Mr Deverill. Stalactites are a formation which take, in some cases, thousands of years to corrode.

A long tense silence

Deverill Gentlemen. I'm going to London. (*pause*)

Landers Where can we reach you sir?

Deverill I shall be at my club. (*a dramatic pause*) Gentlemen – just do it quickly! I want Redlow to survive.

He leaves. Door

Lippert Maniac! What does he think we are – another of his machines?

Landers He's achieved a lot in his time. Give him his due, he fought for this New Town. You can hate the man – but you can't ignore him. He's unsure of himself – that's all.

Gomez It's no use Robert. If it were a case of saving him alone, it just wouldn't be worth the bother.

Landers He's scared Josef – and he just doesn't know how to disguise it. Scared of all the possibilities – of what *could* happen in the next few days. You know I hate to have to tell you, but you two are very alike. The only difference is that Deverill *knows* how to bury his head in the sand. (*pause*) Pity him Josef – because nobody else does.

Fadeout

Pause

Fade in: Ken Richards and a Nursing Sister are walking hurriedly through a hospital corridor

Sister We have to move Miss Marshall from the main ward Doctor. She was beginning to disturb the other patients.

Ken But is she still delirious?

Sister Well, apparently. But it's so terribly difficult to tell. She's just lying there – mumbling to herself the whole time. The extraordinary thing is, about an hour ago, one of the patients in the next bed told us she sat up, looked around the ward, and then just slumped back again. I suppose it is a form of concussion but –

Ken What did Doctor Robeson say?

Sister He's sent for Doctor Ferman. He's coming down from London in the morning.

Ken Have you been able to make out anything she's been saying?

Sister No – not a thing. Just this awful sort of rambling. (*pause. Sympathetically*) What a terrible shock for you Doctor; you are due to be married aren't you?

Ken (*sadly*) Yes.

Sister I'm just amazed there weren't any more injuries. Most of the people they brought in were fairly old. Poor things. They're absolutely bewildered.

They come to a halt

Sister This is the room Doctor.

They enter the room. Door

   (*whispers*) Thank goodness. She seems to be fairly quiet.

Ken (*at bedside, calls gently*) Janet. Janet darling. Can you hear me? (*pause*) It's me – Ken.

Sister I don't think she can hear you.

Ken What's her temperature?

Sister Quite normal. Blood's just a fraction low… but I don't think it's anything to… (*sharply*) Doctor – look! She's opening her eyes…

Ken (*urgently*) Janet. Can you hear me darling?

Janet begins to mumble, almost inaudibly

Sister (*riveted attention*) She's wide awake. She must be…

Janet (*only just distinguishable*) Li… life… life… it's life.

Janet's mumbling stops abruptly

Sister She's closed her eyes again. (*pause*) She must be having a nightmare. Poor little thing.

Ken (*repeating Janet's word, more to himself, curiously*) Life?

Sister I wonder what she meant?

Pause

Ken Sister, I shall be at Mr Wilson's farmhouse tonight. If there's any change in her condition at all, I want you to telephone me immediately. I don't care when it is – but I *want* to know.

Fade out

Pause

Fade in: The sound of Tug Wilson digging a hole in the earth

A car draws up in the background, a car door slams, and Ken Richards approaches

Ken (*puzzled*) Tug. Why're you digging? At this time of night?

Tug 'Cause he's dead, that's why. The dozy thing's dead – he's no good to us now, eh Mickey?

Ken (*very shocked*) Your – your dog, Mickey? (*pause*) What happened?

Tug I don't know, and I don't care. All I know is he's dead and the sooner I get rid of him the better.

Ken Now look Tug – this can't go on. What with those birds, then the rabbit, and now – (*pause*) Did you speak to your wife?

Tug Yeah. I spoke to her.

Ken What was she doing out there in those woods?

Tug She was looking'.

Ken Looking? What for?

Tug Just lookin'.

Ken Now don't be damned stupid man! She was up to something… you know she was!

Tug (*irritated*) And you listen to me Doctor Richards! Don't start goin' around flingin' accusations at folks.

Ken Tug. Listen to me. If somebody's been using poison to kill off animals *I* want to know about it. I want to know why and for what reason.

Tug She didn't put down no poison. Not my Mary.

Ken How d'you know that?

Tug Because if she did, she must've been kept pretty busy. (*pause*) Take a walk over that field sometime Doctor. It's like a graveyard – birds, squirrels, rabbits, fieldmice… the lot!

Ken (*horrified*) What!

Tug And this is where I found the dog. Just lying there in a heap. (*pause. Looking at the dog, sadly*) Maybe he's better off. This is a rotten world to live in.

Almost unnoticed in the background, a car is drawing up

Ken Tug. I'm – I'm sorry about all this. But we've got to do something quickly. Something's killing off all these animals, and we've got to find out what it is.

Tug She wasn't upset, you know. My Mary. She's been motherin' that dog all these years – yet she wasn't upset. (*pause*) You better have a look at her some time Doc.

Ken Of course.

The sound of a man's footsteps approaching

Sorensen (*calls, approaching*) I'm sorry to trouble you, I'm looking for Doctor Richards.

Ken I'm Doctor Richards.

Sorensen Oh Doctor… I am sorry to trouble you sir. They told me I could find you here. My name's Sorensen. A few of us have been exploring the caves – we're camped just up the road at Holly Crag. We could do with your help Doctor. There's been an accident.

Ken Accident?

Sorensen Or at least, we think there has. A couple of our blokes went down this morning. It was only supposed to have been a routine job, but I'm afraid they've met some sort of trouble, footing or something. One of them took a tumble – but we're not quite certain how bad. The other bloke said he's in too much pain to move him, so we thought we'd better get hold of you.

Ken How d'you know about this?

Sorensen We were in radio contact up until a while ago. But the transistor's flaked out on us – we don't know what's going on down there.

Ken (*urgently*) I'll get my things.

Sorensen That's very good of you Doctor.

Tug I'll come with you – nobody knows them caves better than me.

Sharp cut

Pause

A knock on the door of the school laboratory. The door opens

Anna (*peering around the door*) Can I come in?

Gomez Mrs Deverill?

Anna (*closes door, approaches*) I saw the light as I was passing. I thought it was you. (*pause*) Aren't you having any sleep tonight?

Gomez I have to work. We're waiting for some equipment to arrive from London.

Anna It looks very odd in there. That small piece of stone in a huge glass tank.

Gomez It's the school aquarium. We had to borrow it from them.

Anna What does it all mean? Mud turning to stone like that.

Gomez All we can do is to try and find out.

Anna He's pushing you very hard, isn't he? My husband.

Gomez Your husband is a strong-willed man, Mrs Deverill.

Anna Do you hate him?

Gomez Hate is for the non-thinkers, Mrs Deverill. I don't hate anybody – but at the same time it doesn't mean that I have to respect them.

Anna You mustn't blame him. He had to fight his own principles to bring you here.

Gomez It wasn't exactly an easy decision for me to come.

Anna Yes. He's wrong about you. But then he's often wrong about people. (*pause. She moves around the room*) I suppose that's why he doesn't love me.

Gomez (*embarrassed*) Mrs Deverill…

Anna Oh – don't be embarrassed! Everybody knows. (*pause*) He's a lot older than me – we knew it wasn't going to be easy. (*pause*) Unfortunately I'm only just beginning to realise.

Gomez Mrs Deverill. I…

Anna Marriage is such an overestimated institution don't you think. It cuts you down to size. (*looking out of window*) Like those New Town citizens out there.

Gomez Mrs Deverill, I think maybe you should go home. It's getting late.

Anna (*amused, back on mic*) You know, you're very young to be a professor – I always thought professors had white hair and long beards. At least, most of the ones I've met have.

Gomez Please!

The door bursts open. Landers rushes in breathless and tense

Landers Josef! Get your coat on quick!

Gomez Robert. What's the matter?

Landers (*trembling*) The lane, my dear fellow. It's absolutely fantastic!

Gomez The lane?

Landers Holly Mill Lane – the fissure… it's swamped with mud. The whole place is slithering with the stuff.

Gomez (*horrified*) What!

Anna Mud? But it's dried up. I thought the whole thing was as hard as iron?

Landers At the present moment, Mrs Deverill, they've got half the men from the RAF station fighting to push it back. It's bursting out of the fissure all the way along. And the noise! (*with tremendous urgency*) Josef! I don't think they're going to be able to hold it. I just don't think they can do it!

Fade out

Pause

Fade in: Sorensen, the pot-holer, is leading Ken and Tug Wilson through twisting tunnels of the Holly Crag Caves

Sorensen Now, just take your time please Doctor. As we turn the corner here, we have to pass over a ridge. Keep your head down, and keep close to me.

Ken Why the heck you people risk your lives by coming down here I'll never know. It's not *my* idea of a holiday.

Sorensen (*amused*) We all get our kicks in different ways Doctor.

Tug (*in background*) It is so hot down here – it's never been like this before.

Sorensen We'll be all right in a few minutes. There's a wind-shaft just near the waterfall.

Ken Waterfall?

Sorensen Just a small one. It breaks up the stream. (*pause*) Now give me your hand Doctor – and keep your back well into the wall. We're just coming up to the ridge now.

For a moment we hear them struggling as they make their way across the ridge. Then there is a sigh of relief from them all

Are you all right?

Ken (*breathless*) Yes. OK. (*looking around*) Hey! This is quite something, isn't it?

Sorensen Some of the best stalactite formations in the entire Crag. It's possible they were started in the Neolithic period.

Ken Neolithic? D'you mean, you think there was a dwelling down here?

Sorensen If you'd like to have a look over here Doctor. (*to Tug*) Mr Wilson. Could you turn your lamp this way please? (*pause*) Thanks. (*indicating*) You see – here… these carvings?

Ken Good Lord – yes.

Sorensen The three figures. This shape here is a man… and a woman here… and just behind – the child.

Ken Fascinating!

Tug What are they supposed to be doing?

Ken It looks as though they're turning their back on something?

Sorensen Well, there are various schools of thought. Some think they're hiding from a wild animal – you can see the look of fear.

Ken (*absorbed*) Yes…

Sorensen As though they're scared out of their wits. (*pause*) They've got a photo-repro of it in Dover Museum. (*pause*) By the way, have you looked down below?

Ken Yes – now they're stalagmites, aren't they?

Sorensen That's right. They're only babies yet – but give them a few more thousand years!

Ken They're beautiful! But what a fantastic colour – that brilliant green. It's amazing how it stands out down here. Almost illuminous.

In the distant background we can just hear the faint sound of a small waterfall

I can hear water.

Sorensen That's the waterfall. Our blokes are quite near there – we should be able to call out soon. It's quite a narrow ledge along here, so keep close Doctor.

Ken You needn't worry about that – I'm right behind you!

Fade up the sound of the waterfall, then crossfade into the sound of the bubbling, squeaking mud which is moving at a tremendous rate through Holly Mill Lane. We are already in the next scene, with a general chaos in the background as men from the RAF station struggle desperately to control the overflows. The scene is played with an urgent speed

Landers (*calls*) Corporal!

Corporal (*approaching*) Sir!

Landers Can't you block it off at the other end – we can gradually move downwards?

Corporal It's impossible sir. As fast as we shovel the stuff, another lot slides right back again – and you've gotta be so careful sir. If you get any on your hands it burns like mad! It keeps stickin' to the shovel.

Landers How far has it reached up there – can you tell?

Corporal I should say about five or six feet sir. Squadron Leader's sent back for some more help. He's gonna try and get hold of a couple of bulldozers.

Landers Excellent! Thank you very much Corporal. Just do your best.

Corporal Very good sir! (*calls as he leaves*) Come on you blokes! Get a move on!

Gomez Robert. I think we're going to need some barriers here. Do you think you can get someone to do something about it?

Landers (*emphatic*) They'll jolly well have to do something about it! If this stuff reaches much further, it'll be down by the farmhouse. (*desperately concerned*) Josef. I've never seen anything like this before in my whole life. For Heaven's sake – what is it?

Gomez We have to face the fact that there is something forcing the mud out from the root of the fissure. As soon as we've been able to find that –

Landers Yes – but this terrible noise?

Gomez I know, I know. But we can't do anything until we have analysed the mud samples.

Lippert and Anna approach hurriedly

Lippert Josef! There *must* be an acid content of some sort. The soil and the grass are being scorched.

Gomez Scorched?

Lippert It's so deadly. They've just sent one of the RAF boys to hospital. His boots were burnt right the way through.

Anna I can't get hold of my husband – he hasn't checked into his Club yet. I've left a message.

Landers Good. Let me know the moment you hear please, Mrs Deverill.

Gomez John. Can you tell?

Lippert No more than – nine or ten inches at its deepest point.

Gomez Do you think we could separate it?

Lippert How d'you mean?

Gomez Divide it into sections. We could clear each one at a time.

Landers That's a point. Those bulldozers should be here soon.

Gomez As you clear each section, cover the fissure with boards and then some heavy weights.

Lippert That's no good. The boards would burn through. We've already tried.

Gomez Then you'll have to use metal.

Lippert Metal?

Gomez Or stone – or anything you can lay your hands on. The main thing is to seal up that fissure as quickly as we can. Robert. Can I leave you to organise that? I think John and myself should go back to the laboratory.

Landers Yes – of course. Anyway I'd better stay here. I've got the Mayor, the Town Clerk and all the lot of them tearing their hair out down there. I hope to God we come up with something soon.

Anna Josef. What happens if it rains? Will this make things worse? It's very thundery.

Gomez Rain?

Anna It feels as though it might.

Pause

Gomez looks up into the night sky, and talks half to himself, under his breath

Gomez Rain. Yes – maybe it will rain.

Lippert Rain! That's all we need! Rain! At a time like this!

Fade up the sound of the mud then crossfade back to the waterfall at Holly Crag. After a moment, Sorenson's voice, in the background and off mic, echoes in the darkness of the caves

Sorensen (*calls*) Barry! (*pause*) Barry, Keith! Are you there? (*He talks to the others who are still off mic*) They must be down there somewhere. (*calls again*) Oy! Anyone there…?

For the first time, we hear in the close foreground the deep and continuous breathing of the injured pot-holer, Barry

(*calls out*) Look! Look – there he is! Down there.

We hear them struggling to reach Barry

(*approaching*) Barry! Are you all right old son? What is it – the leg?

Barry (*with difficulty*) Yuh. The right one – I think it's broken. Where've you blokes been then?

Sorensen Stay where you are. We've got the Doc.

Ken Somebody's got my bag, please?

Tug Here you are.

Ken (*attending to the injured man*) Tug! Help me tear the trouser leg – quick! Now be careful… (*They tear the trousers*) Now. Does this hurt – here?

Barry (*calls out*) Ouch!

Ken Sorry.

Sorensen Where's Keith then?

Barry He's gone.

Sorensen Gone? What d'you mean?

Barry (*highly emotional and strained*) Gone, gone! What's the matter with you? Don't you know the meaning of the word. He's gone – dead!

Sorensen (*horrified*) Dead! Barry – what the hell are you saying?

Barry He went over the ledge there. (*very upset*) There was nothing I could do about it. (*pause*) If you'd have got here earlier, it wouldn't have happened.

Sorensen (*subdued with shock*) How'd it happen? (*pause*)

Barry (*composing himself*) Soon after we called you, the transistor went dead. We tried again and again, but it was no use. (*pause*) Keith looked round for a place for me to rest up a bit… ouch! Be careful Doc! (*pause*) We got as far as the waterfall, so we pitched down. (*pause*) We hadn't been here more than ten minutes when we heard someone comin' – down the ridge there. I thought it was you.

Sorensen Who was it?

Barry A bloke. An old bloke. (*pause*) How the hell he ever got down here, I'll never know.

Ken (*suddenly looks up, startled*) An old man? Did you say an old man? (*pause*) How old?

Barry (*in pain*) At least eighty – if not more.

Tug Old Ted!

Ken It couldn't possibly be! He'd never have got down here on his own. Not a man of his age. (*pause*) Did he say anything?

Barry That's just it. Keith tried to speak to him, but he wouldn't say a word – just kept right on walking – walking until he reached the edge.

Ken Edge?

Barry And then he stopped. (*pause. Slow, descriptively*) I remember his eyes – a vivid blue.

Tug It *is* Ted!

Barry They just fixed you with a stare. He gave me the creeps.

Ken And then? (*pause*)

Barry He started to sway about. (*reliving the horror*) Keith rushed over and tried to grab him, but then suddenly, for no reason at all – the old boy started lashin' out at him – like a maniac. (*pause*) It turned into a fight. Keith did his best to… I shouted – God knows how I shouted! But I was stuck here – I couldn't move an inch. (*a long tense pause*) It was too late. I couldn't do a thing. (*pause*) They both fell together. (*emphatically*) But the old boy – he had every intention of jumpin' – he *wanted* to – that I swear!

Sorensen Barry. What edge was this? D'you mean – by the water?

Barry Water! (*a strained, mocking laugh*) Take your lamp – and go and look for yourself. No – not that way. Over there.

The sound of footsteps as Sorensen moves about. Barry's voice is now in background

Barry No! Don't go too far! (*pause. Dramatically*) Now. Stand with your back to the wall. (*pause*) Now – look down.

Sorensen I can't see anything. (*looking*) It all looks completely… (*stops, squirms*) Oh my…! (*panics*) Doctor! You'd better come over here…! Come and take a look at this!

A sudden, sharp sound of the mud bubbling down below. It squeals and squeaks, and as we fade out the sound is intensified by the echo in the caves

END OF EPISODE TWO

The Slide
by Victor Pemberton

Episode 3: Analysis

Produced by John Tydeman

TRANSMISSION:	Sunday 27 February 1966	1900–1930 LIGHT
REHEARSALS:	Thursday 3 February 1966	1030–1830
RECORD:	Thursday 3 February	1830–1930 (to H.11)
STUDIO:	B.11	
R.P. No.	TLO 605/553	
EDIT:	Friday 11 February: 0930–1245 (H.54)	
PLAYBACK:	Friday 11 February: 1600–1630 (5108)	

CAST:

Gomez......................................	Roger Delgado
Deverill	Maurice Denham
Landers....................................	Rolf Lefebvre
Lippert.....................................	Allan McClelland
Richards	David Spenser
Anna..	Marion Mathie
Baxter......................................	Geoffrey Matthews
RAF Corporal	Anthony Hall
'Tug' Wilson.............................	Stephen Jack
Mrs Wilson	Miriam Margolyes
Nursing Sister	Eva Haddon
Janet	Elizabeth Proud
Sorensen...................................	Fraser Kerr
Nurse.......................................	Patricia Leventon
AC2 Gibbons	Nigel Graham

S.M.s:	Panel: Amna Smith; Grams: David Cain; Spot: Margaret Rushton
SECRETARY:	Helene Grygar, PABX 2168

Announcer Following the earth tremors, anxiety is growing at the alarming numbers of wildlife dying in countryside surrounding Redlow New Town. In the early hours of the morning, Doctor Richards and his party reach the surface of the Holly Crag Caves, after the discovery of yet another earth fissure.

In the middle of the night, an ambulance is pulling away from the entrance to the Holly Crag caves

Baxter (*aggressive*) Two men, Mr Sorenson! Two perfectly good men – lost their lives because of a hair-brained scheme of no significance. I hope you're proud of yourself!

Sorensen Now look here Inspector – we've been down those caves time and time again. We didn't know we were going to find all that stuff... have a heart!

Baxter You know damned well we've had these earth disruptions. You could have postponed the descent.

Sorensen Most of us are using up our holidays for this Inspector. We don't have time to postpone. (*pause*) Pot-holing isn't a sport you know. It's an important scientific survey. Besides which, my blokes have tackled worse descents than this, I can tell you.

Dr Ken Richards approaches

Baxter How is he Doc? Is he gonna be all right?

Ken It's a break – just below the knee-cap. They'll fix him in the hospital. If anything he's had a bad shock.

Sorensen We're very grateful to you Doctor. I don't know how we'd have got him out without you.

Ken Don't think I enjoyed crawling about in the dark, Mr Sorensen. It's not my favourite form of activity. (*pause*) If you'll take my tip, you and your group will clear out of here once and for all.

Baxter You didn't actually see old Ted down there at all?

Ken (*grimly*) No.

Baxter How can you be sure –?

Ken The description was too perfect to – oh the hell! What does it matter anyway. Two men are dead. You can't bring them back.

Sorensen Barry's a good bloke – he wouldn't lie. I've never known him to get worked up about anythin'. He's a good bloke. (*sighs*) So was Keith. (*pause*) I'm not lookin' forward to seein' his wife.

Baxter How does a man of that age manage to crawl on all fours – and in the darkness? And why?

Ken Suicide.

Baxter (*shocked*) Suicide?

Ken He jumped. They tried to stop him.

Baxter Aw come off it Doc! People who want to do away with themselves don't go to all that trouble.

Ken He struck out like a maniac...

Sorensen I'm tellin' you Barry wouldn't lie. He's not that sort. That old boy suddenly leaped up at them out of the darkness. He's responsible for what happened down there. He was obviously some kind of nut...

Baxter (*confused*) Well – I don't know what I'm supposed to do.

Ken (*firm and urgent*) Then let me tell you Inspector. (*pause*) Seal it up.

Baxter Huh? Seal what up?

Ken Those caves. As soon as you can.

Sorensen (*strongly opposing*) Come off it Doctor!

Ken In a few hours those tunnels are going to be slithering with mud. From end to end, from top to bottom...

73

Sorensen That's putting it on a bit –

Ken You've seen what's happened in Holly Mill Lane Inspector.

Baxter You mean – it's the same thing?

Ken I'd lay my reputation on it. (*pause*) The same oily, oozing mess. The same extraordinary colour – that dreadful green. (*apprehensive fear*) And the sound… bubbling. (*pause. Almost to himself*) What *is* that sound… I wish I – (*pause. As though awakening*) You can't take the risk Inspector. You dare not.

Sorensen (*pleading*) Inspector. Those caves have been down there for centuries. We know there are a lot more signs of a Neolithic civilization… people want to know about it. You just can't destroy them like that – forever.

Pause. He sees the futility of his pleas

(*aggressively*) You'd be destroying scientific knowledge!

Baxter Scientific knowledge can take care of itself, Mr Sorensen. I'm more interested in the protection of the community.

Ken Seal it Inspector. Seal it before it's too late!

Sharp cut to the sound of a train whistle. The train is drawing into Redlow station

Landers and Deverill are walking along the platform

Landers I'm sorry to have to bring you back from London so soon Mr Deverill. I can assure you I wouldn't have done unless it was absolutely imperative.

Deverill It's quite all right Professor. I got your message at the Club last night. I knew it must be urgent. What's happened?

Landers There's been a fresh overflow of mud – in Holly Mill Lane.

Deverill (*shocked*) A – a what? Another one?

Landers In all my experience Mr Deverill, I can't remember anything like it. We've been up half the night trying to get the wretched stuff back into the fissure. As fast as we've cleared one lot, there's another to replace it.

Deverill But I thought they'd sealed it all up with boards or something?

Landers Impossible! The whole lot's burst under the pressure. That farmhouse is going to be in terrible trouble unless we can do something rather quickly. This slide is so destructive.

Deverill Well, provided we can prevent any more damage before it dries up…

Landers Mr Deverill. When I left Holly Mill Lane just under an hour ago, the overflows had stopped. But the mud was dry as before – like solid concrete slabs.

They stop walking. Pause

Deverill (*sternly*) Do you have all the help you need?

Landers Only thanks to those boys from the RAF Station. They've worked miracles. (*pause*)

Deverill (*despondently*) Well, do the best you can.

Landers Of course.

Deverill What about Gomez – and Professor Lippert? Have they found out anything yet?

Landers They've taken some samples of the mud to the laboratory. At the moment they're trying to analyse…

Deverill Professor Landers, I brought Josef Gomez to this country. As long as he remains here he is my responsibility – I hope you try to impress upon him the urgency of this situation. I am not used to having both my time and money wasted.

Landers In Josef Gomez you have one of the most brilliant minds in seismological research. And no one more than he realises the extreme urgency of the situation.

Deverill Brilliant minds sometimes have the habit of thinking too hard Professor.

Pause

Landers If you wish for my withdrawal Mr Deverill, please feel free to do so.

Deverill (*forced dismissal*) That will not be necessary.

Landers How do I know you don't consider an old man like *me* to be a calculated risk and embarrassment.

Deverill Professor, you're missing the point.

Landers (*sternly*) Just before I came to meet you here, I received word that two new fissures have been discovered...

Deverill (*horrified*) What!

Landers In the wells of the Holly Crag Caves. Also – the Americans reported this morning a series of earth tremors – on the shores of Lake Michigan, Chicago. (*pause*) I respect your integrity Mr Deverill – but your own personal feelings have no place in this emergency.

Pause

Deverill (*thinking urgently*) Lake Michigan? (*pause*) That's exactly the same as our own tremors in the Lake District and Scotland. (*pause*) Now look here Landers. I don't care what sort of mud it is. What I want to know is where is it coming from – and how do we stop it.

Pause

Landers Then I think you'd be interested in a visit to the laboratory, Mr Deverill. In a few hours during the night, the specimen taken by Professor Lippert from the overflows has multiplied by more than three times its original proportions.

Fade out

Pause

The school laboratory. Gomez and Lippert are very close to the mic. Anna Deverill is in the background

Gomez (*calls*) All right Mrs Deverill. Will you turn the tap on please.

Immediately we hear the sound of water being fed through a hosepipe into the glass tank. For a moment we listen to it filling up

Lippert I'm still not sure we shouldn't have tried HCl or even H_2SO_4. It might have been a short cut.

Gomez Before we resort to the acids John, let's see what water can do first.

Lippert I can't get over it you know. To think that just a few hours ago that same sample was big enough to fit inside my briefcase. (*pause*) And now look at it.

Gomez What I'm more concerned with is how it manages to change its substance from one period to the next. When I came back in here last night it was wet and clammy, but it was nowhere near filling the base of the tank.

Lippert Then it's obvious it only swells in its liquid state? I've never found a geological formation do that before.

Anna (*in background, calls*) Is that enough?

Gomez That's fine, thank you.

The sound of the water filtering through comes to a halt

Anna (*approaching*) Is anything happening?

Gomez We have to give it time to penetrate. It needs a full immersion.

Anna I think it looks positively repulsive. Like a great octopus just waiting to stretch out.

Lippert I wish it was an octopus. At least we'd know how to treat it. (*pause*) My young son used to stand for hours staring at the wretched things in the Zoo. I've got a feeling he wanted to bring one home for a pet!

Gomez and Anna laugh

Gomez Mrs Deverill. I think you should go home. We're very grateful for your help.

Anna I'm not tired.

Gomez Your husband should be back by now.

Anna (*a sultry mocking*) It's all right Professor. I'm sure he knows how to make his own cup of tea.

Lippert Josef! I think something's happening. (*They all look*)

Gomez Let me see.

Lippert There are some small particles floating off... can you see – like very fine pieces of shell. (*pause*) Is it flaking, d'you think?

Gomez No... (*looking*) ...I don't think so. (*pause*) You may find they are shavings of small pebbles picked up during the overflow. At least it's a good sign that the water has managed to separate them. (*pause*) We must give it a little longer.

They are surprised by a sudden knock on the door of the laboratory

Lippert That's odd. Are you expecting anyone Josef?

Gomez No.

Lippert (*calls*) Come in!

The door opens. Ken Richards peers in

Ken Sorry to trouble you.

Anna Dr Richards.

Lippert Come in Doctor.

Ken closes the door, and enters

Ken I didn't want to disturb you gentlemen, Mrs Deverill. I know you're up to your eyes in it...

Anna Is anything wrong Doctor?

Ken I need some advice. Something's going on in the town, and – frankly, I can't make head nor tail of it – I thought you might be able to help.

Gomez Go ahead please.

Ken It's something I noticed yesterday morning, soon after the tremors – all that business in Holly Mill Lane. (*pause*) Mr Wilson and I – he owns the farmhouse – we were making a short cut across one of his fields, just at the back of the Lane. (*pause*) He did a bit of shooting – we thought we'd bagged a rabbit –

Gomez Yes?

Ken We hadn't. It was a bird. A blackbird.

Gomez You mean, you had shot it – by mistake?

Ken No. (*pause*) We found it lying in the grass, at the foot of a hefty looking oak tree. No bullet-hole. (*pause*) I can assure you, under normal circumstances I wouldn't have thought any more about it. It's not uncommon to find dead birds that have fallen from a nest… except – (*pause*) well – there were a lot more you see.

Lippert More? You mean birds?

Ken Everything. Birds, mice, squirrels, rabbits, wood-pigeons, the lot.

Lippert Good Lord!

Ken It was like a great dumping-ground for dead animals. (*pause*) Anyway, I took a couple of them back to my surgery for dissection. They weren't marked or even bruised. (*pause*) And there were no traces of poison.

Lippert Then what?

Pause

Ken I'd say both of them died from some form of asphyxia.

Lippert Asphyxia?

Ken They'd obviously choked. (*pause*) And there were also very distinct blood clots flooding the brain cells. A haemorrhage in fact.

Lippert (*confused*) Haemorrhage?

Gomez Doctor. Do you have any idea why this should have happened?

Ken That's why I came to you Professor. I just don't know.

Gomez But you obviously have a theory. That's why you did come. (*pause*) You're connecting the mud overflows. Is that correct?

Ken I came Professor, because wildlife is dying off all over the town, and not just in the Holly Mill Lane area. It's my job to try and find out why. And after spending half the night watching and listening to that filthy stuff oozing out into the caves…

Gomez You're quite right doctor. I think there *is* a connection.

Surprised dismay from Lippert and Anna

Lippert Josef!

Anna Josef – in what way?

Gomez It's not the first time I've encountered this situation. There is a small village to the north of Conception in my own country. Wildlife died quite considerably after our 1960 earthquake.

Lippert Did anyone ever discover what it was?

Gomez No. But it's possible the fracture in the earth's crust released some compressed gas. Maybe even nitrogen.

Ken Yes, but in Holly Mill Lane it would have affected everybody – especially those working along the fissure.

Gomez You found no traces of poison in your dissection?

Ken None whatever.

Anna What about insecticide? This is a rural area – they use it all the time on the crops. Hugh's been campaigning against it for years.

Gomez No. This is not insecticide. (*pause*) I am convinced that whatever the destructive force is, we shall find what it is we are looking for in the mud overflows.

Ken Find what?

Pause

Gomez (*smiles*) Come now Doctor. Even you should know that only a complete analysis will…

Lippert (*jumping up excitedly*) Josef! Look at the tank! The water…

Anna It's turned green! All the water in the tank – it's turned green…!

Fade out

Pause

A water jug is smashed to the floor. Almost immediately the Nursing Sister bursts into Janet Marshall's private room at Redlow Hospital

Sister (*shocked*) Miss Marshall! For Heaven's sake – what are you doing in here! Get back into bed immediately!

Janet (*near hysterics*) No – don't touch me!

Sister (*treading on broken glass*) Look at the mess in here. Your water jug's all over the floor… what *have* you been doing?

Janet Why can't you leave me alone? I didn't want to come here in the first place… leave me alone!

Sister And why are these blinds drawn? I thought I gave orders to…

Janet *I* drew them.

Sister Then you shouldn't. It's a lovely day outside…

Janet It was too bright. The sun was hurting my eyes.

Sister All you had to do is ring for Nurse, Miss Marshall. You've only made things twice as difficult. (*calls*) Nurse! (*to Janet*) It's about time you had some sleep young lady. You can't expect your condition to improve whilst you lay here in the dark – day and night – with your eyes wide open.

Janet (*pleading desperately*) You're not going to touch me with that needle again are you? Oh please Sister… please, please don't! (*a panicky breathing*)

The Nurse enters

Nurse Sister?

Sister (*lowered voice*) Oh Nurse. Will you get me a syringe please. You know how many cc's.

Nurse Yes Sister. (*She goes out again*)

Janet begins a very faint sobbing

Sister (*a little more sympathetic*) Now look here my dear. You're not going to help yourself by doing that – are you? You're getting yourself all worked up over nothing. Now why don't you lie back and relax. A little sleep won't do you any harm.

Janet (*pathetically*) I don't want to sleep.

Sister That's silly. I only wish *I* had the chance.

Janet It isn't life when you're not conscious.

Sister Your body must have a chance to unwind my dear. You can't expect it to do that whilst you're wide awake.

Pause

Janet (*calming down*) You – you won't open the blinds – will you?

Sister (*gently*) Of course not – if you don't want me to.

The Nurse re-enters with a syringe

Ah! Thank you Nurse.

Janet (*panicky again*) No! No – please don't! I hate having that needle near me.

Sister (*snaps firmly*) Miss Marshall! Now we're not going to be foolish about this, are we? Keep still please! (*pause. Quietly, to the Nurse*) Hold her arm please.

Janet squirms briefly as the injection is administered

Right! Now you can forget about everything my dear. Just close your eyes…

Janet breathes heavily

Nurse (*whispering*) I don't think it'll do any good Sister. The last one I gave her, she just lay here in the dark the whole time, without saying a word – eyes wide open. She didn't even like it when I switched on the light.

Janet (*in a vague rambling*) It's life… life… born all over again…

Sister Nurse. I think Doctor Robeson's in OutPatients. Run down and ask him if he can spare me a few moments please. I'd feel happier if he had a look at her before we settle down for the night.

Nurse Yes Sister. (*moves to the door*)

Sister (*calls quietly*) Hurry please. (*Nurse leaves*)

Door

Pause. Janet is breathing heavily. Sister speaks quietly and close to her

Sister Miss Marshall. (*pause*) Miss Marshall. Can you hear me?

The sound of the breathing gradually becomes an echo, as also does the voice of Sister

Sister You can't sleep with your eyes open my dear. Come now – try and get some sleep… sleep…

Sister's voice gradually fades out into an echo which is crossfaded with the approaching sound of the mud. For a moment the mud is heard bubbling up in the foreground, until suddenly it stops abruptly as we cut straight into the next scene

Drilling, digging and chipping fills the air in Holly Mill Lane. The airmen and volunteers work on

Landers (*calls*) Sir!

Corporal Sir! (*approaches*)

Landers Take a couple of men – see if you can check that spill at the other end, will you?

Corporal Very good sir. (*pause*) It's pretty difficult stuff to handle, sir.

Landers You'd better warn your people to be careful.

Corporal Yes sir. (*leaves*)

Landers Everything's scorched. As fast as they dig it up, it's as though the whole grass and soil has been burnt. (*pause*) It's quite extraordinary.

Deverill I must say I find it all rather invigorating.

Landers (*surprised*) Invigorating?

Deverill Like standing on the edge of a cliff, looking out to sea. Wanting to know what's on the other side – to catch a glimpse of the unknown. (*pause*) Haven't you ever felt like that?

Landers (*sceptically*) No, Mr Deverill. I'm glad to say I haven't. I get very impatient with things I don't know about, especially problems I can't solve.

Deverill You mean you have a fear of the unknown?

Landers Not fear. Apprehension.

Deverill I'm always much more interested at the end, when I discover why a problem is insoluble. (*pause*) Tell me something Professor. What d'you think the people of this town would do if they suddenly woke up one morning and found their precious homes crumbling around them?

Landers What an extraordinary thing to say! I thought Redlow was your pride and joy?

Deverill It's not the town. They're much the same wherever you go. (*pause*) It's people. They disturb me. They always have. Even when I was a young man at University, they were the one thing I dreaded most. The thought of having to meet new faces – it was a constant horror for me. (*pause*) There was a period in my life when all faces were exactly alike – I couldn't distinguish one from another. All expressions were the same. (*pause*) I suppose that's why I didn't marry for so long. (*almost to himself*) But for me, it took quite a long time for faces to emerge again.

Landers This is not an easy world for us to survive in, Mr Deverill.

Deverill It's not the world's fault Professor. It's people. (*pause*) They're so helpless – like children. Unable to think, to do things for themselves. (*pause*) That's why I'm not so sure Redlow is such a good idea.

Landers (*looking*) That's strange. Have you noticed something?

Deverill What?

Landers The trees... yes – and the bushes over there. (*looking around*) They're drooping... right the way round... can you see?

Deverill (*calmly, showing no surprise*) Yes.

Landers It looks as though... d'you think they *are* dying? (*pause*)

Deverill Yes. (*a half smile*) Yes... I think they are.

A sharp cut

Pause

A door slams in the kitchen of Tug Wilson's Farmhouse. Tug enters

Tug (*disgruntled, approaches*) They got the whole fence on that quarter side down! I don't care what they do from now on, but I'm gonna demand barricades all the way ar...(*stops*) Hallo love. (*pause*) What're you sittin' in the dark for? It's beautiful and sunny out...

Mrs Wilson I'm all right. I like it.

Tug It's not like you –

Mrs Wilson I said I like it. (*pause*) It's too bright outside – it hurts my eyes. (*pause*) Anyway it gives me a chance to think.

Tug Think? At your age? Come on old girl, you're a bit past that now. We both are.

Mrs Wilson Don't call me that.

Tug (*surprised*) What?

Mrs Wilson (*calmly resentful*) I'm not an animal in the yard.

Pause

Tug (*concerned*) Is – anythin' wrong love?

Mrs Wilson I said I was all right, didn't I?

Tug Yes, but –

Mrs Wilson Then stop fussin'!

Pause

Tug (*awkward*) It's because of last night, isn't it? I know I shouldn't have gone out and left you on your own. You must've been scared out of your life. Poor love.

Mrs Wilson Scared? Why should I be scared? (*pause*) I been on my own plenty of times – it doesn't bother me. In fact I prefer it that way. (*pause. Solemn, but contented*) I like to listen to the quiet. It makes… sense.

Tug Quiet! With all that noise goin' on last night!

Mrs Wilson I didn't hear no noise.

Pause

Tug (*close to her, puzzled*) We were scared stiff Mary – you and I. (*pause*) The mud – that noise… it's been pourin' out of the Lane. (*pause*) That first time. You remember love, we were scared stiff…

Mrs Wilson Not any more.

Tug (*irritated, snaps*) What d'you mean not any more! If we get any more of that stuff, it'd float clear through those barricades, right here to the house. (*pause*) I couldn't bear to hear any more of that squeakin' and squealin'. It'd drive me round the bend.

Pause

(*puzzled, irritated*) So what way should I –

Mrs Wilson When I was on my own here last night, I felt lonely and fed up. I didn't want you to go – I was depressed. I started wanderin' about the room aimlessly – lookin' at things… objects… anythin'. (*pause*) For some unknown reason they all started comin' into the focus – standin' out. It was a long time before I found the reason why. (*pause*) It was because they weren't nearly as important as I'd always thought they were. Not one single object in this room was important – not one. (*pause*) And then – I could hear the mud outside. I ran and opened the window. It was dark… I couldn't see a thing… but I knew it was there. I could almost feel its presence. (*pause*) D'you not understand Tug? It wasn't forcing itself. It was a gentle slide… it made me feel better – much better.

Tug tries desperately to break her concentration

Tug Mary love, your – your hands… they're as cold as ice. (*pause*) Look, I been thinkin'. Why don't you go and spend a while with your sister in London. The change might do you a bit of good. I can manage down here…

Mrs Wilson I want to be with you Tug. It's my place.

Tug Just a few weeks…

Mrs Wilson With you…

Tug Once they've got the Lane filled in, things'll be a lot better round here, you'll see.

Mrs Wilson (*gently, assuringly*) But they are better Tug. Surely you can see that dear… they *are* better… much better…

Fade out

Pause

Fade in: The sound of water being splashed about in the glass tank

Lippert (*with effort*) That should do it. We're going to need a new tank Josef.

Anna By the looks of things you'll need some new hands. They're absolutely stained with dye.

Gomez I think we must be prepared to explore the possibility of $MgOH_2$.

Lippert Magnesium? (*pause*) Yes – I see what you mean. It's got that metallic sheen about it… Hey! Wait a minute! What's this?

Gomez What is it?

Lippert Can you see? On the flat side… a sort of white powder.

Gomez Oh yes. (*pause*) Let's get it out of the tank, and have a better look.

Between them they tip the mud sample out of the tank. It falls with a thud onto the bench

Lippert Keep yourself clear please Mrs Deverill. This stuff's got a nasty habit of burning. (*pause*) Josef. There's a nail-file on… yes that's it. Can I have it please. (*pause*) Thanks.

He scrapes the surface of the mud block

Gomez It's like chalk. What d'you think John?

Lippert Salt.

Gomez Salt? Are you sure?

Lippert Rock-salt. I've seen enough of it in the Caspian.

Gomez But it's not possible to get formations this far inland?

Anna What is it?

Lippert Something you normally find in a dried-up salt lake or lagoon. The water evaporates in extreme temperatures – leaves this layer of salt… Josef! The Channel…

Gomez Yes, I know.

Lippert But is it possible? We're several miles from the nearest coastal, aren't we?

Gomez It may be an outlet.

Lippert In which case it's conceivable this mud is the same stuff that's killed off those fish in the Channel – the same way as it's killing off wildlife around here?

Gomez Conceivable – yes. (*with gravity*) But you try and tell me how a normal geological substance such as clay or mud can survive without disintegrating – fully immersed in water?

Pause

Lippert (*sighs*) Yes. That rather leaves us where we came in, doesn't it?

The door bursts open, Landers enters

Landers (*excited, approaches*) Not a word! Not another word! Just let anyone try and tell me where this lot came from!

Lippert What?

Landers tips from a case a whole bunch of sea-shells

Crikey! Sea shells!

Landers We've been digging them up all morning.

Gomez Where? In – not Holly Mill Lane?

Landers In Holly Mill Lane. Some were stuck fast in the mud, the rest we found all along the edge of the fissure. And there are plenty more where *they* came from!

Lippert These are the sort of things my kids pick up on the beach. They've got thousands in their bedrooms.

Landers Give them a few more – with my compliments.

Lippert Sedimentation! That means they *are* following a course – inland from the sea.

Landers (*mocking*) What a clever fellow! Amazing what they teach them at University these days.

Gomez Robert. Do you know where we can get hold of an electrogenerator?

Landers Generator?

Gomez If we can force enough heat into a thermatically sealed container, this may be a way of breaking up the mud. Before we do anything else, why not try an opposing agent?

Landers Anything's worth a try.

Gomez If we had the time.

A tense pause

Landers (*shocked*) Time? You mean, you think there's going to be another…

Gomez All I think at the moment Robert is that, whatever the destructive force in the mud is, I am not convinced that it is only acid.

Landers You're not? (*pause*) Then for Heaven's sake man – what is it?

A sharp cut

Pause

The Nursing Sister and Ken Richards are walking along a hospital corridor on their way to Janet's room

Sister She's in a very distressed condition Dr Richards. This is her third period of sedation, and up to now it's taken practically no effect.

Ken Extraordinary.

Sister It is extraordinary. The poor wee thing can't keep going on like this without sleep. She hasn't the resistance.

Ken What does Dr Robeson say?

Sister He says to give it a few more days. But to be frank with you I'm very worried. She won't let any of my nurses raise the blinds or even switch on the light. It's not natural for a young girl like that. Has she always behaved this way?

Ken (*solemnly*) No. Not at all.Quite the opposite.

Sister (*pessimistically*) Oh dear. I hope it's not going to unbalance her mentally.

They stop, then go straight into Janet's room

In here please Doctor.

Ken Thank you, Sister.

Sister (*whispering*) I shouldn't switch on the light if I were you.

Ken (*hushed voice*) Right. (*Sister leaves*)

Door

Ken is standing in the middle of the darkened room staring at Janet. After a moment he makes an awkward attempt to speak

Hallo. (*silence. No reply*) Aren't you going to say hallo to me? (*silence*) Janet…?

Janet (*sleepiness*) Who is it?

Ken Me, darling – Ken. I've come to see you.

Janet Why?

Ken Do I have to have a reason? (*pause*) Why are you lying here in the dark? It's a beautiful day outside – there's hardly a cloud in the sky. Come on…

He moves to the window and starts to raise the blinds

…don't you want to see the start of the sunset?

Janet (*sits up suddenly*) No! No – please don't. Put down those blinds… (*pause*) …please.

Pause. Ken reluctantly lowers the blinds again

Janet I – I can see you better in the dark.

Pause

Ken (*close to her*) Want to tell me about it?

Janet What?

Ken Why you're sitting here, staring at a blank wall – cutting out the remains of a perfectly good day.

Janet The light hurts my eyes. I prefer being in the darkness.

Ken Since when? What about all those walks we've had – only the other day up on the hill. You know very well you've always liked the fresh air better than me. I remember the time, my girl, when you threw off practically all your clothes to get a sun-tan…

Janet (*not really listening to him*) I think it's horrible.

Ken (*surprised*) Huh? What is it?

Janet The wall. Those marks.

Ken (*turning around*) The wall? (*pause*) Oh that! That's the poor old sun trying to get a look-in through the blinds. (*pause*) I think it's rather beautiful – those deep red lines. (*pause. Turns back*) Come on darling! Won't you come over to the window and watch the sunset with me?

Janet (*empathically firm*) No!

A long pause

Ken (*close to her*) Janet. Will you tell me something? (*pause*) The pain. After your fall, when you woke up – you had a pain in your head. Is that what's troubling you?

Janet (*coldly*) No.

Ken (*desperately*) Then darling – what is it?

Janet (*impatient*) Nothing! I keep telling you I'm quite all right. (*pause*) If only…

Ken If only what?

Pause

Janet My eyes. If only for a few minutes… I could close my eyes. Just for a few minutes…

Fade out

Pause

Fade in: A car comes to a halt outside the Deverills' home

Gomez There we are Mrs Deverill.

Anna Thanks for the lift Josef. How about coming in for a drink? Hugh won't be home for a while.

Gomez Thank you – I won't. I must go straight back to the laboratory.

Anna I'm afraid it's going to be another long night for you. D'you really think there is going to be danger – I mean for the town?

Gomez Who can tell? We have a lot of questions to answer before we know that.

Anna I wonder what it'd be like? (*with relish*) I mean if Redlow was suddenly faced with a real disaster – something like you've had plenty of times in your own country.

Gomez Something I do not wish for anyone.

Anna Oh – nor me. (*pause*) But it's rather like watching an airliner in the sky, isn't it? You know it's full of people, and it's bound to be going or coming from somewhere. (*pause*) But somehow – you become mesmerised by it, and quite unconsciously you search for a sign that shows something's not quite right. You expect something to go wrong, and after a while – almost wish it would. (*pause*) I wonder why?

Gomez A horrible thought.

Anna The excitement I suppose. (*pause*) You know, I find it odd that you and my husband can't seem to hit it off, because in many ways, you're really quite alike.

Gomez (*bored with a repetitive question*) So I've been told.

Anna Josef. Would you be offended if I asked you a personal question?

Gomez I don't know. It depends.

Anna Why is it you've never married?

Gomez I don't see what interest –

Anna (*intimately*) You're not particularly good looking – but handsome. Above all though, considering your background, you're a man of considerable charm. (*pause*) You see Josef, I find it hard to believe someone like you would be willing to sacrifice stability – just for the sake of an old microscope or something. There's much more to you than that.

Gomez Is there?

Anna Do we scare you? (*pause. Amused*) No. We don't scare you. (*pause*) D'you know what *I* think? I think – at some time in your dark and mysterious past, you were let down by one of us ghastly creatures. Am I right?

Gomez (*unmoved by her teasing*) You're very inquisitive Mrs Deverill.

Anna I knew it! She must have hurt you very much – did she?

Pause

Gomez Yes.

Anna (*jubilant*) You see! I know more about you than you could ever possibly know yours…

Gomez She died. (*Anna stops abruptly*) Giving birth to our son. She was my wife, you see.

Anna (*distraught with shame*) Josef… I – I'm most terribly sorry. I didn't realise you… (*pause*) But it's no good you know. You can't let it go on haunting you for the rest of your life. If she loved you, she wouldn't have wanted it that way.

Gomez It was a long time ago, Mrs Deverill.

Anna And I suppose that means you'll never think about marriage again?

Gomez Who can tell? Maybe.

A long pause

Anna I'd better go in.

Gomez I think so.

She gets out of the car, slams the door

Anna You know Josef, sooner or later you're going to have to learn to forget.

Gomez Not at all Mrs Deverill. My greatest problem is that I *have* forgotten – much too soon. (*pause*) Goodbye.

He starts up the car again and drives off quickly

Anna (*calls*) Thanks again for the lift… (*She starts to walk back to the house, when she stops abruptly, startled*) Oh – Hugh! Darling – I didn't see you. (*pause*) I – I didn't know you were back.

Deverill It's all right my dear. (*smiling*) Even the railways have a habit of being punctual – particularly when you don't want them to be.

A sharp cut

Pause

The Wilson's farmhouse. Mrs Wilson, in her bedroom upstairs, off, calls to her husband downstairs

Mrs Wilson (*off, calls*) Tug! Tug – are you down there?

Tug (*awkwardly*) Er – yes. Yes love, I am.

Mrs Wilson What're you doing?

Tug Just – just goin' out to have a smoke. That's all. You have a little rest love. I won't be long.

Mrs Wilson Well – I'm going to bed. Don't forget to lock up.

Tug I won't.

Door upstairs. Ken Richards is with Tug downstairs

Ken What is it Tug?

Tug (*whispers*) Keep your voice down. I don't want her to know you're here.

Ken (*lowers voice*) What's up? Is she ill?

Tug Maybe she is, and maybe she ain't. I don't know. But it's not like her – and it's not my Mary. (*pause*) She's been ramblin', and I can't make head nor tail of it.

Ken Rambling?

Tug Goin' on about things that don't mean anythin'. When she talks she looks straight through yer – as though you don't even exist. I'm sure she doesn't hear a thing I say.

Ken When did this start?

Tug The first time was when I tackled her about those birds we found. She said somethin' funny then. That whatever it was that killed 'em, it was probably all for the best.

Ken Extraordinary.

Tug And then again, just a little while ago, I found her sittin' all alone in the kitchen – in the dark. Even though it was broad daylight outside.

Ken The dark?

Tug Couldn't see a thing. She'd got the blinds down – and she lashed out at me when I went to open 'em. But when I did… (*pause*) it was a funny look on her face… peculiar. (*pause*) I tell you I'm scared Doc. It's not like my Mary at all.

Ken I think you'll find she's just tired out. This business in the Lane has been a bit of a shock.

Tug I keep thinkin' of old Ted – those caves.

Ken (*sharply*) Then don't. It won't do any good.

Tug (*sadly*) When I put my arms round her, she didn't even want me to kiss her, but when I did it was terrible – like kissin' a block of ice.

Ken (*taking notice*) Cold?

Tug Absolutely freezin', poor love. And yet, *she* didn't seem to worry – didn't even feel it.

Pause

Ken (*shielding the urgency*) All right. Keep her in bed for as long as you can. If she needs a sleeping pill, I'll let you have one. But if possible, I'd prefer you to try and do without.

Tug She's been ill before, and I always knew how to treat her. But not like this – not this way. (*pause*) You know somethin' Doc? These last couple of days, when I seen that sun disappearin' behind the back of those trees, I've been getting' a funny feelin' in my stomach. Like somethin' I never had before. (*with fear and apprehension*) As though somethin' was not quite right – somewhere. (*pause*) Maybe it's that stuff in the Lane, I don't know. But I'm scared. Imagine it – me – Tug Wilson – scared to face the darkness. (*with* *desperation*) What is it Doc? What's wrong with me? What's goin' on round here…?

Slow fade out

Pause

A door is opened and slammed. Anna Deverill, in a temper, approaches her husband

Anna (*angrily*) That was grossly unfair. A beastly thing to do!

Deverill (*unconcerned*) I beg your pardon, my dear?

Anna I've just been reading that interview you gave to an American reporter in London. Those disgusting things you said about Josef.

Deverill (*sarcastically*) 'Josef'?…

Anna He's a decent, kind gentleman. It's not fair to treat him like this.

Deverill I apologise my dear. I hadn't realised I was hurting your feelings…

Anna Oh for God's sake stop being so childish Hugh! How many more times do I have to tell you that the only reason I went to the laboratory was to see if I could help…

Deverill A great sacrifice. It's all right. I know, my dear.

Anna What's the matter with you these days? Are you suffering from some kind of persecution mania or something?

Deverill (*restrained anger*) Let's drop the subject shall we, my dear? I've had a splitting headache all day…

Anna I don't see you as the jealous lover Hugh. It doesn't suit you.

Deverill (*attacking*) I said – drop it! (*tense pause. He adopts an ultra-unpleasantness*) Please – dear.

Pause

Anna (*restraining*) Hugh. Let's get away from here. Right away from all the pettiness, the small minds.

Deverill (*politely*) No, my dear. My place is here. (*pause*) It's very bright in this room…

Anna Somewhere we can forget about them all – learn to live a life of our own, have some fun like we used to…

Deverill (*ignoring her*) …so hurtful to the eyes.

Anna (*retaliating*) Have you thought what's going to happen when Josef sees that interview? Suppose he decides to stop everything, and walk out on you?

Deverill He will be replaced.

Anna, exasperated, moves to the door, opens it

Anna Why do I even bother to talk to you? (*turns around*) Shall I tell you something Hugh? When I first met you, you were really someone to admire – to look up to. (*pause*) But not any more Hugh. Everything inside you seems to have shrivelled up. These days you only live to exist. I don't know you any more.

Deverill (*unmoved, unemotional*) Would you mind very much if I drew the curtains, my dear? I really do find the light in here very strong. (*pause*) It hurts my eyes.

Anna (*raging*) I couldn't care less if you sit in the dark for the rest of your life!

She storms out, slamming the door behind her. Pause

Deverill (*to himself, smiling*) No, I'm sure you don't – my dear.

He draws the curtains. Quick cut

The night is still and lifeless. An RAF Corporal and an Aircraftsman are on guard duty in Holly Mill Lane. They speak in hushed voices

Gibbons Corps! Hey Corps!

Corporal Yuh?

Gibbons D'you think there's a chance this stuff *will* get on the move again?

Corporal Well, they wouldn't stick us on guard out here if it wasn't.

Gibbons It's a cheek though.

Corporal What is?

Gibbons Callin' in the RAF to clear up this dump. We're supposed to be airmen.

Corporal (*mocking*) Well AC2 Gibbons – since you're a clerk in the Registry, I don't think we need worry too much about a close definition of the word, do you? Apart from the fact that I'm sure your fellow countrymen aren't particularly concerned about the way in which you serve them – whether it's at the controls of a Canberra Jet Bomber, or sittin' on an upturned orange box in Holly Mill Lane.

Gibbons I still think it's a liberty. And anyway, we've got rid of most of the mud.

Corporal And what would you do if those concrete blocks suddenly popped out of that hole in the road, and Mother Nature sent another dose of slithering muck to greet you?

Gibbons I wouldn't stay around to thank her.

Corporal Spoken like a true Englishman.

Pause. A marked silence

Gibbons It gives me the creeps you know. Everything's so quiet. Not even an owl.

Corporal I could sing to you – if that'd help?

Gibbons (*ignoring him*) You know what I mean! (*pause*) At night in the country you always hear something. Either birds or animals – or... something. (*pause*) It gives me the creeps. (*pause*) What about a drink?

Corporal What's the matter with you son? You forgettin' Queen's Regulations or somethin'? We're on Guard Duty...

Gibbons I got some whisky from the NAAFI...

Corporal Oh well... under the circumstances I suppose...

Gibbons Hand us over my rucksack. (*pause*) Ta. (*sorts around*) It's a dead cert I'm not gonna get through this night unless.

Corporal (*abrupt*) Shut up!

Gibbons (*puzzled*) Huh? What is it?

Corporal Can you hear somethin'?

Pause. Absolute silence

Gibbons No?

Corporal (*puzzled*) Water. I could have sworn I heard runnin' water.

Gibbons Aw Gord! Not again!

Corporal I'm goin' over the other side to have a look-see. You hang on here for me.

Gibbons You're jokin' of course! You won't get *me* stayin' here all on me tod! I'm comin' with you...

Fade out

Pause

In the small room adjoining the laboratory, Gomez and Landers prepare to switch on the electrical generator

Gomez (*calls*) Are you connected at that end Robert?

Landers (*background*) Yes, I think so. (*pause*) You're sure it's not going to blow up on us or anything? I feel most unsafe!

Gomez (*amused*) I wouldn't rely on it. Anyway, if we can get it up to a hundred degrees, we'll at least have some idea of the effects. (*pause*) Are you ready?

Landers Ready!

Gomez Right...

Immediately he switches on, we hear the running sound of the electrical generator

Landers Is anything happening?

Gomez (*half shouting*) I don't know yet.

Landers It looks awfully hot inside there – doesn't look as though it's drying.

Gomez Can you give me a reading?

Landers (*reading the indicator slowly*) Seventy-five, eighty... eighty-five... ninety... ninety-five... that's it – a hundred. Shall I turn it off?

Gomez No. Give it a few minutes. We can always boost it up if we have to.

Landers Right!

Gomez I'm going in to see if John's found anything under the microscope. Can you cope for a while?

Landers That's all right old boy! I'll shout good and loud if I need you!

Gomez opens the door, and goes out into the laboratory closing the door behind him. Immediately the sound of the generator is cut out into distant background. Lippert is immersed in his microscopic investigation

Gomez What can you see, John?

Lippert Difficult to tell. The piece of mud I chipped off was really a bit too big for this thing. Mind you it'd be better if I could get hold of my own microscope. I'm sure this contraption was used by Madame Curie!

Gomez is leaning close trying to get a better look at the mud specimen

Gomez Can you trace the salt?

Lippert Oh it's rock-salt all right, except it's even more incredibly fine. More like evaporite. (*pause*) I've seen something similar in Rye.

Gomez Rye?

Lippert A small coastal town in Sussex. (*pause*) You know, if we could follow the tracks of the compression waves caused by those tremors, I'll lay you a dozen to one they'd lead to a salt marsh of some description.

Gomez A coastal area?

Lippert Why not? These seismological disturbances you found on the Channel sea-bed were obviously caused by some violent disruption further down – maybe as much a mile or so. God knows what's been happening down there, but the force must be pretty... (*He stops abruptly*) Hey! What the hell's this?

Gomez What?

Lippert (*looking hard*) There are some small particles... (*pause*) Yes – it is you know! There's a movement.

Gomez (*puzzled*) Movement? What are you talking about?

Lippert Josef. Either I'm going stark raving mad, or this stuff's turning back into a substance – right in front of me. (*pause*) Wait a... minute. (*still looking hard*) Take a look down there. Tell me what you can see.

Gomez takes over the microscope

Now – am I mad, or aren't I?

Gomez (*grimly*) No John, you're not. They *are* tissues.

Lippert (*horrified*) But Josef – don't you see what this means? (*pause. A tense strain*) For Heaven's sake man – make sure... make quite sure!

Gomez (*empathetically*) I am sure.

Lippert An – an organic matter in a geological substance? (*stunned*) It's incredible! It's damn well incredible! Just a few minutes ago that thing was dead solid. That means –

Gomez It means that it has the ability to multiply – but only in its liquid state.

Lippert (*half dazed*) Multiply! But how much? (*pause*) Josef, we've got to get the medics on to this. I've never seen anything like it before. It's way out of our field.

Gomez No! Before we say anything to anyone, let's first complete our own analysis. If there are living organisms in the mud, we've got to find out where they come from, and how they are formed. (*pause*) And most of all, somehow we've got to determine the extent to which they are able to multiply.

Lippert (*pleading desperately*) Josef! That one small sample we took from Holly Mill Lane multiplied itself more than three times overnight. At that rate of expansion it could completely swamp this area in forty-eight hours. I tell you it's out of our hands...

The telephone rings. He answers it

Hallo? (*pause*) Oh yes Inspector. (*pause*) It's – what! Are you sure? (*pause*) Well, yes we did, but we had no idea it could poss...(*pause*) hell!

Gomez What is it?

Lippert All right Inspector – yes. (*pause*) Of course we will. (*pause*) Right you are – you do that. We'll be down as soon as we can. (*slams down the receiver*)

Gomez Holly Mill Lane?

Lippert (*restrained fear*) Every one of the concrete blocks are out.

Gomez No!

Lippert Mud's seeping out of every crack in the road. It's sliding further than it's ever done. They've got every available man they could muster fighting like hell to clear it. (*pause. Dramatically*) Josef. It's going to multiply, isn't it? The blasted stuff's going to multiply.

A loud sound of smashing glass from the next room

(*shouts*) Robert! (*They dash into the room*) Robert are you... Josef! Look at the tank!

There is no sound of the generator as they walk on broken glass

Gomez (*urgency*) Grab hold of his arms – quickly!

Lippert But the mud – look at the mud! It's running out – it's running all over the place...

Gomez (*shouts impatiently*) Do what I say! Grab hold of his arms! Let's get him out of here – before it's too late!

For the first time we hear the gradual sound of the bubbling mud sliding out of the broken tank. Fade up to crescendo then fade right out

END OF EPISODE THREE

The Slide
by Victor Pemberton

Episode 4: Heart Beat

Produced by John Tydeman

TRANSMISSION:	Sunday 6 March 1966	1900–1930 LIGHT
REHEARSALS:	Monday 7 February	1030–1830
RECORD:	Monday 7 February	1830–1930 (to H.11)
STUDIO:	B.11	
R.P. No.	TLO 605/550	
EDIT:	Monday 14 February	1015–1245 (H.54)
PLAYBACK:	Monday 14 February	1500–1530 (5108)

CAST:

Gomez	Roger Delgado
Deverill	Maurice Denham
Landers	Rolf Lefebvre
Lippert	Allan McClelland
Richards	David Spenser
Anna	Marion Mathie
Baxter	Geoffrey Matthews
RAF Corporal	Anthony Hall
'Tug' Wilson	Stephen Jack
Mrs Wilson	Miriam Margolyes
Mrs Luke	Noel Hood
Nursing Sister	Eva Haddon

S.M.s: Panel: Amna Smith; Grams: David Cain; Spot: Margaret Rushton

SECRETARY: Helene Grygar, PABX 2168

Announcer An explosion has rocked the school laboratory where Professor Gomez and his colleagues are conducting their experiments with the mud samples. But as night draws on, the impossible task of clearing the mud from Holly Mill Lane continues…

It is late evening. A surge of excited activity surrounds Holly Mill Lane as the RAF airmen, volunteers and citizens of Redlow New Town wrestle feverishly with the new and more powerful overflows of mud from the fissure

The shovelling and scraping continues at a hectic pace, as the sound of the bubbling, squelching, and almost shrieking mud fills the night air in the background

The crowd suddenly shout out in panic and run for safety as a large and heavy tree topples to the ground

Baxter (*shouts out*) Get those people out of here! What're you tryin' to do – start a panic or somethin'?

The shovelling resumes

Corporal!

Corporal (*off*) Sir! (*running in*)

Baxter Who's in charge of your party?

Corporal Squadron Leader Jones sir.

Baxter Ask him if he can do something about the flow at the other end. We've gotta try and block the mud off before it reaches the farmhouse.

Corporal I'll tell him Inspector, but we're havin' a bit of a job with these trees. They're topplin' over like nine pins. It must be getting' at the roots or somethin'.

Baxter Well, do your best son!

Corporal Right! (*about to dash off*)

Baxter And Corps. You may have my full authority to stop any of those photographers breakin' the cordon. OK?

Corporal (*dashing off, calls*) Will do!

The shovelling, scraping continues energetically

Baxter (*shouts*) Come on then you blokes! Put your backs into it!

Tug (*dejected*) It won't do no good. It's gone too far – the whole thing. They don't stand a chance.

Baxter We can try Mr Wilson. The least we can do is to try.

Tug I'll bet you it stretches for over a quarter of a mile now. A great sea of mud. It's even right the way round the back of my place. If they can't stop it now, they never will.

Baxter (*shouts again*) Make your trench deeper! It'll drop down into it. (*to Tug*) Now listen to me Mr Wilson. We'll get this muck cleared. If we have to call out troops from every part of the country, we'll get it cleared.

Tug It wouldn't be so bad if you knew what you was fightin'. But one minute it's as solid as rock – the next, it's like this. I tell you – it's an Act of God. (*looking around*) It's taken me years of hard work to get this bit of land workin' the way I wanted. Huh! And all for this. A slithering mass of green slime. (*sighs*) It's heart-breakin' I tell you. Heart-breakin'!

Baxter (*sympathetically awkward*) I'm sorry Mr Wilson. I heard about the chicken run. Bad lucky.

Tug Hundred and fifty of 'em. I had some of the best prize fowls in this part of the country in there. They always did well for me on Maidstone Show day. (*pause*) I couldn't believe my eyes when I saw it. Just a pile of broken timbers and feathers. Like a slaughterhouse – only there weren't nothin' but mud. If that's what it really is.

Baxter Mr Wilson. You're goin' to have to evacuate you know. You *and* your wife.

Tug Evacuate?

Baxter We daren't risk you in that house much longer whilst all this is going on.

Tug (*stubbornly*) Nobody or nothin' gets me out of my house. Me and Mary've worked all our lives for it – 'specially now the kids have gone.

Baxter Mr Wilson. As fast as we clear one shovel of this mud, there's a whole heap to replace it. It's sliding at a tremendous rate. Even you can see that. By morning it could quite easily be right on your front doorstep.

Tug We'll take our chances.

Baxter Then that's up to you Mr Wilson. As far as I'm concerned my first duty is to protect life before property. I'll get a working party in there to help you with your things as soon as ever you like. But I want you to understand this right here and now Mr Wilson, that if you and your wife decide to stay put under these circumstances, neither me nor anybody else will accept responsibility for what happens. I hope that's quite clear?

Pause

Tug (*quietly defiant*) We stay put.

Baxter (*curt and businesslike*) Very well Mr Wilson. Then from now on, the responsibility is all yours – and yours alone!

Sharp cut

Pause

In the school laboratory, Lippert sweeps up the broken glass from the generator container, whilst Gomez attends to Professor Landers who has been shocked by the force of the impact

Lippert (*sweeping glass*) From now on we use nothing but steel. Reinforced, double-layer steel! The glass in this container's been smashed to smithereens.

Landers (*unnerved*) Josef. You'll have to tell them. You dare not keep this a minute longer. You'll *have* to tell them.

Gomez Drink the rest of your brandy Robert. You'll feel better…

Landers (*drinks nervously*) I mean, good God, man. If those mud samples do contain some kind of organic matter, this could be the most phenomenal scientific discovery in geological history.

Gomez We have to be quite certain first.

Landers You saw it under the microscope didn't you – both of you?

Gomez (*curiously*) Yes. It follows a pattern of natural organic movement, but to what extent we have to make quite certain before we make dramatic revelations of this kind.

Landers Dramatic or no, that machine blew up right in front of my very eyes. It's a wonder I wasn't killed.

Gomez It's incredible that it could have happened so quickly. I was only out of the room for a few moments. Can you remember how it started exactly?

Landers Condensation.

Gomez Condensation? Inside the container?

Landers Yes. The window misted up – I couldn't see a thing after that. Suddenly a crack appeared right through the glass – from top to bottom. I got a terrible shock – made a dive for the switch. But it was too late. The blasted thing blew up practically right into my face... The impact knocked me to the floor – I felt quite dazed. It wasn't until you and John rushed in I saw that... that foul mess oozing out down the side of the table, onto the floor at the side of me. (*pause*) Where did it all come from Josef? Where?

Gomez I think we have got to face the fact that the application of heat to the mud is quite possibly an aid to the multiplication.

Landers Multiplication! You mean – all those organic cells – they're increasing all the time?

Gomez There can be no other explanation. (*pause*) We watched it under the microscope Robert. It moved. Right in front of our very eyes – it moved.

Lippert *And* changed its shape, form and colour. The specimen *I* put under the 'scope was a solid hard splinter. It hadn't been there for a couple of minutes when it started floating about – like slime from a snail. Put me right off I can tell you! (*shivers*)

Landers An unidentified geological substance containing living organisms. Have either of you stopped to realise just how terrifying a prospect that is?

Gomez Robert. When I first saw the mud in Holly Mill Lane, I knew that we were going to be against something quite unique. Things now seem to fit into place. Why shouldn't those seismological disturbances in the English Channel have been caused by the mud's unsuccessful attempts to overflow onto the sea-bed. So what should it do?

Lippert Find another outlet.

Gomez Precisely! And isn't Redlow Town just a few miles from the Channel coastline?

Landers You're quite right. The epicentre of those earth tremors *was* here.

Lippert But Josef. What about the other fissures, the overflows in the North of England *and* in the States?

Landers Something must be disturbing the level of the mud, forcing it out from beneath.

Gomez *I* don't think so.

Pause

Lippert (*with trepidation*) Then – what do you think Josef?

Pause

Gomez The mud is organic. Why shouldn't it be capable of exercising its own force?

Stunned silence

Landers We can't keep this to ourselves. Not any longer.

Gomez No Robert. First of all let John continue his analysis.

Lippert (*with urgency*) I'll see if I can get a breakdown of the particles – find out the type and the group.

Landers But the people have to be warned. We can't let them go on thinking...

Gomez Let them think *what* they like – and for as long as they like, Robert. When we're absolutely sure, we'll know what precautions to advise. Until then, I'll go down to Holly Mill Lane and see what I can find.

He goes to the door and opens it

Landers Josef. I – I'm terrified. For the first time in my life – I'm terrified.

Gomez (*smiling affectionately*) My dear Robert. When you're working in the dark – who *isn't*?

He leaves. Door. Sharp cut

Pause

In the school garage, Gomez has some difficulty in starting up his car. After a moment Anna Deverill, strained and emotional, enters

Anna (*approach*) Josef! I *must* see you.

Gomez (*looks up, surprised*) Mrs Deverill? What are you doing here. It's late.

Anna I had to get away from the house for a while. I felt so shut in. I saw your car lights through the garage door…

Gomez Is anything wrong?

Anna Couldn't sleep that's all. So much on my mind.

Gomez (*suspiciously*) Really?

Anna I'm worried about Hugh. He's not eating, keeps moping around the place – he won't even talk. All he's done today is to sit in a darkened room with the curtains drawn. It's so unlike him.

Gomez He's tired. All this has been a great strain on him.

Anna No. I know my husband, Josef. He's a changed man.

Gomez In what way changed?

Pause

Anna Jealous for one thing. He's not been like that all the years we've been married. Oh he tries to pretend he's not – but he is. (*pause. Searchingly*) He practically accused me of having an association with you. Did you know that?

Gomez Oh?

Anna (*smiling*) Ridiculous – isn't it?

Gomez I would think so.

Pause

Anna (*uneasy*) I – I wish you'd try and convince him otherwise. Life would be much easier – he'd listen to you.

Gomez I'm sorry Mrs Deverill. I have no wish to become involved in domestic disagreements between you and your husband.

Anna (*immediately, but calmly resentful*) Professor Gomez. I have no intention of trying to involve you in anything, and that is not the reason I came in here. I may not love my husband any more, but I do still respect him.

Gomez I'm glad to hear it.

Anna You're a very vain man, Josef. D'you know that?

Gomez (*smiling*) D'you think so?

Anna All those test tubes and books of yours don't fool anyone. You find it difficult to contain your feelings inside as any other man. (*pause*) It's taken my husband quite a few years to discover what his true feelings are. I hope it won't take you as long.

Pause

Gomez Forgive me Mrs Deverill. I hadn't realised what an unhappy woman you are. I'm very sorry…

Anna (*proudly*) At the present moment Professor my only concern is for my husband's health. It's not your sympathy I want. It's your help.

A sharp cut

Pause

The telephone rings in the surgery of Dr Ken Richards. He picks up the receiver and answers

Ken (*sleepy*) Dr Richards.

Sister (*at other end*) Good morning Doctor. Sorry to wake you. It's Sister Roberts, Redlow General.

Ken Yes Sister?

Sister I'm afraid we've had some trouble during the night Doctor. We've lost your young lady – Miss Marshall.

Ken (*sits up with a jerk*) You've what!

Sister When Nurse went in about half an hour ago she found the room in a terrible state. Everything's been ripped to pieces…

Ken Ripped to… what're you talking about Sister?

Sister Curtain, sheets, pillow-cases. She'd even tipped a waste-bin all over the floor. It's quite incredible.

Ken (*horrified*) Oh my – (*confused*) D'you know what's happened to her?

Sister No idea Doctor. She's left all her things behind except her dress and a raincoat. She obviously just upped and walked out in the early hours. Anyway, I think you ought to come over and have a look for yourself.

Ken Have you called Doctor Robeson yet?

Sister Oh yes. I've done what he said. I've called the police.

Ken Police!

Sister It's not only Miss Marshall we're worried about Doctor. We've seven other patients missing from the ward next door…

Fade cut

Pause

Fade in: Eggs being fried

Tug (*at the side of his wife, worried*) Don't cook me breakfast love, I don't feel a bit hungry. (*pause*) Come on. You been doin' quite enough bustlin' around. Sit down and talk to me for a few minutes.

Mrs Wilson Leave me Tug. I'm quite all right.

Tug But I'm not hungry

Mrs Wilson Leave me.

Tug sighs, goes to window. Background

Tug (*off*) They're still out there. Hordes of 'em. (*pause*) More like Piccadilly Circus on New Years Eve. You'd never think it was Sunday morning. (*mocking*) What do they think they're doin'? That stuff's set firm – they'll never chip it away now.

Mrs Wilson D'you want bacon with your eggs – or sausages?

Tug (*moving back to her*) Don't mind.

Pause. He suddenly grabs hold of her

Tug Come on!

Mrs Wilson (*objecting*) No Tug – what're you doing? Let me be…

Tug (*calmly, firm*) Now come and sit down. I wanna talk to you. What's so wrong about wanting to talk to my own wife.

She sits at the table with him

That's better.

Mrs Wilson What's there to talk about?

Tug We used to talk a lot together in the old days – you and me. When the kids were still at school. Why don't we any more?

Mrs Wilson Tug –

Tug Mary. I want us to get away from here.

Mrs Wilson Away?

Tug I mean right away – from Holly Mill Lane, from Redlow…

Mrs Wilson But I like it here. It's our home. Why should we leave it?

Tug Because it's different now. It's not like it used to be. Things have changed.

Mrs Wilson (*suggestion of a smile*) Are you scared Tug?

Tug Scared? What of? (*pause*) No. I'm not scared of the mud. At first I thought I was. But I'm not.

Mrs Wilson Then why leave?

Tug Because – because we've reached a time in life when we ought to start thinkin' about doin' different things. Learn to enjoy ourselves – instead of bein' tied down to this place twenty-four hours a day. Do it before we're too old.

Mrs Wilson The eggs are burnin'… (*He stops her from getting up*)

Tug No Mary! Listen to me! (*pause*) We could go down to Jack Percy in Torquay – you'd like that. Bit of sea air – do you a world of good. (*trying to make light*) You and his missus got on like a house on fire. (*laughs*) You two'd soon solve all the world's problems…

Mrs Wilson No Tug.

Tug But Mary – there's so much I want to do. So much I want both of us to do. We've got enough money saved to take us round the world and back if we want. What's the use in spendin' the rest of our days diggin' and ploughin'…

Mrs Wilson You don't know how to face things, do you Tug? You never could.

Tug (*close to her, near pleading*) Mary love – please. If you won't do it for yourself, do it for me. (*pause*) Please!

Pause

Mrs Wilson Better make it sausages. The bacon's a bit streaky.

She gets up. Returns to stove. Pause. Tug angrily jumps up and moves to window again

Tug (*shouts angrily*) All right then!

With a brief, hefty movement he draws back the curtains

Mrs Wilson (*panicking*) Tug! No. What're you doin'? Leave those curtains closed…

Tug I'm sick of the dark!

Mrs Wilson rushes across to try to stop him

I'm sick of wanderin' around this place like a half-awake zombie. God gave us good light to feast our eyes on. So let's see it...!

He opens the window. Immediately we hear the sound of the drilling and digging in the yard outside. In the very distant background, the sound of churchbells

Mrs Wilson (*pleading*) Tug – please don't. I can't stand the light. It hurts my eyes...

Tug (*face to face*) But why Mary – why? You've always loved the sunshine. Ever since you was a young girl. What's happened to you Mary? What's happened?

Mrs Wilson Please Tug!

Tug Come on – let's go to church. We'll just about make it if we hurry...

Mrs Wilson No!

Tug (*taken by surprise*) But – you never miss church? It's one of the things you look forward to all week.

Mrs Wilson (*snaps sharply*) I don't wanna go to no church – not never again! They're all hypocrites – every one of them. I despise them!

Tug Mary!

Mrs Wilson Church! What does it mean? It's just crosses and stones and bells. It don't mean nothin' – nothin' at all!

Tug (*sadly stunned*) If I thought you meant that Mary my love, I'd have given up hope for you a long time ago. That I can assure you...

Fade up church bells for a moment then crossfade congregation leaving church, after service

Mrs Luke (*off, calls*) Mrs Deverill! (*approaches*) Mrs Deverill.

Anna (*turns around, surprised*) Oh – Mrs Luke. Good morning.

Mrs Luke I was very surprised not to see your husband in church this morning. Is he in London?

Anna No. It's just that he couldn't spare the time. He's rather immersed in his work at the moment.

Mrs Luke Poor man! Such a burden to carry. This business in Holly Mill Lane is rather taking its toll on all of us, isn't it? I noticed that there were fewer men at the service than there's ever been before. (*sighs*) Where is it all going to end?

Anna If you'll excuse me Mrs Luke. I promised to get back...

Mrs Luke (*stops her*) Mrs Deverill. I don't want you to think I'm prying into your affairs my dear – I know how worried you must be. (*lowers voice*) But I have enough respect for your husband to offer him a friendly word of advice.

Anna Yes?

Mrs Luke I met Andrew Thompson just before the service – he and his wife. You know he's on the Town Council...

Anna Of course.

Mrs Luke There's a lot of discontent at the Town Hall Mrs Deverill.

Anna Discontent?

Mrs Luke Apparently they've asked your husband three times to attend Emergency Council meetings – to discuss the mud. Three times in two days. Did you know that?

Anna (*vague*) Er – no. As a matter of fact I didn't.

Mrs Luke He refused every time. Under the present circumstances I would have thought the first duty of an MP is to keep in close contact with the local authorities. And why is he still refusing to call on the Government for help?

Anna Refusing?

Mrs Luke Mr Thompson says your husband is quite adamant. He apparently says the town is his responsibility. He says he won't call on the Government until it's absolutely necessary. *When's* that going to be, I'd like to know? I do wish you'd speak to him Mrs Deverill.

Anna (*politely*) I will, Mrs Luke. Thank you.

Mrs Luke I'd hate him to get involved in some nasty publicity – especially with all these newspaper fellow about. I mean – you know what they're like.

Fade out

Pause

A hill overlooking Holly Mill Lane. There is a slight breeze, but the weather is still close and warm. Gomez and Inspector Baxter look down as we hear the sound of the drilling and digging in the far distant background

Baxter My father used to bring me up here when I was a kid. Used to be quite a beauty spot, though you wouldn't think so to look at it now.

Gomez It's good to feel fresh air again.

Baxter You oughta get some rest you know, Professor. You've been out here most of the night. You'll crack up if you're not careful. Even I've had a couple of hours.

Gomez There's a lot to be admired in the English countryside you know. Everything is so much richer – more full.

Baxter Huh! You mean *was*, don't you? (*looking around*) What happened to the grass? (*pause*) What's happened to the trees? (*slowly, descriptively*) Burning, withering, fading. (*pause*) I tell you – for some reason or other, Mother Nature's got it in for us.

Gomez (*looking*) Inspector. What's that place over there? Can you see… on the banks of the river – on the other side of town…

Baxter (*looking*) Oh that – yeah! That's the old windmill. Hasn't been used for years. (*pause*) Some old Dutch crank built it – sort of status symbol I suppose. Although I believe he did use it for a flour mill for quite a time. Why?

Gomez It's just that the grass around it looks more faded than on the other side of the river.

Baxter Yeah, that's true. Last time I was over there the place was runnin' wild with weeds and grass. It's a good place gone to pot, if you ask me. (*pause*) Look Professor. I – I wanna ask you a straight question – oh you don't have to worry about levelling with me. I don't easily panic, but –

Gomez Go ahead – please.

Pause

Baxter How much farther's all this gonna go? I think I've got a right to know.

Gomez I'm sorry Inspector. I wish I could tell you. I think you'll agree this is one of those freaks of Nature that needs a lot of study before we can hope to understand it.

Baxter It's not easy to come to terms with something you're not used to. With something you don't expect.

Gomez As far as Nature is concerned Inspector, we should always be ready to expect. We have no right not to be prepared. My own countrymen learned that a long time ago.

Baxter Yes. Us poor old English're a bit like that aren't we? We're more than capable of tackling most things, but we're hardly ever ready for it until after it's happened!

Gomez Who is?

Baxter I don't care for myself, of course. It's... well, d'you know what I had to watch them do this morning?

Gomez No?

Baxter Bury a horse. Beautiful creature... couldn't have been more than eighteen months old. Tug Wilson found him in his stable. (*sighs*) And it's like that all over the place – wherever you go. One long trail of dead cats, dogs, pet rabbits, birds... like a slaughterhouse. And no one knows why. (*pause*) But they're gonna want to know Professor. Any minute now, they're gonna want to know. Because it's pretty heart-breakin' I tell you. Even *I* can't bear to see it. They seem to think that just because you're a flat-foot, you don't care. You don't notice. But I do.

Gomez You've got to realise, Inspector: this – disturbance, or whatever you like to call it, is a threat, not only to you people down here, but perhaps to people all over the world. The danger is bound to be increased when the scientist doesn't know. When he's up against something he's not encountered before. It's the same in all areas of research.

Baxter Then you think there *is* a connection between the earth tremors we've had down here, and the ones in the north and in the States?

Gomez Inspector. All I can ask you to do – all I can ask anyone to do, is to bear with us. To trust us for as long as you can.

Baxter (*noticing someone approaching*) Hallo... who's this coming up?

The RAF Corporal is heard approaching, out of breath

Baxter It's that RAF Corporal. Gord – what's up now! (*calls*) Up here Corps!

The Corporal arrives breathless

Baxter What's up?

Corporal Sorry to trouble you, sir. Message for Professor Gomez. From the other gentlemen.

Gomez Yes?

Corporal They'd like you to get back to the laboratory as quick as you can please sir.

Gomez (*moving off*) Did they say what it was?

Corporal No sir. Just to tell you to make it as quick as you can. It's somethin' very urgent...

Fade out

Pause

Sister and Ken Richards are in the lift on the way up to Janet's room in the hospital

102

Ken …but even people. It's a terrifying thought. Have you questioned all the other people in the ward?

Sister Nobody seems to know anything Doctor. The whole business seems to have been carried out in absolute secrecy. That's why we can't help thinking that it must have been planned.

Ken What sort of cases were they?

Sister Two of them were quite elderly, but nearly all of them were road casualties, or injuries from the earth tremors. Concussion – that sort of thing. Much the same as Miss Marshall. It's very suspicious.

The lift stops. Gates open and close. They start to walk along a corridor

Ken And are the police going to start a search?

Sister What else can they do? Legally, any one of them is entitled to walk out whenever they wish. The locker room at the other end of the ward had been broken into. They took all their own clothes. (*pause*) I wouldn't have worried quite so much, except for what one of the other patients told the policemen.

Ken What's that?

Sister Well, she said she woke up in the middle of the night because she thought she heard a strange sound.

Ken What sort of sound?

Sister She just couldn't identify it. You know how you forget things when you wake up. (*pause*) Anyway, when she opened her eyes, she vaguely remembers seeing one of the two old ladies – standing at the foot of her bed, still in her nightgown. She was just staring down at her.

Ken Yes?

Sister When she tried to speak to her, the old lady swiftly moved away, and went straight back to her bed. She didn't think any more about it. That's why she didn't call the Nurse. (*pause, sighs*) However, the poor old soul was missing this morning. And nobody heard a thing.

Ken Extraordinary.

Sister You see, as I said before Doctor, it's not for me to say, I know, but after being in such close contact with your Miss Marshall for these last few days, I should say her giving us the slip like this is a serious pointer to her mental stability.

Ken (*sighs*) I know what you mean, Sister, and I only hope you're wrong. And this thing you say about Janet being violent takes quite a lot of believing. It's so completely unlike her.

They stop walking and pause outside Janet's door

Sister Well – that may be as it is, Doctor. But before you take any notice of me, I suggest you take a look in here at her room.

She opens the door. Ken is immediately shocked

Ken Oh my – ! This?

Sister I'd hardly call this the work of a normally balanced young girl. Would *you* Doctor…?

A very sharp cut

Pause

A door slams off. Anna returns home from church

Anna (*off, calls*) Hugh! (*pause*) Where are you?

She enters lounge. Finds Deverill still sitting alone with curtains drawn

    (*approaches*) Darling. It's a beautiful day outside. You should try and get some fresh air. Let's draw the curtains.

Deverill (*sharply*) No!

Anna But it's so gloomy in here –

Deverill (*firm, but polite*) Just leave them alone please. I'm perfectly all right, if you'll just leave me alone.

Pause. Anna refuses to accept an atmosphere

Anna You were missed in church today. Nearly everybody said it wasn't the same without you sitting in your usual place…

Deverill will not be drawn into conversation. Anna chats on non-stop

Anna Even the vicar. He said he thought he'd never see a Sunday morning with that front pew empty. Mind you, you weren't the only one. There were hardly any men in church at all. I suppose most of them are down at Holly Mill Lane?

Deverill I suppose they are.

Anna realises the gay chatter will not work. She kneels down beside his chair, and makes a direct plea

Anna Darling. After service I – I saw Mrs Luke.

Deverill Really?

Anna Why haven't you been to any of the Emergency Meetings at the Town Hall?

Deverill I don't go to meetings at the Town Hall. They bore me.

Anna Andrew Thompson says the Council have asked you three times to attend, but you keep refusing. Why, Hugh?

Deverill I shouldn't concern yourself with Mr Thompson's political opinions my dear. I'm well accustomed to his agitations, both here and in London.

Anna But he's a powerful man, Hugh. He's only got to say a word to those press men, and it'll be splashed across every front page in the country. (*pause*) Is it true that you're not going to ask the Government to declare Redlow a distressed area?

Deverill Yes.

Anna But why? The situation in Holly Mill Lane is completely out of hand. They've been working day and night to clear that mud. And still without success. If there are no more outbreaks…

Deverill (*gets up and walks around*) Everybody's always offering service. Always knowing what the situation demands better than anyone else – better than those who are qualified to know. (*pause. Across the room*) When are people going to realise this is my town, I can do what I want with it.

Anna (*pleading*) It's their town too! I want you to try and restore some of the respect these people used to have for you.

Deverill (*face to face*) People don't interest me any more Anna. They made this world for themselves. It's up to them to try and live in it the best way they can!

Anna If things get out of hand – if you let them Hugh – they'll only blame one person. Is that what you want? Do you want to destroy yourself?

Pause

Deverill (*smiling benevolently*) Let things take care of themselves my dear. It's the only way.

Pause

Anna Then there's nothing I can do for you any more.

She makes her way to the door. He stops her

Deverill (*fixed smile, close*) Anna – darling. (*pause*) Where did you go last night?

Anna (*defensive*) Last n –?

Deverill You left this house shortly before eleven o'clock last night. You did not return until a quarter to twelve.

Anna I went to get some air.

Deverill Ah!

Anna Because I'm tired of sitting all day in a room with the curtains drawn. Tired of being scared to open my mouth – to breathe the same stale, stagnant air. As though I was being locked up.

Deverill I trust the learned Professor Gomez was able to offer you – a comfortable alternative?

Pause. She tries to push past him

Anna Will you get out of my way please Hugh!

Deverill You haven't changed a bit – have you my dear? Just like the good old days – a long time ago… or is it?

Anna (*snaps back*) What's wrong with you? Don't you trust me anymore?

Deverill You'll never change, Anna, will you? Not that I expect you to. It wouldn't be fair…

Anna Hugh! Please get out of my way…!

Pause

Deverill (*holds her as she struggles*) Anyway I'm sure you'll find the Chilean climate much more agreeable my dear. (*smiles*) At least it'll be a novelty.

Fade out

Pause

Fade in: A powerful magnification of the high whining sound of the mud bubbling. In the far distant background, almost unnoticeable, we hear a very faint pulsating throb of a heartbeat. After a moment of this, the tape recorder is switched off abruptly

Gomez Fascinating! How on earth did you manage to record it John?

Lippert It took me over two hours. Every time I put the lead wires in, they just burnt away. You've got to be so careful the way you handle the stuff.

Landers Josef. Surely this proves beyond a shadow of doubt the mud's a living thing? The way it moves, this extraordinary sound.

Gomez I think it proves an awful lot Robert. But what it doesn't prove at the moment is the extent. (*pause*) Yes, we have seen there is clear evidence of living organic movement – but what kind? Is it vegetation? We know very well it is possible for certain kinds of plant life to exist in a solid geological formation.

Lippert I remember seeing blades of grass sprouting out of volcanic lava in New Zealand. Just a few days after it had set.

Gomez But I think what we have here goes beyond the normal bounds of clear definition.

Landers What do you mean, Josef?

Pause

Gomez John. Let's have the tape-recorder on again. But this time can you see if you can shape the background a little?

Lippert I don't know. I'll try.

He runs back some of the tape

Lippert Why? What're you thinking?

Gomez I have a feeling somewhere in the middle we have an indication – something staring us right in the eyes.

Tape is now at the still position

Lippert OK. All set!

Turns on the recorder. Once again we hear the mud sounds, but this time the heartbeat pulsating rhythm is much more prominent

Gomez (*listening hard*) Yes. Yes you see. I thought so.

Landers What? It sounds exactly the same to me.

Gomez Listen carefully, Robert. (*pause*) Do you mean to tell me you can't hear it?

Lippert I can! (*listens for a moment*) You mean – that throbbing sound?

Gomez That's it. (*almost in time with the heartbeat*) The same... rhythmical... pulsation... (*pause*) Can you hear it now, Robert?

Landers I can hear it, but I'm damned if I know what it... (*stops*) Good Lord! Yes... I know... I see what you mean now. Josef! You don't – it can't possibly be a...

Gomez (*grimly calm*) Oh yes Robert. Indeed it possibly can. Every living creature must have a centre. It has to.

Lippert Incredible!

Landers Incredible? It's – terrifying! I can't believe it. I just can't believe it!

Gomez Do you see now Robert? It's alive. This monstrous thing is alive. That's why we haven't been able to control it in Holly Mill Lane. That's why we haven't been able to stop it in the caves. There *must* be a centre.

Landers Then for God's sake man, let's find this centre – destroy it before it's too late. Before it breaks out anywhere else.

Gomez Find it? Yes, we'll find it, when we know where – and how many.

Landers (*puzzled*) How many?

Gomez It's expanding, growing all the time. In just a few days it has increased and developed beyond all known proportions. Are we to believe that just one centre can be responsible for so much? Do *you* believe that Robert? Do *you* John? (*pause*) Or should we believe that the mud is not one source – but many – made up of hundreds, maybe even thousands of different centres. (*pause*) But whatever it is gentlemen, I tell you this. This mud is creeping up on us. Slowly but surely – it *is* creeping up on us all…

Fade up tape recording, but giving full prominence to the heart beating, gradually fading out the usual mud sounds. Let the heartbeat continue for a moment or so until it quickly and suddenly stops, as we make a sharp cut

Pause

A canary is singing in a cage. Mrs Luke knocks on the door of Ken Richard's surgery

Mrs Luke (*to canary*) Here Binky, Binky, Binky… (*makes kissing sounds to the bird*) Come on Binky darling. Doctor soon take care of you.

Door opened

Oh – good evening, Doctor. I *am* sorry to bother you like this – especially on a Sunday evening…

Ken (*a bored sigh*) Yes Mrs Luke? What is it?

Mrs Luke It's Binky. I think she's suffering. I got a bit worried when you think what's happening to all those poor animals and birds around.

Ken What's wrong with it? (*looks at the bird*)

Mrs Luke She just won't eat her food, and she was very sick after the grapes…

Ken Grapes?

Mrs Luke Apart from her seed, I wouldn't dream of giving her anything but the best white grapes.

Ken All right Mrs Luke. Leave it with me. I can't promise to do anything tonight – I've still got quite a few calls…

Mrs Luke Thank you, Doctor. (*to canary*) Binky, Binky!

Hands canary to Doctor

Ken Good night Mrs Luke. Call in tomorrow. (*closing door*)

Mrs Luke Oh Doctor! I'm very glad to see Miss Marshall's back on her feet again. You must have been worried?

Ken Miss –? I beg your pardon?

Mrs Luke Yes. Your Miss Marshall. She's out of hospital, isn't she? Well she must be, because I saw her.

Ken You – saw Miss Marshall? Janet?

Mrs Luke Why – yes.

Ken (*desperately*) Mrs Luke. Quickly now – please tell me where?

Mrs Luke Near the old Dutch Mill. By the river.

Ken What time was this?

Mrs Luke Ooh – I'm not quite sure. Couple of hours ago I suppose. I was on my way home from evensong at the church.

Ken Did you – did *she* speak? Was she all right?

Mrs Luke We didn't exactly speak. I waved, but I don't think she actually saw me. She was too busy talkin' to that other woman.

Ken Woman? Which one?

Mrs Luke That Mrs Wilson from Holly Mill Lane. Nasty thing she is. Never could bear the woman…

Ken And they both went towards the Dutch Mill?

Mrs Luke No, no, no. Only Miss Marshall. Mrs Wilson left her after a few minutes – made her way back towards town.

Ken Did you actually see where she went – I mean Miss Marshall. Did she go into the Mill?

Mrs Luke Doctor Richards. It's not my habit to go around snooping on people. I mean, what business is it of mine where the young lady goes? (*pause*) Yes. I think she did go into the Mill, as a matter of fact. I must say, I did think it was a bit funny at the time.

Ken Mrs Luke. Do you know the Mill?

Mrs Luke Well, yes of course – don't you?

Ken I've only seen it once. Will you take me there?

Mrs Luke (*taken by surprise*) Well… er… I – I d–d…

Ken (*dashing inside*) I'll just get my coat!

Mrs Luke But what about Binky? (*calls*) Doctor! What about my Binky…? (*The canary sings in his cage*)

Fade out

Fade in: the Deverills' home

Deverill No gentlemen, I'm sorry. I cannot agree.

Landers But Mr Deverill, I can assure you Professor Gomez has proved to us without doubt the unparalleled dangers that exist in this mud.

Deverill What 'dangers'?

Gomez At this stage, I think it would be inadvisable to inform you of the precise nature of our discoveries, Mr Deverill.

Deverill (*very cool*) Oh really Professor? Why is that?

Gomez I'm not prepared to say further than that.

Landers We don't want to start a panic, that's why! But we must have your full co-operation Mr Deverill. We need more men, more equipment to put an immediate halt to the overflows – both in Holly Mill Lane and the caves.

Deverill Can't be done, I'm afraid.

Landers But for Heaven's sake, sir, why not? The government should be informed immediately of the gravity of the situation – declare Redlow and surroundings a disaster area.

Deverill This is a local matter. It does not concern the Government.

Landers But it's no longer just a local matter. This is now a national emergency. We refuse to accept the responsibility for not stopping a menace which could threaten the very foundations of this town, and perhaps a lot more.

Deverill Nobody's asking you to accept responsibility for anything Professor. (*calmly*) I merely ask you to reduce your measure of alarm.

Landers (*bewildered*) Alarm! Mr Deverill, you amaze me! All three of us have been up half the night trying to –

Gomez Mr Deverill. (*completely composed*) We have found that the mud contains living organisms.

Long pause

Deverill (*disinterested*) Oh – really?

Landers Do you understand the significance of that sir? Do you understand that we're going to have to face an enemy that science has never before encountered?

Deverill Science was created by the people, for the people, Professor. I find your theory preposterous.

Landers It's not a theory sir. It's a fact! For heaven's sake Josef – tell him.

Gomez (*unwilling to be emotional*) I don't think that's at all necessary Robert. I'm sure Mr Deverill is more than aware of his own responsibilities. Especially towards his own countrymen.

Deverill I leave *my* countrymen to make their own decisions, Professor Gomez. I'm sure a man of your background will find that rather difficult to comprehend.

Landers (*disgusted*) Mr Deverill – please!

Gomez (*quite unmoved*) I quite agree with you Mr Deverill. I can assure you that I am the last person to comprehend my own background. In many ways I still consider it to be one of the most painful episodes of my life. That is, of course, if you are referring to my political life. (*pause*) You see, it took me a very long time to realise both my mistakes and my inequality. I came from a poor family, and I have no one but myself to blame for exploiting this for political purposes. (*pause*) Unfortunately, by the time I did eventually come to realise how pointless my life had been, it was too late. I could do nothing about it. (*long pause*) When I first read about you Mr Deverill, I was still a young man at university. I used to read your speeches with great interest – you were something of a hero amongst our older generation. (*pause*) But believe me, it didn't need a very high standard of education to understand what sort of person you really were. Oh – not that you didn't mean every word you ever said. It's just that it's not easy admitting how dishonest one can be – not only to others but to oneself. (*pause. Almost to himself*) I'm afraid that's the hardest part of all. (*moves to door and opens it*) Unfortunately you never did admit it, did you, Mr Deverill. And still haven't.

Deverill (*completely unstirred*) Goodbye Professor Gomez.

Door

Landers (*stunned*) Have you any idea what you've just done?

Deverill (*disinterested*) Yes, I think I do. The man was becoming an incredible bore. His departure seems just about the most satisfactory compromise I can think of.

Landers I hope you're wrong, Mr Deverill. For the sake of yourself and all of us – I hope you're wrong.

Fade out

The sound of water rippling by. Ken and Mrs Luke have arrived on the banks of the River Holly

Mrs Luke How extraordinary. All those dead fish floating on top of the water. D'you think the river's polluted or something Doctor?

Ken I don't know. I'll have to inform the Health Department first thing in the morning. They can send someone down.

Mrs Luke How awful! I've often seen dogs and cattle drinking the water down here. Perhaps this is where all the trouble's coming from?

Ken Is that the Mill – over there on the other side of the river?

Mrs Luke Yes. You know I think we're being a little unwise – searching around a disused building. It'll be dark in jut a few minutes.

Ken How do we get across?

Mrs Luke There's a small footbridge down there. (*indicating*) About a hundred yards.

Ken If you give me the torch, Mrs Luke, I'll go over on my own. You can wait here if you like. I won't be long…

Mrs Luke Certainly not! I'm not hanging around here on my own in the dark. (*proudly*) Anyway, it's best to have a woman around. They always know how to deal with any eventuality. (*moving off*) Come on.

Fade out

Pause

The door of the Mill is kicked open. Ken and Mrs Luke stand in the open doorway

Mrs Luke Can you see anything?

Ken No. Looks as though it's full of junk – and cobwebs. Let's have a look inside.

They enter. Bare floorboards

Mrs Luke It smells of old rope and dead fish.

Ken (*calls, echo*) Janet! (*pause*) Janet darling! Are you in here?

Mrs Luke She must be out of her mind if she is.

Ken How many floors are there – can you remember?

Mrs Luke Three I believe. The old fellow who used to own the place lived on the top floor. Mind you, if it had been me…

Ken Ssh!

Silence

Mrs Luke (*whispers*) What is it?

Ken (*hushed voice*) I thought I heard something.

Continued silence

Mrs Luke (*swallows hard*) I'm not at all scared you know. (*proudly*) I don't believe in ghosts.

Ken (*calls out again*) Janet! Is that you? (*silence. Dejected*) No.

Mrs Luke Perhaps she went back to the farmhouse. We should have checked with Mrs Wilson fir…

Sound of something being dropped or moved beneath them. Mrs Luke jumps with surprise

Oh dear!

Ken (*across the room*) There it is again! Is there another floor down below?

Mrs Luke No. Only the landing-stage. It was only big enough to take a couple of small rowing boats. Should we look there, d'you think?

Ken How do we get down?

Mrs Luke There's a trap-door – just at the side of your feet.

Ken (*reaching down*) This? (*takes hold of handle*)

Mrs Luke Now do be careful, Doctor. I shouldn't think anybody's been down there for years. The steps might be dangerous.

Ken pulls open trap-door. Immediately sound of water from river rippling by. He starts to go down steps

Ken (*calls*) Janet! Damn!

Mrs Luke What's the matter?

Ken The bulb in your torch is like a red-hot nail. D'you have any matches… no, it's all right – I've got some.

She joins him on steps

Now be careful Mrs Luke. It's very slippery on these steps.

Mrs Luke What a dreadful smell. Everything's so stale.

Ken strikes match unsuccessfully

Ken Damn!

Mrs Luke The sooner they pull this place down the better.

He strikes match

I've always said these buildings are so unsightly, especially along the edge of the r – (*shouts out*) Doctor!

Ken (*calls*) Janet darling!

Mrs Luke Doctor! The corner… at the side of you… look!

Ken Where… oh my… (*inwardly*) Janet! (*shouting out*) Janet! Get away from there!

Immediately the air is shaken by the sound of the pulsating heartbeat heard earlier in the lab. It reaches a heightened proportion before being gradually faded out

END OF EPISODE FOUR

The Slide
by Victor Pemberton

Episode 5: Danger Point

Produced by John Tydeman

TRANSMISSION:	Sunday 13 March 1966	1900–1930 LIGHT
REHEARSALS:	Tuesday 8 February	1030–1830
RECORD:	Tuesday 8 February	1830–1930 (to H.11)
STUDIO:	B.11	
R.P. No.	TLO 605/551	
EDIT:	Monday 14 February	1015–1245 (H.54)
PLAYBACK:	Monday 14 February	1530–1600 (5108)

CAST:	Gomez......................................	Roger Delgado
	Deverill	Maurice Denham
	Landers....................................	Rolf Lefebvre
	Lippert.....................................	Allan McClelland
	Richards	David Spenser
	Anna...	Marion Mathie
	Baxter.......................................	Geoffrey Matthews
	RAF Corporal	Anthony Hall
	'Tug' Wilson.............................	Stephen Jack
	Mrs Wilson	Miriam Margolyes
	Mrs Luke..................................	Noel Hood
	Nursing Sister	Eva Haddon
	Janet	Elizabeth Proud
	Dr Robeson	Michael Kilgarriff
	Vicar	Noel Howlett
	Sergeant Johnson	Wilfred Babbage
	Journalist 1	Peter Marinker
	Journalist 2	Hector Ross
	Journalist 3..............................	Brian Hewlett
	Journalist 4..............................	Anthony Jackson
	Policeman	
	Operator	

S.M.s:	Panel: Amna Smith; Grams: David Cain; Spot: Margaret Rushton
SECRETARY:	Helene Grygar, PABX 2168

Announcer Janet Marshall has disappeared from her room at Redlow Hospital. In the darkness of the old Dutch Mill on the banks of the River Holly, Mrs Luke and Doctor Richards find the girl crouching by a wall. Desperately they struggle to get her out into the open air…

Late evening. The darkness is still, except for the waters of the River Holly rippling by

A moment passes until we hear the approach of Ken Richards and Mrs Luke struggling to hurry Janet Marshall out of the old windmill

Ken Take her other arm Mrs Luke.

They reach the open air, and both breathe freely

    That's it!

Mrs Luke Thank God for the fresh air. I thought I was going to suffocate in there.

Ken, with some effort, manages to close the door

    Hadn't we better see if we can get hold of someone right away? Before the mud gets a grip down there?

Ken (*to Janet, slow, precise*) Janet. (*close to her*) Darling – listen to me. (*pause*) What were you doing down there – by the landing stage? (*no reply*) Tell me.

Janet (*distant*) You shouldn't have come. You should have left me.

Ken (*with urgency*) Janet. That mud was seeping through the wall. In just a few minutes you'd have… (*stops. Quietly*) What were you doing, crouching all alone in the dark? (*no reply*) Won't you talk to me?

Janet There's nothing to talk about.

Ken I want to help you.

Janet I don't need your help. Nobody's help.

Ken Why did you leave the hospital like that?

Janet Because I couldn't bear it any longer.

Ken But in the middle of the night?

Janet It was the best time. The only time. I didn't want to go through another day with all those people sneaking in and out – staring at me – as though I was some sort of caged animal.

Ken It's not safe for you to be wandering around on your own in the middle of the night. (*pause*) Darling – you're ill –

Janet (*snaps*) Stop saying that! How many more times have I got to tell you that I am not 'ill'. I just want to be left alone that's all.

Ken sighs. Pause

Ken (*hardening*) Janet. What happened to all those other people.

Janet I don't know what you're talking about. What other people?

Ken (*firm*) I want to know! Seven patients disappeared from the ward next to your room at the hospital. And all at exactly the same time. Now what's happened to them?

Janet I have no idea.

Ken Now listen to me Janet. Some of those people are old and infirm. They're in no fit condition to go wandering around the countryside in the darkness – and all alone. Especially –

Janet (*faint suggestion of a smile*) Especially?

Ken It's – dangerous. At this particular moment. (*pause. Pleads*) Look. If you know where they are you've got to tell me. We've had half the County Constabulary out looking for them all day. Their relatives are going half out of their minds.

Janet I'm sorry.

Pause

Ken (*brusque, businesslike*) Mrs Luke. Can you drive?

Mrs Luke (*surprised*) Why – yes. Not for years though. I have a bicycle.

Ken Will you take my car and drive Miss Marshall straight back to the hospital...

Janet No!

Ken If you ask for Doctor Robeson, he'll know what to do.

Janet I'm not going back to that place. Not ever!

Ken (*firmly*) Now listen. Janet, if you think anything of me, anything at all, you'll do as I tell you. You'll go back to that hospital and let them take care of you. If you don't – well, it's up to you.

In the far distance the clock tower sounds eleven o'clock

Mrs Luke Eleven o'clock. What are you going to do Doctor?

Ken They're so busy trying to get rid of the mud on the other side of town, nobody seems to know it's over here as well. The sooner somebody knows the better. I'm going to see if I can get hold of the Inspector.

Mrs Luke He said something about them going to seal the Holly Crag Caves with gelignite – at about half-past eleven.

Ken I'll just about make it. I'll call the hospital and tell them you're on your way over. You can meet me there.

Mrs Luke Right.

Ken Are you sure you can cope?

Mrs Luke (*proudly*) Perfectly!

Ken (*to Janet*) Janet. Don't let me down – please. (*dashing off*) See you.

Mrs Luke is now alone with Janet

Mrs Luke Are you ready my dear? (*pause*) Now we're not going to be silly about this are we? You'll find I'm just as determined as you are. Right then –

They start to move off

Wait a minute. (*They stop*) What have you got in your hand? No – the other one...

Janet (*turning her eyes from the light*) Turn that torch away from my eyes... turn it away!

Mrs Luke Let me see... (*squirms*) Oh! Miss Marshall – how could you! A little sparrow... a poor, dead little sparrow...

Fade out

Pause

A loud explosion as gelignite brings rocks tumbling down to seal the entrance to the Holly Crag Caves

Baxter (*shouts out*) Keep clear of those rocks! Don't anyone move in 'til it's settled! (*pause*) Sergeant Johnson!

Johnson (*off. Calls*) Sir!

Baxter As soon as the dust clears, take a few of your blokes round the back of the Crag – make sure there's no mud comin' out anywhere. I want this place sealed in once and for all, OK?

Johnson Right you are, Sir! (*moves off in the background*)

Ken Inspector. Can't you get some of your people down to the Mill? I'm scared it's going to start flowing out any minute.

Baxter I'm sorry Doctor, there's nothin' I can do 'til I've got this mess cleared up. If we don't get these Caves sealed now, there'll be no holding the mud.

Ken Can't you get any more help?

Baxter I've got half my blokes here, the other half down in Holly Mill Lane – and most of 'em haven't had a wink of sleep in twenty-four hours. There's nothin' I can do 'til the rest of the troops arrive from Shorncliffe Barracks. (*pause*) But how the hell we're gonna keep track of all these overflows I just don't know. That makes five now.

Ken (*shocked*) Five!

Baxter Apart from the Lane, the Mill and here, there's one just at the back of the Regal Cinema.

Ken The Regal! But that's practically inside the town. There's a main shopping area…

Baxter I know, I know. They had to clear the cinema during the last performance tonight. Just in case.

Ken Where's the other?

Baxter Centre Heights.

Ken The new apartment block?

Baxter Yup! It's about a twenty-five yard gap in the lawns at the back, right alongside the fountain. (*apprehensively*) It's all happenin' Doc. I tell you – it's all happenin'!

Cut

Pause

Fade in: Josef Gomez's hotel bedroom

Lippert Don't be a fool Josef. I can't believe you'd walk out just because of the power-crazed ramblings of a man like Deverill. It doesn't make sense. It isn't you.

Gomez My dear John. To be able to continue the type of work we are doing here, it's necessary to have a belief that, although your ideas are not necessarily the right ones, you can at least count on the confidence and trust of those who believe in what you are trying to attempt. Can you honestly say that we have this trust?

Lippert No, I can't…

Gomez You see!

Lippert But only from those who matter the least.

Gomez scoffs

Listen Josef. I haven't always agreed with everything you've said – even when you tried to publish those Channel findings of yours, years ago. My pals at university said you were a crank, and I stood right behind them, sure. (*pause*) But when you've got somebody to hide behind, Josef, it's easy to shout 'crank' – and good fun too. Especially when you don't know yourself.

Gomez (*teasing*) Does that mean you've changed your opinion? Don't you think I'm a crank any more?

Lippert I don't know. But I'm prepared to find out – if you'll give me the chance.

Pause

Gomez It's no use John. I can't go on, with this man hating me so much.

Lippert D'you know what surprises me about you Josef? The reasons why you find Deverill so important.

Gomez Don't be silly… I don't think he's important.

Lippert But you must do. Because you make him so.

Gomez I haven't been involved in politics since I was a young man at university. But still this man insists on my past to provoke me.

Lippert (*dismissing*) Your past! Your past! Who the hell cares about the past. It's the future we're concerned with Josef. A future my kids are going to be able to live in safely. (*pause*) Somebody's got to show people there are still plenty of scientists around who aren't content with just trying to find a way to blow up the world, and as far as I'm concerned nobody stands a better chance of getting us out of this present crisis than you.

Gomez I don't know about that.

Lippert You know what goes on beneath the crust of this tired old planet of ours more than anyone else I know. And you know it!

Gomez (*adamant*) I'm going home John. I have to.

Lippert To Chile?

Gomez Yes. At least they need me there.

Lippert We need you here.

Gomez I'm sorry.

Pause

Lippert Don't you care about people any more Josef? People out there in the middle of the night – fighting to clear a monstrous freak of Nature that could threaten their very existence. (*pause*) Don't you care Josef? (*pause*) Because I do. They may not be worth it, some of them, but we're no different to them, whether we like it or not.

Gomez Give me one good reason why I should bother to help them, when they can't – won't – trust me. Just one reason.

Pause

Lippert I can't Josef. All I know is that you have to help them. You *have* to.

Fade out

Pause

Redlow General Hospital. Ken anxiously questions Sister and Doctor Robeson about the non-arrival of Janet and Mrs Luke

Ken For Heaven's sake Sister, what d'you mean she's not arrived? I left her with Mrs Luke over an hour ago. They were coming straight here.

Sister I'm sorry Doctor Richards. I gave strict instructions to the porter on the gate to bring them up as soon as they were here, but so far there's been absolutely no sign of them at all.

Robeson All right Sister, thank you. You can leave it with me now. Ken. Can you come in for a minute.

Ken goes into Robeson's examination room. Door

(*lowering his voice*) Now look. Something's got to be done about this you know.

Ken What d'you mean?

Robeson I mean Janet. As soon as we can get her back here, she must go to Psychiatry.

Ken Oh don't talk nonsense Bernie!

Robeson I'm telling you she'll have to – or we'll have to, well – wash our hands of the whole business.

Ken Do what?

Robeson We lost seven patients from Ward Eight last night – and two more died today.

Ken (*shocked*) Died!

Robeson Admitted they were fairly elderly, but their condition has never given cause to alarm. We're keeping a close watch on all the other wards tonight. (*pause*) Look Ken. I've known you and Janet a long time now. I've always thought her not only a good-looker, but pretty reliable and level-headed. Now if you know anything that should make me think otherwise, I reckon you should tell me about it.

Ken Janet's as sane as you and me.

Robeson Are you sure?

Ken I'd stake my reputation on it.

Pause. He moves about the room

Robeson Have you any idea why she kept herself in a darkened room all the time she was here?

Ken No.

Robeson The last time I examined her, her eyes were wide open even though she'd been pumped with sedation. Every time I tried to raise the blinds she screamed blue murder. There's something wrong somewhere. (*pause*) To your knowledge, you're sure she's never had treatment?

Ken What sort? If you mean psychiatric, the answer's no.

Robeson Not necessarily psychiatric. (*pause*) Ken. Have you ever thought about hypnotism?

Ken (*bewildered*) Hypnotism? What're you talking about?

Robeson D'you remember old Doctor Luther – at the Middlesex Hospital?

Ken Wasn't he the old boy who was always plugging the use of hypnotic treatment in asthmatic disease?

Robeson That's him.

Ken Why?

Robeson Just that I went to a few of his lectures. Most of it was a lot of old bunkum I thought, but one or two of the practical demonstrations were quite interesting. (*pause*) He used to have this marvellous gimmick of putting his patients to sleep, making them open their eyes, and then convincing them that the light was too strong for them – even though they were in a darkened area. (*pause*) It's an interesting thought, although I must admit I'd forgotten all about it until –

Ken Until you saw Janet?

Robeson Frankly – yes.

Ken She's never seen a hypnotist in her life – she's had no reason to. Even if she had, she'd have told me.

Robeson No asthma, bronchitis, nerves…

Ken Bernie, I tell you if she had, she certainly wouldn't have turned to hypnotism. It's not her at all.

Robeson Oh well, perhaps you're right. Let's hope when we find her, we'll be able to prove otherwise. But it's an interesting thought – isn't it?

A sharp cut

Pause

Mrs Luke in a distressed condition is in a telephone kiosk. She struggles to dial 999

Operator (*at the other end*) Fire, police, ambulance. Which service do you require please?

Mrs Luke (*breathing heavily*) Please – please help me.

Operator I – I'm sorry. I can't quite hear you. Can you speak up a little please?

Mrs Luke (*raising voice*) Please help me!

Operator I – I will my dear. If you'll just tell me which service. Is it an ambulance you want?

Mrs Luke No, no! I don't want an ambulance.

Operator The police?

Mrs Luke Yes! Yes, get me the police – quickly!

Operator One moment please.

The sound of the operator transferring the call to the County Constabulary

Pause

Policeman (*at the other end*) County Constabulary…

Mrs Luke Police? Is that the police?

Policeman Yes madam? Can I help you?

Mrs Luke Come quickly! You've got to come quickly!

Policeman (*writing*) Where are you madam? Look at the number of your telephone… just tell me where you are.

Mrs Luke (*with difficulty*) It's – the junction. The corner of the junction…

Policeman Junction… yes.

Mrs Luke Near the Mill, the river.

Policeman I've got it! Are you hurt? It'll only take us five minutes to get there.

Mrs Luke No – I'm all right. Just hurry… as soon as you can. There's been an accident…

Fade out

Pause

The following afternoon: once again the mud has hardened to a solid mass. Troops, who have now joined the airmen, help the crowd of civilians who are working at fever pitch to chip away at the overflow adjacent to the Regal Cinema, on the fringe of the town

Gomez, Landers and Lippert inspect the overflow with Inspector Baxter. Drilling is heard in the distant background

Baxter The main thing is to get that stuff away from the back wall. If there's any more pressure, the whole lot's gonna cave in.

Landers Yes, and probably the cinema with it.

Gomez Inspector, how long do you think you can hold the mud back in this sector? Is it possible to erect some kind of barricade?

Baxter It's possible all right sir, but it won't do no good. We put up solid concrete blocks at Mr Wilson's farmhouse, but they just toppled over like a pile of matchboxes. The house doesn't stand a chance now – it's surrounded on all sides. The foundations'll never take the strain. (*pause*) I tell you gentlemen, somebody's gonna have to do somethin' soon. We just can't keep up the pace.

Landers I've already spoken to the Town Council. They've agreed not to wait for Mr Deverill any longer.

Sergeant Johnson approaches

Baxter What's up Sarge?

Johnson The London Road, sir. We're diverting the traffic.

Baxter Why?

Johnson The mud's half way across. The boy's have been tryin' all day to clear a channel, but it won't budge – not an inch. We're sendin' everythin' round via the by-pass.

Baxter (*sighs*) Right. If you need any more help, let me know. I've got some troops comin' in from Shorncliffe in the next hour or so.

Johnson Right sir. (*leaves*)

Gomez (*impatient, irritated*) Why, why, why is there this change of substance during the day? I feel the answer is so close – staring us right in the face.

Landers What is it John?

Lippert (*crouching*) Seems to be more rock salt here than in any of the other overflows. But again – these thin, green streaks. They mean something – I *know* they mean something.

Gomez Five fissures in four days. And in that time, the mud has progressed in Holly Mill Lane alone at the rate of over a quarter of a mile each night. (*to Landers*) You realise Robert, these new overflows could penetrate the main thoroughfares of the town within a matter of hours.

Landers Inspector. I don't care what you do, or who you get, but it's imperative you spare no effort to seal these last overflows before they extend any further into the town limits. If necessary… get every man, woman and child out here.

Baxter I'm beginnin' to think some people forget I'm just a cop around here.

In the background the sound of an electrical explosion. Everybody is taken by surprise

Landers Good God! What's that?

Baxter (*looking out*) That sounds like Centre Heights way. Excuse me gentlemen. (*dashes off, calling*) Sarge!

Lippert There's a great pall of smoke over there, whatever it is.

The sound of a fire engine racing off in the background. Anna Deverill approaches. She is very distressed

Anna (*calls*) Professor!

Landers (*turns around, surprised*) Mrs Deverill?

Anna Professor. I need your help. My husband.

Landers What's happened?

Anna He's called a press conference at the Town Hall for five o'clock.

Landers Well, what's wrong with that?

Anna He has absolutely no authority to do so. He hasn't consulted with London, the Town Council, or even the Party. I'm terrified of what he's going to say.

Landers For Heaven's sake why?

Anna Because at the present moment he's in no fit state to talk to anyone. He just can't be held responsible for anything he says.

Anna Redlow's full of reporters and journalists Mrs Deverill. I don't see what he can possibly tell them that they don't already know?

Anna Would you say the destruction of this town is inevitable Professor? Because that's what my husband thinks.

Shock and dismay from everyone

Landers/Lippert (*together*) What!

Landers Has he gone out of his mind or something?

Anna I can assure you I'd be the last to admit it, but there's no doubt at all this has greatly unbalanced him.

Lippert But this town – it was your husband's own idea. He can't possibly mean what he says.

Anna In the last few days, Professor, my husband has come to hate Redlow and everything to do with it. He blames himself for participating in something he firmly believes is a monument to Man's corruption. (*pause*) I tell you gentlemen, if you allow my husband to go through with this press conference, he'll expose everything and everybody. It'll be the end of his political career.

Gomez Mrs Deverill. Are you trying to tell us that your husband would actually welcome the destruction of this town?

Anna Last night he told me that when – not if, mind you, but when the mud destroys Redlow, it'll be a salvation.

Lippert Robert. He's got to be stopped.

Landers Mrs Deverill. For what time has he called this conference?

Anna Five o'clock – in the theatre at the Town Hall.

Lippert It's five now.

Anna But you'll have to hurry. When I left five minutes ago, the place was already packed to capacity.

Fade out with the sound of more fire engines racing past in the background

Pause

Hugh Deverill addresses the great assembly of British and foreign journalists, some of whom are science correspondents. He speaks in a voice which echoes through the hall. Sometimes it is energetic and forceful, and at other times vibrating with abuse and emotion

Deverill In front of you gentlemen, at the side of me here on the platform, you see a scale model of a town. A town greatly revered by my colleagues and friends on the Town Council, and everyone else. (*pause*) And you ladies and gentlemen. How do you feel about it? Do these gleaming white skyscrapers thrill you, inspire, excite your emotion? Because here it is – a towering tribute to Man's determination to create. (*pause*) By now you are familiar with the events of the past few days, which have brought so many of you hurrying from far corners of the globe. (*pause*) Now why is that? Is it because you really believe Nature has struck a cruel blow against this small corner of the English countryside? Paralysed a daily routine – a way of life that has continued for countless generations? (*pause*) Or can it be that somewhere inside each one of you, there are more decisive questions yearning for an answer?

Speculative mumbling from the assembly. At the back of the hall, Landers, Gomez and Lippert speak in hushed tones

Lippert Somebody do something! We can't let him go on like this.

Landers Look at the state of him. He's an absolute wreck!

Gomez Wait a few minutes. I want to hear what he's going to say.

Deverill continues as the mumbling subsides

Deverill Most of you people here today have described what has happened down here as an evil freak of Nature. But my friends, I can assure you it is not! Whatever evil there is – is in ourselves!

More mumbling

(*absorbed*) Have none of you ever tried to find a way out of stagnation? Tried to find a new way of life, a new way of thinking? A better way? (*pause*) Well *I* have! And that's why I'm glad the chance has come at last.

An outburst of speculation. He speaks above them

The world, ladies and gentlemen, is on the brink of a new and exciting existence. Soon the circle will be broken, the flower will wither. Death is not something to be feared. It is not finality.

The assembly is buzzing with bewilderment

Landers The man's off his head!

Lippert For God's sake don't let him go on like this. He's ill!

Gomez I wonder?

Landers (*moving off*) We'll see if we can get down nearer the front. Follow me.

Deverill (*speaking above the din*) We may look to the stars ladies and gentlemen, but it won't do any good. *Our* hope for the future is right here on Earth. We don't have to be scared of the darkness any more. Darkness is the new giver of life – darkness. And do you know why? (*almost shouting to be heard*) Because the sun, ladies and gentlemen, is no longer the creator.

An uproar breaks out as we fade out

Pause

Fade in: A room at the Redlow Hospital. Mrs Luke is sobbing, watched over by Ken Richards and the Nursing Sister

Ken (*comforting*) It's all right now Mrs Luke. Don't distress yourself. We know it's not your fault.

Mrs Luke (*sobbing*) She must have been mad or something. She could have killed both of us. (*turning to Ken*) Doctor. I'm telling you she went quite berserk – like a wild animal. Your car's an absolute wreck. (*stifling her sobs*)

Ken It doesn't matter in the slightest Mrs Luke. Just try and remember exactly what happened. Why did she suddenly go like that? Was it something you said?

Mrs Luke No. She just wouldn't speak – not for a long time. For most of the time she sat in the front seat at the side of me – just staring dead in front of her at the road. Every so often I could see her face reflected in the wing mirror – all white and drawn. (*with emotion*) And her eyes. They were so determined.

Ken Tell me how the accident happened?

Mrs Luke It was those two stupid old people. They seemed to spring out from nowhere – right out of the darkness. They suddenly stepped out in front of the car, and started waving frantically at me. Before I could do anything, that wretched girl had grabbed hold of the steering wheel, and we were going straight for them. There was nothing I could do – she was far too strong for me. (*pause*) But then, it was quite extraordinary. Just as we were about to hit them, she screamed out and swerved the car right off the road. We ended up at the bottom of the incline – glass everywhere. I don't know how we weren't killed.

Ken What happened then?

Mrs Luke I suppose I must have blacked out for a few minutes, but I do remember seeing that girl scrambling up the grass verge with the two old people. Where they went from there, I don't know.

Ken Sister. Could either of these two old people be from the Ward?

Sister I don't know Doctor. From the description, it sounds a bit like Mrs Thompkins and Miss Kirby. But it's hard to say. There are so many of them missing now – it's hard to keep track.

Mrs Luke It was so awful to see them all standing on the road at the top – just staring down at me. (*distressed*) D'you know, I really think they were wishing me dead. Even though I kept calling to them to help, they just ignored me. It was so heartless.

Ken So in fact, Janet wasn't hurt badly?

Mrs Luke I don't see how she could have been. She was out long before me.

Ken Mrs Luke. Have you any idea in which direction she went? Was it back towards town?

Mrs Luke I've told you, I don't know. I suppose I must have blacked out for nearly an hour. All I can tell you is that it took me ages to break my way out of that car on my own. I practically collapsed when I reached the telephone box.

Ken If you can remember anything – anything at all. I don't have to tell you how imperative it is we find her as soon as possible.

Mrs Luke I feel so guilty to have let you down like this. You should never have trusted me with her. (*pause*) She's a very sick girl, Doctor.

Ken (*grave and serious*) I know.

Mrs Luke To think of her wandering around the countryside all alone like that, in the dark. And then hiding in disused buildings, carrying those poor little creatures about with her…

Ken (*looks up, surprised*) Creatures?

Mrs Luke Yes. Soon after you left us I found she was holding on to a poor, dead little bird. A little sparrow. When I tried to take it away from her she just pushed me aside, and threw it into the river. I think even you'll have to agree Doctor, it's a pretty warped mind that wants to do things like that. Very warped indeed.

Fade out. Pause

At the press conference, Deverill faces a barrage of questions from the journalists without involvement

1st Journalist Sir! I'd like to ask you why Redlow has still not been declared a disaster area. Surely an appeal to the Prime Minister is well overdue?

Deverill We're perfectly capable of dealing with our own problems in our own time.

2nd Journalist But the situation's getting out of hand. You can't possibly deny the implications of such a –

Deverill (*completely oblivious*) Implications? What implications?

3rd Journalist (*jumps up angrily*) Mr Deverill! Hasn't anyone bothered to tell you? People are already being evacuated from their homes in four different areas of the town.

2nd Journalist (*angrily*) Do they have to wait until it reaches *your* home before something's done!

Shouts of agreement from everyone. Deverill snaps back angrily at the criticism

Deverill Why are you blind? (*shouts*) Why are you all so blind?

The noise in the hall subsides

  For the first time you are privileged to witness a new evolution – a turning-point in the history of mankind. (*with emotion*) I implore you not to scorn it! Do not look to the mud as an enemy. (*triumphantly*) It is our salvation!

The awed silence is suddenly broken by the voice of Professor Landers, who is standing at the side of the hall

Landers (*calls*) That's just where you're wrong Mr Deverill!

As he approaches the platform, there is an excited buzz of speculation

  For your information, in case you don't know, this mud constitutes a danger, unprecedented by all previous freaks of Nature on this planet…

An outburst of shock from all present

(*speaking above the noise*) …and in the interests of public safety, ladies and gentlemen, I beg you to disregard anything you have heard from this man during the course of the last hour. His platitudes are not only unauthorised, but wild and dangerous.

Buzzing throughout the hall, gradually subsiding

I'm sure most of you will know both me and my colleagues. You will also know that we were invited by Her Majesty's Government to investigate this extraordinary situation in the Redlow area, caused by these sudden and unexpected earth tremors and mud overflows. A situation which has, and cannot fail to baffle the scientific mind. All you ladies and gentlemen gathered here are well acquainted with the innumerable natural disasters which frequently ravage the surface of this earth. (*pointing hard at them*) But now I ask you to consider this. What kind of disorder is it that can produce tremors, fissures, and a discharge of an unidentified substance, in an area which is generally accepted by us all to be outside the seismic belt?

A wave of excited speculation

(*composing himself*) These are questions, ladies and gentlemen, which – I am distressed to have to tell you – are still unanswered. (*pause, solemn*) How great our danger is, I will let you decide. I will let *you* decide. I will ask nothing of you, other than you listen to the latest evidence at our disposal.

Deverill (*shouting out*) Don't listen to these men! They bring you nothing but lies!

Landers (*ignoring Deverill*) It's up to you, ladies and gentlemen.

2nd Journalist (*shouts*) Let them speak!

There is complete general agreement. Landers waits for the noise to subside

Landers Very well. (*turns to Gomez and Lippert*) Professor Gomez and Professor Lippert. Will you come up here please?

We fade out on the renewed buzz of speculation from the assembly

Pause

A fire has broken out in the Centre Heights apartment block. The scene is one of general chaos, as fire engines race to and fro in the background

Baxter How long has it been like this Sarge?

Johnson About twenty minutes sir.

Baxter Anybody still in there?

Johnson Yeah, I'm afraid so. A few bods in the top flats. Trouble is the lifts cut out soon after the fire broke out. I think it's burnt through the main cable. They can only get down by usin' the stairs. And that's a hell of a way through all that smoke. I'm afraid there's not gonna be much left of Centre Heights after this.

Baxter How'd it start? Anybody know?

Johnson Oh it was definitely in the basement, that we do know. A couple of the porters smelt the fumes. Unfortunately the generator blew out just as they got there. They're in a pretty bad way.

Baxter The generator? So it was an electrical failure?

Johnson Oh it was electrical all right. The whole building was blacked out from top to bottom. That blasted stuff.

Baxter What're you talkin' about? What stuff?

Johnson Well – the mud.

Baxter Mud?

Johnson In the basement. It was full of it – over a foot deep. The Fire boys had a fit when they saw it. (*pause*) I thought you knew sir?

Baxter (*obviously shocked*) No Sergeant. As a matter of fact – I did not.

The RAF Corporal approaches, breathless

Hallo Corps. What now? Holly Mill Lane?

Corporal I think you'd better get down there right away Inspector. It's Mr Wilson.

Baxter Tug Wilson? What's up?

Corporal He's barricaded himself inside the farmhouse.

Baxter What!

Corporal Him and his missus. We thought we'd give him a hand to move some of his stuff out, but every time we get anywhere near the place, he takes a pot-shot at you.

Baxter Don't give me – . You mean Tug and his missus? Firing at you?

Corporal You don't have to believe me Inspector. Just come down there and try pokin' your head out. Both of them have got a couple of 303's. And I'll tell you this. If somebody don't get them out of there in the next half-hour or so, that mud's gonna be on the move again, and this time it's not gonna be at all funny. 'Cause the mud's already pressin' against every wall of that house.

Fade out. Pause

At the press conference, Gomez, his voice strong and urgent, addresses the assembly

Gomez For many years, ladies and gentlemen, we scientists have struggled to understand the reasons why the earth begins to shake, to tremble, then open out into great chasms. To try and discover what great energies it is that clash beneath the surface of this great crust we walk upon. (*pause*) We know it could be for many reasons. Perhaps volcanic, a landslide, or in some cases even the movement of a rock formation. But, as Professor Landers has told you, the one thing we have known until now, is that such disturbances have nearly always been confined to those areas of the world which we quite often refer as the seismic belt. (*pause*) Those of you who live as I and my countrymen do, under the constant threat of these impending disasters, will appreciate the real horror of being in an earthquake. The feeling of helplessness, of being completely in the hands of Nature. (*pause*) But, ladies and gentlemen, I make no pretence of the fact that what I and my colleagues have witnessed here in Redlow during the past few days has both fascinated and shocked us. (*buzz of murmuring throughout the hall, gradually subsiding*) Let us for the moment disregard the complexity of the very fact that the British Isles are outside the normal seismic belt. Then let us try to find out why the situation which has developed here is such a critical one. (*pause. He points towards the model of the New Town*) In front of you ladies and gentlemen, you see a scale model of Redlow New Town. The first fissure, that is to say the first fracture in the soil's crust, appeared... here. (*points*) The area known as Holly Mill Lane. (*continues to indicate*) And then – here... here... here... and... here... (*pause*) Five distinct fractures, not all in one place, but, ladies and gentlemen, look at the model... (*dramatically*) and see for yourselves the circular, almost perfectly symmetrical pattern formed around the town.

More speculative buzzing in the hall

2nd Journalist Professor. Are you trying to tell us there is some kind of significance in the positioning of those fissures?

Gomez If we want, we can merely regard this positioning as a coincidence. That is, except for one thing. (*pause*) The overflow of this substance which we have come to think of as mud, which I must tell you now I firmly believe to be a dangerous threat to us all. This mud, ladies and gentlemen – is a killer!

An uproar from the assembly

(*speaks above them*) For all we know, it may have been lying in the bowels of the earth for perhaps thousands of years, but I can tell you that my own investigations have proved that the mud was unable to find an outlet on the sea-bed of the English Channel. (*pause*) Now, it has found that outlet, and I am convinced that it intends to hold on to it at all costs. (*grimly*) Because, ladies and gentlemen, there is no doubt this mud has the intelligence to do so.

The hall is again seething with excited speculation. In the middle of this, an American journalist stands up

American journalist (*tending towards sarcasm*) Professor Gomez. I'd like to ask you sir, what theories you have as to the cause of these disruptions? Would you rule out the possibility of – nuclear testing, for instance?

Gomez No sir. I would not.

More buzzing throughout the hall

American journalist (*smiling*) Oh, come now sir – you must forgive my saying, but your past sympathies with, shall we say, pacifist-inclined groups, are well known to us all. (*speaking above the objections*) This is hardly the platform for a nuclear disarmament campaign. (*He ignores shouts for him to sit down*) Be honest with us sir! Can you really expect us to believe that a geological substance is capable of determing its own movements?

Long pause. Gomez is unmoved by the attack

Gomez No. I can't expect you to believe that. I can't expect anyone to. Because to try to convince is a tremendous responsibility to have to bear. (*pause*) That's why, ladies and gentlemen, I'm going to ask you to listen to my colleague, Professor Lippert.

More buzzing throughout the hall, as Lippert stands up

Lippert Our samples, ladies and gentlemen, were taken from the overflows of fissures in both Holly Mill Lane and the Holly Crag Caves. Their appearance remained green and slimy in appearance, rather like the discharge from a snail or slug – except for periods during the day, when they reverted back to a solid block formation. A microscopic examination at first showed nothing except the presence of small particles of rock salt. It was not until a later stage that we realised the specimen was – multiplying itself at a tremendous rate every few seconds.

More buzzing throughout the hall

American journalist Multiplying? How could it possibly do that Professor?

Lippert (*curt*) My analysis of the samples proved beyond the shadow of a doubt, the existence in the mud of – living organisms.

An uproar from the assembly

American journalist (*stunned*) Living organisms!

Lippert My colleagues and I have come to the conclusion that the mud is a single, living thing… (*overriding the excitement*) …capable of an acid-like destruction of anything or anybody it comes into contact with.

American journalist For Heaven's sake man! D'you realise what you're saying?

Lippert The mud is a living thing, containing an unmissable heartbeat, which we have measured at the rate of seventy-two revolutions per minute. And that, my friend, I am sure you will know, is comparable to that of any adult human being!

American journalist (*stunned with disbelief*) But if this is true, this surrounding of Redlow could be the first step towards the ultimate destruction of the town.

Lippert Not only this town, my friend. (*solemnly*) Remember this. Every minute we allow this monster to exist, it doubles and perhaps even trebles its strength. Time is against us, ladies and gentlemen. Make no mistake about it. Either we find a way to destroy it now, or we let *it* destroy *us*, completely and irrevocably!

The conference bursts into chaos and confusion, as the journalists rush to release their news. On this, we fade out

Pause

The sound of a .303 bullet and its ricochet fills the air

Baxter (*shouts*) Tug! Put that damned thing down! Don't be a fool man. Get out of there before it's too late.

Corporal I should keep behind cover if I was you Inspector. He'll blast your head off, if you're not careful.

Baxter How much longer have we got?

Corporal I shouldn't imagine more than a few minutes at the most. The top of the mud's already got a shine on it. There's a sure sign it's beginnin' to soften up.

Baxter Couple of maniacs! What the hell do they reckon they're tryin' to prove?

Vicar Inspector.

Baxter Vicar. What're you doin' here sir?

Vicar I want to speak to the Wilsons. Will you let me past, please?

Baxter Are you mad sir? The pair of them have got a couple of 303's. They're not particular where they take aim. Take my tip sir, keep well clear of this. There's nothin' you can do for them now.

Vicar Mr and Mrs Wilson are my parishioners. They're chuch-going folk. I'm sure they'll listen to me.

Baxter You put one foot out there, sir, and they'll blow your head off. Believe me.

Vicar (*pleads*) I've got to try. I have to. (*pause*) Please?

A long pause

Baxter (*calls out*) Sergeant Johnson!

Johnson (*off, calls*) Sir!

Baxter See if you can get hold of a megaphone, and let me have some light on those windows up there. And for God's sake man – keep your head down!

Fade out. Pause

Now alone in the vast conference hall, Deverill, embittered and lost, stares down at the model of Redlow New Town. The door at the back of the halls open, and Anna calls to her husband

Anna Hugh! (*no reply. She walks a few steps towards him*) Hugh darling. It's no use, staring at the model like that. It won't help – everyone's gone. (*pause*) Come on. I've got the car outside. Let's go home.

Deverill I have no home.

She moves right in closer to him

Anna (*with sympathetic concern*) Hugh. Why did you do it? What made you say all those things? Your whole dream – everything you've ever fought for – all gone in just a few minutes. (*pause*) Why?

Deverill (*staring hard at the model*) Look at it. *My* town. *My* dream.

Anna You made it a reality. You've helped to create a new conception in Man's standard of living. They wouldn't have their town if it wasn't for you – and they know it! You should be proud.

Deverill That's what you think is it? Proud to have been a part of Man's plans for ruthless corruption. Is that it?

Anna (*bewildered*) Corruption? How can you possibly say that when thousands of people have now got a roof over their head?

Deverill Corruption, expansion, domination… call it what you like.

Anna Domination?

Deverill Look at the way these buildings stretch up towards the sky – flaunting their domination. Monuments to greed, a lust for power. An attempt to deny Nature its very right to exist. (*neurotically*) D'you think I'm proud of that? Proud to be an accomplice to evil?

Anna Hugh – stop talking like that! You're ill –

Deverill Yes. You wanted me to create this, didn't you? You encouraged me. Well it's no good. Only Nature has the right to create. Only She has the power to stop us from exploiting corruption and evil – don't you worry about that.

Anna (*stunned and disbelieving*) Hugh! What are you saying!

Deverill (*forcefully*) The Earth was created for and by Nature. When are you going to realise that?

Anna Hugh! (*struggling*) Let go of my arm! You're hurting me!

Deverill They think they know. But they don't! None of them! When the darkness comes, they won't be able to shield behind the sun any more.

Picks up walking stick

Anna (*terrified, shouts out*) Hugh! What are you going to do with that walking-stick! For God's sake put it down!

Deverill (*releasing her, shouts*) But – not any more!

Anna stifles her terror as Deverill suddenly starts to lash out at the model of the New Town

Anna Hugh!

The sound of the destruction of the model continues, and then stops abruptly. For a moment or two there is silence, but for the exhausted heavy breathing of Deverill

Hugh! What have you done? The model. You've destroyed it.

Deverill (*breathless*) Something I should have done – a long time ago. (*pause*) And… it's still not too late!

He hurries off past her, throwing down the walking stick. He stops at the back of the hall to call back

(*shouts*) Not too late!

He leaves the hall, slamming the door

Anna (*to herself*) Hugh. (*calls*) Hugh!

Distressed, she begins to sob as we fade out

Pause

The siege of the farmhouse has begun. The Vicar, off, appeals to the Wilsons through a police megaphone

Vicar Mr Wilson! (*pause*) Mr Wilson, can you hear me?

A window is pulled open, on mic

Tug (*shouts*) Get out of there Vicar! This has got nothin' to do with you.

Vicar For Heaven's sake man, use your senses. The mud is already beginning to soften. Get yourselves out of there before it's too late.

Tug Nobody takes away what belongs to me!

Vicar But don't you understand? You're endangering your lives. Those walls won't be able to take the strain for much longer.

Mrs Wilson Don't listen to him Tug. He's just tryin' to trick us. He's no different to the rest of 'em. (*puts her head out of the window and shouts*) Go back to your church Vicar! Tell *them* some of your lies. You don't mean nothin' to us now! Go back!

Vicar (*pleading*) Please! I beg of you both. Your house will be rebuilt, but don't sacrifice yourselves for an unworthy cause. Don't abandon your faith – everything you've ever believed in. We'll help you – I promise we'll help you.

Mrs Wilson You see! All that talk. He *is* tryin' to trick us!

Vicar Please Mr Wilson! Mrs Wilson!

Mrs Wilson Give me that rifle!

Tug (*struggling with her*) No Mary! (*The rifle fires*) You fool! What're you tryin' to do – kill him or something? (*He slams the window closed. Raging with scorn*) Don't you *ever* try that again! We're not murderers!

Mrs Wilson You're a fool, Tug. Don't you think I can see through his lies and his promises. It's always been like that, and it always will – whilst we let it.

Tug He's always been a good friend to us. He's never deceived us. I don't see why we should start disbelievin' him now. (*pause, regretful*) Perhaps he's right. Perhaps we are causin' a lot of misery for no reason.

Mrs Wilson No reason? This is our house Tug. We built it, you and me – with our own bare hands. You tell me there's no reason for wantin' to hang on to it?

Tug (*walking around*) If it's true what they say, if it *is* dangerous…

Mrs Wilson (*scoffing*) Dangerous!

Tug I don't wanna take no chances. Anyway, I can't bear bein' locked away like this. It's like an oven in here. (*struggling with his collar*) I feel as though I'm bein' throttled.

Mrs Wilson (*close to him, comforting*) It's not so bad is it love? At least we're together. That's what you always wanted, isn't it?

The first sound of wooden beams creaking

Tug What's that?

Mrs Wilson (*unnaturally calm*) It's nothin'. Don't worry love…

Tug (*looking up*) The – the ceilin' – look. It's shakin'…

Mrs Wilson It's all right love. This is what we've been waitin' for, you and me… all our lives. This is just the start. Don't it make you feel good, my love?

The sound of things tumbling over. The wooden beams showing first signs of collapse

Tug (*panicking*) The walls… it's… all gonna cave in on us! We've gotta get out of here quick!

Mrs Wilson (*very intense*) We've beaten them now Tug. You and me, we've beaten the lot of 'em. Put your arms around me! Go on!

Tug (*finding it difficult to breathe*) I'm suffocating I tell you! I've gotta have some air.

He smashes the window

Outside we hear the mud reverting back to its clammy substance

(*shouts out*) Help! Somebody help us!

The creaking of the beams is now an unbearable, near deafening sound

Mrs Wilson Hold on to me Tug! Hold on… and we'll never be parted again…

At last we hear the ceiling and walls collapse. A dreadful feeling of crumbling as the house disintegrates into a pile of rubble, and the mud slides on relentlessly

Fade out

END OF EPISODE FIVE

The Slide
by Victor Pemberton

Episode 6: Time Limit

Produced by John Tydeman

TRANSMISSION:	Sunday 20 March 1966	1900–1930 LIGHT
REHEARSALS:	Wednesday 9 February	1030–1830
RECORD:	Wednesday 9 February	1830–1930 (to H.11)
STUDIO:	B.11	
R.P. No.	TLO 605/552	
EDIT:	Wednesday 16 February	1015–1245 (H.54)
PLAYBACK:	Wednesday 16 February	1500–1530 (5108)

CAST:

Gomez	Roger Delgado
Deverill	Maurice Denham
Landers	Rolf Lefebvre
Lippert	Allan McClelland
Richards	David Spenser
Anna	Marion Mathie
Baxter	Geoffrey Matthews
RAF Corporal	Anthony Hall
Mrs Luke	Noel Hood
Sergeant Johnson	Wilfred Babbage
Margaret Griffith	Joan Matheson
Pilot	Anthony Jackson
Control	Brian Hewlett

S.M.s: Panel: Amna Smith; Grams: David Cain; Spot: Margaret Rushton

SECRETARY: Helene Grygar, PABX 2168

Announcer Tug Wilson and his wife have been trapped in their farmhouse, which has been reduced to a heap of rubble by the surging force of the mud overflow. Redlow New Town itself is now a major disaster area…

An RAF helicopter is flying low over the rooftops of Redlow New Town

Pilot 'C' Charlie calling Redlow Control. 'C' Charlie calling Redlow Control. Are you receiving me? Over.

Ground Control (*at the other end*) Control to 'C' Charlie. Control to 'C' Charlie. Receiving you. Go ahead please. Over.

Pilot Am following a course due west of the Holly River. Just coming over the town centre now. Looks pretty hectic down there. What are they doing anyway? All those trucks and lorries. Like a ruddy circus. Over.

Ground Control They're getting the hell out of there chum. Wouldn't you? Over.

Pilot Too true! The streets look as though they're crawling alive with that stuff. (*pause*) Now look Control. Listen carefully please. This is my third circuit around the town. Have you got that? Over.

Ground Control Go ahead please. Over.

Pilot So far I've seen two lots of fissures with mud in a small field at the back of the skyscraper block – that is what's left of it. Then there are a couple more alongside the railway line – about two hundred yards outside Redlow Station. I should warn them if I was you. Oh yeah – and I'm not quite sure but I've got an idea there's another one in the churchyard at St Peters. At least, it looks as though there are a few trees down. Got that? Over.

Ground Control Thank you 'C' Charlie. Message received and understood. Please complete one more circuit, then return to Base. And whatever you do chum, keep your eyes open! Over.

Mix the sound of the helicopter in the air into the same sound passing over the heads of the crowd below. It is morning. Mud has overflowed from the drains in a small side street. Efforts are made to dig, drill, and chip at the hardened mud surface

Baxter (*calls*) Sergeant Johnson!

Johnson (*off, calls*) Sir!

Baxter Take two men and get those people out of that house! I gave you orders to get everybody out of this street by eleven o'clock. Now what's up with you? Have I got to do everythin' myself?

Johnson I can't help it Inspector. It's some old dear trying to get the boys to put her piano on the truck. It's a hell of a job.

Baxter (*ruthlessly*) Well get her out of there! Unless she wants the whole street to come down on top of her.

Johnson Yes sir! (*dashes off*)

Lippert Is that likely, d'you think Inspector? Are the foundations shaky?

Baxter I really don't know sir. But after last night – with the Wilsons – I'm not takin' any chances. There's no gas, water, electricity. We can't even get a telephone line through to London. Somethin's jamming it all up – and I won't give you more than two guesses what that is. It's been seepin' up through these drains in the road all night.

Lippert You mustn't blame yourself you know. What happened to the Wilsons was not your fault.

Baxter No sir? Then whose fault was it? (*pause*) I've known Tug Wilson and his missus for years. Ever since I left the beat. He was always a bit of a dope – obstinate, big-headed, full of himself. But he was as much a part of the countryside round here as the soil itself. I was a fool not to have realised that last night. It might have done some good. (*pause*) When are we gonna see the back of this Professor?

Lippert (*grimly*) We have to move first. That's all I can tell you.

Baxter Well, I hope somebody comes up with a bright idea sooner or later. Before it's too late. (*pause*) It's not the mud that scares me, you know. It's people.

Lippert People?

Baxter D'you know what they were doin' in the town last night? Right in the centre – the main High Street?

Lippert No?

Baxter Looting. The sane, level-headed British public – smashing shop windows, and swipin' everythin' they could lay their hands on. None of 'em were professionals, none of 'em had criminal records. They were just the ordinary man-in-the-street, that docile creature you'd probably find mowin' his garden lawn on a Sunday morning. (*pause*) Still – I don't suppose you can blame him really. When the unexpected turns into a nightmare, it's bound to turn him into an animal. I mean – it's only natural, ain't it?

Pause

Lippert Inspector. How can I get down into those sewers?

Baxter (*shocked*) Do what sir?

Lippert There's obviously a fracture down there somewhere. It's just possible we can do something, *if* we can find out which way the mud is moving.

Baxter I'm sorry sir – I can't allow that. It's much too dangerous for you to go wandering through the town sewers on your own.

Lippert That's easily settled. Come with me.

Baxter (*clearing his throat nervously*) I – er – don't know about that sir. You've told us yourself, that mud's alive. You never know what it might be capable of doin'…

Lippert Not during the day Inspector. You can see for yourself – it's as hard as concrete. Come on. It won't take more than ten minutes. I just want to have a look.

Baxter (*very reluctant*) Oh – very well sir. I'll see if I can get hold of a torch. But this I warn you Professor Lippert. One peep out of that stuff whilst we're down there, and you won't see me for dust. That I promise you…!

Lippert (*laughs, moving*) Come on!

Fade out

Pause

Fade in: The taped sound of the mud's heartbeat as played on a recorder in the laboratory. After listening to it for a moment, it is suddenly switched off

Gomez So? What do you think now Doctor?

Ken No doubt about it. It's an unmistakable heartbeat. Quite incredible!

Gomez And would you say it compares with the beat of a regular human heart?

Ken Almost identical. In fact I'd like as many pennies as the number of times I've listened to this inside my own patients. The only difference is that this is much stronger, more firm. (*clearly stunned*) But is this really possible? A living organism in a geological substance?

Landers You've had the chance to study the mud sample under the microscope Doctor. What more proof do you need?

Ken It's just that it takes quite a bit of getting used to. (*pause*) This of course answers quite a few questions.

Landers Such as?

Ken Well, if we're to believe that this mud is alive, with functioning brain cells, then we must also believe that it's capable of exercising its own intelligence.

Landers You mean, equal to that of a human being?

Ken (*grimly*) And maybe more Professor. In fact the evidence at our disposal is now too overwhelming to think otherwise.

Landers I don't quite follow you?

Ken During the past few days our surgeries throughout the town have been crowded with patients complaining of almost identical symptoms.

Gomez What kind of symptoms Doctor?

Ken On the face of it, quite ordinary really. Headaches, sickness, nausea. But the interesting thing is the depression which follows.

Gomez Depression?

Ken It's difficult to describe really, but from nearly all these people we've had reports of them doing the most extraordinary things – things which are so completely alien to their own personalities. And in some cases this has led to direct physical violence.

Landers Yes Doctor, but isn't this a perfectly natural reaction? The hospital are still treating hordes of people for shock after the earth tremors.

Ken I'm sorry Professor, but I believe there's much more to it than that. And so do my colleagues. That's why they've asked me to come and see you. To be perfectly frank with you gentlemen – we're concerned.

Gomez The mud. You think there's some connection. Is that it?

Ken Believe me Professor – I don't know. What's happened around here during the past few days I'd never have thought possible in my wildest dreams.

Landers Would anybody?

Ken An old man throwing himself into the mud in the Holly Crag Caves, people disappearing from the hospital wards in the middle of the night. Even Mr Deverill with that absurd press conference of his last night. (*pause*) And Janet. My own fiancée who doesn't even know me any more… roaming around the countryside God knows where. (*pause*) And then, what about the wildlife. Birds, cattle, sheep, cats, dogs – dying off by the score – and for no reason. I tell you gentlemen – *something's* happening!

Pause

Gomez Let me see if I understand you Doctor. You and your colleagues obviously believe that certain sections of the community are being subjected to some kind of – mental pressure. Is that correct?

Pause

Ken Yes.

Gomez An outside pressure, trying to force its way in.

Ken Yes.

Gomez And that outside force – is the mud?

Pause

Ken (*reluctantly*) Yes.

Landers But this is preposterous! How can the mud, even with its brain cells and heartbeats, exercise *any* sort of pressure over the human mind?

Gomez In a way, my dear Robert, that we should have realised long ago. (*to Ken*) Will you tell us Doctor? Or shall I?

A long pause

Ken Hypnotism, Professor. The art of hypnotism.

A sharp cut

Pause

The front door of the Deverills' home is wide open. From the street outside, we hear the sound of heavy lorries rumbling by every few minutes. In the hall of the house, Anna Deverill collects things together in readiness for the evacuation. She does not notice her friend, Margaret Griffiths, a Welsh MP, standing in the open doorway

Maggie (*off, calls*) Hallo! Anybody at home?

Anna (*turns around, surprised*) Maggie! What are you doing here? I didn't know you were in Redlow?

Maggie (*entering*) I got a lift in from Maidstone. There's a blockage on the line just outside town. Even the boat train passengers had to be diverted.

Anna goes to the front door and slams out the noise

Anna This noise!

Maggie How long's it been like that?

Anna The whole night. I haven't slept a wink. I suppose you know, we're what you call a distressed area now. We're all being bundled off to the RAF camp at Redlow. I'm supposed to be out of here by eleven – hence the mess.

Maggie (*confidently*) How are you my dear?

Anna You really want to know? (*pause*) I'm scared Maggie. In fact I've never been so scared in my whole life. The bottom seems to have dropped out of everything in the last few days.

Maggie That doesn't sound a bit like you Anna. You've always known how to cope in the past. I have a feeling New Town life doesn't appeal to you?

Pause

Anna Why've you come down here? Did – *they* send you?

Maggie I suppose you could call me a sort of advance guard. There was a secret meeting at Chequers during the night. They're all shaking from the knees upwards. I think you'll find my arrival the first of many. (*pause*) Anna. What's happened to Hugh?

Anna (*on the defensive*) Why ask me? You've known him just as long.

Maggie Now don't be silly, girl! I'm not down here as a politician. Hugh's my friend – and so are you.

Anna He's a very sick man. That's all I know.

Maggie But this wild press conference of his last night. He attacked everyone. The Government, the Party, the Council – even his own original conception of the town. The whole country's buzzing with it. What's gone wrong for Heaven's sake? It's so unlike him.

Pause

Anna (*coldly*) Perhaps you'd better see for yourself. He's in here.

She opens the door of the lounge and enters

(*calls gently*) Hugh. (*no reply*) Hugh, there's someone to see you. (*no reply*) Hugh?

Maggie Hallo boy! Don't you want to see me? It's Maggie. (*pause*) Whereabouts are you? I can't see you in all this dark?

Deverill (*softly*) What d'you want?

Maggie (*turns around sharply*) Oh – there you are. Why? Do I have to have a reason to visit an old friend? (*pause*) Can't we have some light?

Deverill Leave those curtains alone!

Maggie But it's a lovely day outside. Anyway it's silly to sit and talk in the dark. So impersonal.

Deverill I prefer it. (*pause*) What d'you want?

Pause

Maggie (*tactfully*) We were wondering – some of us were wondering – when you're coming back?

Deverill Back? Where to?

Maggie To Westminster. We haven't seen you at any of the meetings over the last few days. There was one at Chequers last night. Most of the defence people were there. (*pause*) We – we missed you.

Deverill And you came all the way from London to tell me that? That my colleagues, my associates, my 'friends' – all miss me. Is that it?

Maggie What's the matter with you Hugh? Don't you care about Redlow any more? Your town? You know very well, all the Government wants to do is…

Deverill (*a highly-strung outburst*) Government! My dear, dear friend. When are you and all the rest of those fools going to realise that the time is coming when the only form of 'Government' will be the Earth itself?

Maggie (*shocked and bewildered*) Hugh! What are you saying? You can't sit by and see the town swallowed up – right in front of your very eyes.

Deverill (*close to mic, almost maniacal*) Maggie! Oh Maggie, can't you feel it? The vibration of an exciting new life…?

A long pause

Maggie (*impatiently*) How much longer do you intend to lock yourself away like this?

Deverill (*straightening up*) For as long as I wish.

Maggie And how long is that supposed to be?

Deverill *I* shall know.

Maggie Very well. (*pause*) Then I shall take Anna with me…

Anna No, Maggie…

Maggie If you want to stay here and rot, you can do so. But don't expect your wife to rot with you. (*pause, a last attempt*) Oh Hugh. What's happened to you? Can you so easily forget those fifteen years of hard work? (*pause*) I can't believe you're willing to let it all go – just like that. (*pause. Curtly*) Very well.

Anna Maggie. Maggie – what are you doing?

Maggie (*at the window*) If you won't let God's good light in – *I* will!

136

Deverill (*shouts out*) No!

Maggie draws the curtains apart

Maggie Look out there Hugh! Take a good look – and feel the sun on your face! (*stops, horrified*) Oh my God! Look at you!

Deverill (*protecting himself*) My eyes! Somebody help me! My eyes!

Fade out with Deverill groaning out his misery

Pause

Lippert and Inspector Baxter are climbing down the iron steps into the town sewers

Baxter Mind how you go now sir. These steps are a bit slippery.

Lippert It's all right thanks – I'm OK.

They reach the bottom of the steps and take a breather

I must say it all looks very clean. I always imagined town sewers to be filthy.

Baxter Oh no. The whole system's pretty new. They only finished doin' it about six months ago. (*looks around*) So? Which way?

Lippert Shine the torch over there can you? (*looks around*) Yes. Well. I reckon if we follow the stream for two or three hundred yards – that way… it should bring us almost directly underneath the High Street… (*jumps with a start*) Lord! What's that?

Baxter (*smiling smugly*) Don't worry Professor. It's only a rat. I mean – you're bound to find them down here, aren't you?

Lippert (*nervously*) Er – yes, quite.

Baxter As long as we don't find anythin' worse than that, we'll be all right… I hope! This way sir.

Fade out as they tread their way carefully at the side of the rippling sewer stream

Pause

The sound of piano strings shaking as an upright piano is being moved across the hall

Corporal Take it over your side a bit Gibbons…hey! Mind my blasted foot!

Mrs Luke (*bossy*) Be careful there you two! I don't want it chipped – this is my best French polish.

Corporal (*breathless*) If you don't mind my sayin' so madam, you'd hardly call an upright piano an article for essential evacuation, now would you?

Mrs Luke Your only concern young man, is to get it out onto that lorry in one piece. It happens to be a very valuable piece of antique furniture left to me by my dear mother. One scratch or chip out of it, and I wouldn't hesitate to sue the RAF Minister or whoever he is. In fact I'd sooner this piano was saved than myself.

Corporal (*under his breath*) You can say that again.

Mrs Luke What was that?

Corporal I said it'll be difficult to get it on the lorry.

Mrs Luke That is not my problem. You don't think I particularly like the idea of being thrown out of my own house and home do you? It's just perfectly ridiculous. There's no mud in here.

Corporal You've already been told Mrs Luke. The foundations of the whole block are very shaky. We're not even sure if the mud's not jamming up everythin' down below. That's why you haven't got any gas or electricity, or even water.

Mrs Luke Well, all I'm saying is that they'd better make us comfortable in that billet place of yours or I shall write a letter to my MP. It won't be the first time I've written to Mr Deverill.

Corporal (*bored*) Yes madam.

Mrs Luke Now be good enough to go about your work and get that piano onto the…

He stops her abruptly

Corporal (*snaps*) Be quiet!

Mrs Luke I *beg* your…!

Corporal Shut up will yer!

Mrs Luke (*shaking with indignation*) How dare you! I shall report you to your…

Corporal Listen. (*pause*) Can't you hear it?

Mrs Luke Hear it? Hear what?

The first sounds of the building beginning to shake

Corporal We're shakin'. (*The noise increases*) Let's get out of here!

As they run out of the house, the building begins to collapse. Mrs Luke screams out. In the middle of the crumbling masonry, we hear the muffled sound of the piano strings

Fade out

Pause

Lippert and Baxter are still treading their way carefully along the edge of the sewer stream

Lippert I should think we're just below the High Street now. Can you see anything Inspector?

Baxter (*looking around*) No. Not a thing. (*They stop walking*) Have you noticed something though?

Lippert No?

Baxter Look in the water.

Lippert (*looking down*) Good Lord! Dead rats. Look at them all – there must be about a dozen of them.

Baxter That's why I was a bit surprised to see that one alive when we first came down. These things have been floatin' on top of the water all the way along.

Lippert In which case – we can expect the worst. (*pause*) Where does that alley lead to?

Baxter (*slightly away from him*) Dead end I should think. Anyway, there must be quite a few exits down here. One for nearly every street… hey! That's funny.

Lippert What?

Baxter Over here. (*Lippert joins him*)

Lippert What is it?

Baxter (*lowering voice*) Can you hear anything?

They listen. Silence, except for the rippling water

Lippert Not a thing.

Baxter (*almost whispering*) Put your ear up against the wall... no – closer. (*pause*) There! Can you hear it now?

For the first time we hear the sound of a man or woman breathing. It echoes along the wall

Lippert (*whispering*) Yes! (*listens*) It – it's somebody breathing. Quick! Shine the torch in front of you.

They are both staring dead ahead

Baxter I can't see a thing. Not a damned thing.

Lippert Give me the torch. I want to look down this alley. (*He takes the torch*) Those rats! There must be dozens of them floating in the water.

Baxter Yeah! And have you noticed the colour of the water now? Real dirty green. If you ask me, the best thing we can do is to get the... (*stops, shouts out*) Professor! Quick! The torch!

Lippert Where?

Baxter Dead ahead of you – there! Someone – crouching on the ground.

Lippert (*staggered*) Oh my – ! It's a woman.

Baxter (*calls out*) You there! Hey you!

The sound of the woman shying away, frightened

Who are you? What are you doing down here? (*as though addressing a child*) Don't be scared. I'm not going to hurt you... (*The woman suddenly runs off*) Hey! Come back! (*He starts to follow her*)

Lippert (*calls*) Inspector! Don't go any further. There are more of them... look – on the other side. They're all huddled together – around the bottom of the steps. A whole lot of them – crouching on the floor. Look at their faces. They're watching us... d'you see their eyes? They're watching us...

Baxter (*shouts*) What are you doing? Get out of there – all of you! Did you hear me...?

A man tries to speak. He mumbles, as though deaf and dumb

(*gently*) What is it? What are you trying to say? (*pause*) Who are you? What are you doing down here?

Suddenly the sound of the small crowd shying back into their corner, and then this is broken by the even greater sound of the mud squeaking and bubbling

Lippert (*panic-stricken, shouts out*) Inspector! Inspector! The mud... look at the mud! It's all over the walls... Come on! For God's sake let's get out of here!

Fade out with the sound of the mud which also contains, very faintly in the background, its own heartbeat

Pause

Fade in: the laboratory

Landers Hypnotism? That's quite a hypothesis Doctor. I hope you know what you're saying?

Ken Do you believe the existence of this form of science, Professor?

Landers Science? So that's what you call it, is it?

Ken There are many people who believe that hypnotism can be a great aid to medical treatment.

Landers And do you?

Ken (*smiling*) I prefer to keep an open mind.

Gomez So what you're suggesting Doctor is that, by means of hypnotism, the mud is exercising some kind of mental pressure on the human mind.

Ken I think it's a possibility.

Landers Then why only certain types of people? Couldn't it do the same to all of us?

Ken Hypnotism is only accepted by the mind which is susceptible to it. It could not penetrate a human mind whose willpower is against it.

Landers That's true. I remember seeing a hypnotist at our local Music Hall once. He got very embarrassed when, out of six volunteers from the audience, he was only able to put one dear old lady to sleep. Even then I think it was just an excuse for her to have a nap.

Gomez Then this would also account for the death of wild and plant life. The mental pressure would be too great for them?

Ken Exactly. Hypnotism is usually administered during a state of deep sleep. The subject only acts on external suggestion.

Landers But these people haven't been put in a deep sleep have they?

Ken How can we possibly know? They shut themselves away in the darkness, and to them the world outside doesn't exist. Believe me gentlemen, I've watched the glazed expression in their eyes – so vacant, so unreal.

Landers This is all beyond me. If all this is true, what's the mud's objective? Is it purely to destroy?

Gomez Ultimately – yes. But if it is to destroy the surface of the Earth, first of all it must eliminate human habitation.

Ken And the only way to do this is by mental domination.

Gomez Precisely! It must prove to its subjects that *it* is the new Creator of Life – and that the only way to that new life is through death.

Landers Good Lord! That's almost exactly what Deverill said.

Ken (*shocked*) Deverill?

Gomez And the only effective way to destroy human life, is to persuade it to destroy itself.

Landers Suicide!

Ken That seems feasible. It's an almost obvious conclusion to all these depressions.

Landers Then how?

Gomez When it is ready, draw everything towards it.

Ken Like a magnet.

Gomez In the first case it would be easy to gain control of the mind that is either senile or infirm. Hence your great number of patients Doctor – and especially those missing from the hospital wards.

Ken (*sadly*) And Janet. In her condition, her mind could never take the strain.

Landers So you think Josef, when the time comes, these people are just going to throw themselves into the mud – like human sacrifices? God. What a terrifying thought!

Ken (*desperately concerned*) We've got to stop them. Whatever we do – we've got to stop them.

The door bursts open. Lippert is excitable and breathless through running

Lippert Josef!

Gomez (*looks up sharply*) John… what's happened?

Lippert They're all down there. The whole lot of them. We've got to get them out!

Landers What're you talking about old boy? Who's down where?

Lippert Those people – from the hospital…

Ken What!

Lippert And a good few more. We were down in the sewers. The whole place is crawling alive with them.

Landers Have some brandy old boy. You look like death.

Pours brandy

Lippert It was terrible. I've never been so shocked in all my life. It was so unexpected. A whole sea of faces just – staring at you.

Ken You mean these people are hiding down there – in the sewers?

Lippert They're like frightened mice, all bunched together in the darkness – crouching on the floor. (*swallows brandy*) I tell you – it's terrifying! Those faces – yellow and half-dead.

Gomez We must get them out immediately.

Lippert It's impossible. They're trapped.

Ken Trapped?

Lippert There's mud streaming down the walls – I don't know where it's coming from. They're completely cut off. The Inspector and I had to run for our lives.

Gomez (*puzzled*) But the mud – it's solid. Surely it's no danger?

Lippert Go and look for yourself how safe it is. I tell you that stuff down there's alive. We dare not go near the stuff.

Ken (*desperately, to himself*) Janet! Oh – Janet…

Landers (*tensely*) Josef. Do you realise what this means? They're being – collected together down there. The whole lot of them.

Gomez (*grimly*) Yes Robert. They're being collected. Now all they have to do is to wait…

Fade out

Pause

At the Deverill home, Anna pushes open the door of the lounge. She calls out gently but firmly to her husband, who is still sitting in the dark

Anna Hugh. Hugh, can you hear me? (*no reply*) I'm going now. (*pause*) The men will be here in a few minutes – I've collected together as many things as I can. (*no reply*) Hugh. Did you hear? I said I'm going.

Deverill (*quietly smouldering*) Yes. I heard you.

Anna (*trying not to show her nervousness*) I – I sent Maggie away. I told her that whatever happened I wouldn't go without you. That was the – the right thing to do, wasn't it darling?

Deverill Why are you standing in the doorway? Are you scared of me?

Anna (*proudly*) Of course not. Why should I be scared of you? You're my own husband.

Deverill Close it then. Go on. Close the door.

Pause. She closes the door. Pause

Come over here, my dear.

Anna (*anxiously*) Hugh… darling… we haven't the time. I've told you, the men will be here at any moment. Why don't you put on a coat and – and let's go.

Deverill Over here.

Pause. She moves towards him

Anna It's getting dark outside darling. We shan't be able to see anything. There's no electricity…

Deverill What's wrong with the dark? Don't you find it so much more relaxing?

Anna Please darling…

Deverill Sit here – at the side of me. (*She crouches beside him*) There! That's better. (*pause*) Your hands – they're so warm…

Anna Yours are freezing.

Deverill …but so beautifully smooth. But then – you're a very beautiful woman Anna. You always were.

Anna I'm sorry about Maggie, darling. I didn't know she was going to do that. I didn't know she was going to open those curtains, really I didn't. I know you prefer the dark.

Deverill Do you know what my father used to do when I was a child? If ever I displeased him – just once – he'd lock me in the cellar. In the darkness. A small child all alone – the master of his own little world. It was a very strange feeling. (*pause*) Sometimes I could sense the spiders crawling down the walls. I couldn't see them, but I knew they were there all right.

Anna (*squirming*) Please darling!

Deverill I remember once sitting on my usual stool in the darkness, when suddenly I could feel this wretched thing crawling slowly up my bare leg. But I didn't move – not an inch. I sat there for as long as I could without taking any notice of it. Eventually it would stop still on my leg, and you could almost hear the two of us in the darkness, trying to decide what to do next. But he always went, and I was the winner. (*pause*) I suppose it was a sort of game? Maybe that's why I'm not scared of the dark.

Pause

Anna Hugh. Let's go. (*She starts to get up*)

Deverill Stay with me.

Anna No! I've told you… Hugh! Please let me go… you're hurting me… (*She is struggling*)

Deverill I can't see you any more – but at least like this we're equal. (*pause*) Don't struggle, my dear. You and I went meant to stay together. We should never be apart.

Anna (*finding it difficult to breathe*) Hugh! You're hurting me!

Deverill This is your chance to prove to me that these years haven't all been wasted. Our chance, Anna, to go hand in hand into a new Creation. You and me Anna… you and me…!

Fade out with Anna struggling to release herself from Deverill's grasp

Pause

Fade in: A billet hut at RAF Redlow. The general flurry of people moving in. Mrs Luke is sobbing gently to herself in a corner

Corporal There, there Mrs Luke. Don't you go upsetting yourself. I know it's been a terrible shock for you – losin' your house like that.

Mrs Luke (*sobbing*) Nobody knows. Nobody knows – until it hits them. One's own home. One's whole life – gone in five minutes. (*angry more than upset*) We might have been killed.

Corporal (*comforting*) Yes, but we weren't killed were we Mrs Luke? Now dry up those tears, and I'll see about getting' everybody a nice cup of tea. Would you like that?

Mrs Luke (*regaining her attack*) I would've thought the first thing to do is to see about getting all those poor people a decent place to sleep in – instead of *this* filthy barn!

Corporal (*resentful*) This filthy barn, as you call it madam, happens to be the blokes' own sleepin' quarters. We've all given up our billets to house you people. If *we* get any kip tonight, it'll have to be in the hangars.

Mrs Luke I have not slept in one of those dreadful iron bed things since my days with the ENSA during the war. (*She bounces on the bed. The spring twangs unmelodiously*) There! D'you see what I mean? (*She jumps with a start at the sound of a distant explosion, off*) Oh! Good gracious – what was that?

Everyone is very frightened. The Corporal goes to the window

Corporal (*looking out*) Somethin's gone up in town. The whole sky's lit up. Phew! I reckon that's quite a blaze…

Fade up the sound of flames coming from a building on fire. Hold, and keep in background during the following scene

Fire engines, crowd running etc

Baxter (*shouting amidst the chaos*) Get those people behind the barrier! Oy! You blokes! Clear that road will yer! They'll have the whole lot down on them in a minute. (*shouts louder*) Sergeant! (*dashes off*)

Pause. The blaze continues

Gomez What is it Robert?

Landers The main Post Office I think. Somebody said it was a gas main explosion down below.

Gomez I'm not surprised. All those pipes must be absolutely jammed.

Landers I don't think my nerves can stand much more of this. You know, we'll have to clear that laboratory if this goes on much longer. It's getting too close for comfort. When the devil is all this going to stop!

Maggie That's what a lot of people would like to know.

Landers (*taken by surprise*) I beg your –

Maggie It's Professor Landers isn't it?

Landers Yes?

Maggie I'm Margaret Griffiths, from the Home Office.

Landers Miss Griffiths! I had no idea you were down from London. Nobody told me. This is my colleague, Professor Gomez.

Maggie (*coldly*) Professor.

Gomez How do you do.

Maggie (*looking at the blaze*) It's a pretty sight, isn't it? (*pause*) Did you know this was to have been some sort of show-place for Redlow? Huh! Our Postmaster-General ought to see it now. (*pause*) So gentlemen. What do you intend to do?

Landers Do?

Maggie Do you want us to sit tight and see the town crumble all around us? Is that the idea?

Landers (*angry*) Miss Griffiths. Both me and my colleagues have been working night and day to try and find the cause of this outbreak.

Maggie It's not the cause we're interested in Professor. It's a remedy we want. A way to save this town. A town that was built *by* the people, and *for* the people. What started off as a freak of nature in a confined area has now been allowed to develop into a full-scale threat to us all. (*pause*) Professor Gomez. You were called in because of your superior knowledge of geological disturbance. Haven't you even the faintest idea how to get rid of this stuff?

Gomez No Miss Griffiths. I'm afraid I have not.

Maggie Then somebody must have. There are scientists down here from all parts. Some of them must know what...

Gomez Miss Griffiths. To our knowledge, what has happened here in Redlow is something that has never before been experienced throughout the history of mankind. (*intense*) Somewhere beneath the surface of this tired Earth there is a hard core. How far down we may never know. But it is our enemy. Its aim is to destroy us, to crush whatever human life is left after – (*looking around*) all this. (*pause*) This mud, Miss Griffiths, is the army of that core. Tentacles from the head of the octopus, the nerve-centre of the thousands of brain cells spreading themselves across the land. And make no mistake about it, if we allow it to, it will not stop here.

Maggie Then what you said at that press conference last night was –

Gomez We are no longer fighting a geological disruption Miss Griffiths. This is war. War between two human minds – a battle of the giants – one of them more powerful than we have ever dared imagine.

Pause

Maggie What do you need?

Gomez Something I am afraid that nobody can give us. (*sighs*) Time. We must have time to find out who or what is the real enemy of this monster. *Why* it is the sun is no longer the creator?

Landers Miss Griffiths. I think you will have to advise the Prime Minster that unless we can come up with something by tomorrow evening, our chances of saving Redlow are practically negligible.

Pause

Maggie (*sadly*) Isn't it strange how quickly a dream can become a nightmare. (*pause*) Gentlemen. I'm sorry I threw politics at you. I promise you, I won't do it again.

Baxter approaches

Baxter I'm sorry madam, I can't allow you to remain in this area any longer. In a few minutes the Civil Defence are using the air raid siren. That'll mean the mud's on the move again. You'll find most of the women and children over at RAF Redlow.

Maggie Thank you Inspector. I'm just going. (*pause*) I'll be praying for you gentlemen.

Gomez Pray for us all Miss Griffiths.

Maggie leaves

Fade out with fire engines, flames, shouts and general chaos

Pause

Lippert is leading Ken Richards through the sewer tunnels

Lippert (*whispering*) I'm sorry Doctor, but I think this is a pretty hare-brained idea of yours. These sewers are absolutely full of mud. You've only got to look at the rock salt on the walls. It must be omitting some sort of vapour. For Heaven's sake let's turn back. It's too dangerous.

Ken I can't. I've got to find Janet. What sort of a person do you think I'd be if I just went off and left her to die down here.

Lippert All right. But I'm going no further than the end of this block. The first alley where we saw them is just on the left. (*They begin to move*) Now keep your back to the wall, and whatever you do – don't move without me.

They continue to make their way along the tunnels for a moment or so

It's so blinding dark down here you can't see a… Stop!

They stop abruptly

Ken What is it?

Lippert There's someone there. I can hear the breathing.

We hear the breathing for a brief moment

Yes! Look there – right ahead!

Ken It's a girl! (*calls*) Janet!

Lippert Come back you fool! D'you want to get yourself killed!

Ken Give me the torch. I tell you it *is* her! (*calls*) Janet!

He runs off down the tunnel

Lippert Doctor! Come back! (*shouts*) There's a mud bank just in front of her! (*shouts louder*) Doctor!

Fade out

Pause

The Deverill home. Gomez rushes into the front hall to find Anna alone and very distracted

Gomez Mrs Deverill! I came as soon as I got your message. What is it?

Anna (*restrained*) Hugh tried to kill me.

Gomez What!

Anna He made me go in and sit beside him in the dark. It was terrible. I think his mind's now gone completely. He was like a maniac.

Gomez (*looking around*) Where is he now?

Anna I don't know. Still in the lounge I think. (*shaking*) It was a miracle how I managed to get away from him. All I could do was to run out of the house as fast as I could. There was a soldier on duty at the end of the road. I told him to find you. (*pause*) The terrible noise coming from that room – as though the whole place was being torn apart. And the groans.

Gomez Wait here.

Anna No Josef! You mustn't... he'll kill you!

Gomez Give me the oil-lamp. (*He takes it*) Right. Now keep back.

Gomez slowly opens the door and enters

> (*calls firmly*) Mr Deverill. (*no reply*) Mr Deverill. Are you in there? (*a shocked sigh at what he sees*) All right Mrs Deverill. You can come in. He's not here.

Anna enters the room

Anna That's strange. I didn't hear him go... (*shocked*) Josef! Look at the room! What's he done?

Gomez (*walking around*) Is there another way out?

Anna The door in the corner. It leads straight out into the garden. (*looking around her*) The curtains – they're torn to pieces. And the furniture...

Gomez (*closing the corner door*) I can't see anything. He must have gone. (*He joins her*) You must leave here immediately.

Anna (*half-dazed*) He just sat here in the darkness. I couldn't see him but I knew his eyes were watching me – all the time. When his hand touched me it was cold – like ice. He knew I was scared of him... he could feel my heart racing.

Gomez What made him try to kill you?

Anna I don't know. It all happened so quickly. He grabbed hold of my throat and started to squeeze... I felt the life draining out of my body. (*pause*) But it was his strength... I've never known Hugh to be like that before, especially for a man of his age. It was so unnatural. (*pause*) He must hate me very much.

Gomez (*sympathetically*) No. What you see in your husband now is a puppet. He's no longer able to think for himself.

Anna He's so alone. I think, most of all – that's the thing I can't bear.

Gomez We shall get him back, Mrs Deverill. He and all those other people. (*almost threateningly to himself*) We must!

A sharp cut

Pause

In the sewers, Ken and Lippert are facing Janet Marshall who is separated from them by a ridge of mud which can only just be heard at their feet

Ken (*gently, to Janet*) Janet. Look at me darling. Don't you know me?

Lippert (*holding him back*) For God's sake man – don't take another step. The mud's active. It's waiting for you to move in.

Ken Janet – please!

Lippert Can't you see? She's a prisoner!

Ken Look at her face – her eyes. She doesn't even know me. Oh God. What's happened to her?

Lippert She can't hear you man. You can see she's only allowed to obey one voice. It's a trick to get you over there. Whatever you do, don't move!

Ken She looks so sad, so tired… (*pause*) I've got to get her back. I just can't leave her down here like this.

Lippert She's under command. She doesn't know you, doesn't want to. Once you try to make contact that stuff is going to go for both her and us.

Ken (*hand outstretched*) Janet. Listen to me darling. I'm going to take you away from here – out of this place. Now. If you keep perfectly still – I can just lift you across.

Lippert No Doctor, no!

Ken Janet. Listen to me… (*firmly*) *to me!* (*pause*) Now. Give me your hand…

Lippert Don't be a fool man!

Ken (*pleading*) Please Janet, please!

Pause. Janet slowly raises her hand to meet Ken's

That's it darling, that's it! Now – just a little bit further… go on – you can do it!

Lippert Don't do it Doctor! There's a pressure. Can't you feel it in your head. There's a pressure.

Ken (*an almost strangled whisper*) Our… fingertips are…almost touching… (*reaching out as far as he can*) I've got you darling… I've… almost got you…

At this precise moment the mud immediately swells up, and its squeaking, bubbling sound echoes out its rage. Almost simultaneously, Janet lets out a penetrating scream

Lippert It's moving! Doctor – don't touch her! The mud's moving towards us… hurry! (*rushes off*)

Ken is still standing and staring

Ken Janet! (*calls*) No Janet… don't leave me… (*shouts*) Janet! *Please!*

As he shouts after Janet, who is scuttling away from him, we hear the screech of the air raid siren from the street above. We fade out with this, together with the sound of the mud containing the background heartbeat

END OF EPISODE SIX

The Slide
by Victor Pemberton

Episode 7: Out of the Darkness

Produced by John Tydeman

TRANSMISSION:	Sunday 27 March 1966	1900–1930 LIGHT
REHEARSALS:	Thursday 10 February	1030–1830
RECORD:	Thursday 10 February	1830–1930 (to H.11)
STUDIO:	B.11	
R.P. No.	TLO 605/553	
EDIT:	Wednesday 16 February	1015–1245 (H.54)
PLAYBACK:	Wednesday 16 February	1530–1600 (5108)

CAST:	Gomez......................................	Roger Delgado
	Deverill	Maurice Denham
	Landers.....................................	Rolf Lefebvre
	Lippert......................................	Allan McClelland
	Richards	David Spenser
	Anna...	Marion Mathie
	Baxter.......................................	Geoffrey Matthews
	RAF Corporal	Anthony Hall
	Sergeant Johnson	Wilfred Babbage
	Margaret Griffith.......................	Joan Matheson
	TV Interviewer..........................	Henry Stamper
	Man in Crowd	Nigel Graham
	Soldier......................................	Henry Stamper

S.M.s:	Panel: Amna Smith; Grams: David Cain; Spot: Margaret Rushton
SECRETARY:	Helene Grygar, PABX 2168

Announcer The lost people of Redlow New Town have been found hiding in the sewer tunnels beneath the deserted streets. In the main square above, Inspector Baxter waits anxiously for Doctor Richards and Professor Lippert...

It is just before sunrise. The streets of Redlow New Town are completely deserted. The mud is once again lifeless

As we fade in, the marked stillness is only relieved by the almost surreal peal of a solitary church bell in the far distance. After a moment, footsteps echo as they approach across the cobbled stones of the main square and come to an abrupt halt

Baxter Any signs?

Johnson No sir. Not yet.

Baxter Just the two of them you said? Lippert and the doctor – is that right?

Johnson Yes, sir. I've been listening for the last two hours, but I can't hear a thing. Sounds dead. Trouble is, these sewers stretch for miles.

Baxter (*sighs*) Okay Sarge. We'll give 'em another ten minutes or so, then we'd better go and get some kip. If they wanna risk their own necks – let 'em. I've had enough wanderin' about those tunnels down there. (*stretches*) Anyway, it'll be sun-up in a few minutes.

Johnson (*listening to the bell*) I wish he'd pack that up. Sounds like a funeral dirge.

Baxter We all have our own way of showing feeling Sarge. Vicar's been in that church for fifteen years. I reckon he's got the right to ring that bell if he wants.

Johnson It's not feeling that's gonna save this town. Not now. Look at the place. You'd never think it was a Tuesday morning would you? (*a meaningless laugh*) Market day! More like a battlefield.

Baxter They'll build again.

Johnson If they get the chance.

Baxter They've got to. They just have. (*pause*) Anyway, I'd sooner listen to his bell than hang here in silence. (*pause*) I think it's that that scares me more than anythin' else. The silence. Not bein' able to hear a thing – not a damned thing! Knowin' that mud's all around, watchin' us – like a lot of eyes… waitin'… (*pause*) Oh God – I'd give anythin' to hear the birds singin' away in those trees again.

The lid of the sewer shaft begins to move

Johnson (*excitedly*) Inspector! They're here!

Baxter Quick! Give 'em a hand!

They assist Lippert and Ken Richards out of the sewer exit

Baxter Okay Professor! I've got you… hold on now! All right Doctor?

Ken Yes, thank you.

They are now both straightening up

Lippert (*breathes deeply*) Fresh air! Thank the Lord!

Baxter You've been down there for hours. We were just about to give you up.

Lippert It's taken us all our time to find a way out. By tonight those tunnels are going to be choked with mud.

Baxter What about Miss Marshall, Doc? Any signs?

Ken (*unresponsive*) Yes. She's down there.

Baxter Was there no way to – ?

Lippert She was cut off from us… we couldn't take the risk…

Ken (*steps back bitterly*) I could have reached her! I was almost touching her hand.

Lippert You try to reach any of those poor devils down there, and the mud'll get you just like them!

Ken So we just leave them all down there – old and young alike – to rot away when that damned stuff's good and ready. Is your conscience big enough to take the responsibility Professor? Because mine isn't.

Lippert We have no alternative. The only way we can help them now is to find some way to break this 'influence', or whatever it is the mud has over them.

Baxter You say 'them'. Have you any idea how many?

Lippert It's impossible to tell. Thirty, forty, maybe even more. The sewers are absolutely crawling with them. They crouch in corners hiding from us, guarded by their jailer, their poor tired eyes peering out of the darkness. Lost, dazed, tormented souls. (*pause. Grimly*) I felt so hopeless. Knowing they were there, and not being able to do a thing for them.

Baxter Well I tell you this much Professor – somebody's got to, that's for sure. We've done all *we* can. From now on, it's up to you blokes. It's up to you…

Fade out

Pause

Fade in: The sound of a small sample of mud bubbling at the bottom of a glass tank. After a moment the lid is slammed firmly on top, and the mud sound is cut out immediately

Gomez (*shaking Landers*) Robert. Robert, wake up please.

Landers begins to stir

Landers (*yawning, stretching*) Oh… sorry old boy. Must have dropped off for a few minutes.

Gomez An hour and a half to be exact. It's seven-thirty.

Landers Is it really? (*stretching*) Oh well, when you get to my age you need your rest. Any luck yet?

Gets up, joins Gomez at tank

Gomez No. The mud sample's been on the move most of the night. The only interesting thing that seems to have happened is the rock particles have disappeared from the side of the tank. D'you see?

Landers (*looking*) Yes… Good Lord! Look at the wretched stuff. It's swelled much more than it was last night.

Gomez At least three or four times I would say. We'll have to get rid of it soon. It's too dangerous to keep in here for much longer.

Landers You know, that bubbling really is like volcanic lava, isn't it? Reminds me of some of those eruptions I saw in New Zealand.

Gomez Would you like to blow out the lamp.

Moves to window

Gomez I'll raise the blinds. We could do with some fresh air in here.

Landers I know. This light's a strain on the eyes – especially on my poor old worn-out things.

Gomez raises the blinds

Gomez It's beautiful! Hardly a cloud in the sky.

He opens the windows and we immediately hear the sound of the solitary church bell in the distance

Gomez If somebody had told me they had such sunlit days in England, I would never have believed them. (*breathes deeply*) Better?

Landers Much better.

Gomez (*looking upwards*) Let's hope the heavens are with us today. (*pause*) If they could just send us some wind... a little breeze. Everything is so still, so lifeless and unreal. In fact it is difficult to believe there is any life left out there at all. We could be a boat in the middle of an ocean...

Landers (*shouts out excitedly*) Josef! Quick!

Gomez (*rushing to him*) What is it?

Landers Look at the mud sample... look!

Gomez Let me s... (*stunned*) Robert!

Landers It's absolutely incredible! I was watching it... I was watching it I tell you!

Gomez It's solid again. Completely solid. (*a gradual understanding*) Of course! (*raises voice triumphantly*) Of course!

Landers (*stunned with disbelief*) I watched it transform. Josef... I watched it transform. Right in front of my very eyes!

Fade up and out church bell

Pause

Fade in: A street in Redlow. A team of workers resume drilling and digging. Anna Deverill approaches

Anna (*calls*) Inspector! Inspector Baxter.

Baxter Mrs Deverill? What are you doing here? The town's out of bounds to all civilian personnel.

Anna Inspector. You've got to find my husband.

Baxter (*irritated*) Mrs Deverill. Take a look around you will you please. I've got fifteen hundred blokes tryin' to clear this stuff from the streets.

Anna (*urgent*) I'm warning you – he may be dangerous.

Baxter Dangerous?

Anna In his present condition he's capable of doing anything.

Baxter (*dismissingly*) Who isn't?

Anna Inspector! He tried to kill me.

Baxter He what!

Anna But he doesn't know what he's doing. He's confused and tired. Don't you see, we can't hold him responsible for anything he might do. But we've got to try and reach him before he does anything dangerous.

Baxter When did this happen please?

Anna Last night. Just before eleven. He ran out of the house.

Baxter You have no idea where he was heading?

Anna None at all. But he did take the car. (*pause*) Hugh has never done anything like this before. He's no killer. He'd never want to harm me. There's something inside him that's pushing him to the borders of insanity. Some evil force that's taken over his complete soul. (*distressed*) Inspector. I beg you to get him back before it's too late.

Pause

Baxter (*calls out*) Sergeant Johnson!

Johnson (*calls, off*) Sir!

Baxter Take a party of men. Put someone on patrol at every one of the sewer entrances.

Anna (*horrified*) Sewers?

Baxter If anyone tries to get past, fire a warning shot over their heads. Okay?

Johnson Right sir! (*dashes off*)

Anna The sewers. He couldn't go down those... he couldn't...

Baxter I don't know what he'd do, Mrs Deverill. I don't know what anyone would do. But after what's been happenin' to people round here in the last few days, I don't take any more chances...

Fade out on drilling, digging etc.

Pause

Fade in: A car approaches at breakneck speed, and suddenly skids to a sharp halt. Footsteps are heard running towards it

Corporal (*out of breath*) I'm sorry sir! You'll have to turn around. The road's blocked from now on.

Deverill (*leaning out of the window, angry*) Get that thing out of my way. I'm going into Redlow.

Corporal I'm very sorry sir. The town's out of bounds to all civilian personnel until further notice. If you want permission to... (*stops, horrified to see Deverill's face*)

Deverill What's the matter with you? What are you looking at?

Corporal Your – your face sir. Are you all right?

Deverill (*immediately withdrawn*) I *am* perfectly all right! Now will you get out of my way!

Corporal But it's scratched sir... you're bleeding. Let me get you a doctor.

Deverill (*speaks neurotically fast*) I do not need a doctor. I do not need anyone. I've got to get into that town, and I've got to get in quickly. (*a near hysterical whisper*) They *need* me! Don't you understand that! They *need* me!

Corporal (*calmly defiant*) Turn your car around please, sir.

Deverill (*shouts back*) Damn it man! Do you know who I am?

Corporal No sir, I do not. My orders are that no one passes this barrier without permission from my Commanding Officer. It's not my business to know *who* you are sir, so you'll be saving yourself a lot of time and trouble if you just turn right around and go back where you came from. And if you'll take my tip sir, you'll see a doctor as soon as you can. Those scratches look as though they need to... (*stops abruptly*) Hey! What the heck are you doing?

Deverill Now! Are you going to get out of my way?

Corporal Put that gun away! Are you mad or somethi...

Deverill fires a shot. The Corporal lets out a cry as he slumps to the ground. Deverill immediately starts up the engine again and races off, breaking down the barrier as he goes. We fade out with the sound of the Corporal groaning

Pause

Fade in: A small group of people are gathered together in the laboratory

Gomez (*joyful, enthusiastic*) The sun! Don't you see my friends? The answer has been up there in the sky all the time. At last we know who is the real enemy of the mud.

Maggie Fascinating. But what does it mean?

Lippert It means that somewhere in the solar system there's a filament of light capable of penetrating the mud's pores.

Gomez But only when those pores are open – when they are breathing.

Maggie And that's during the night?

Gomez Precisely! The only time when it is safe to shed its protective crust. All through the night this laboratory has been in darkness except for one small oil lamp. We have watched the organic movement in this small mud sample multiply beyond recognition. (*He walks over to the window*) But – immediately I came over to this window and raised the blinds, that organic life came to a complete halt! Right in front of my very eyes! (*comes back again*) The sun! We should have realised before.

Landers So what you're suggesting Josef is that this is some kind of battle between the mud and the sun?

Gomez (*emphatically*) Yes!

Landers But why?

Gomez Throughout the history of mankind there have always been those who have prayed to the sun as a kind of God – the creator of heaven and earth. You only have to look at something like the Inca civilisation, the worship of the Sun God. The sun as the Creator.

Maggie But I don't see what this has got to do with the mud?

Gomez Don't you see? If we are to believe that the mud is a living thing, capable of generating its own influence on human life as we know it, then we must also believe that if the mud is to claim the earth for itself, it must first destroy everything on the surface created *by* the sun.

Maggie Fantastic!

Lippert It's the only logical explanation. For all we know the mud may have been lying in the bowels of the earth since the beginning of time itself – just straining to get out. This is why we've had these freak earth tremors.

Gomez But that is not all, I can assure you. Before the mud can start any form of life for itself, it must first of all rid itself of the human and natural environment. Nature, my friends, has turned this into a psychological warfare.

Landers Dr Richards. You've had a chance to see these people hiding down in the sewers. What d'you think the effects are likely to be?

Pause

Ken (*sadly expresses his fears*) I don't think there's any doubt. The mud intends to absorb the human mind, take it into its confidence by means of hypnotic transference – and then (*sighs*) eliminate it, I suppose.

Maggie In what way Doctor?

Ken How can one possibly foretell! (*angered with worry*) I'm not a hypnotist – I'm no magician! (*pause*) One can only presume the mud intends to hold on to those people down there until it's ready to do… (*distressed*) …well, whatever it intends to do.

Lippert The mud has the power to draw these people towards it – like a magnet.

Landers Mass suicide…

Ken Or murder.

Maggie How horrible! When do you think this is going to happen?

Gomez At the present moment, the mud has been sliding in from four or five distinct corners of the town. By tonight they can't fail to meet up –

Lippert Right in the centre of the town.

Gomez It is then we shall reach the danger point for these people. If we are going to prevent this, we have to do something by nightfall.

Landers What for Heaven's sake?

Maggie Do you mean to tell me that out of all the scientific knowledge Man has acquired, he can't come up with anything to prevent this extermination?

Pause

Gomez There *is* something.

A general sharpness of interest

Gomez But it may not work.

Landers For Heaven's sake man, we've got to try. What is it?

Gomez The mud is like a giant octopus. Its head – the nerve centre – is somewhere beneath the surface of the earth's crust. If we can find a way to burn through the tentacles, the thousands of little brain-cells that are causing this multiplication…

Landers How the heck do we do that?

Gomez Strike at a time when it is unable to protect itself, when its pores are wide open…

Maggie During the night.

Gomez As soon as the sun sets…

Landers Yes. But what do we strike with? We can't build a sun in the middle of the night.

Gomez We don't have to build a sun, Robert. (*pause*) Look at the diagram on the board again. Tell me. Which of the spectrums in the solar system would you say is the most likely to penetrate into the mud's pores?

Lippert It couldn't be ultra-violet – especially if there was any cloud around. Anyway, it's not nearly deep enough.

Ken What about infra-red?

Gomez Yes Doctor? What about it?

Ken Well, I would have thought infra-red is about the deepest heat you could get. It's used quite consistently in the hospitals – especially for rheumatic conditions. If you could harness enough…

Gomez (*urgently*) How?

Ken Well, as far as I know there's a pretty strong infra-red filament in xenon discharge lamps. They use them in most photographic or film studios. If you could get your hands on some of those…

Landers You'd need hundreds of the things to cover the entire town!

Gomez No! We could take it section by section. If the first experiment works – we can repeat it.

A sudden, quick urgency now prevails

Miss Griffiths. What can you do for us?

Maggie How many would you need – these lamps?

Gomez To start with – I should say twenty. We could line the edge of Holly Mill Lane. But they *must* be installed by sunset this evening.

Maggie Don't worry – you'll have them!

Ken I warn you they're pretty powerful these lamps. I should think they'll light up the whole sky.

Gomez As long as that is all they do Doctor, I shan't worry.

Ken What d'you mean?

Gomez I don't think I have to remind you what happened the last time we used generated heat. Even the most minute particle of mud expanded beyond all proportions. If this should happen again, the dangers will be greater than we ever dare imagine.

Ken You mean, the whole thing may – may multiply…?

Gomez Quicker than ever before. There is not just one but maybe thousands of living organisms lying in that mud out there. For all we know this experiment may only succeed in increasing them. If that should happen my friends, I don't have to remind you of the consequences.

Maggie Increasing them? But – you're a scientist. Don't you know?

Gomez No, Miss Griffiths, I'm afraid I do not. You see, unfortunately there are times when even a scientist – just does not know…

Fade out

Pause

Fade in: A police car approaches the spot where the injured RAF Corporal is fighting for breath. The car door slams and Baxter hurries to the scene

Baxter How is he?

Johnson Not so good. The bullet grazed his spinal cord. He's lost a lot of blood. Anyway, we've got a description.

Baxter Deverill?

Johnson Yes. It's him all right. His car smashed through that barrier like a bulldozer. I reckon you were right after all. He's tryin' to make it to those sewers.

Baxter bends down to talk gently to the Corporal

Baxter It's all right now old son. You just lie still… you're gonna be all right.

Corporal (*struggles to speak*) You… have to get him… before he gets there… he's going to them…

Baxter Who's he going to son? Who?

Corporal They… need him… he told me… he's going to them…

Baxter (*slowly*) Try and remember who it was…

Corporal His face… (*a last effort*) his… face…

Pause

Johnson We'd better get him to hospital. He's lost quite a lot of blood.

Baxter (*pause, he stands up*) What was this he said about Deverill's face?

Johnson Scratch marks all over – as though he'd been clawed. Sounds as though he's in a pretty bad way himself. Apparently there were some dead birds and things on the back seat of his car.

Baxter Put out a general alarm to pick up Deverill – dead or alive.

Johnson (*shocked*) Dead or – ? Inspector, we can't do that. We don't have the authority to shoot to kill, you know that.

Baxter (*snaps back*) Dead or alive Sergeant – and that's an order!

A loud ricochet as a shot is fired from a .303 rifle. We are now in the main market square

Anna Murder! It's cold blooded murder to fire at innocent people like that.

Gomez They are not firing *at* them. They're shooting above their heads to keep them away from those sewers. Once they get down there we shan't see them again.

Anna But the poor devils are wandering around like lost souls. Can't somebody do something... get hold of them?

Gomez The only thing we can do is to keep them away from the mud. In their present state of hypnotic influence, if we tried to touch any one of them, there is no knowing what the shock might do. We dare not take the risk.

Anna It's like coming out of a bad dream.

Gomez You know, you're not helping yourself or anyone else by staying here.

Another rifle shot is heard in the background

Anna They'll do that to him won't they? Shoot him down like a rat in a sewer.

Gomez That's nonsense and you know it. Nobody is going to shoot your husband. It's our help he needs.

Anna It's all right. It wouldn't make any difference to me. In fact, after seeing him the way he was last night – maybe it'll be a good thing.

Gomez I don't believe you.

Anna Don't you?

Gomez I don't believe you really hate him as much as you try to pretend. You can't shut him out of your life as easily as that. You can't shut out the world.

Anna (*voice hardening*) I don't need you to tell me that Professor. (*pause*) But for one moment early this morning, I thought I had. (*looking upwards*) Up there – on that hill overlooking the town. (*pause*) Oh I know everything seemed to look exactly the same – even though I knew it wasn't. But there was a moment – one brief moment – when the world became a blur. It didn't exist any more... people, places, things. (*bitterly*) And I was happy – *very* happy. Alone in a vast wilderness. (*long pause*) But I soon focused again, found it quite a shock to see I wasn't alone after all. The world was still there. (*pause*) But I wish it wasn't. Oh God, I wish it wasn't.

Lippert and Landers, both very excited, run in

Lippert Josef! The RAF are sending in three lorries from Maidstone. They're coming through now.

Gomez With the equipment?

Landers Enough lamps to cover the whole of Holly Mill Lane.

The first sound of the lorries approaching

Lippert The electricians say they must have at least forty-five minutes to synchronise the entire circuit with Maidstone.

Gomez What time is it now?

Landers Exactly five-thirty. The sun goes down at six thirty-eight.

Gomez (*looking at his watch*) Sixty-eight minutes. (*tense and dramatic*) Gentlemen. Those lamps go on at sunset, or the battle is lost – for *all* of us!

A sharp cut

Pause

Footsteps echo in a deserted street. They approach and come to a halt, on mic

Landers Ladies and gentlemen. Ladies and gentlemen. May I have your attention please.

The crowd stop to listen

Countdown for this operation will begin in five minutes from now. May I remind you the lamps on either side of the Lane are of extreme high density. You should protect your eyes from the glare, and keep well back from the experimental area. We rely on your co-operation. Thank you.

Pause

Anna Doctor Richards! (*approaches*) Doctor Richards. Is it true what they're saying?

Ken (*looks back, surprised*) Mrs Deverill… what's the matter?

Anna Are those lights going to kill the people down in the sewers?

Ken Mrs…

Anna (*shouts*) Tell me! I want to know!

Ken (*snaps back angrily*) I don't know! I only wish I did.

Anna (*troubled and confused*) But how? In Heaven's name – how?

Ken Gomez seems to think that if the light does penetrate the mud's brain cells, it might do the same to… It's a chance we've got to take.

Anna And you mean to tell me you – a doctor – are going to let them do it? Let them kill off all those defenceless people?

Ken We have no alternative, Mrs Deverill! And anyway, we don't know this is going to happen – not until the actual moment the lamps are turned on. (*desperately*) Don't you think I'd put a stop to this if I thought… if anyone thought…

Anna (*almost dreamily*) They say his face was scratched from top to bottom. Why Doctor? Why?

Ken (*with effort*) What's happened to your husband Mrs Deverill, is a tragic breakdown of resistance. He's a strong-willed man, and that's why one side of his brain is in direct conflict with the other. Like the meeting of two parts of a schizophrenic. One hand refuses to do what the other wants it to. And unless we can stop it, the part of his mind controlled by the mud intends to destroy the other part.

Anna (*squirms*) How horrible!

Ken He's down there – somewhere, I know it. (*sighs*) *And* Janet – and all those other people who didn't ask for this. (*pause*) But if we want them back again Mrs Deverill, we have to kill that mud… you know that…

Landers (*over the tannoy system*) Three minutes to countdown. Stand well back please.

The crowd begin to flurry again as we fade out

Pause

Fade in: The echo of whispers continues in the sewer tunnels

Johnson What's happening sir?

Baxter (*looking down the shaft*) Can't see a thing. It's so dark down there.

Johnson I've got some matches.

Baxter No. (*stands up*) If they can see a light they'll probably scarper. We can't take any chances now. (*pause*) How long's this been going on?

Johnson (*turning round*) About half-an-hour you said didn't.... (*stops*) Hallo.

Baxter What?

Johnson He's gone.

Baxter Who's gone?

Johnson That young boy... he was here... on guard duty... (*pause*) Oh Gord! I hope he's not... now I come to think of it he was actin' a bit funny himself... somethin' about a headache.

Baxter Any minute now. That sky's gonna be lit up like a bomb. I hope the hell they know what they're doin'.

Johnson Reminds you of the Blitz don't it?

A movement is heard on the steps of the sewer shaft

Baxter Ssh!

Johnson (*voice hushed*) What is it?

Baxter (*voice hushed*) There's someone there. Quick! Lie on your stomach and don't say a word.

Gradually we hear the sound of the people coming up from the sewers. This time there is no whispering but a quiet shuffle as they climb out and move off

Johnson They're comin' out! Look at them. The whole lot of them Inspector! We've got to do something. We've got to get hold of them...!

Baxter Stay where you are! Once they're out – they're out for good. If they see us here it'll stop all the others. Somethin's makin' them move out of there. Keep your head down.

Johnson But their faces. Look at their faces... yellow... and their eyes... those old people! Where are they going? Inspector! Where are they going?

Fade up the sound of the people shuffling off, and mix into the sound of the crowd, now even more nervous, in Holly Mill Lane

Lippert (*approaching, breathless*) Josef! There are small cracks appearing in the surface of the road in the Main Square. The engineers have just told me.

Gomez The Main Square? That's in the centre of town.

Lippert I'm afraid so – yes.

Gomez (*pointedly*) So we were right! The middle of the circle. All four sides are going to meet.

Maggie But what does that mean?

Gomez It means, Miss Griffiths, that if we miss our chance tonight, all four banks of mud are going to become one.

Lippert By morning the whole town'll be swamped. It'll give way like matchsticks.

Maggie But will we have time to stop the other overflows?

Gomez Once we know the infra-red can reach the nerve-centre of the mud's brain cells, the growth will stop. It will not be able to expand any more.

Lippert But if it continues to move even with the flood of light on it – then look out for trouble.

Anna runs towards them, very upset

Anna Josef! Please – you've got to stop those lights! You've got to!

Maggie (*surprised*) Anna? What are you – ?

Anna If he turns them on, every one of those people down in the sewers is going to die.

Maggie What!

Anna It's inhuman!

Gomez (*calm and oblivious*) You're hysterical, Mrs Deverill. Please get out of the way.

Anna If you kill the mud, you kill all those poor devils with it.

Maggie Professor. Is this true?

Anna Of course it's true. (*shouts at him*) Tell them! Go on, tell them what a murderer you are!

Maggie Professor Gomez. I – I didn't know that this was… perhaps we'd better postpone the whole thing?

Lippert (*looking outwards*) You're too late. (*deadly serious*) Look. The sun's almost gone.

An anxious murmur throughout the crowd. A woman overcome by the tension stifles a cry of fear. And then, all is silent, but for the hushed tones of the TV interviewer describing the scene

Interviewer And now – all faces, all thoughts are one, as we turn our eyes towards that great ball of fire slipping majestically behind the hillside above us. The moment is near. Figures turn to silhouettes as the deep red glow becomes – twilight. (*pause*) The sun is gone. (*pause*) And now – the silence.

A sudden flutter of excitement from the crowd

Wait a minute! (*excitedly*) Something's happening out there! (*looking*) Yes! To the right of your picture ladies and gentlemen. Someone has run out… he's in the middle of the mud overflow.

Anna (*off, shouts*) Hugh!

Landers (*on the tannoy system*) Sixty seconds.

Lippert That damned fool! What's he doing out there!

Various people shout out Deverill's name

Gomez Deverill! The mud is going to change any moment. Get out of there!

Anna (*shouts hysterically*) Hugh… please!

Deverill, now half-crazed, stands alone in the middle of the mud overflow, defying the hysterical shouts from the crowd

Deverill (*shouting*) Don't come near! Don't touch me! You won't be able to hurt me any more – *none* of you!

Maggie (*completely shocked*) He's mad. The poor devil's gone completely mad. Just look at his face!

Lippert (*calls*) Somebody get him out of there!

Gomez Keep away from that mud! There's nothing we can do.

Landers (*through the tannoy*) Forty seconds.

Anna Don't let them turn on those lights... Josef!

Gomez (*shouting out desperately*) Deverill – listen to me! You're in great danger. The mud wants to kill you. It wants to keep you for itself – for all time.

Deverill (*completely oblivious*) No longer do we have to look to the sun. At last we are being given the chance to destroy the evil created by Man. A chance to destroy the evil that is in *us*... (*addressing the crowd*) ... in you, and me, and all of us who have allowed this corruption.

Gomez Deverill! You've got to believe me! The *mud* is evil. The only thing it wants of you is your destruction.

Maggie Somebody do something! We can't leave him out there to die.

Lippert We can't go out there – it's too dangerous.

Anna But the mud's not moving yet. (*hopefully*) Perhaps it's not going to?

Gomez We can't take the chance. If we don't get those lamps on the moment the mud's pores open, they'll close up immediately – like an oyster.

Landers (*through the tannoy*) Twenty seconds.

Anna (*pleading desperately*) Maggie! Don't let them do it! Please don't let them do it!

Lippert There's nothing we can do. The switch is under remote control from Maidstone.

Maggie (*looking out*) What's he doing now? He's turned to the crowd...

Deverill (*addressing the crowd*) Man was never give the Earth. He took it for himself. He used the sun to help him create his own lust for power, his greed, his evil. But now we are free to think for ourselves. We can destroy this evil (*shouting*) ... right here and now... you and me!

Gomez No Deverill – no!

Deverill Who of you – will follow me off this path of corruption.

Lippert (*shouts out suddenly*) Look at the crowd! The people from the sewers!

A great flurry of movement in the crowd

Keep them back! They're trying to reach him!

Shouts and screams from the crowd as they struggle with the people from the sewers who try desperately to reach Deverill

Gomez The mud! Keep those people away! (*staring*) It's beginning to move...

The slow, gradual bubbling of the mud. Landers begins the countdown

Landers (*through the tannoy*) Five, four, three, two, one...

A gasp from the crowd as the lamps are turned on. A woman screams out from the middle of the crowd. Deverill groans with pain as the light penetrates his eyes, and picks him out in the darkness

Deverill (*groaning*) My eyes! Take the light off my eyes! I can't see!

Anna (*shouts out*) Hugh!

Gomez (*struggling with Anna*) No, Mrs Deverill! There's nothing you can do...!

Anna Let me go...! (*sobs*) Please let me go...

Maggie (*squirms with horror*) The mud's giving way. He's going to be pulled under… please! Somebody do something. I can't bear much more of this…

The mud begins to bubble even louder. The crowd draw back horrified

Man in crowd (*shouts out, panic-stricken*) It's spreading!

Policeman Get back there will you!

Lippert (*close to Gomez*) Josef it's no good. Look – the lights are making no difference. The mud's swelling up more than ever.

Gomez (*sad and dejected*) Get them out of here.

Lippert Get them – ? What are you talking ab –

Gomez (*snaps back*) I said get them out – all of them! Do you want them to be killed. Can't you see the organisms are increasing!

Landers (*approaching, tense*) Josef. The mud's already over the marker line. Do we move back the lamps?

Gomez No.

Landers But they might explode.

Gomez Keep them where they are! We'll keep the power running as long as we can. Get a party of men down here. For the time being we can divert the flow.

Maggie It's happening isn't it? The light really *is* multiplying the mud's organisms?

Gomez Unless we can block the flow, I don't think there's any doubt that within two or three hours they are going to meet – right in the centre of the town.

Maggie Then for Heaven's sake – why doesn't somebody turn off those lamps…

Lippert (*shouts out suddenly*) No! Josef – Look! Something's happening…

We gradually become aware that the bubbling sound of the mud is changing to that of a squeaking, squealing

Landers (*looking out*) What's that red glow at the other end?

Lippert (*excitedly*) It's burning! The whole lot's catching fire – all the way along! Look at the marker line… the mud's shrivelling up…

The mud is emitting a terrifying squeaking sound

Maggie It's horrible! Horrible!

Lippert (*deliriously happy, shouting out*) It's not horrible, Miss Griffiths! It's wonderful! (*laughs*) The most wonderful thing I've ever seen…!

The overexcited crowd let out a loud cheer and we fade out on the sound of the flames crackling furiously

Pause

Fade in: Holly Mill Lane. The crowd have dispersed, but people are heard milling about busily. In the background an ambulance rushes by, and we can still hear the faint crackle of the mud. Flames in the distance

Lippert When I think of all those poor devils down in the sewers just waiting to be told when to come up and destroy themselves. It's terrifying.

Landers Well, thank God we got there in time. If those people in the crowd hadn't have stopped them… we were lucky, that's all.

Baxter D'you think so sir?

Landers What d'you mean Inspector?

Baxter I was just looking around, that's all. Somehow I don't feel very lucky. (*pause*) It's funny isn't it? When you think what difference a few days can make to your life. Oh I've no doubt, once they've got rid of the mud they'll soon put this town together again. But I'll never feel the same – when I walk through those streets again. (*pauses, brightly*) I must say, I'm lookin' forward to hearin' those birds sing again.

Lippert Yes, and I intend to be a sun-worshipper for the rest of my life.

They laugh. Ken Richards approaches

Landers Hallo Doctor. How's Miss Marshall?

Ken I've sent her back to hospital. If she stays there this time – I think she'll pull through.

Landers I was terrified when I saw her trying to reach the mud. She was fighting like a maniac to get there.

Ken Yes. You see, when the infra-red finally penetrated the mud's nerve-centre, this immediately snapped the hypnotic influence over the human brain. The sudden release of energy on these people must have been tremendous. It's a wonder it didn't cause a haemorrhage.

Landers And – Deverill?

Pause

Ken (*sadly*) I'm afraid not. We were too late. (*pause*) Is all this ever going to happen again Professor?

Landers (*smiles*) If you mean are we likely to have another earthquake, young man, I suggest you ask Mother Nature. She always seems to have a little something tucked up her sleeve. Oh, I've no doubt we shall go on dropping our bombs and fighting each other, but when Nature's tired of all this, I can assure you – she knows exactly when to show her disapproval...

Pause. Mix to another part of the lane

Gomez You are – going home?

Anna (*dazed*) Home? What home?

Gomez (*awkwardly*) I – I just hoped it would never be like this. I would have done anything to prevent...

Anna That last moment – when he stumbled and fell. He looked so lost... so old... unreal. There was a moment when I thought he recognised me... just a faint trace of his old smile. (*pause*) I remember Hugh when he had a warm sense of humour. He could laugh louder than anyone. (*pause*) I never wanted him to die.

Gomez There... was so much – I wanted to say...

Anna (*kindly*) We have nothing to say Josef. Not now. Not any more. (*pause*) Goodbye.

She leaves. Pause. Landers approaches

Landers Josef! They've moved the lamps over the other side of town. They'll have most of it clear by morning. (*pause*) Well – don't look so gloomy. We've won a battle you know.

Gomez Have we?

Landers Well? Haven't we?

Gomez I wonder? Maybe it's just the beginning.

Landers Come off it old boy! I've had quite enough for one week thanks all the same! (*thinks again*) But we have stopped the mud – haven't we?

Gomez The mud? Yes I think so.

Landers Well then?

Gomez Robert, my friend, yes. We have won a battle. We have managed this time to face something that Man has always feared. The unknown. (*pause*) But, for how long I wonder? (*pause*) Do you remember what Deverill said about Man's insatiable lust for domination? Well, maybe he was right. Maybe one day either we or Nature are going to unleash something that we know nothing about. Whether it is in the seas, the atmosphere…

The voice begins to echo as if in a cave

…or in the bowels of the Earth. (*pause*) And the next time? What will we do… the next time?

We hear the first sound of the mud bubbling, gradually building up to a crescendo. A deafening echo in a cave, and then – a gradual fade out

THE END

Kill the Pharaoh!

L ike so many other people, I hate war. Having lived and struggled through one myself, the thought of even one single person being sacrificed to the insanity of conflict seems to me to be utterly obscene. In 1967, war was once again dominating our lives: not in Britain, but on the other side of the world, in Vietnam and also in the Middle East.

6 June has always been an important date in the calendar of war, being the anniversary of the D-Day landings in Normandy – the subject not only of Steven Spielberg's *Saving Private Ryan*, but also of many British epic war films of that period. However, although 5 June 1967 was relatively calm and peaceful in Studio 6A on the sixth floor of BBC Broadcasting House, in the Middle East war broke out between Israel and the Arab states. Need I say that this was hardly the best moment to start writing an eight-part adventure serial set in modern Egypt!

Scheduled for broadcast in August of that year, the timing couldn't have been worse. With John Tydeman producing and a sturdy cast of BBC Drama Repertory Company stalwarts clutching their scripts, *Kill the Pharaoh!* needed rewrites from the first day of rehearsal, for despite the fact that the war itself only lasted for six days, the BBC were very sensitive about upsetting any of the countries who had been involved in the real conflict. I remember so well arriving at the studio to be told that certain passages in the script of Episode 1, which was called *Village of the White Scorpion*, would have to be replaced – no easy task, for when I first started writing the serial two months before, it had been very tightly plotted. Nonetheless, rewrites were necessary; and whilst the cast read through as much of the script as they could, I was led into a small announcer's studio to rework the plot so that Middle Eastern sensitivities would not be offended.

At the heart of the story was Elizabeth Warwick, an NHS doctor from London who soon found that her eagerly awaited holiday in Egypt would turn out to be a nightmare of international crime and intrigue. It was my intention from the start that as many characters as possible should be suspected of being involved in the sinister plot, including the smooth-talking Police Inspector Mahmoud, who was also an antique dealer (and practically everything else!). In my notes I say that he is 'Arab by nature and humour, but European when it is convenient for him to be so.' He was played by a very fine and distinguished actor called James Thomason, who had been a leading member of the BBC Drama Repertory Company for many years. Another shady suspect was Fuad Yassif, a slightly ambiguous character, 'a young Arab who speaks English extremely well, having spent a lot of his childhood in the company of English archeologists in the Valley of the Kings.' Guess who played him? Yes, you could be right – David Spenser!

But the central character of Elizabeth Warwick was played by Sheila Grant, an actress I had long admired. Although most of her work had been in radio, she had appeared in several films, and also on stage in the West End and provincial theatre. Once again this was an actress who, on radio, quite often did not look at all like the character she was playing. Although she was in her mid-forties at the time, as Elizabeth Warwick her rich, articulate voice completely conveyed a much younger woman, strong-willed and not easily scared. Elizabeth was an independent minded woman, forever facing up to the perils of the dark forces of a hostile environment, and there was never one moment throughout the serial when Sheila Grant did not perfectly convey that firm and dominant character.

Although the political elements of the story were of that period, some of the situations exist today. However, making explicit comments in a radio drama about the tensions between Arabs and Jews when they had just fought a bitter war was an explosive issue. By the time the actors and actresses took up their roles in front of the microphone, I had been persuaded to tone down what I really wanted to say about the never-ending tensions in the Middle East. Nonetheless, thanks to John, the cast, the control room crew, and my regular rewriting forays into the announcer's tiny claustrophobic studio, I like to think that the story held up well.

Although *Kill the Pharaoh!* was devised for radio drama, it had a very visual element to it. Having been brought up as a child in the Second World War, I had always been a dedicated film fanatic. During the London blitz, and regardless of the bombs that rained down on us during that time, I went to the 'pictures' as many times as I could, more often than not three or four times a week. There were, of course, no multiplex cinemas in those days, so one 'bunked in' to all the different cinemas in the neighbourhood – and I do mean 'bunked in' or sneaked in, because I had a real love of horror films, which carried an 'H' certificate, meaning that no minors were allowed into the show. Many a time I had to hide under the seat when the usherette appeared, shining her torch along the rows, searching out under-age intruders like me! During a showing of the original version of *King Kong*, the manager yanked me off by my collar, and cast me out into the back yard of the cinema, where I discovered a lump of chewing gum stuck to my jersey after lying flat on the floor under the seat! No matter. I did the same thing all over again later, and eventually even managed to see the complete film. Mind you, I also loved musicals, war films and adventure thrillers, so you can imagine what influenced me when I came to writing for radio and, later, for television.

For *Kill the Pharaoh!* I was fortunate enough to have visited Egypt and the Valley of the Kings on holiday a year or so before I started writing the serial, so I was able to see in my mind's eye the locations I wanted to sketch in for listeners. The Valley of the Kings, the last resting place of many of the Pharaohs of ancient Egypt, is so full of mystery, grandeur, and a quite creepy atmosphere, that it was no wonder I chose to set part of the action down there. With Pharaonic tombs and desert, the majestic River Nile just a stone's throw away, the remains of massive ancient temples, and a relentlessly hot sun, Luxor was, for me, a perfect background for a story of murder and intrigue. A few years later, of course, I used a similar setting for my contribution to the *Ace of Wands* television series, *The Power of Atep*. I was clearly still mesmerised by those images from modern Egypt's historical past – so much so that, in the same year that I wrote for *Ace of Wands*, I joined forces with my friend David Spenser to write two serials for BBC Children's Radio, *Shadow of the Pharaoh* and *Pharaoh of the Nile*. Must have been my Pharaonic period!

In many ways, it was very strange sitting in the green and pleasant countryside of England writing about the bleak landscapes and towering monuments of ancient Egypt. Just a few months before embarking on the radio serial, David Spenser and I moved into a timber-framed cottage in Essex. Surrounded by fields of wheat, chestnut, greengage, apple and pear trees, and rolling hedgerows inhabited by a very lively population of English birds, it hardly seemed the perfect place to summon up the hot sands of the Luxor desert. However, as I sat for hours staring out of my study window, fingers poised over the keys of my beloved old typewriter, it was the sounds of Egypt that pushed me on: the strange pipe music that accompanied the Dance of the Dervishes in Episode 7, the sound of boatmen singing along the Nile, local Egyptian shoppers in a village market and, of course, the call of the muezzin. In those days, that rich, exotic sound, echoing out from the top of a minaret, was only really known if you were lucky enough to have visited a Muslim country. Today, of course, as the world begins to change, it can be heard in many non-Muslim countries, but in *Kill the Pharaoh!* it was very much used to identify a particular place, and to heighten tension in one part of the story, as in the final episode of the serial, which I called quite simply *Muezzin*.

Episode 8 was set in Cairo, and in particular the City of the Dead. The first time I visited this vast cemetery set amongst the bustling metropolitan precincts of Egypt's capital city, I was completely overwhelmed. There, the act of death is not so much for grief but for celebration, the celebration of a life. Amongst the grand and not so grand headstones on the hundreds of graves, you will find family members and friends having a picnic, either on the anniversary of their loved one's death, or on a particular religious holiday. The sheer expanse of the place is quite astonishing; and, for me, it proved to be an ideal setting for the closing sequences of the serial. I will not ruin the plot for you by commenting on what happens, but it is a breathtaking climax, where ancient and modern come together in a desperate race against time.

1967 turned out to be a very busy year for me, for in between writing radio drama scripts, I managed to earn my keep by doing work as an extra in both film and television, an idea put forward, as already mentioned, by my old friend Cedric Messina. The previous year I had made what for me was a stupid decision to do a non-speaking part in *Doctor Who and the Moonbase*, which I have seen on various *Who* websites classifying me as being an 'actor'. I can assure you that, as far as I am concerned, I am no actor, never have been, and never wanted to be! I did it only once more, in a large-scale BBC TV version of Terence Rattigan's stage play about Lawrence of Arabia, *Ross*, but I'll come to that later. I did, however go on to do quite a lot of work as an 'extra' or 'crowd' artist, in such major international films as *Those Magnificent Men in their Flying Machines*, *The Yellow Rolls Royce* and *Operation Crossbow*. It was certainly fascinating to watch how such epics were made, and to be working in the background with such big names as Shirley MacLaine, George C. Scott, Terry-Thomas, James Fox, Sarah Miles, George Peppard and Alain Delon; but my interest was always in what was going on in the script, and behind, not in front of, the camera.

After I had finished *Kill the Pharaoh!*, I met with my very dear friend Peter Bryant, a man of immense talent both as actor and producer, who was instrumental in the casting of Jon Pertwee as Doctor Who. Peter, who had only recently taken over the series as Producer, asked me to join the team as Assistant Script Editor, which I readily accepted, and enjoyed enormously. During the short period I was there I became full Script Editor on the classic Gerry Davis/Kit Pedler story *The Tomb of the Cybermen*, which under Peter's supervision became one of the highlights of a very successful season. However, in those days the BBC did not encourage Script Editors to write their own work whilst working under contract for the Corporation, so I left, at my own request, to write my own six-part serial for *Who*, *Fury from the Deep*.

Fortunately I already knew the current Doctor, Patrick Troughton, who had been a friend since David Spenser had worked with him on location in Crete for a BBC TV serial called *Paul of Tarsus*; and I had also casually met Deborah Watling and Frazer Hines in my role as Assistant Script Editor during *The Evil of the Daleks* and *The Ice Warriors*. To say that it was fun working with them is an understatement. Apart from the fact that both Patrick and Frazer were wicked practical jokers, they were always professional, and together with Deborah they brought that trio to life in a way that made such an endearing combination. As for Deborah, well I've always thought her to be a good actress, both on television and on the stage. And she has done a few nifty performances in films as well, apart from being a lovely person, which is not surprising when you consider that fine acting family she comes from.

Fury from the Deep turned out to be one of the most costly *Who* serials that had yet been made. What with location filming at Pegwell Bay in Kent in the middle of winter (a luxury to have such an amount of filming and special effects at that time), a huge gas refinery set built in the BBC Ealing Film Studios, and more sets at Lime Grove, it was quite an undertaking for director Hugh David and his crew. But they all did a fine job, and I have nothing but admiration for them.

Needless to say, although some people were anxious that *Fury* was a little too frightening for children, its success certainly helped me to get more work in television, and I only mention it briefly here because the opportunity came at a time whilst I was deeply involved in writing for radio drama. However, there was also an awful lot of 'extra' work going on too, and that certainly helped me to understand more about the way television drama worked.

Soon after *Fury*, I was offered a three-month contract on a radio soap opera called *Waggoners' Walk*. I wasn't at all overjoyed by the prospect of working with a team who had been together for some considerable time, but the producer needed someone to replace one of the writers who, I seem to remember, had taken a leave of absence. In the event, my fears were thoroughly justified. My arrival for my first meeting with the team was not exactly welcomed with open arms. They all gave me the impression that I couldn't possibly understand the complexities of writing for a show that required continuous action, and the moment I suggested a story for some of the regular characters, the raised eyebrows around the table instantly told me that this assignment was not for me. Mind you, the Producer didn't help much, for I was treated very much like a 'new boy'. To be fair, quite a lot of us writers resent other writers. I'm no different, except that when I like someone else's work, I am always there to admire and congratulate. Don't get me wrong. Soap operas have been at the centre of radio and television drama for years, and it is thanks to the teams of writers that they have been kept alive for so long with such good stories. The older readers among you will remember *Mrs Dale's Diary* on BBC Radio, which eventually became *The Dales*, starring the late Jessie Matthews. Then there was *Dick Barton, Special Agent*, and the legendary *Journey Into Space*. Great teamwork, for which I honestly do have the greatest admiration. It's just that I myself found it difficult to work with a team of writers who seemed to me to be feeling very insecure. Sour grapes? No. Just disappointment.

After all that rewriting, I was relieved that *Kill the Pharaoh!* was received well. When I submitted a film version synopsis of the radio serial to a Hollywood film company in London, the response was very positive, with a comment that it was an absolutely intriguing story. But – as with so many ideas – money and 'not the right time' finally killed off the project! Fortunately, the few political elements that remained in the radio scripts caused offence to no one, and I was relieved not to have been responsible for a break in diplomatic relations between the United Kingdom and the warring nations of the Middle East!

It would be several years before I wrote another play for radio. A lot of the time in between was devoted to writing synopses for the growing number of television series. However, as I have already mentioned, in 1970 I was persuaded by my friend Cedric Messina to take a small role in his epic television production of Terence Rattigan's stage play, *Ross*. With Ian KcKellen already cast as Lawrence of Arabia, and a star-studded cast that included Edward Fox, Charles Gray and John Westbrook, I shook my head so violently that it nearly fell off. Even though the part was only a few lines, I was adamant that acting was not for me. But the lure of a location in the Sahara desert proved too much for me to reject, and so I was thrown in at the deep end. Cast as a nasty Turkish corporal, with an oily black moustache, I looked and felt like a nerd out of water. And talk about self-conscious. Ian was great fun to be with, as was David, who had been cast as Lawrence's Arab friend, Achmed; but they both knew how nervous I was, especially as I had to walk up to the two of them in the very first shot of the film. The moment I reached them they gave me such a teasing look that I flunked one of my only two lines! Nonetheless, thanks to Cedric, the whole experience, both in North Africa and in Studio 1 at the BBC Television Centre, turned out to be a rewarding one. And I must just add that working with Cedric was, for me, a joy. As a director/producer he was meticulous, and as a friend he was the essence of loyalty. Yes, he had his enemies amongst his colleagues, but to my mind that was because they resented his great ability to get programmes made. He is sorely missed.

So then we come to 1972, when radio was streaming through my mind again. But for some unknown reason I was beginning to think in a different direction. What I had learnt over those past few years was giving me a yearning to try something new, and my instinct was gradually leading me into the world of the supernatural...

Kill the Pharaoh!
A thriller serial for radio in eight episodes
by Victor Pemberton

Episode 1: Village of the White Scorpion

Produced by John Tydeman

REHEARSALS:	Tuesday 15 August 1967	1030–1730
	Wednesday 16 August 1967	1030–1730
RECORD:	Wednesday 16 August 1967	1730–1830
STUDIO:	6A	
R.P. No.	TLN33/DA847H	

CAST:
Elizabeth	Sheila Grant
Mahmoud	James Thomason
Mr Wilder	John Humphry
Fuad	David Spenser
Charles Villiers	Rolf Lefebvre
Margaret Villiers	Marion Mathie
Achmed Araby	Haydn Jones
Abdullah	Antony Viccars
1st Boatman	Nigel Anthony
2nd Boatman	Anthony Jackson
3rd Boatman	Ian Thompson
1st American	Barbara Mitchell
2nd American	Margaret Robertson
Arab Policeman	Nigel Anthony
Arab	Anthony Jackson

S.M.s: Panel: Amna Smith; Grams: Keith Salmon;
Spot: Enyd Williams

SECRETARY: Judy Munk, PABX 2168

Modern Egypt. Open with the shrill call of the muezzin. Gradually mix in the sound of the Cairo-Luxor express train speeding south

Mahmoud (*in Arabic*) Ismah lee, hathea alkursie mahjoz? (*Excuse me, is this seat taken?*)

Elizabeth I'm sorry. I don't speak Arabic.

Mahmoud (*very courteous*) Ah! Then I will speak English. Is this seat taken please?

Elizabeth Oh, I do beg your pardon. No of course not.

169

Mahmoud (*closing door*) Thank you dear lady, thank you. (*sits. A sigh of relief*) Ah! The air-condition. I always say if one has to travel on a train in Egypt, one must always pay the extra for the air-condition.

Elizabeth (*feeling the heat*) Will it get much hotter, d'you think?

Mahmoud (*amused*) Dear lady, we have only just left Cairo. By the time we reach the South, those poor devils in the second class will not be able to breathe.

Elizabeth ~~So much for my travel agent. He assured me I'd find Egypt much cooler in October.~~

[*Pause*]

Mahmoud ~~Then~~ it is your first time [down] to Luxor?

Elizabeth Yes.

Mahmoud Welcome!

Elizabeth Thank you.

Mahmoud ~~These days the whole world come to Luxor.~~ [Dear lady, Luxor belong to the people, not to the politicians.] You will have much to see.

Elizabeth ~~To tell you the truth~~ I feel as though I already know the place. My father used to tell me so much.

Mahmoud ~~He was with the British Army perhaps?~~

Elizabeth ~~No.~~ He was an Egyptologist.

Mahmoud (*delighted*) Ah!

Elizabeth Sir Richard Warwick. ~~Perhaps you've heard of him?~~

Mahmoud (*taken aback*) War…! Sir Richard Warwick? Excavator of great tomb at Harshak – in the Valley of the Kings?

Elizabeth Yes, that's right.

Mahmoud ~~(excitedly) Dear lady! This is fantastic coincidence! I knew him! I knew him well.~~

Elizabeth ~~Really?~~

Mahmoud ~~Of course!~~ [This is wonderful!] All Egypt remembers this man. But for him the great tomb would still be ~~hiding beneath~~ [covered by] the sand.

Elizabeth Do people still go there – to see the tomb?

Mahmoud There is nothing to see dear lady. It is ~~of~~ great sadness to me that since departure of your father the tomb has remained exactly as he found it. A lonely figure in the sand and dust, high up in the hills above ~~the~~ Valley of the Kings. (*a sad sigh*) And still we have no hope to find ~~the~~ name of the Pharaoh who may once have rest there.

Elizabeth With all due respects, if your Government ~~hadn't removed my father and certain other foreign archeologists…~~ [had allowed my father to continue his work…]

The door opens abruptly. A policeman enters

Policeman (*brusquely*) Ashoof-ul-pasport fadlak? (*May I see your passport please?*)

Elizabeth (*a little confused*) What does he want?

Mahmoud He is policeman. He ask to see your passport.

Elizabeth Oh. (*takes out passport*) There you are.

The policeman examines the passport. Pause

Elizabeth Is this a normal procedure on ~~the~~ [your] trains?

Mahmoud ~~Not at all.~~ [Our country is still in state of emergency.] I think maybe they look for someone.

Policeman (*handing back passport*) Shoukran. (*Thank you.*)

Elizabeth Thank you. (*softly to Mahmoud*) I don't think he likes me very much you know!

[**Mahmoud** Sssh! This is policeman!]

The policeman shakes a man who has been sleeping in the corner. The man groans irritably

Policeman (*roughly*) Ar-ragil da rakab, al'atr min wain? (*Where did this man get on the train?*)

Mahmoud The policeman ask how long the man in corner has been on train. Do you know?

Elizabeth Most of the time I think. Since Cairo.

Mahmoud (*to policeman*) Min Masr. (*At Cairo.*)

Policeman (*grabs hold of the man roughly*) Imshie, ante maoqoof lilhapis. (*Come on! You're under arrest!*)

The man begins to struggle

Elizabeth What's happening? (*disturbed*) What are they doing?

Mahmoud They are going to take him off the train.

The man creates a loud disturbance as he struggles with the policeman. Suddenly he stops in front of Elizabeth. We hear him breathing fast and heavily as Elizabeth cowers back from him

Elizabeth (*nervously*) W–What's wrong with him? Why's he staring at me like that?

Mahmoud Don't be frightened dear lady. (*condemningly*) He is drunk.

The man is pushed out of the compartment door

Elizabeth Well! (*sigh of relief*) That was charming.

Mahmoud He will be taken off the train at the next station – until he has time to recover ~~his wits~~.

Elizabeth (*firmly*) That man was not drunk.

Mahmoud (*surprised*) No?

Elizabeth I happen to be a doctor. He looks a very sick man, but whatever it is, I can assure you he ~~is~~ [was] *not* drunk.

The sharp scream of the engine horn as the train speeds on. Gradually mix in the sound of the hustle and bustle of the platform at Luxor Railway Station. A group of excited children are shouting "Bakhshish! Bakhshish!"

Mahmoud (*approaching, shouts*) Imshie ya wolid! Imshie! (*Get out of the way! Go on!*)

Elizabeth Poor little things. I only wish I did have some money to give them.

Mahmoud (*firmly*) No! They do not need the money!

Shouts angrily at the defiant children

Children laughing: "Bakhshish! Bakhshish!"

How can we ~~expect to~~ build a ~~country~~ [new nation] when fathers send their children out to beg!

Elizabeth (*awkwardly*) I'm sorry. I hadn't thought about that.

Mahmoud (*calmer, lightly*) Of course not. (*pause*) Excuse my ask dear lady – why do you wait here on platform?

Elizabeth (*looking around*) A friend of my father is supposed to be meeting me. I don't know what's happened to him.

~~Mahmoud We Egyptians are notoriously unpunctual. Are you sure he will recognise you?~~

~~Elizabeth Well he should do. He has a photograph.~~

Mahmoud If I may suggest, railway station is not good place for unaccompanied lady to wait. The sun takes only a few moments to set. Soon it will be dark. To which hotel do you go?

Elizabeth The Winter Palace. But it's quite all right, I can easily find my [own] way...

Mahmoud Dear lady, Luxor is [only] small town. It is no trouble for me. I am sure you will find message waiting at hotel. (*pause*) Please.

Pause as Elizabeth decides

Elizabeth (*smiling*) Very well. Thank you.

Mahmoud Splendid! I tell you ~~what~~. We shall take an Arabana – a horse-carriage. If we hurry, we shall still see the sun disappear behind the Temple of Luxor. (*moving off*) Now dear lady, you are *really* in ~~the~~ Land of the Pharaohs!

As they move off the children once again follow them with teasing shouts of "Bakhshish! Bakhshish!"

Fade out

Pause

Fade in: the hotel reception desk. Elizabeth opens an envelope and reads a letter. Pause

Elizabeth (*despondently*) Oh ~~Lord!~~ [dear!]

Mahmoud I hope is not bad news?

Elizabeth It's a letter from my friend. The one who was supposed to meet me. [He says] His father's been taken ill. He can't leave the village.

Mahmoud (*sympathetically*) Ah! A disappointment.

Elizabeth He wants me to take a boat and go out there first thing in the morning. (*putting letter away*) It must be pretty serious. He'd never have done this.

Mahmoud What village is this?

Elizabeth A place called Hasia. D'you know it?

Mahmoud (*with surprise*) Hasia?

Elizabeth Is it that bad?

Mahmoud No. Just that it is small village – five, maybe six miles from Luxor. On the banks of the Nile.

Elizabeth Sounds fun.

Mahmoud I hope you will think so, dear lady. The Nile is in bad flood. For many years we not have such disaster.

~~Elizabeth Oh dear. I hadn't realised.~~

172

Mahmoud ~~You remember on train from Cairo, I show you from train window.~~ ~~From Alexandria as far as Sudan, there is much damage, homes under water,~~ ~~people die. Very bad dear lady, very bad.~~

Elizabeth ~~How dreadful!~~

Mahmoud However, if you need help to get boat, I am [entirely] at your ~~service~~ [disposal]. My shop is very close to quayside.

Elizabeth You have a shop?

Mahmoud I am dealer in rare antiquities. None better in whole Upper Egypt. (*lowers voice, confidingly*) And of course for the daughter of Sir Edward Warwick I give very special price. (*takes out card*) Here. I am going to give you my card. There! Do you see? Mahmoud. That's me!

Elizabeth (*amused*) Oh yes. Well I'm Elizabeth Warwick, and I'm very pleased to know you Mr Mahmoud. And I shall most certainly visit your shop.

Mahmoud Splendid! Splendid! We shall talk, drink mint tea, and talk some more. But if I may warn you dear lady, when you go to ~~the~~ village of Hasia, please to be careful.

Elizabeth [Careful?] Why?

Mahmoud (*awkwardly*) You may find it a little, shall we say – primitive.

Elizabeth (*haughtily*) It's quite all right Mr Mahmoud. I don't think you need worry about that. I am *not* used to afternoon tea and cakes – even in England.

Fade out. Pause

A dinner gong is banged loudly and irregularly. Mix in to dining room

Villiers Do sit down Miss Warwick!

Elizabeth ~~I do hope I'm not barging in~~? [Thank you.]

Villiers ~~Not at all.~~ The waiter told us you were joining our table tonight. It's an honour for us. You're quite a celebrity around here. We saw your picture in the local newspapers.

Elizabeth Oh really?

Villiers I'm Charles Villiers. This is my wife Margaret.

Elizabeth How d'you do.

Margaret (*tipsy, speech slurred*) Hallo ~~duckie~~! Welcome to the Land of the Pharaohs. Hope you've brought your mosquito spray. You'll [certainly] need it.

Elizabeth Are you on holiday, Mr Villiers?

Villiers More or less. Maggie and I've been saving up for this for ten years. It's been a bit of a struggle, but we've [finally] made it.

Elizabeth Are you interested in Egyptology?

Villiers Only what I've read. My Unit was out here for a time. ~~Oh - before Suez.~~ In the good old days. (*a weak laugh*)

Elizabeth (*icily*) It's a beautiful country, isn't it?

Villiers Well, I don't know about beautiful, but it's certainly fascinating.

Margaret (*rambling*) Palm trees, desert and (*slaps a mosquito*) mosquitos!

Villiers I was very sorry to hear about your father passing on like that. It must have been a big shock for you?

Elizabeth Yes.

Villiers It's terribly sad to think he never had the chance to finish off his work up at that tomb. (*pause*) Tell me ~~something~~ Miss Warwick. Is it true that when your father ~~dug up~~ [excavated] that place he found it absolutely empty?

Elizabeth Yes. It's true.

Villiers But surely, in most of the tombs they found not only the remains of the King, but most of his treasures?

Elizabeth In this case, nobody knows if this *was* the tomb of the King. The very fact that it was not in the Valley itself, but in the hills above.

Villiers And the treasures?

Elizabeth If there were any, they could have been taken by robbers at any time, right back through the centuries.

Villiers Fascinating!

Margaret (*pouring wine, rambling*) When I'm dead and buried, I don't want anyone to dig *me* up again.

Villiers (*snaps*) Maggie! That's enough wine!

Margaret (*drinking messily*) Oh Charlie! Don't be a bore...

Villiers (*grabbing the glass from her*) Did you hear what I said! [No more wine...!]

The glass is knocked over

Margaret Now look what you've done! You've spilt it all over my dress.

Villiers (*awkwardly to Elizabeth*) Sorry about this Miss Warwick. (*a weak laugh*) Too many cocktails before dinner I'm afraid.

Elizabeth It's quite all right... (*slaps a mosquito*) Dash the mosquitos! I do see what you mean. They've got a nip like a pin.

Villiers Yes. I'm afraid you've come at rather a bad time for the mozzies. They're all over the place. A menace.

Margaret (*disgruntled, relishingly*) That's nothing! You wait 'til you get to that village downstream.

[*Pause*]

Elizabeth (*looking up sharply*) I beg your pardon? What village?

Villiers (*quickly covering up*) We mean, you're bound to be having a look at some of the villages along the Nile. Most people do. Some lovely little places...

Elizabeth Really? (*sceptical, cautious*) I thought the Nile was in flood.

Villiers Yes, but –

Margaret *They'll* bite you. Yes – they'll bite you all right!

Villiers (*menacingly*) Maggie! (*to Elizabeth*) I'm sorry Miss Warwick. I think I'd better ~~get her~~ [take my wife] upstairs. She's not ~~really fit enough to have dinner tonight~~ [feeling very well]. If you'll excuse us?

Elizabeth Of course.

They stand

Villiers Oh by the way, if you do happen to need a boat at all, we can put you on to a good boatman.

Elizabeth Thank you.

Villiers Nice little chap. Took us on our trip to Aswan and back. Just mention our name [– Villiers]. He'll know.

Elizabeth Good. I'll do that. How do I find him?

Villiers You'll find him down on the quayside near the hotel. Ask for Araby. Achmed Araby.

A sharp cut to the quayside where a large group of laughing, but good humoured, Boatsmen are teasing the highly amused Elizabeth

1st Boatman Lady! You want boat? I have best boat in whole Upper Egypt!

2nd Boatman Lady! This man lies! His boat will sink after two minutes. Two minutes, lady!

3rd Boatman (*the superior one*) Look lady. Do not listen to these men. They are peasants. (*quietly confiding*) *My* boat is best for you…

2nd Boatman For you lady, I give special price. Ten piastas to go to Banana Island. Ten piastas lady! Where in whole Luxor you find such a bargain?

An old man shouts "Bakhshish! Bakhshish!" in the background. This sends the whole crowd into a gale of laughter. Elizabeth shouts above them

Elizabeth How many more times do I have to tell you? I do not want to go to Banana Island…or Crocodile Island… or anywhere else.

A groan from the crowd

Now then. Which of you is Achmed Araby?

A sudden silence

Well?

Achmed (*a calm youthful voice*) Here is Achmed.

Pause. Elizabeth is very wary of him

Elizabeth Are you sure?

Achmed (*brightly, cheekily*) Sure! *I* am Achmed, Son of Nile. My boat is best of all. You have made wise choice lady. You will see!

Elizabeth Which one is your boat Achmed?

Achmed (*points*) There! The one with the white sail – the blue wood. 'Horous' – God of the Sun.

Elizabeth I want to go to the village of Hasia.

Without warning, the crowd quickly disperses

(*looking around, surprised*) W–What's wrong? Where are you all going?

Achmed (*solemnly*) My boat is not for hire today.

Elizabeth What are you talking about? You just said –

Achmed Not today. There is no breeze – the water is too difficult. I ['Horous'] will not sail today.

Pause

Elizabeth Twenty piastas…

Achmed Not today.

Elizabeth (*losing patience*) What's wrong with you? Don't you want the business? One minute you say you will, the next you won't! (*pause. Calmer*) Look Achmed. I was recommended to you by Mr and Mrs Villiers. Do you know them?

Achmed They my friends – sure!

175

Elizabeth Then why won't you take me to Hasia? ~~What's wrong with it? It's only a village, isn't it.~~

Achmed Many floods.

Elizabeth I know there are floods, but I still have to get there just the same. I have to meet a friend.

Achmed (*looking up, curiously*) What friend you have in Hasia?

Elizabeth A young man called Fuad Yassif. Do you know him?

Another silence from Achmed

He used to work in the Valley – with my father.

Achmed I don't know this man.

Elizabeth But if you know the people in Hasia, you must know Fuad. He's lived there all his life.

Achmed (*defiantly*) I don't know this man! My boat is not for hire today.

Achmed starts to walk away

Elizabeth (*shouts angrily*) All right Achmed Araby! If your boat is not for hire today, I'm sure the Tourist Board will be only too happy to make sure it is not for hire *any* day.

Achmed stops walking

Elizabeth Now! Are you going to take me to Hasia – or aren't you!

A sharp cut. Pause

Fade in: Achmed's boat is creaking its way down the Nile

Elizabeth You're a very good boatman Achmed. For how long?

Achmed Lady, I am born of Nile. Before me, my father and his father.

Elizabeth And do you never leave Luxor?

Achmed Oh yes! I have been to Cairo, *and* to Alexandria. Very beautiful.

Elizabeth You mean, you go all the way to Alexandria by boat?

Achmed Of course! 'Horous' like to have the holiday.

Elizabeth laughs

Ah! There is your village.

Elizabeth (*looking*) Where?

Achmed There! By the big trees. Do you see?

Elizabeth Oh yes. It looks very beautiful. (*pause*) I can't see anybody... ~~oh God!~~ [Oh – and just] Look at [all] that flood water. ~~The poor devils!~~

The boat creaks on. Mix in the sound of Elizabeth banging on the door of a hut

Elizabeth (*banging, calling*) Hallo! Hallo, is there anyone in there? (*no reply. Silence*) Hallo! (*bangs again*) ~~Damn!~~ Where ~~the hell~~ are they all! (*pause*) Oh well, here goes.

She slowly pushes the creaking door open, and wades in ankle deep in water. Immediately we hear the sound of flies and mosquitos buzzing around. Now inside, she calls again

Hallo! (*no reply. She wades in a little further*) Hallo. Is anyone in here?

The silence is suddenly broken by the asthmatic breathing of a man. Elizabeth turns around with a start

Abdullah (*breathing with difficulty*) Who are you English woman? What are you doing in my house?

Elizabeth (*recovering from her shock*) Oh! I'm terribly sorry. I didn't see you standing there in the corner.

Abdullah What do you want?

Elizabeth I've been wandering around the village for the last half-hour. There doesn't seem to be anyone about. (*pause. Awkwardly*) The flood water is very deep.

Abdullah You should not come to Hasia.

Elizabeth I'm looking for someone. A friend.

Abdullah What 'friend'?

Elizabeth Yassif. Fuad Yassif.

No reply from Abdullah

I was supposed to meet him here.

Abdullah I don't know this man.

Elizabeth (*puzzled*) Don't – know him? But he lives here. He's lived here all his life.

Abdullah There is no such man in Hasia. All the people gone.

Elizabeth *Where* have they gone? (*pause*) I may be able to find my friend.

Abdullah Go back to Luxor. You are not welcome here English woman.

He starts a violent fit of coughing

Elizabeth You're ill. (*sympathetically*) Please let me help you.

Abdullah (*cowers back*) You will not touch me! [Not touch me!]

Elizabeth I don't want to hurt you. I'm a trained Doctor. (*pause*) Look. You can't stay in this place. The flood water is stagnant. You're leaving yourself wide open for any amount of disease.

Sound of mosquitos buzzing is prominent

Elizabeth (*impatiently*) You can see for yourself. Look at the mosquitos in here! It's uncivilised!

Abdullah lets out a hearty, asthmatic laugh

Abdullah Uncivilise? (*laughs louder*) Yes. How many times I hear this word in my life. (*calmer*) Always they tell Abdullah to start 'new life'. Once it was the British. Now – even the Arab. (*sadly*) When will you let me live old life before I start the new?

The sound of a man groaning, off

Elizabeth What was that? There's someone in the next room.

Abdullah No!

Elizabeth I tell you –

Abdullah (*grabs hold of her arm, warningly*) Go back to Luxor. (*close, almost whispering*) You have seen nothing – nothing!

Elizabeth What do you mean I've seen... (*pause*) Who have you got in that room? (*voice hardening*) Let go of my arm Mr Abdullah. I'm going in there!

Abdullah (*snaps*) No! Come back!

She breaks loose from him and wades to the door of an adjoining room. She draws back the curtain. She is appalled by what she sees

Elizabeth ~~My God!~~ Look at the state of this man! Who is he?

Abdullah My brother is sick. You cannot help him.

Elizabeth Sick! You must be out of your mind keeping him here in all this stench. Get out of my way. I want to have a look at… (*horrified*) Oh my – ! Who did this to him? This man has been ~~beaten up!~~ [attacked!]

Abdullah After one night my brother will be well again.

Elizabeth (*deadly solemn*) Oh no. After one night your brother will not be well again. This man is going to die.

A long silence

Abdullah It is the will of Allah.

The man groans again

Elizabeth You must help me get him to a hospital.

Abdullah He will not go hospital. He stay here, where he belong.

Elizabeth (*scathingly*) Then your brother will die.

Abdullah In this village, we are not afraid to die.

Elizabeth Are you mad? How can you leave your own brother to…

Abdullah (*close to her*) Why you come Egypt, English woman? Your father is dead now.

Elizabeth (*startled*) My – . Then you *do* know who I am.

Abdullah (*bitterly*) You bring us nothing but trouble.

Elizabeth What's happened to Fuad? Where is everybody…?

Abdullah (*tauntingly*) Why you stand with back to wall? (*closer*) Do you – scare of me?

Elizabeth (*firmly defiant*) No, my friend. I am *not* scared of you!

Abdullah Good! Good! (*swiftly, suddenly*) Then look to the wall – there! By your face.

Elizabeth stifles a gasp. Abdullah laughs

You do not have the white scorpi in England, no? Here. (*takes hold of the scorpion*) I make gift to you.

Elizabeth You fool! Don't touch it! That's a white scorpion. It's deadly!

Abdullah (*mocking, highly amused*) Scorpi! Scorpi!

Elizabeth (*cowering back*) You maniac!

Abdullah Did they not tell you in Luxor, they call Hasia the Village of the White Scorpion? She is our friend. (*very close, almost a whisper*) Look. Do you see? She does not move in my hand. She stops – to watch you.

Pause

Elizabeth Get out of my way.

Abdullah Look to the shadows English woman. Even now they begin to fall across the river. In half hour it will be dark. Without boat you will have long journey.

Elizabeth What d'you mean without… (*gradually realises*) Oh no! Achmed! (*shouts*) Achmed!

Abdullah begins to laugh, Elizabeth rushes out through the water (*off, shouting*) Achmed!

We fade out with Abdullah laughing boisterously, asthmatically

Pause

The hotel entrance

Villiers She's not back.

Margaret What did you expect?

Villiers We'll give her another half hour, then I'll check.

Margaret If you ask me our little friend Achmed is playing a double game. He's far too fond of the bakhshish.

Villiers I don't think so.

Margaret Well *I* do.

Villiers You're not asked to think. Just keep off the booze [sober]. Anyway, why this sudden concern? You're not usually so considerate.

Margaret The whole thing makes me feel quite sick. I wish we could just forget about it and go back home.

Villiers We will – when we've finished what we have to do.

Margaret That may be too late. (*nervously*) Charlie, I don't like it. She's out there in that village… in the darkness… all alone…

A very sharp cut to the sound of Elizabeth's frenzied shouting in the darkness of Hasia

Elizabeth (*shouts echoing*) Achmed!

Pause, wades through water

Achmed Araby! Where are you!

The air is filled with night sounds: crickets, bullfrogs, cicadas, a dog howling in the far distance, and the lapping of the water against the river bank. She calls again

Achmed! (*still no reply. To herself, angrily*) Damn you! (*pause*) If it wasn't so dark I could find my [own] way out of this…

She stops as she hears someone wading through the water towards her

Who's that?

The movement continues, closer

Achmed! Is that you?

The movement comes to a halt. Silence

(*a nervous breathing*) I know you're there. (*silence*) I may not be able to see you, but I know you're there. (*pause. Shouts*) Did you hear what I said! (*still uncertain*) Abdullah?

Achmed (*wickedly amused*) You my friend lady – sure!

Elizabeth (*angrily*) Achmed! What the hell d'you mean by leaving me out here alone! Where've you been?

Achmed River too strong for boat, lady. Achmed wait other side.

Elizabeth (*scathingly*) Don't you ever dare do that to me again. Do you understand, Achmed Araby?

Pause

Achmed (*sorrowfully*) Yes lady.

Elizabeth (*snaps angrily*) Now tell me! What's happened to all the villagers? What have they done with Fuad Yassif? (*more anger*) I want to know!

Achmed (*shying back*) Gone, lady. All people gone...

Elizabeth *Where* have they gone?

Achmed Into hills, lady. Too many the floods.

Elizabeth Is Fuad with them? (*close, pleads*) Please Achmed! If you know, you've got to tell m... (*stops dead*) What's that ~~glare~~ [blaze] over there? (*looking*) It's a fire!

Flames in background

Achmed (*solemnly*) We go now, lady.

Elizabeth My God! That's Abdullah's house.

Achmed We go back to boat...

Elizabeth I tell you I was there just a little while ago. Look! It's burning. We've got to do something.

Achmed (*holding her*) No lady, no! It is the will of Allah.

Elizabeth What d'you mean it's... (*gradually realises*) His brother. Abdullah's brother. He's dead, isn't he? That's why they're burning the...

Achmed You must understand, lady. For Arab – it is no shame to die.

Elizabeth (*distressed*) Yes – but that poor man...

Achmed We believe is more honour to die than to live. (*pause*) So it has always been. (*with great dignity*) So must it be now.

Fade up the sound of flames crackling fiercely

Mix into this the voice of Mahmoud, who is reading a quotation to two elderly American tourist ladies in his shop. They listen spellbound

Mahmoud (*with a great sense of the theatrical*) "When Man remains after death, his deeds are heaped beside him. What is there is there for all eternity. He who reaches other world without wrong-doing shall exist there like a God."

A romantic sigh from the two ladies

1st American Wonderful!

2nd American You make it sound so, so real, Mr Mahmoud.

Mahmoud Ah dear ladies, you are kind. But these are not words of Mahmoud. They were written by the Pharaoh Kheti.

1st American Nevertheless –

Mahmoud (*with amazing rapidity*) But! For five hundred piastas – *only* five hundred – you can have scarab necklace found in great Pharaoh's tomb. Original necklace!

2nd American Goodness!

1st American Five hundred! Gee! Isn't that kinda expensive?

Mahmoud No expensive lady. Cheap! Only for you do I give special price. (*lowers voice confidingly*) You see, my dear [dead] mother was American lady.

1st American (*warily*) Well... I don't know...

The shop door opens. Overhead bell

Mahmoud Ah! Miss Warwick! Welcome! Welcome! (*surprised*) Dear lady – what has happened? Your clothes – they are wet…

Elizabeth (*approaching*) I'm sorry to barge in on you like this Mr Mahmoud, but I *must* see you at once.

1st American (*delighted to find an excuse*) Well, we'll see you later Mr Mahmoud, goodbye. (*moving off*)

2nd American (*rushing off*) Bye!

Mahmoud (*a little sadly*) Goodbye!

The two American ladies leave. Door

Elizabeth Mr Mahmoud. I've just got back fron the village of Hasia. D'you remember the man the police took off the train yesterday? In our compartment?

Mahmoud Oh yes. The man who was drunk?

Elizabeth I found him in a filthy looking hut owned by a man named Abdullah. Somebody had beaten him up. He was in a dreadful state.

Mahmoud But this is terrible! We must call the Hospital [immediately].

Elizabeth It's too late. The man is dead.

Mahmoud And the other villagers?

Elizabeth Gone. The whole village. I can't understand what's been going on out there. Who was this man? D'you think he was following me or something?

Mahmoud Leave this to me dear lady. I will inform police immediately. (*pause*) But what of your friend? Was he not in the village to meet you?

Pause

Elizabeth No. And I don't believe he had any intention of doing so.

Mahmoud (*bewildered*) Not – ? Dear Lady, what do you mean?

Elizabeth That message I got at the hotel. *I* don't think Fuad wrote it. (*a tired sigh*) Somebody wanted to get me out there. That's all I know.

Mahmoud Dear lady, ~~you have had great shock on first day in Luxor. Now~~ you must go back to hotel – rest. I myself will telephone Police Inspector. He is very good friend. After dinner you go see him at Police Station. Tell him all you see at this village.

Elizabeth But if anything *has* happened to Fuad…

Mahmoud (*sympathetically*) *If* it has, dear lady, we are going to know about it. That I promise you.

Sharp cut. A telephone ringing. ~~A door opened and slammed, off.~~ Elizabeth grabs hold of the telephone receiver

Elizabeth (*breathless*) Yes?

Villiers (*at other end*) Miss Warwick?

Elizabeth (*half-heartedly*) Oh yes, Mr Villiers?

Villiers We were in the hall downstairs. Saw you go up. What sort of a day have you had?

Elizabeth (*caustically*) Interesting.

Villiers The river's ~~so~~ beautiful, isn't it?

Elizabeth Very.

Villiers Did you manage to find Achmed Araby – the boatman?

Elizabeth Oh yes – I found *him* all right.

Villiers ~~Isn't he marvellous? And 'Horous' is one of the cleanest boats on the river.~~

Elizabeth ~~Very competent.~~

Villiers Look Miss Warwick. Maggie and I are going down for a quick drink before dinner. What about joining us?

Elizabeth Thank you all the same Mr Villiers. I really am rather tired. I'm eating in my room tonight. It's been a long day.

Villiers Of course. I quite understand. Get yourself a good night's rest. Do you the world of good. We'll see you some time tomorrow.

Elizabeth Right.

Villiers Goodnight.

Elizabeth Goodnight.

Replaces receiver. Almost immediately she picks up the receiver again and dials two figures. A single buzz until a woman receptionist answers

Woman (*at the other end*) Can I help you?

Elizabeth (*a tired voice*) Oh yes. This is Miss Warwick in Room Twenty-two. I shan't be eating in the dining room this evening. I'd like something in my room please.

Woman (*writing*) Room… Twenty-two. Yes, madam.

Elizabeth How long will it be please?

Woman Few minutes only madam.

Elizabeth That's fine. Thank you.

Woman Thank you madam.

Receivers replaced. As she replaces her receiver, Elizabeth is immediately startled to find someone staring at her from a corner of the room

Elizabeth Who are you? (*fast, nervous breathing*) What are you doing in my room?

No reply from the intruder. Pause

I only have to pick up that telephone…

Picks up telephone receiver. An immediate buzzing

Man (*calm, but firm*) Put down the receiver.

Pause. The receiver is still buzzing

(*firmly insistent*) Please!

Elizabeth replaces the receiver

Thank you.

Elizabeth What do you want?

Man You are – a little older than I expected…

Elizabeth If it's money you want –

Man … but still very beautiful…

Elizabeth (*snaps angrily*) Did you hear what I –

Man … you have your father's eyes.

A shocked silence from Elizabeth

Yes ~~Miss~~ Elizabeth. I am Fuad Yassif.

Elizabeth Fu… (*hardening*) No. I don't believe you.

Man Your father took many pictures. You have only to look.

Elizabeth Those pictures were taken a long time ago. (*pause*) If you are Fuad Yassif, why didn't you meet me off the train last night?

Fuad There was something I had to do –

Elizabeth (*angry*) Your instructions were to —

Fuad My father died.

~~**Elizabeth** Died?~~

Fuad We had to take him into the hills. There was no time to stop you from going to the village…

Elizabeth (*unwillingly*) You might have left a message.

Fuad I tell you there was no time!

Silence

Elizabeth All right Fuad, I believe you. Now tell me. What is it you want?

Fuad (*puzzled*) Want?

Elizabeth You've brought me out all the way from England. Why?

Fuad You – *know* why.

Elizabeth (*smugly*) [Then –] Tell me?

Pause

Fuad (*hesitant*) The – the tomb at Harshak.

Elizabeth What about it?

Fuad (*lowers voice, compellingly*) Your father told me that one day you and me would share a King's fortune.

Elizabeth (*amused*) And how would we do that – Fuad?

Fuad Don't play games with me!

Elizabeth (*unnaturally confident*) Show me your hands Fuad.

Fuad (*very irritated*) What are you –

Elizabeth Please.

Pause. He stretches out his hands

Thank you.

Pause. She is looking at them

My father often used to talk of a little boy with beautiful hands. Long, thin fingers – almost delicate at the touch…

A knock at the door

Fuad (*panicking*) The maid! They've brought your food!

Elizabeth …and gentle. Almost like a woman…

Another knock at the door

Fuad Please Elizabeth – please!

Elizabeth These hands are very rough. They're used to hard work. (*close to mic*) Can I really trust you Fuad? (*forcefully*) Can I?

A sudden impatient tapping on the door, which we linger on for a moment as we gradually mix into the sound of someone typing in the next scene

We are now in Luxor Police Station, where Elizabeth is waiting to see the Inspector

Wilder (*approaching, talks with a slight stammer*) Excuse me. I'm [awfully] sorry to trouble you.

A surprised murmur from Elizabeth as she looks up

It is Miss Warwick, isn't it?

Elizabeth Why – yes.

Wilder The Inspector told me you were coming here to the Police Station. I thought I'd come and see if I could be of any help. My name's Wilder. I'm from the British Consulate in Luxor.

Elizabeth Oh – how d'you do.

Wilder Heard about the frightful time you had in that village. I do hope you're feeling better now?

Elizabeth Much, thank you.

Wilder It's really nice to have such a distinguished visitor in our midst. (*confidingly*) Especially a British one. (*pause*) Unfortunately your father was a bit before my time. I never had the pleasure of meeting him. But I gather from the locals he was highly respected [out here].

Elizabeth Yes.

Wilder No doubt you'll be carrying on the good work up at Harshak?

Elizabeth (*firmly*) No.

Wilder (*a little taken aback*) But I thought –

Elizabeth I'm here as a tourist Mr Wilder. Nothing more.

Wilder (*awkwardly*) Oh – I do beg your pardon. I rather thought… well, the way Inspector Mahmoud was talking…

Elizabeth (*shocked*) Inspector – who did you say?

The door of the Inspector's office opens, and the beaming Mahmoud appears, approaches

Mahmoud Ah! Dear lady. And Mr Wilder – welcome, welcome!

Elizabeth (*taken completely by surprise*) You!

A very sharp cut. Pause

Fade in: Mahmoud's office

Mahmoud You see dear lady, in Luxor I have many jobs. Antiques, restaurant, taxi service, and in spare time I am Official Tourist Guide. (*aside*) Police job I like not much.

Elizabeth But why didn't you tell me?

Mahmoud Dear lady – you did not ask!

Wilder Inspector. I think it's about time you told Miss Warwick one or two things about that village.

Elizabeth You mean Hasia?

Mahmoud My men have already reached this village. About half-an-hour ago.

Elizabeth Yes? And?

Wilder Apparently what you told the Inspector is true. Well – almost.

Elizabeth And what's that supposed to mean?

Mahmoud It means dear lady that there are floods, and there is the wreckage of a burnt out house.

Elizabeth Well, there you are.

Wilder But the village is not deserted.

Elizabeth What! Don't talk nonsense man! If you don't believe me, get hold of that Abdullah character.

Mahmoud Yes. Which brings us to another question. This house – the one you saw burning – you say there were two men…

Elizabeth Yes.

Mahmoud One very sick?

Elizabeth Yes.

Mahmoud And the other? This Abdullah?

Elizabeth Nothing wrong with him except sheer arrogance.

Wilder There were two charred bodies in the wreckage Miss Warwick. Not one.

Stunned silence from Elizabeth

Elizabeth (*with disbelief*) [What?] What are you saying?

Wilder Just that something is going on in that village that we don't know about. You should never have gone there in the first place.

Mahmoud I should have warned you dear lady. Hasia has reputation of its own. Even the police are reluctant to, shall we say, interfere in domestic affairs. (*pause*) But now. We must find your Fuad Yassif.

Elizabeth That won't be necessary. I've already seen him.

Mahmoud What?

Wilder Where was this?

Elizabeth He came to my hotel this evening. The whole thing has been a misunderstanding. His father died up in the hills. That's why he wasn't able to meet me.

Pause

Wilder (*troubled*) But – [Miss Warwick]!

Mahmoud (*deliberately overriding him*) We are very happy for you Miss Warwick. This is great relief.

Elizabeth Thank you. All I want to do now is to forget the whole thing, and try to enjoy myself for the next [a] few days.

Mahmoud Of course.

Elizabeth And so if you'll excuse me (*gets up*) I'm very tired. I think a good night's rest will do me the world of good.

Mahmoud I am at your disposal – any time.

Elizabeth You're very kind. Goodnight Mr Wilder.

Wilder Anytime you're passing the consulate [my office], drop in. I'm on the first floor.

Elizabeth (*moving to the door*) I will. Goodnight Mr – I mean Inspector Mahmoud.

Mahmoud Dear lady.

Opens door for her, off mic

Goodnight.

Closes door

Wilder Nice girl.

Mahmoud (*returning to mic*) Charming.

Wilder She knows the score all right. Still. I suppose being a Doctor, you'd have to. (*pause*) I was looking up her father's file just before I came here tonight. She had a brother you know. Michael. Killed in the Suez fighting.

Mahmoud (*half to himself*) Yes.

Wilder You know?

Mahmoud Of course.

Wilder You never –

Mahmoud ~~I am policeman Mr Wilder.~~ It is my job [Mr Wilder].

Wilder (*sighs*) Well, at least we don't have to worry about our Miss Warwick any more – especially now she's found this Fuad Yassif chap.

Mahmoud picks up telephone

Mind you, you've got to hand it to her. It takes a lot of guts for a woman to go wandering down the Nile all alone. And in the dark.

Mahmoud (*on telephone*) Khalie wahid yetba'a Al-Engieliezieya. (*pause*) Aywa. (*Get someone to follow the English woman – Yes.*)

Replaces receiver

Wilder (*looks up surprised*) What are you doing that for? Why are you having her followed?

Mahmoud For her protection, Mr Wilder. That is all.

Wilder But – why?

Mahmoud Because the man called Fuad Yassif was killed in a car crash – just one month ago.

Sharp cut to the shrill call of the muezzin which continues over our closing announcements

END OF EPISODE ONE

Kill the Pharaoh!

by Victor Pemberton

Episode 2: Into the Darkness

Produced by John Tydeman

REHEARSALS:	Thursday 17 August 1967	1030–1730
RECORD:	Thursday 17 August 1967	1730–1830
STUDIO:	B.10	
R.P. No.	TLN33/DA848H	

CAST:

Elizabeth ....Sheila Grant
Mahmoud.................................James Thomason
Mr Wilder ....John Humphry
Fuad ....David Spenser
Charles ....Rolf Lefebvre
Margaret Villiers......................Marion Mathie
Achmed Araby..........................Haydn Jones
Bertie Pringle ....Barry Lowe
O'Hara ....Denis McCarthy
Captain Aziz ....John Justin

S.M.s: Panel: Amna Smith; Grams: Keith Salmon;
Spot: Enyd Williams

SECRETARY: Judy Munk

Mix the opening call of the muezzin into quayside effects at Luxor. Early morning, and the Nile ferry boat is about to make its first crossing of the day to the donkey station for the Valley of the Kings

There is the usual chaos, as tourists mingle with the excitable but good-humoured Arab crowd, all travelling with livestock. Goats, cattle, sheep – and in the background dogs barking their irritation. Amongst the tourists are Charles and Margaret Villiers

Villiers (*calling above the din*) Miss Warwick! Miss Warwick – over here! We've kept a place for you.

Elizabeth Warwick struggles her way through the crowd

Elizabeth Oh – Mr Villiers! (*approaching*) Thank you so much. (*a sigh of relief*) What chaos! Is it like this every day?

Villiers It is if you want to cross the Nile first thing in the morning, my dear. Always best to get here early.

Elizabeth But fancy bringing all their livestock onto a passenger ferry boat. Surely they're not all going to the Valley of the Kings?

Villiers I'm afraid that's something you'll have to get used to, Miss Warwick. In Egypt most of the Arabs take their livestock around with them wherever they go. They're almost part of the family. (*amused*) Ask Maggie here, she'll tell you.

Margaret By the time we get to the other side, you'll have more fleas on you than you'd ever thought…

She lets out a yell as a goat bleats disapprovingly at the side of her

Get away from me you nasty thing!

A roar of Arab crowd laughter

Villiers So where are you making for today Miss Warwick? The Harshak Tomb?

Elizabeth Possibly. I'm not quite sure yet.

Villiers Must be quite a big day for you – seeing for the first time all the good work your father did. Let's hope you won't be too disappointed.

Elizabeth Why?

Villiers The authorities have rather let the place go to rot. No one goes up there any more.

Margaret You know Miss Warwick, the tomb is very deserted – well off the beaten track. Not the sort of place for a girl to go wandering off on her own. I know *I* wouldn't.

Elizabeth I shall be quite all right. I'm meeting an Arab friend. He used to work in the tomb with my father.

Villiers Good! No worries then. As long as you've got someone with you. I mean it can be pretty dangerous up there on those hill tracks – especially if you're not used to them.

Elizabeth (*not having realised this*) Hill tracks?

Villiers (*pointedly*) Why yes. The Harshak Tomb isn't in the actual Valley itself. You have to climb up there (*indicating*) – to the top of the Theban Peak. You knew that – didn't you Miss Warwick?

The boat's engine starts up

Ah! We're off!

A sarcastic cheer from Arab crowd

Margaret Oh no! Look who's running along the quayside. It's that awful man!

Elizabeth (*looking out*) Who is he?

Villiers Bertie Pringle. He's staying at our hotel. We usually try to avoid him.

Margaret Just look at him in that ridiculous Arab headdress. It's so embarrassing! Oh come on boat… get a move on!

The boat chugs off amidst Arab chatter. Mix in the sound of footsteps echoing across the stone floor of the Town Mortuary. Eventually, they come to a halt

Mahmoud (*a relieved sigh*) So Mr Wilder! Do you not feel good to have the air-condition?

Wilder (*continuing his stammer*) Yes I do Inspector, but I hardly find the Town Mortuary the ideal place for relaxation.

Mahmoud But the luxury to breathe again after the heat outside…

Wilder Yes. Too bad our friends in the boxes over there can't enjoy the same luxury. (*pause*) You say this is where they brought the body of Fuad Yassif after the car crash?

Mahmoud Yes. Military Police found him on hill just below Theban Peak – or what was left of him.

Wilder Then how can you be sure it was the real Fuad Yassif?

Mahmoud That is the point Mr Wilder. We are not sure. It is why we come to Mortuary to find out.

Wilder But this man who met Elizabeth Warwick at her hotel last night. Why is he posing as Fuad Yassif? What does he want?

Mahmoud Also we must find out.

Wilder She may be in danger.

Mahmoud My men keep watch at all times…

Wilder It only needs one mistake…

Mahmoud (*surprised assurance*) At *all* times, Mr Wilder. At *all* times.

He walks around

Let us remember, if this man is the real Fuad Yassif, your lady will have nothing to fear. After all… (*pause*) he was close friend of Sir Richard Warwick.

Wilder Yes, as a child.

Mahmoud And now… (*deadly serious*) …he is a man.

Pause. He rejoins Wilder

Mr Wilder. Can you tell me why your Miss Warwick come to Luxor?

Wilder Well you should know. Your people in London issued the Visa.

Mahmoud Visa! (*a dismissing laugh*) Very funny!

Wilder (*indignantly*) Her passport *is* perfectly legal, if that's what you're implying.

Mahmoud Holiday? You think is true?

Wilder I don't see why not. Plenty of people do, you know.

Mahmoud But Miss Warwick is different – is she not?

Pause

Wilder (*confused*) Different? In what way?

Mahmoud She is daughter of man who discover tomb. Tomb without a mummy, without a treasure.

Wilder Now look here Mahmoud. That tomb has been empty for years – nobody cares a damn about the place.

Mahmoud No?

Wilder Well, of course they don't… there's nothing to see. (*trying to convince*) The Harshak Tomb is nothing but a bare shell, you know that.

Mahmoud Yes.

Wilder So I can't see any possible reason why Elizabeth Warwick – or anyone else – should suddenly want to take an interest in the place.

A brief pause

Mahmoud (*very serious*) No, Mr Wilder. Neither can I.

189

A sharp cut to a toot from the ferry boat hooter. The engine of the small boat is still chugging its way across the Nile. Bertie Pringle, the Cockney tourist 'expert' is reading a quote from his Edwardian guide book

Pringle (*with great assurance*) ..."but once outside the Tomb of Ramses, the visitor will not fail to become aware of the intense heat, and servants should be instructed in advance to provide necessary refreshments for the return journey by carriage. Ladies are well advised to carry their parasol..."

Margaret Parasol? What an absurd book!

Pringle (*indignantly*) Not at all Mrs Villiers. It happens to be one of the most authoritative guide books you can get. There's not a stone in Egypt it doesn't know about.

Margaret (*under her breath*) I bet!

Elizabeth But isn't it just a bit out of date, Mr Pringle? Surely servants and parasols went out years ago?

Pringle (*sadly*) Yes, I suppose so – more's the pity.

Elizabeth You resent the change?

Pringle It's not the same Egypt I first came to when I was a kid. There's no respect now. These people don't even trust us any more.

Elizabeth I would have thought that inevitable –

Villiers Well – I don't trust them I can tell you that. They're only out for what they can get...

Pringle You can say that again!

Elizabeth But you wear the Arab headdress, Mr Pringle. That shows you must still think something of these people?

Pringle Not at all Miss Warwick. You know, when in Rome and all that.

Margaret But we're not in Rome. (*wryly*) This is Egypt – the United Arab Republic. Things are going to be different now.

Pringle What about you Miss Warwick? Do you like the Arab?

Elizabeth I respect them, if that's what you mean?

Pringle Is that a fact? You do amaze me.

Elizabeth (*cool*) Really? In what way?

Pringle Well, I mean – after the way they treated your father...

Elizabeth I can assure you, Mr Pringle, if my father had been alive today, this is where he'd have been – right here on this boat with me. You see he loved the Arab – and Egypt. As far as he was concerned the Nile is a lot deeper than most of us like to think.

Pringle (*withholding amusement*) Well let's hope he was right, Miss Warwick.

Another toot from the boat's hooter

Villiers (*background, shouts out*) Here's your chance to find out! Welcome to the Valley of the Kings!

A sharp cut. Return to echo effect at Town Mortuary

Wilder A Christian? Fuad Yassif? Are you sure?

Mahmoud That is what it say in file Mr Wilder. Here. You may look for yourself.

Wilder (*takes file, looks*) The only son of a Muslim family who suddenly becomes a Christian. Why?

Mahmoud He work for many years with Europeans. Perhaps is natural?

Wilder He was very young. Only twenty-three.

Mahmoud Tragic.

Wilder There's no photograph.

Mahmoud Alas – no.

Wilder Then I don't see how you're going to find out if this man with Elizabeth Warwick is a fake or not.

Mahmoud (*smugly confident*) We shall find out.

Wilder (*irritated*) Do you mind telling me how?

Mahmoud Before we know about second Fuad Yassif – we must look to the first.

Pause

Wilder (*a little squeamish*) You mean – you'll exhume the body?

Mahmoud (*with a teasing delight*) You have not seen dead body before, Mr Wilder?

Wilder Usually I try not to see them – after they've been buried. (*pause*) Which graveyard?

Mahmoud The Roman Catholic Church here in Luxor.

Wilder I don't think they'll like that very much. Are you sure they'll give you permission?

Mahmoud I think we may rely on Captain Aziz to take care of this.

Wilder (*alarmed*) Captain Aziz? What's he got to do with all this?

Mahmoud Captain is in charge of Military Police. We work together very closely. Patricularly on matters of security.

Wilder Security? So now I suppose you think Elizabeth Warwick is some kind of spy?

Mahmoud We only wish to protect this lady.

Wilder I hope you do, Mahmoud, because I hold you entirely responsible for that girl's safety. If anything happens… (*pause*) Where is she now?

Mahmoud Her Fuad Yassif take her to the Valley of the Kings.

Wilder (*horrified*) Fuad…! You've let her go out there alone with that man – after what happened in the village of Hasia last night?

Mahmoud Do not be alarmed my friend.

Wilder Alarmed! (*angrily*) Are you out of your mind or something? She should have been warned about this man…

Mahmoud (*emphatic*) No! To catch the gander – we must watch the goose.

Wilder She could be killed!

Mahmoud (*assuringly*) Always we have watch the goose. From the first moment.

Pause

Wilder (*puzzled*) Are you telling me you've been following Elizabeth Warwick – ever since she arrived in Egypt?

Pause

Why Mahmoud? For Heaven's sake – why?

Mahmoud Because, my friend, although Sir Richard Warwick have many friends in Egypt, he also have – many enemies. (*walking around*) And not all of them rest here in Mortuary.

Sharp cut to the neighing of donkeys. At the donkey station for the Valley of the Kings

Fuad I am glad you have come Elizabeth. Welcome!

Elizabeth (*reticent*) Thank you. Which way do we go?

Fuad There is a road which leads to the western slope. Then we must start up to the Peak.

Elizabeth I've been told the tracks are rather primitive. Do we have a Guide?

Fuad There is no need for a Guide.

Elizabeth Why not?

Fuad You forget. Fuad Yassif is very familiar with the journey to Harshak. You trust him – don't you Elizabeth?

Elizabeth Do I have any choice?

Fuad Maybe.

Elizabeth Which is?

Fuad To go alone.

Elizabeth It's probably safer.

Fuad (*amused*) Probably.

Pause

Elizabeth How long will it take? It's getting very hot.

Fuad In one hour and a half we shall be at the Harshak Tomb.

Elizabeth Do we have a car?

Fuad No car. The road is too bad.

Elizabeth No car? Then how are we expected to… you mean we have to go all the way up that mountain… on one of these things?

Fuad But of course. What did you expect?

Neighing of donkeys. Gradually mix to nearby quayside effects. Passengers disembarking etc.

Villiers Achmed, are you sure about this? Absolutely sure?

Achmed (*very excitable*) Yes, Mr Villiers. Sure! Sure!

Villiers Where did you see this man?

Achmed The Cafe in Markaz Square. Two times I have seen – with my own eyes. Two times!

Margaret Charlie, it must be him! It's got to be!

Villiers Well, there's nothing we can do about it now. We'll have to wait 'til we get back this evening.

Margaret No Charlie – don't be a fool! We've got to go to that cafe *now*…

Villiers (*firmly*) We'll wait until this evening, I tell you. If we turn back now it'll look too suspicious. Achmed – go and get the car. We'll do some sightseeing in the Valley.

Achmed Yes! (*goes*)

Margaret (*sadly*) We're going to lose him. I know we're going to lose him…

Villiers (*sympathetically*) Maggie. Now listen to me. We've waited a long time for this chance, and we're not going to waste it just for the sake of a few hours. We're going to find that boy, I promise you. But we're not going to throw everything away we've been working on all these months.

Pause

Do you understand?

Margaret (*reluctantly*) Yes.

Villiers All right then. So let's just go out to the Valley and… (*stops suddenly*) That's odd.

Margaret What is it?

Villiers The girl. She's got someone with her. An Arab. They're going up to Harshak by donkey.

Margaret She said she was meeting a friend.

Villiers Yes. But look who's also following the track.

Margaret (*looking, surprised*) It's Pringle. Mr Pringle! But he said he wasn't going up to Harshak. I thought he was going into the Valley.

Villiers (*with caution*) Yes. So did I.

Cut to the exterior sound of a school bell being rung vigorously. We are in the Theban Village School of Harshak. Arabic children, arriving for lessons, are shouting, laughing in background

Mahmoud (*in background*) Ya awtad, rouh 'awam. Aizeen titakhartu fil-madvasah. (*Quick! You children will be late for school.*)

The teacher, Mr O'Hara, an Irishman, stops ringing his bell

O'Hara (*surprised*) Inspector Mahmoud. This is an unexpected pleasure. What brings you to Harshak so early in the day?

Mahmoud (*approaching*) Is long time since we meet, Mr O'Hara. But your school look better than always. (*looking at children*) Never have I seen so many children.

O'Hara They seem to come from all over the place.

Mahmoud It is good work you do in the village. Our Government should be grateful.

O'Hara The Government let me stay, Inspector. I'm the one that's grateful.

Pause

What can I do for you?

Mahmoud Did you know Miss Warwick have come to Luxor?

O'Hara Miss Who?

Mahmoud Daughter of Sir Richard.

O'Hara (*obviously shocked*) Elizabeth? Elizabeth Warwick – here?

Mahmoud Since last night.

O'Hara But I was a close friend of her father's. All that time we worked together up at the Harshak Tomb. She might at least have written to say she was comin'.

Mahmoud But you have never met this lady?

O'Hara No never. She was only a kid during the excavations. But Sir Richard used to show me some of her letters. They were very close you know.

Mahmoud She also had a brother, did she not? The one that was killed at Suez.

O'Hara Michael Warwick – oh yes. But there lies a very different tale. There was no love lost between father and son. The boy was a dirty word as far as the old man was concerned.

Pause

Mahmoud Mr O'Hara. Do you know why Miss Warwick should have come to Luxor?

O'Hara Presumably a holiday. Isn't that why most people come?

Mahmoud Then you have not heard of the man Fuad Yassif?

Pause

O'Hara (*cautiously*) Who?

Mahmoud Yassif. Fuad Yassif. It was he who have invite Miss Warwick to Luxor.

O'Hara (*dismissingly*) Is that a fact? Well I'm glad at least someone knew she was comin'.

Pause

No Inspector. I can't say I know the feller.

Pause

Mahmoud Mr O'Hara. For how many years now do you have the School here in Harshak?

O'Hara Oh you should know that Inspector. Must be all of fifteen years – if not more.

Mahmoud Fifteen years. Is long time – to teach peasant children to face the world with a better mind.

O'Hara You needn't worry about that Inspector. Most of these kids have a mind of their own. The only thing I have to offer them is a basic education.

Mahmoud But you must love them very much… after fifteen years?

O'Hara Yes. I suppose I must do. The little rogues.

Mahmoud And even after they have gone, you do not forget them?

O'Hara Forget? I bet you I remember the names of every one of the little devils.

Mahmoud (*impressed*) Really?

O'Hara Off by heart.

Mahmoud Very strange.

O'Hara What's so strange about it?

Mahmoud That you should not remember the name of the small boy – Fuad Yassif.

Pause

O'Hara (*puzzled*) Boy?

Mahmoud (*innocently*) Why yes. According to the file, he was a pupil for two years – here with you at the School in Harshak.

Fade up children playing. Mix in the plodding of donkeys' hoofs on the dusty tracks of the Theban hills. Elizabeth is clearly affected by the extreme heat, and buzzing of flies.

Elizabeth (*calls*) Fuad! (*no reply*) Fuad, please – not so fast!

The donkeys stop

This heat's killing me. I can hardly breathe.

Fuad (*a short distance away*) It is not good to stop for too long. The sun is very strong.

Pause

(*reluctantly*) One minute then.

A sigh of relief from Elizabeth as Fuad returns to join her. Donkey comes to a stop. Flies still buzzing fiercely

You had better drink some water.

Takes out water bottle

Elizabeth (*clearing throat*) It wouldn't be so bad if it wsn't for all this dust. And tehse flies have got teeth like pins. How much further do we have to go for goodness' sake?

Fuad First we must get to the other side of the Peak. Then we shall be at the Harshak Tomb in one half-hour.

Elizabeth (*relaxing*) It's such an odd feeling up here. To be able to look down on the Valley of the Kings – laid out like a giant graveyard.

Pause

What an incredible place it must have been in its time.

Fuad (*pouring water into cup*) Of course. It still is.

Elizabeth I wonder.

Fuad You don't approve of our new Egypt?

Elizabeth Everyone keeps telling me about the new Egypt. Personally I never found anything wrong with the old one. At least the Pharaohs built an Egypt that no one could ever forget.

Fuad Every country needs to progress. Even England knows that.

Elizabeth Progress? Yes – now there's a word that covers a multitude of sins. I seem to have heard that one before.

Fuad Here, drink some water. It will help to cool you down.

Elizabeth Thank you. (*takes cup, drinks*) Why should a Pharaoh build his tomb on the slopes of a mountain? Why not alongside all the others – in the Valley itself?

Fuad So you do believe Harshak is a Pharaoh's tomb?

Elizabeth (*guarded*) I believe as much as anybody wants me to believe. Or as little. Just like those ants down there.

Fuad Tourists? (*dismissingly*) They come to look with the eyes – not with the heart.

Elizabeth And yet they don't seem to come up here.

Pause

Perhaps it's too dangerous – even for the ants.

Fuad (*recitatively*) "Beware the Goddess of the Western Peak. She strikes instantly, and without warning."

Elizabeth What's that?

Fuad An ancient text.

Elizabeth What does it mean?

Fuad That danger is always with us.

Pause

Elizabeth Is that what *you* believe?

Fuad I am an Arab. I have to be prepared to face danger at all times. Even death.

Pause

Are you afraid to meet death, Elizabeth?

Elizabeth (*close to irritation*) How extraordinary. You know you're the second person to ask me that since I arrived. What is this obsession the Arab has for death.

Fuad For the Arab, death is no disgrace. Like the Pharaohs, it is an ambition we work towards – from the day we are born.

Elizabeth Well that's fine, as long as you don't forget that, with a bit of luck – there's an awful long time in between.

Fuad (*with faint amusement*) Perhaps

Pause

Shall we go?

Elizabeth (*finishes water*) Right!

Fuad (*digging donkey*) Ruh! Ruh!

A loud neigh from the donkey as the animal jumps with a start. Elizabeth shouts out in a panic

Elizabeth Fuad! The donkey!

The donkey scuffling, neighing

Fu… ad!

Fuad (*calm, without anxiety*) If you keep still Elizabeth, the animal will not move.

Elizabeth Don't be a fool man! He's standing right on the edge… d'you want me to go over the top? Get him away…!

The donkey calms down, and there is now complete silence

(*a tense calm*) Did you hear what I said? Get him away from this edge.

Pause

I am not afraid, Fuad. I am not afraid.

Fuad Perfectly still…

Pause

Elizabeth You wanted this didn't you? That's why you dismissed the donkey boy. You wanted this…

Fuad (*stifled anger*) Still!

Pause

Now. Give me your hand.

Elizabeth I tell you he'll back over the top…

Fuad (*quietly insistent*) Give me your hand.

Pause. She is stretching out her hand

Now. Very slowly… get down from the saddle… no – take your time…

At last she gets down. A sigh of relief from Elizabeth as the donkey snorts indignantly

(*cynically*) I'm sorry Elizabeth. I hadn't realised you trust me so little.

Elizabeth Not at all Fuad. I trust you – just as long as you don't try something like that on me again… ever.

Another loud snort from the donkey. Fade up the sound of flies buzzing, and gradually mix in the sound of the whirr of an 8mm cine camera

In the background, a car approaches along the dusty tracks, and pulls to a halt. Villiers calls from the car to the photographer, Bertie Pringle

Villiers Mr Pringle! Hey – Mr Pringle! Can we give you a lift?

Pringle stops filming, joins the Villiers

Pringle (*surprised*) Oh – Mr Villiers, it's you. What're you doin' up this far?

Villiers Isn't it a bit hot standing up here taking pictures all on your own?

Pringle Oh no – I love it. You get a marvellous panoramic view of the whole Valley from up here – 'specially on this Japanese job of mine. It's got a terrific zoom lens.

Margaret Can't we give you a lift?

Pringle No thanks all the same Mrs Villiers. I much prefer it this way. I get car sick in the heat.

Margaret Well, rather you than me…

Villiers But you're not going up to Harshak.

Pringle That old dump? No, I don't think so. Getting half way up the Theban Peak is quite enough for me for one day. I'll probably end up in the Rest House with a glass of local beer and a siesta.

Villiers Right. See you back at the hotel tonight then?

Car starts up again

Pringle Okey-doke! Cheers!

The car drives away. We stay with the Villiers inside the car

Villiers (*calls*) Goodbye!

Margaret (*calls*) Bye!

Car driving along

Is he going up there d'you think?

Villiers Of course. Where else?

Margaret I told you we should have got up there before the girl. There's going to be trouble. I know it. (*to Achmed*) Achmed. Are you sure there isn't another road we can branch off on?

Achmed (*driving*) No lady. Tracks not good – too little room.

Margaret Charlie, I don't like this. (*feeling heat*) Oh damn this place! What I couldn't do for a drink…

Villiers (*looking over shoulder*) Hallo. That's odd.

Margaret What?

Villiers Achmed. Stop the car.

Car draws to a halt again

Margaret What is it?

Pause. Silence but for flies buzzing

Villiers Yes, I thought so. He's gone.

Margaret What are you talking about? Who's gone?

Villiers Pringle. He's left the road. I can't even see him any more.

A quick fade, slight pause, and then the whirr of an overhead electric cooling fan. We are in Wilder's office at the British Consulate

Wilder (*cool and official*) No Captain Aziz. I'm sorry, but if you want that type of information you'll have to apply through the normal diplomatic channels. We're only a Consulate you know.

Aziz (*impatient, brusque*) Mr Wilder. I am neither a diplomat nor a police officer. As a soldier you have my word that all information I receive will be treated with the utmost secrecy.

Wilder Miss Warwick is already under close police observation. I really can't see what the military…

Aziz The military is not interested in the petty criminal, Mr Wilder. Only in state security.

Wilder State sec…!

Pause. He laughs

Oh no Captain – even you!

Aziz (*restraining anger*) It amuses you?

Wilder Well what are you trying to tell me? That she's some kind of female James Bond or something?

Aziz Political subversion by the foreigner does not come new to the Arab. We have learnt to live with the infiltrator – until the time comes to expose him.

Wilder Subversion? Now look here old chap. Miss Warwick happens to be here on a tourist visa issued by your Embassy in London.

Aziz Her movements have not been those of a tourist. Last night she was in the village of Hasia.

Wilder Well? What's so wrong about that?

Aziz A dervish village – also well-known for its political bias. Miss Warwick was ill-advised to go there.

Wilder I'm sure she'd be the first to agree with you.

Aziz You forget her father was deported by the Government of my country.

Wilder Yes. So were a lot of other European archaeologists…

Aziz Her brother, an officer in the British Army – killed fighting the Arab…

Wilder Plenty of people lost their lives at Suez…

Aziz (*angrily*) Mr Wilder! Revenge is good enough reason for the spreading of subversive propaganda.

Wilder (*calm, dismissingly*) Oh really Captain. What's wrong with you chaps? You seem to be scared of your own shadows these days.

Aziz We have good reason to be. The outside world has much to gain from our inexperience.

Wilder You're going on as though this girl came here to blow up the Aswan Dam or something. I think you're forgetting she's a guest in your country – not an enemy.

Aziz Everyone is a potential enemy until proved otherwise.

Wilder (*sighs*) Yes. I suppose that's why nobody seems to understand each other any more.

Aziz gets up. Moves to door

Aziz Until Miss Warwick is able to do this, I am afraid I must hold you entirely responsible for her conduct.

Opens door, stops

You see, Mr Wilder, when I was at University in England, every person was fascinated in ancient Egypt – the old way of life. But for we who have to live and work here, life has to be something more than just old stones and temples. One day, Egypt is going to be known as something more than just the land of the Pharaohs. Things are going to change – because they have to.

Fade out

The huge iron doors of the Harshak Tomb are pushed open with a thump. Immediately we hear the screeching and fluttering of bats echoing throughout the passages. Fuad leads Elizabeth into the tomb

Elizabeth Good lord! What's that?

Fuad Only the tomb bats. They won't harm you.

Elizabeth The air smells foul in there. Doesn't look as though anyone's been here for years.

Fuad There is nothing here to interest the tourist. (*looking around*) Now somewhere around there should be an oil lamp… ah!

He finds the lamp

Now – matches.

Finds matches, strikes one and lights the lamp

Elizabeth (*looking around, wanders*) What a place!

Pause

It's so different – not a bit how I'd imagined.

Fuad Different?

Elizabeth It's much smaller. (*looking up*) And the ceiling. It's set very low. I always thought Pharaonic tombs were much more spacious.

She has wandered off

Everything's so bare. Not one single wall decoration.

Fuad (*calls*) Elizabeth! Don't go too far. It may not be safe. Try and keep close to me.

Elizabeth (*coming back*) You don't have to worry, Fuad. I'm not superstitious about a tomb.

Fuad It was not the tomb I was thinking about. Only the inhabitants.

Elizabeth (*puzzled*) Inhabitants?

Fuad The cobra. (*smilingly*) Shall we go?

A sharp cut. Pause

Flies buzzing. A track above the Theban Hills

Margaret (*exhausted by heat, low voice*) Can you see anything?

Villiers He's talking to three men. One of them looks like a European.

Margaret Who are they – can you see?

Villiers No. The sun's too strong. I can't see a thing. (*to Achmed*) Achmed. D'you know any of them?

Achmed I think one man come from the donkey station at quayside…

Margaret (*suddenly swats a fly angrily*) Damn the flies!

Villiers (*trying to quieten her*) Get down will you Margaret! D'you want Pringle to see us?

Margaret I tell you I'm bitten all over. I'm sick to death of stewing in this heat. Why can't we go back to the car?

Villiers (*to Achmed*) Achmed. How much further do we have to go?

Achmed Very soon now mister! Very soon!

Villiers (*to Margaret*) You see!

Margaret (*disregardingly*) I don't care. I can't stand this any longer. (*gets up, voice raised*) I must have a drink…

Villiers (*angrily*) Will you sit down and shut up!

Achmed (*excitedly*) Mr Villiers! Quick! They look at something.

Villiers What?

Achmed Do you see? Up there?

Villiers Give me the binoculars. (*looking*) Yes…

Margaret Are they looking at us?

Villiers (*casually*) No, I don't think so. They seem to be looking up at the Harshak Tomb.

Sharp cut. Pause

O'Hara is walking with Inspector Mahmoud to his car. Gravel path

O'Hara Fuad Yassif. Well, if there was such a boy working in Sir Richard's party, I certainly never knew him. And as far as being a pupil at this school, you're more than welcome to check my school lists Inspector.

Mahmoud But you do agree, there were children working for Sir Richard? Arab children.

O'Hara Of course. The place was swarming with them nearly all the time. But they were just hangers-on as far as I remember.

Mahmoud Mr O'Hara. Last night I was at the Department of Antiquities. Professor Fawzad insists that the tomb at Harshak is of no importance.

O'Hara He's probably right.

Mahmoud But Sir Richard –

O'Hara Sir Richard was a determined and patient man. He worked for years on the theory that other Pharaonic tombs would be found outside the Valley of the Kings. That much he was right.

They stop walking

Mahmoud But Harshak is an empty shell.

O'Hara That no one cares about.

Mahmoud Except Miss Warwick.

O'Hara Miss Warwick?

Mahmoud I think maybe soon she will go there. Today perhaps.

O'Hara She's going all the way up to that tomb – alone?

Mahmoud Not alone. She has friend. Fuad Yassif.

He opens car door. Gets in

O'Hara Yassif? But I thought you said he was dead – killed in a car crash?

Mahmoud Maybe he is, my friend. Maybe he is.

Driver starts up engine

But tomorrow we will find out – when we open the coffin of Fuad Yassif in the graveyard at Luxor.

The car pulls away. Mahmoud calls back

Until soon, my friend! Goodbye!

As the car drives off at great speed, we mix the sound of the fading police siren with footsteps echoing along the gravel passages of the Harshak Tomb. The footsteps come to a halt. The voices of Elizabeth and Fuad echo in the main hall

Elizabeth (*in background, calls*) Over here Fuad. I want to have a look at this wall.

Fuad moves towards her

Could you hold the lamp a little higher please. (*pause*) Yes, you see. My father was right. There were hieroglyphics here, but they've obviously been scratched out. I wonder why?

Fuad Tomb robbers. There must have been many over the centuries. It was quite common.

Elizabeth Yes, I know. But why break into a place like this? There were never any treasures. They must have known it wouldn't be worth the time and effort.

Fuad Perhaps.

Elizabeth wanders around

Elizabeth I suppose this was intended to be some kind of main hall. At least the ceiling isn't so low in here. (*making a discovery*) Ah! This must be the south wall.

Fuad You seem to know it?

Elizabeth I remember it from my father's diagrams.

Fuad But no photographs?

Elizabeth (*disturbed*) He never allowed photographs to be taken down here. You must have known that?

Fuad (*unmoved*) Yes. Of course.

She walks across to tap the wall

Elizabeth Yes. Well there's nothing on the other side of that except stone and sand. (*sighs*) It's really quite a barn of a place, isn't it? Though I must say it does have quite an extraordinary atmosphere. Its own special kind of peace.

Fuad No. There was never peace here.

Elizabeth (*walking back to rejoin him*) I don't follow you? What do you mean?

Fuad When they broke into nearly all the other tombs in the Valley, everything was still and quiet. As though one was peering into Eternity itself.

Pause

But not here.

Elizabeth Why?

Fuad strolls around the hall. He is reliving an important moment in his life

Fuad During the excavations, we worked for months digging in the sand and rock outside. Nobody knew why. We just followed your father – because something told us we had to.

Pause

He was like a child. Not for one minute did he ever stop to think that what he was looking for just did not exist. But he was determined. When we slept, he worked on – sometimes through the night by the light of a candle. He had such dedication and faith.

Pause

One day, the heat outside was unbearable. Everyone stopped what they were doing and went to sleep in their tents. But not Sir Richard. With just a handkerchief to cover his head, he sipped mint tea, staring down at the sand, as if it would suddenly come to life.

Pause

And of course – it did. (*slowly, descriptively*) His eyes suddenly focused on a few particles of sand which began to move. Almost hypnotised, he watched the head and eyes of a cobra – staring at him over the top of the sand. His blood was cold, and he couldn't move until the serpent had emerged and slithered away. (*pause. Recovering voice control*) Your father had found the entrance to the tomb.

Elizabeth The red cobra. Yes. He talks a lot about that in his diary. How he tore away at the sand with his bare hands, helpless until someone heard him shouting out. (*pause*) But you sound as though you were sorry he found the tomb?

Fuad To me it was the first step towards death.

Elizabeth You're superstitious? It seems unlike you.

Fuad There's something restless here. That's all I know.

Elizabeth (*crossing the hall again*) You could say that about all the tombs in the Valley from what I've heard. (*pause*) But I will admit – this one is rather special. I don't know why.

Pause

Fuad (*on mic*) Elizabeth.

Elizabeth Mm?

Fuad What did your father tell you about this tomb?

Elizabeth (*cautiously*) As much as he told you, I imagine.

Fuad It is Pharaonic, isn't it?

Elizabeth You know, there's no doubt about it, this tomb is cut diagonally into the hill. I thought that as we made the approach…

Fuad Where is the King's Chamber?

Elizabeth King's Chamber? Is there one?

Fuad I've told you not to play games with me! Now tell me. You promised! Your father promised! (*pause. A hushed anger*) Elizabeth! I want to know!

Elizabeth (*ignoring him*) Hallo. What's this mark on the wall? (*inspecting it in background*) It looks as though it could have been a cartouche or something…

yes – d'you see? The double-headed cobra… quick Fuad! Bring the lamp over here… (*no reply from Fuad*) Fuad! Did you hear what I…

On mic, Fuad blows out the oil lamp. This startles Elizabeth

Fuad! What the hell d'you think you're doing?

No reply

You don't scare me you know.

She is feeling her way back on mic

I can hear you moving around in the dark.

Pause

Don't think I'm going to tell you anything until you light that lamp again. (*no reply. Shouts angrily*) Fuad! Did you hear what I said…!

Quiet unexpected, she is shocked to hear the iron doors of the tomb slamming in the extreme background. Again she shouts out

Fuad! No…! Please… don't leave me…!

She suddenly stops dead as her foot touches something on the ground. Her voice is hushed, almost strangulated

Fuad! There's… something here… it's touching my foot… there's something crawling along the floor… (*a strangulated scream*) Fuad… FUAD…!

The scream is cut by the shrill call of the muezzin, over which we read our closing announcements

END OF EPISODE TWO

Kill the Pharaoh!

by Victor Pemberton

Episode 3: Strangers in a Cafe

Produced by John Tydeman

REHEARSALS:	Friday 18 August 1967	1030–1730
RECORD:	Friday 18 August 1967	1730–1830
STUDIO:	B.10	
R.P. No.	TLN33/DA849H	

CAST:	Elizabeth ....Sheila Grant	
	Mahmoud...................................James Thomason	
	Mr Wilder ....John Humphry	
	Fuad ....David Spenser	
	Charles.....................................Rolf Lefebvre	
	Margaret....................................Marion Mathie	
	Achmed.....................................Haydn Jones	
	Abdullah (man attacking Elizabeth)	
	....Antony Viccars	
	Bertie ....Barry Lowe	
	O'Hara ....Denis McCarthy	
	Captain Aziz ....John Justin	
	Michael (stranger).....................Christopher Bidmead	
S.M.s:	Panel: Amna Smith; Grams: Keith Salmon; Spot: Enyd Williams	
SECRETARY:	Judy Munk	

The call of the muezzin is mixed into the high-pitched screeching of the bats in the Harshak Tomb. Elizabeth Warwick, who is alone in the dark where Fuad Yassif had left her, tries to shield herself from the fluttering wings of the bats all around her

Elizabeth (*shouts with tremendous effort*) Get away! Get away! (*louder*) Is anyone there? Please! Somebody help me!

Without warning the bats flutter off to the background as we hear footsteps running in to approach. They stop. Now there is silence but for the heavy but disturbed breathing of Elizabeth

Who's there? (*no reply*) Fuad? Fuad, is that you? (*still no reply*) If you think you're going to scare me, it won't work. (*no reply*) Did you hear what I…

She jumps with a start as somebody strikes a match

Oh – it's you!

Villiers (*with concern*) Miss Warwick. What are you doing down here in the tomb – all alone?

Elizabeth (*with relief*) That's a very good question, Mr Villiers. I might ask you the same.

Villiers Maggie and I heard you shouting as we were going past the entrance. Scared the life out of us. We weren't going to come in.

Elizabeth Mr Villiers. Would you mind looking around the floor? I'm sure my foot kicked something.

Villiers Yes, of course. Just let me light another match.

He takes out and lights another match

(*looking around*) You have to be very careful in these tombs you know. They're full of scorpions and snakes and goodness knows what.

Elizabeth So I've been told. Can you see anything?

Villiers Not a thing. Unless you mean this?

Elizabeth (*cautiously*) What is it?

Villiers A piece of rope. (*coming back*) Just an old piece of rope. I don't somehow think that'd do you much harm, Miss Warwick. Do you?

Elizabeth (*laughing, relieved*) No, Mr Villiers. Somehow I don't think it would.

Her laughter echoes through the tunnels of the tomb. Mix to the sound of digging in the graveyard of the Roman Catholic Church in Luxor

Mahmoud (*calls*) Tigi hina bi sur'a! (*Be as quick as you can please!*)

A few garbled mutters from the gravediggers

Wilder (*reflectively*) "How long will a man rest i'the earth ere he rest?"

Mahmoud Ah! A wise man was your Mr Shakespeare. You know, sometimes I think maybe he was really an Arab.

Wilder I can assure you, Mahmoud, this little circus of yours is not very popular with the Priest over there. Exhuming a body from consecrated ground.

Mahmoud Let us consider for a moment. For why does this young man – whoever he is – wish to bring Miss Warwick to Luxor? Is he really a friend of Sir Richard?

Wilder Well, he'd have to be, wouldn't he?

Mahmoud You think so?

Wilder Naturally.

Mahmoud Why?

Wilder He'd hardly have got her to come out here all the way from England unless he was. The expense alone.

Mahmoud I think Miss Warwick is not without money, my friend.

Wilder Yes, but even so –

Mahmoud No. Maybe Luxor have more to offer this lady than we think.

Pause. Digging continues

Wilder Of course you know what baffles me about all this. The fact that nobody seems to care about the danger this girl has been in. You told me yourself about that drunk who tried to attack her on the train down from Cairo. (*pause*) I tell you it all adds up. Somebody's trying to get at her.

Mahmoud Let me assure you, my friend. Whilst she us in Luxor she will receive our full protection.

Captain Aziz approaches

Ah! Captain Aziz. What news?

Aziz Al gama'a biyoul inn… (*My men have just reported…*)

Mahmoud Er – Captain. I think is better to speak in English.

Pause

Aziz (*holding back resentment*) The English woman.

Mahmoud } (*eagerly*) Yes?

Wilder } What's happened?

Aziz She and her friend went to the Harshak Tomb.

Mahmoud Ah! So it *was* the first place…

Aziz One of my men followed them. He is now dead.

Wilder What!

Mahmoud How did this happen, Captain?

Aziz They used the old donkey tracks to reach the Peak. My man lay at the foot of some rocks. His throat has been cut.

Wilder How terrible!

Mahmoud The donkey tracks. I wonder why not the new road to Harshak? It is so much quicker.

Wilder Which means they must now be inside that tomb. The two of them – alone together. (*panicking*) We've got to get them out of there.

Mahmoud No!

Wilder Don't be a fool man! If this man with her is Fuad Yassif, it's obvious he's trying to threaten her.

Mahmoud At the moment, we do not know that he is Fuad Yassif.

Wilder Then for Heaven's sake – when are we going to know?

A loud triumphant shout from the gravediggers as one of their shovels hits the top of the coffin

Mahmoud They have reach the coffin! *Now*, Mr Wilder! *Now* we shall know who lies in the coffin of Fuad Yassif!

A sharp cut to the buzzing of flies outside the entrance to the Harshak Tomb. Villiers helps Elizabeth up the steps, where Margaret Villiers is waiting for them

Villiers Now… mind how you go my dear. That's right. Give me your hand.

Elizabeth (*inhales deeply*) Thank goodness for the fresh air.

Margaret You poor thing. What a dreadful thing to be locked down there in the dark.

Elizabeth It's my own fault, Mrs Villiers. I should have taken a torch with me. The hurricane lamp must have blown out.

Villiers Well, that's odd. There was no hurricane lamp down there.

Elizabeth Oh, I'm sure there was, Mr Villiers. Probably you didn't notice it.

Villiers I could have sworn –

Elizabeth Tell me something. I didn't notice you two were coming up the Harshak. You told me you were spending the day in the Valley.

Margaret (*awkwardly*) Well, yes –

Villiers (*interrupting quickly*) We decided to change our mind.

Elizabeth Why?

Villiers Well –

Margaret It's those binoculars you see.

Elizabeth Binoculars?

Margaret He's like a child with them. We bought them in Port Said on the way down.

Villiers Much better than a camera. You can see everything. They're German.

Margaret That's why we came up this far. It's such a marvellous view. As a matter of fact we watched you go into the tomb – from right the way down there – oh, past those rocks.

Elizabeth (*rather cool*) Really?

Villiers You – and your friend. By the way, what happened to him?

Elizabeth Happened?

Villiers We saw him go in – but he didn't come out again.

Elizabeth You didn't – ? (*casually*) Are you sure?

Villiers Positive.

Elizabeth How long were you out here?

Margaret All the time. I mean, we couldn't have missed him – could we?

A sharp cut to the squeaking sound of the coffin lid being prised open in the graveyard in Luxor

Mahmoud and Wilder are crouched on the edge of the grave, their voices lowered

Mahmoud (*enjoying the macabre*) You do not enjoy to look on the face of a dead man, Mr Wilder?

Wilder Not when it's been lying in a grave for a month. It's probably half-decomposed by now. I wish they'd hurry up…

The creaking lid begins to move

Mahmoud Ah! The lid is beginning to move!

After a struggle, the lid opens with a thud

Now…!

A gasp from the group around the grave

Wilder Good Lord! It's empty!

Mahmoud So! The cat has run away!

General excitement continues in background

Wilder But why? Don't they check the coffins around here before burial?

Mahmoud We shall see what the Priest has to say. (*calls*) Tigi hina bi abouna O'Hara! (*Boy! Get the Priest for me!*)

Wilder So the man with Elizabeth Warwick probably is the real Fuad Yassif?

Mahmoud We shall see.

Aziz Inspector Mahmoud. I am going to place these two people under arrest. The English woman – and the man with her.

Wilder Arrest?

Mahmoud No, Captain. I think not.

Aziz The decisions are no longer yours to take…

Mahmoud And you will not interfere in a police investigation, Captain.

Aziz (*angrily*) One of my men has been killed. Murdered! These people must be punished!

Wilder You can't arrest a British subject.

Both men ignore Wilder

Mahmoud What I think you do not fully understand, Captain, is the reason *why* your man has been killed. *Why* we find it necessary to have these two people followed.

Aziz They are potential enemies of the state. This is now a military…

A tense pause

The woman is a foreigner.

Wilder She's nothing of the sort! She has a British passport.

Aziz I am warning you, Inspector. If you allow these people to get away, Cairo will hear about this. (*as he leaves, he calls back*) Hasib! (*I'm warning you!*)

Wilder Mahmoud. Will you listen to me? You've got to tell that girl about the man with her. She has a right to know.

Mahmoud All in good time, my friend. All in good time. First, we must wait.

Wilder Wait! By that time she could have her throat slit. (*pause. Tries to be more calm*) Why? Why must we wait?

Mahmoud Because, my friend, I think our Miss Warwick she is good bait.

Wilder Bait? What on earth are you talking about?

Mahmoud Come now, Mr Wilder. Even in England you must know. Always to catch the fish – one must have good bait.

A sharp cut to the sound of a cooing hoopoe bird, a local species. A waiter is serving tea to hotel guests on the front verandah as Elizabeth returns from Harshak

O'Hara They're beautiful creatures, aren't they?

Elizabeth (*stops, surprised*) Oh – er – yes.

O'Hara They're called the hoopoe bird. Actually they're quite common in this part of Egypt. You find them right the way down the Nile – even in Aswan. Silly little things, especially that long beak… no, don't go. Won't you stay and have a drink with me?

Elizabeth It's very kind of you, but –

O'Hara Don't be surprised, Elizabeth. They told me you were staying at this hotel. I've been waiting for you.

Elizabeth I'm sorry. I don't seem to know…

O'Hara James O'Hara. I'm an old friend of your father. We worked together up at Harshak.

Elizabeth Mr O'Hara. I'm terribly sorry. You must think me… of course I'd love to have a drink with you.

O'Hara Ah! Well done! Sit down my dear. You know it really is rather remarkable. You've got the same eyes… oh yes…

Elizabeth It's funny. I know I must know you, but I can't remember my father ever writing…

O'Hara Well, I know you my dear. Every expression, every little nod of the head. He loved you very much, you know. He used to read us all your letters.

The waiter approaches

Waiter Sir?

O'Hara What'll it be, my dear?

Elizabeth Just a cup of tea, please.

O'Hara (*laughs*) Ah! Home from home, huh? (*to waiter*) Fingatain shai mih fadlak. (*Two cups of tea, please.*)

Elizabeth You speak Arabic?

O'Hara You can't live in a country for fifteen years without speaking the language. They only let me stay on because I run a school up at Harshak.

Elizabeth Things must have changed a lot?

O'Hara Well, they'd have to, wouldn't they? Most new countries do.

Elizabeth Do you never want to go back home?

O'Hara Home is where you hang your hat, isn't it? No. I suppose this is as near to a home as I'll ever get. (*pause*) Mind you, it's a pity you have to get rid of the old before you can build the new. Egypt's a bit like that. (*pause*) But their biggest mistake was gettin' rid of folk like your father. (*lowers voice*) They could do with him around the place today, I'm tellin' you.

He has completely won Elizabeth's trust and confidence

Elizabeth Oh, Mr O'Hara. I only wish I could tell you what it means to me to find someone like you down here. Someone I can trust – a real friend of my father… at last!

O'Hara You're a nice girl, Elizabeth. A very nice girl.

Slow fade out on the hoopoe bird

Pause. An Arab bazaar in Markaz Square, Luxor. This is a busy thoroughfare, street traders, excitable chatter etc. In extreme background, prayer chanting from the nearby Mosque

Villiers Achmed! Achmed… wait a minute! (*approaches*) Are you sure this is the right place? Markaz Square?

Achmed Sure, mister, sure! This is where Achmed see the man. Sure!

Margaret Which cafe is it?

Achmed Over there, lady. The one on the corner… where the big man smoke the hashish…

Margaret There! That filthy place!

Achmed No lady, beautiful… beautiful!

Villiers I don't like the look of it. Too many people. They seem to be coming out of the Mosque on the other side.

Margaret Achmed. Now listen to me. This man you saw. He *was* English?

Achmed (*emphatically*) English! English!

Margaret But what did he look like?

Achmed No very big –

Margaret Yes?

Achmed But more big than Achmed.

Margaret His eyes? What about his eyes?

Achmed (*trying to think*) Brown eyes… little eyes – like you, lady.

Margaret Charlie, I tell you it is him! It must be.

Pause

Villiers They're all getting pretty het up at something on television. I don't know whether we ought to… (*pause*) All right, Achmed. Take us across there.

Achmed (*change in tone*) No! Achmed stay here.

Villiers What do you mean, no? You promised.

Achmed Achmed promise only to bring you to Square. Know too many people.

Villiers What difference does that make?

Achmed No want to have trouble. Maybe someone try to kill Achmed. Bad for business.

Pause

Villiers (*irritated*) All right. We'll go alone. Do they speak English? (*no reply*) Achmed, I said, do they speak…

Margaret You're too late. He's gone.

Bring up Arab street effects, hold for a moment then gradually mix in the voice of a BBC cricket commentator broadcasting a county match on short wave transmission. Knock on the door of Elizabeth's hotel bedroom

Elizabeth Come in! (*door opens. Surprised*) Mr Wilder.

Wilder (*approaching*) I'm sorry to trouble you, Miss Warwick – I wonder if I could have a few words with you?

Elizabeth Of course. Come in. (*Wilder closes door*) Does this worry you?

Wilder Not at all.

Elizabeth turns down the radio

Is that coming from London?

Elizabeth Yes. It's a County Match. I'd have missed it if Mr Villiers hadn't lent me his transistor.

Wilder I had no idea women liked cricket.

Elizabeth Why shouldn't they?

Pause

Wilder No reason. (*pause*) Miss Warwick. I really came to give you a few words of warning.

Elizabeth Oh? So this is an official visit?

Wilder It depends.

Elizabeth On what?

Pause

Wilder You've been out to the Harshak Tomb today, is that right?

Elizabeth Yes.

Wilder Why?

Elizabeth I would have thought it perfectly obvious. I suppose you could call it a sort of pilgrimage.

Wilder And that's all?

Elizabeth Mr Wilder. I do rather get the impression that I'm sitting in the hot seat. Am I supposed to have done something wrong?

Wilder The man who went with you. Who was he?

Elizabeth I told you at the Police Station last night. His name's Fuad Yassif, and he's a friend of my father.

Wilder You've checked on that, have you?

Elizabeth Look. He invited me here…

Wilder Why did you use the donkey tracks to get to the tomb.

Elizabeth Because I imagine it's the only way.

Wilder It isn't. (*pause*) There's a new main road.

Pause

Elizabeth Oh – really? Well, it seems you know exactly what I've been doing today…

Wilder What happened up at the tomb?

Elizabeth Happened? I looked around. Why, is that against the law?

Wilder A man was killed up there today. They found his body on the rocks just below the tomb. (*pause*) Did you happen to know that by any chance?

Pause

Elizabeth No. As a matter of fact – I didn't. I was locked in the tomb for nearly an hour and couldn't find my way out.

Wilder Locked?

Elizabeth Fuad had to leave before me. I stayed behind for a bit and the hurricane lamp blew out. It's as simple as that.

Wilder (*not believing a word*) Oh really?

Elizabeth Mr Wilder! I didn't come all the way to Egypt to be treated like a first-year schoolgirl!

Wilder (*unmoved*) Whilst you are here you are the direct responsibility of the Consulate. The sooner you realise that the better. It's our duty to protect you.

Elizabeth How many more times do I have to tell you people that I don't need protection.

Wilder (*now irritated*) This is an Arab state, Miss Warwick…not Lords' cricket ground. Here an English woman no longer receives special privileges.

An indignant snort from Elizabeth

Here, every move, every turn you make – is watched. (*pause*) I don't know why you came to Egypt, but whatever the reasons are – I implore you to be careful. Don't provoke these people. They're just waiting for a chance to pounce on you.

Pause

Elizabeth Is that all, Mr Wilder?

Wilder (*a little hurt*) Yes.

Elizabeth Then if you'll excuse me, I'd like to shower before dinner.

Wilder Of course. (*goes to the door, opens it*) Miss Warwick. Will you do something for me?

Elizabeth Yes?

Wilder If there's something you feel you want to tell me – something I ought to know – will you promise to come to the Consulate?

Elizabeth (*like the obedient schoolgirl*) Yes, Mr Wilder. Of course.

Wilder Goodbye.

Elizabeth Goodbye.

Wilder leaves. Door shuts

Angrily she turns the radio up almost to full blast. For a brief moment we listen to the slow drawl of the cricket commentary. Mix gradually to Arab political speakers on a TV set in the background of the Arab cafe in Markaz Square

Margaret (*voice hushed, nervously*) Charlie. How much longer are we going to sit here? I'm scared.

Villiers Just keep your voice down. They're more interested in their television set than me. Drink your tea and don't take any notice.

Loud cheer from the cafe crowd in response to a remark from the TV speaker

Margaret What's it all about? What's he saying?

Villiers I don't know. Probably political. We'll give it another five minutes. If this bloke doesn't turn up by… Good Lord!

Margaret What?

Villiers Look who's just come in.

Pringle approaches

Pringle Mr and Mrs Villiers! Well – this is a surprise! I haven't seen you in this cafe before. How'd you find it?

Villiers We were shopping in Markaz Square. You know the place well do you?

Pringle Oh yes. I'm quite a regular here. I like to get off the tourist tracks whenever I can. All that red plush and travellers' cheques. No. You get the real atmosphere in a place like this. (*pause*) Mind if I join you?

Villiers Not at all.

Another cheer, wild applause from the crowd

Have you any idea what this is all about?

Pringle Oh, you know. Bit of old propaganda. It's like that on the telly most nights here. It's either that or a belly dancer – and you can bet your life what this lot prefer. And me!

Margaret (*anxiously*) Mr Pringle. You say you spend quite a lot of time in here?

Pringle That's right, Mrs Villiers.

Margaret Have you – do you ever notice any other tourists?

Pringle Well – no. I can't say I do. As I told you, that's the main reason I come in here. I mean I can't somehow see tourists sittin' down to a plate of sheep's eyeballs – can you?

Margaret Mr Pringle. Are you sure you wouldn't remember a man – a young man?

Villiers (*shutting her up*) Maggie!

Margaret Not very young – but good-looking. He'd be about thirty…

Pringle (*confused*) I'm sorry. I'm not sure what you…

Villiers It's all right, Mr Pringle. Don't worry…

Margaret (*suddenly bursting out*) What do you mean don't worry! Don't you care? Don't you care whether we find him or not?

Villiers Will you shut up!

Margaret No! I will not shut up! Not any longer! Mr Pringle. Please. If you remember… you might just… remember…

Villiers The whole cafe is watching you.

Margaret (*to Pringle, desperately*) If you do…

Pause

Pringle (*covered with confusion*) I'm sorry, Mrs Villiers. I've never seen any tourists in here.

Margaret begins to sob

Margaret Oh… damn! (*She dashes off*) Damn!

Villiers (*calling after her*) Maggie! Come back!

Pringle (*embarrassed*) Mr Villiers… is there anything – er…

Villiers It's all right, Mr Pringle. I'm sorry about this… really sorry… She's just a bit tired… If you'll excuse me, I'd better run after her… (*going*) See you back at the hotel… Goodbye!

Pringle Goodb… (*calls*) Hey! Mr Villiers! Aren't you gonna stop to see the belly dancer?

Loud round of applause into which we bring up the Arab TV speaker. Hold, but fade out background cafe effects

In his antique shop, Mahmoud is also watching the same telecast. The bell above the front door rings, as Wilder enters

Mahmoud Ah! Mr Wilder. Welcome to my shop, welcome!

He turns off the TV set

Wilder (*approaching*) Oh please, don't let me disturb you.

Mahmoud Not important. I have seen this man many times before. Always it is the same speech. (*pause*) So! What is the news of Miss Warwick?

Wilder She's back at the hotel.

Mahmoud Excellent! Excellent! You see. You have not to worry.

Wilder Something happened up at that tomb. I just wish I knew what. Anyhow, you wanted to see me?

Mahmoud Yes. (*pause*) Mr Wilder. Do you know of the name – Villiers?

Wilder Villiers? (*thinking*) Yes. Aren't they staying at the same hotel as Miss Warwick?

Mahmoud Room number twenty-six I think. They are British subjects.

Wilder British? That's odd. I don't think I've met them.

Mahmoud And at the Consulate? Perhaps you know of them?

Wilder Well if we do, I'm sure they're not on the list. Why?

Mahmoud Today they were at the Harshak Tomb.

Wilder Really? Do you think there's some connection with the trouble up there?

Mahmoud Perhaps. But it is interesting that already they have been in Luxor for many weeks, and only today they have decide to go to the Harshak Tomb.

Wilder On the same day as Miss Warwick?

Mahmoud (*pointedly*) Yes, Mr Wilder. On the same day as Miss Warwick. (*pause*) Mr Wilder. I am going to ask that you do for me a favour.

Wilder Yes?

Mahmoud picks up the telephone, dials

Mahmoud I am going to telephone hotel. I would like for you to ask the Reception the name of the people who have occupy the room number twenty-six. Will you do it?

Wilder Well – yes, if you want. But why. I thought you said the Villiers –

213

Mahmoud (*into telephone*) Hello? Is that the Winter Palace Hotel? (*pause*) Hold the line please. Here you are, Mr Wilder.

Wilder takes the telephone

Wilder (*into telephone*) Good evening. This is Mr Wilder from the British Consulate. I wonder if you could do something for me please. I believe you have some British guests staying in your room number twenty-six. (*pause*) Yes, that's right. Would you mind telling me their names please? (*pause*) Yes, of course.

Chinkling sound. Mahmoud is holding some gold-chained necklaces

(*to Mahmoud*) What are those you're holding?

Mahmoud The necklace of the 'Key of Life' – symbol of eternity for the great Pharaohs. It is made of pure Egyptian gold.

Wilder Yes. But is it genuine?

Mahmoud My friend! What kind of shop do you think Mahmoud have? (*pause*) No. I do not think is genuine. But it *was* found in the tomb of Harshak this morning…

Wilder (*into telephone*) Oh hallo. Yes, I'm here. (*pause*) Yes? (*pause*) Who? (*pause*) Are you sure? (*pause*) No, it's quite all right. (*pause*) Yes. Thank you. Goodbye.

He replaces phone

Mahmoud So?

Wilder They say the room is occupied by a Mr and Mrs Charles Berkeley – from London.

Mahmoud Berkeley. Yes. That is the name we have on the police tourist register. But to everyone else – they are Mr and Mrs Villiers. Do you know why, my friend? Do you know why?

Wilder No. But I know that name from somewhere. Berkeley. Berkeley…

Bring up chinkling of the Key of Life necklaces. Mix to sound of ice cubes being dropped into a glass, followed by gin being poured. Margaret Villiers, the worse for drink, is propped up at the bar of the hotel. She takes a deep gulp

Elizabeth Having one for the road, Mrs Villiers?

Margaret Huh…? Who's… oh – it's you.

Elizabeth It can't be much fun drinking on your own. Mind if I join you?

Margaret It's a free country – as they say.

Elizabeth (*sitting*) Where's Mr Villiers tonight? Is he out?

Margaret Out, upstairs, downstairs… I don't know. I don't care. Why should I care? He doesn't. (*lowers voice*) He hates me.

Elizabeth Oh come now. I'm sure he doesn't.

Margaret I tell you he hates me! He always has. He doesn't know how to love. (*pause. She gulps more gin*) And he hates you too – did you know that?

Elizabeth (*taken aback*) Me? (*casually*) Why?

Margaret He knows all about you – and your father – and your brother…!

Elizabeth Mrs Villiers, I'm not quite sure I know what you…

Margaret You don't think we came all the way out here to this fly-ridden hole just to see a lot of broken-down old tombs, do you?

Elizabeth Look, Mrs Villiers. If you tell me about it, I may be able to help you…

Margaret Help me! Ha! That's a laugh that is! You help *me*. All you've got to do is to tell me what they've done with my boy… (*calls*) My son.

Elizabeth Your – son?

Margaret They said he deserted his regiment. He didn't! He'd never do a thing like that. Not my Brian.

Elizabeth Your son – is a deserter from his regiment. From where?

Margaret From Suez. He was in the landing in fifty-six. The same regiment as your brother…

Elizabeth Michael?

Margaret They were friends together.

Elizabeth But Michael was killed in action. He's buried in the British War Cemetery.

Margaret They were friends I tell you! Brian was always telling us that one day he and your brother would come down here and carry on where your father left off. (*pause*) He's around here somewhere. I know he is. (*pause*) You don't have any children of your own, do you, Miss Warwick? No. Of course you don't. You've got all your life ahead of you. Well, let me tell you something. I haven't. I've only got one person to love me – and I want him back. Do you hear me? (*half-sobs*) I want him back.

Elizabeth (*comforting*) Look, Mrs Villiers. Believe me, I don't know where your son is. If I did know I'd…

Margaret Oh, get away from me! Leave me alone!

Elizabeth Mrs Villiers! Please…

Margaret And stop calling me that! It's not my name. My name is –

They have not noticed Villiers' arrival

Villiers Berkeley. Margaret Louisa Berkeley.

Elizabeth Oh – Mr Villiers. I'm sorry, I didn't notice you.

Long awkward pause

Well – if you'll excuse me I think I'll take a little stroll down to the river before I turn in. (*as she leaves*) Goodnight, all.

Villiers Goodnight.

Margaret (*nervously lowering her voice*) I didn't tell her anything, Charlie – honest! (*no reply*) I promise!

Villiers Are you ready for bed, my dear. You must be very tired.

Sharp cut to cicadas. Elizabeth and O'Hara are taking a stroll down by the river's edge

O'Hara Just don't let it worry you, my dear. If the boy's a deserter, there's nothin' you can do about it.

Elizabeth It was just that I felt so sorry for the poor woman. She seems so alone. If only I'd known her son was in the same regiment as Michael… Oh well. (*They stop. She sighs*) It is beautiful, isn't it?

O'Hara You don't see a sky like that in London.

Elizabeth I've never seen so many stars. They must have been a wonderful guide for the architect you know.

O'Hara You only have to look at the Pyramids at Giza for that.

Elizabeth Yes. (*the idea suddenly occurs*) Yes. Do you think it was like that at the Harshak Tomb? Could it have been worked out mathematically?

O'Hara I doubt it.

Elizabeth Then you think the same as the rest of them? Father was wrong. It isn't a Pharaoh's tomb?

O'Hara I think if it was, it was never occupied. As much as I hate to admit it, I think that tomb is pretty much of a white elephant. You'd do well to forget all about it. Try and gave yourself a little bit of fun whilst you're here.

Elizabeth Perhaps you're right.

Pause

O'Hara Well, I must be off home. As it is I don't like drivin' over these mountain tracks after dark. (*pause*) Take care of yourself my dear.

Elizabeth I will.

O'Hara Don't forget to call on me if you feel like it. (*going*) And don't wander around down here on your own too long. I should get back to the hotel. Goodbye, Elizabeth.

Elizabeth (*calls*) Bye!

As his footsteps disappear into the distance, Elizabeth sighs. After a brief moment she is startled by a movement behind her

Who's there? (*no reply*) Who is that?

Another movement as someone steps out in front of her

What do you want? (*no reply*) I have no money.

Arab man (*sneeringly*) English woman!

The man grabs hold of Elizabeth

Elizabeth Get away from me! Get away...! Mr O'Hara! Mr O'Hara... please help me...

In the struggle the man tries to push his hand over her mouth, but he dashes off as O'Hara runs back

O'Hara (*approaching*) Elizabeth! (*nearer*) Elizabeth!

Elizabeth is lying on the ground, breathing heavily

For mercy's sake, child – what happened?

Elizabeth (*being helped up*) A man... attacked me. I thought he was going to strangle me!

O'Hara I knew I shouldn't have left you. You should have come straight back to the hotel! Did he take your purse?

Elizabeth (*coldly*) No.

O'Hara No? Are you sure?

Elizabeth Here it is.

O'Hara He couldn't have seen it.

Elizabeth He saw it all right.

O'Hara But my dear child – he might have killed you. Why?

Elizabeth Yes. Why?

Sharp cut to sound of Arabic music accompanying the belly dancer on the TV set in the cafe in Markaz Square. A strange young man of about 30 with a cultured

English voice approaches Bertie Pringle who is joining in the general cafe festivities

Stranger (*smooth and commanding*) Pringle.

Pringle (*turning round, nervously*) Oh… it's you! (*gulps heavily*) I didn't know you was comin' tonight. I was just watchin' the belly dancer on the…

Stranger Did you follow my instructions?

Pringle Yes, yes I did! Just like you said.

Stranger Where is he?

Pringle Upstairs. Shall I come with you?

Stranger No. Wait here. (*pause*) Does he know I'm coming?

Pringle No – honest.

Stranger Good. (*starts to leave*) And Pringle. Try not to spend too much of my money – will you, please?

Bring up Arabic belly dancer music for a moment. Cut it out sharply as the stranger enters the room above the cafe. Music now in extreme background. Fuad Yassif calls out from an adjoining room

Fuad (*off*) Pringle! Is that you? (*no reply*) Pringle…! (*as he approaches, he stops dead. Immediately his tone becomes nervous as he recognises the stranger*) Oh – it's you.

Stranger Good evening, Fuad. (*pause*) Why did you come here?

Fuad I had to. There was nowhere else to go. No one knows that I am here.

Stranger I'm afraid you're wrong there. You were followed.

Fuad Followed? No. It's impossible!

Stranger You were followed by the two English people – Mr and Mrs Villiers. That was very careless of you…

Fuad I'm – sorry.

Stranger In fact, Fuad, two mistakes in one day – is more than careless. It's dangerous.

Fuad There was nothing I could do out at that tomb. She's not going to tell us… she's just not going to…

The stranger punches out at Fuad, who falls to the ground with a thud

No, please! Please – let go of my hair…!

Stranger It's all right Fuad. I forgive you this time. I know you won't let me down again. I've already lost one good man on that train. I'd hate to lose another.

Fuad (*struggling*) My hair! You're hurting my…

Stranger (*almost whispering*) Tomorrow Fuad. Tomorrow you will try again. I want that girl brought to me. Do you understand? (*as he pulls Fuad's hair*) I want Elizabeth Warwick brought to me…!

Fuad lets out a penetrating scream. Cut to the shrill call of the muezzin. Hold under announcement

END OF EPISODE THREE

Kill the Pharaoh!

by Victor Pemberton

Episode 4: The Hunter

Produced by John Tydeman

REHEARSALS:	Monday 21 August 1967	1030–1730
RECORD:	Monday 21 August 1967	1730–1830
STUDIO:	B.10	
R.P. No.	TLN34/DA850H	

CAST:	Elizabeth	Sheila Grant
	Mahmoud	James Thomason
	Mr Wilder	John Humphry
	Fuad	David Spenser
	Charles	Rolf Lefebvre
	Margaret	Marion Mathie
	Achmed	Haydn Jones
	Bertie	Barry Lowe
	O'Hara	Denis McCarthy
	Captain Aziz	John Justin
	Michael	Christopher Bidmead
	Abdullah	Antony Viccars
S.M.s:	Panel: Amna Smith; Grams: Keith Salmon; Spot: Enyd Williams	
SECRETARY:	Judy Munk	

The call of the muezzin is broken by the commanding Arabic voice of Director of Antiquities, Dr Fawzad. He and Elizabeth Warwick are walking around one of the main showrooms of the Department in Luxor

Fawzad The Harshak Tomb? No, Miss Warwick. Is better for you to forget this place.

Elizabeth (*irritated*) Forget?

Fawzad The tomb is worthless – you must know that. Ever since your father first excavated…

Elizabeth My father spent the best years of his life digging out that tomb. Valuable years. And now you tell me the Department of Antiquities are just going to leave the place to rot in the sun – as a rest home for cobras and scorpions.

Fawzad Miss Warwick. Your father was a greatly respected man. But you cannot expect my Department to spend what little money we have on preserving something which is of no archaeological importance.

Elizabeth Doctor Fawzad. How can you say such a thing? Surely the fact that such a tomb exists –

Fawzad My dear young lady. See for yourself.

They come to a halt

These photographs were taken after your father's excavations. Do you see? Not one single hieroglyphic, cartouche, or anything else. Not even a sarcophagus or remains of a mummy. How are we supposed to know what such a place is if there are no recognisable means of identification?

Elizabeth Perhaps this particular Pharaoh didn't want to be identified?

Fawzad Miss Warwick. The tomb is an empty shell. It is not even in the Pharaonic Valley.

Elizabeth In which case there must be a reason.

Fawzad (*despairing sigh*) Well, whatever it is – we shall never know.

Elizabeth We would have – if my father had been allowed to continue his work.

Fawzad Miss Warwick. Although I did not agree with your father's theories, I would like you to know that I personally did not approve of such an action. Even though Sir Richard was a sick man when he left Egypt.

Elizabeth Not as sick as all that, Doctor. Don't forget there are quite a few things in the Cairo Museum today that wouldn't be there if it wasn't for my father.

Fawzad No, I do not forget this, Miss Warwick. But I hope that one day we too shall have a Museum in Luxor – *better* than the one in Cairo. Then perhaps these things will be returned to their rightful home.

Pause

Elizabeth I must go. Doctor Fawzad, I – I hope I haven't been too rude? I'd like to call on you again if I may?

Fawzad You will be welcome any time, Miss Warwick – any time at all.

Elizabeth (*going, then stops*) Oh yes, there was just one thing.

Fawzad Yes?

Elizabeth There's a piece of broken fresco they dug up from the road – somewhere near the Tomb. Do you know it at all?

Fawzad 'The Hunter'? Yes. You will find it in the grounds of the Temple of Luxor. Near the Statue of Ramses. But I should not give it too much importance.

Elizabeth But worth taking a look?

Fawzad Of course. But, Miss Warwick, if you will take from me a few friendly words of advice. Keep away from the Harshak Tomb. The people around are very superstitious about it. They believe it is haunted.

Elizabeth You needn't worry, Doctor. I don't scare too easily. Not even if there's a mummy's curse!

Fawzad Nonetheless, I am concerned about this sudden interest in the tomb. If it goes on I will have to have it sealed up.

Elizabeth Sudden interest?

Fawzad You are not the first person to ask me about it recently. Only yesterday there was a man here. Also English.

Elizabeth Really? Do you know who he was? What does he look like?

Fawzad Small, with spectacles. Rather facetious I thought. Now… what was his name…?

Elizabeth Small? With spectacles… good Lord! You don't mean…

Fawzad Ah yes! I remember. His name was Pringle. Mr Pringle.

Sharp cut to Wilder's office at the British Consulate

Wilder Now then, Mr Pringle. What's on your mind?

Pringle (*ultra-polite*) Well, Mr Wilder, I didn't want to have to come to the Consulate and bother you, but it's like this, see. I'm a bit suspicious about this English couple that's stayin' at the same hotel as me. Mr and Mrs Villiers.

Wilder Suspicious? In what way?

Pringle Well, for one thing I don't even think that's their real name.

Wilder (*on his guard*) Really?

Pringle Berkeley. That's the name they gave at the Reception desk.

Wilder Berkeley?

Pringle And so I ask myself why? Why register under a different name? That is, unless you've got something to hide.

Wilder And you think they have?

Pringle Well, I wouldn't have – until I met them in that cafe last night. The one in Markaz Square. I mean it's all right for me. I lap up the local atmosphere, but it's not the sort of dump you'd expect a respectable English couple, is it? Especially all on their tod.

Wilder On their own?

Pringle Yeah. But they were lookin' for someone. A young bloke. Mrs Villiers got very worked up about it – 'cos this bloke wasn't there. Which made me put two and two together. (*pause*) Do you know what I think, Mr Wilder?

Wilder No – what?

Pringle I reckon they've come down here to try and contact their son. And I'll bet you a quid to a farthin' that the son – is a deserter – from the Army.

Wilder Deserter?

Pringle And believe me, Mr Wilder sir, there's nothin' I can't stand worse than a white feather. *I* fought for my country… in the Second World War. And I'm proud of it!

Wilder But Mr Pringle, how can you be sure that this person the Villiers are looking for *is* an army deserter?

Pringle Well I can't be absolutely sure, can I, Mr Wilder? But let's face it, if he is, he'd have to stay out here. If he put his nose back in Blighty, he'd soon get it cut off!

Wilder (*deep in thought*) And you think the Villiers have already made contact with him, do you?

Pringle I should think they're bound to've. But look, Mr Wilder sir. I don't want you to think I came here to try and stir up trouble for the Villiers. That's the last thing I want to do. You do know that – don't you?

Sharp cut followed by a pause

Arab children reciting an English nursery rhyme in a classroom at the village school of Harshak. Children suddenly stop dead as classroom doors opened roughly at the back of the room

O'Hara (*calls, angrily*) Captain Aziz! Would you mind telling me what the hell you think you're doing! This happens to be the middle of a lesson.

Aziz So I see.

Footsteps as he walks between the desks to Mr O'Hara. He stops

I had no idea it was necessary for Arab children to learn their lessons in a foreign language.

O'Hara The lessons at this school, Captain, are varied, and carefully chosen.

Aziz To include the English language?

O'Hara To include any subject that is going to improve the general standard of education.

Aziz Then I hope it will be put to a good use. To improve them as citizens of the United Arab Republic.

O'Hara Not only to the Republic, Captain – but also to themselves. Now perhaps you'd be good enough to tell me the reason for this interruption? We have work to do.

Aziz walks up and down the aisle

Aziz I want to ask the children a question. I have been told that they are scared of sounds which are coming from inside the Harshak Tomb.

O'Hara They have their superstitions, just like the rest of us. Isn't that perfectly natural for children –

Aziz I do not believe that Arab children scare so easy! The Harshak Tomb is not haunted. There is no mummy's curse, no 'hidden treasure'. (*back to O'Hara again, quiet and threatening*) And Mr O'Hara, I do not believe these children are scared of anything.

Pause

O'Hara In that case, Captain, perhaps you'd better ask the children yourself.

Aziz No, no, Mr O'Hara. *You* are the teacher. They will understand *your* language more better than mine.

Pause. O'Hara addresses the class but in perfect Arabic

O'Hara Ya awlad, ad dabit yis'al idha kan aiyi had minkum yikhawf il aswat ti turbat Harshak? (*Children! The Captain asks if any of you are scared of the sounds in the Harshak Tomb.*)

Immediate response of scare and panic from the children

There you are, Captain. Does that answer your question?

After a pause, Aziz turns around and angrily strides out of the room without uttering a word. He slams the door after him

(*addressing the class*) All right, children! Shall we continue?

Sharp cut to chirping of birds in grounds of the Temple of Luxor. Background sounds of tourists wandering about

Mahmoud 'The Hunter'. That is the name of the fresco. Did you know that, dear lady?

Elizabeth Yes, Inspector. I did know that, thank you.

Mahmoud But of course. Your father have mention it in his book. Is very interesting picture, no?

Elizabeth Very.

Mahmoud These – here. They are the animals who have been killed?

Elizabeth Correct. Three hippopotami.

Mahmoud And the two men?

Elizabeth The hunter in the foreground is either a nobleman or king. The one behind, pointing the arrow – I should think he's probably a slave-bearer.

Mahmoud Is unusual – do you not think?

Elizabeth What is?

Mahmoud That the Pharaoh does not hunt alone. Always I have thought that the symbol of the royal manhood was that the Pharaoh should hunt alone?

Elizabeth Well, that depends if the man in foreground *is* a Pharaoh. After all, there's nothing to identify him. If there was a cartouche, it's been broken off.

Mahmoud Fascinating! You see, dear lady, you *are* your father's daughter. You show great knowledge of Egyptology.

Elizabeth Purely a hobby, I assure you.

Mahmoud Ah! Is a wonderful thing! So many times I have stood in the shadows of this Temple. I have watched the sun turn to the colour of blood, and for me there comes a moment when it seems Egypt belongs to the Pharaohs again.

Elizabeth Maybe it does. It's just that we haven't noticed.

Pause

Mahmoud But at least we still have the pleasure to try to find out about things we do not know.

Elizabeth Such as?

Mahmoud Oh many things, dear lady – in this Temple alone. For instance – the fresco. Can you tell me what happened to the other animal?

Elizabeth Other animal? There are only three hippopotami. And you can see them here – they're all dead.

Mahmoud Yes. But the man behind the Pharaoh. Do you see? He points his arrow towards another animal – that we cannot see.

Pause

Elizabeth Yes, that's odd. I must say I've never noticed... Good Lord! Yes!

Mahmoud Dear Lady. What is it? What do you see?

Elizabeth Inspector. You can't see another animal – because there isn't one. Look at the man in the background. He's not pointing his arrow at an animal. He's pointing it directly at the Pharaoh's back!

Sharp cut to loud splash as the anchor of Achmed's boat is thrown into the water

Villiers All right, Achmed, now keep the boat like that. If we stay at anchor on this side of the river they won't notice us.

Achmed Cannot stay too long, Mr Villiers. Current of water very strong.

Margaret She's looking at the same fresco.

Villiers Yes. But I'd like to know who that is with her. Achmed, do you recognise the man standing with Miss Warwick over at the Luxor Temple?

Achmed No. I cannot see his face because he… Mr Villiers!

Villiers What is it?

Achmed The man! He is Mahmoud, Chief of Police.

Villiers   } What!
Margaret } Oh my – !

Villiers Are you sure?

Achmed Yes, I know him! I have seen him many times in the town. Inspector Mahmoud.

Villiers Then she's told him.

Margaret No! She couldn't…

Villiers What do you mean, she couldn't? After what you told her last night. By now the police will know the whole damned story. They'll be out looking for Brian, and he'll be sent straight back to England for court martial. Well, my dear, I hope you're satisfied with yourself.

Margaret But I didn't tell her anything – I promise!

Villiers You told her our son is an army deserter.

Margaret Yes, but she doesn't know what he looks like.

Villiers I don't think that'll be very difficult to find out. Especially if you get a couple more drinks down you. No. This means we have to change our plans.

Margaret How?

Villiers We've got to stop looking for Brian.

Margaret No, Charlie…!

Villiers At least for the time being. Whatever he's doing up at that tomb, we've got to try and divert attention from it.

Margaret But what happens if the British Consulate find out about – well, who we are?

Villiers You might have thought about that before you drank yourself into a stupor last night. Achmed. Mrs Villiers and I are not going up to the Harshak Tomb any more for the time being. So I want you to go up there instead.

Achmed No! No, no, Mr Villiers. Not for Achmed.

Villiers What do you mean – not Achmed? I want you to go up there and watch the place for us. If you see anything of the same young Englishman I want you to come down and tell me right away, is that clear?

Achmed Tomb have many ghosts. Bring bad luck to Achmed.

Villiers I'm warning you, my friend, if you don't do what I say this time, it'll bring you more than bad luck. In fact, there'll be just one more ghost to add to that tomb.

Fade out

Pause

Fade back to the Temple of Luxor

Mahmoud Incredible! Absolutely incredible! You see, Miss Warwick. After only a few days in Luxor you have discovered something that has just been staring into the face of us all for years. The murder of a Pharaoh!

Elizabeth Now let's not jump to hasty conclusions, Inspector. We have no proof that the hunter in the fresco *is* a Pharaoh. The angle of the picture has been painted very badly. Do you see here? This is the edge of the river, and the tablet has obviously been broken off. So you see, the man in the background may still be pointing his arrow at another animal. Maybe a hippopotamus – or even a crocodile.

Mahmoud I think not. The crocodile is not so much to Luxor. Only sometimes in the river at Aswan.

Elizabeth Yes, but in those days the river here was infested with crocodiles. No. I still think the river's edge shown in the fresco is the one right here – in Luxor itself. But it's interesting that the tablet was found so near to the Harshak Tomb.

Mahmoud (*loudly yawning*) Dear lady. I think is maybe time for you to return to your hotel. Already we are approaching the midday sun. The streets are beginning to empty.

They begin to walk

You can take the horse-carriage. It will be much cooler.

Elizabeth Good! At least it'll stop you following me, won't it?

Mahmoud Follow? Dear lady – me!

Elizabeth Oh come off it, Inspector, you know very well you've spent the last hour dodging in and out of those columns like a weary James Bond.

Mahmoud Dear lady, how can you say such a... (*laughs*) For your protection, dear lady, for your protection.

Elizabeth You're very kind, Inspector, but I promise you I can take care of myself.

They stop walking

Mahmoud (*calls to cabbie*) Sayyid issit lil Winter Palace Hotel. (*Take this lady to the Winter Palace Hotel.*)

Driver Hadiv. (*Yes sir.*)

Mahmoud helps Elizabeth into the carriage

Mahmoud Have a good sleep!

Slams carriage door

Elizabeth Thanks! And the same to you.

Mahmoud Miss Warwick. Do not be offended if I say something to you.

Elizabeth Of course not. What?

Mahmoud Take care. Whatever you do, wherever you go – take care.

Elizabeth But why?

Mahmoud Because there are some who may – misinterpret your reasons for coming to Egypt. And also because I wish only for you – a good holiday. Do you understand?

Pause

Elizabeth Yes, Inspector, I do understand. But I want you to know I'm enjoying my holiday – very much. I promise.

The driver calls to the horse as the carriage draws off

(*calls back*) Goodbye!

Horse's hooves disappear. Mix to sound of telephone ringing in Wilder's office

Wilder (*picks up receiver*) Wilder. (*pause*) Yes, Jean? (*pause*) Oh, London – good! Put them through, will you please.

Pause. He sorts through some papers on his desk

Hello? Hello Reggie – is that you? (*pause*) Yes, I'm fine! (*pause*) Stinking hot! (*pause*) Any luck with the Berkeley thing? (*pause*) It *is*? Yes, I thought so. (*pause*) Yes. Go ahead. (*He begins to write*) Second Lieutenant Brian Leslie Berkeley. Service number 78129. Yes – got that. Does it show which date he was first reported AWOL? (*pause*) Seventh of December, 1956. How old was he? (*pause*) So that would put him at about thirty-two now. (*pause*) No, that's fine, old boy. Thanks a lot. (*pause*) Haven't the faintest idea, but I'm going to have a try. (*pause*) Right! See you! Cheers!

He slams down the receiver, but immediately picks up another one

Hallo, Jean. Check up on any army deserters in November/December '56. (*pause*) No. Suez and Port Said... and Jean. See if you can get hold of Miss Elizabeth Warwick for me. With a bit of luck she may still be at the hotel in the middle of her siesta.

Sharp cut to horse's hooves moving just a little faster over the deserted streets of Luxor

Elizabeth (*calls*) Driver! (*no reply*) I say – driver! I think we're going the wrong way. I asked for the Winter Palace Hotel. It's not in the town. It's across the river. (*still no reply*) Driver. Did you hear what I –

Without a word the driver suddenly puts the horse into a full gallop

(*shouting*) Help! Somebody help me!

Horse's hooves suddenly go onto echo as the carriage pulls to a sharp halt in a back alley

You fool! You mad, stupid...! What the hell do you think you're trying to do – kill me? (*still no reply*) What do you want? Why have you brought me to this alley?

Driver (*menacingly*) Stay where you are – English woman.

Elizabeth (*horrified*) You! Abdullah!

Abdullah So, English woman. You do not forget your old friend from the village of Hasia?

Elizabeth But I thought you were dead. You and your brother. Your house – it was burnt down.

Abdullah bursts out into his now recognisable asthmatic laugh

They found two bodies!

Abdullah (*menacing again*) I told you to go from Egypt, English woman! Why do you not go, heh?

Elizabeth Last night. Yes. It was you who tried to strangle me, wasn't it? Down by the river – you!

An asthmatic chuckle from Abdullah

Why? Why are you doing this to me? What do you want?

Abdullah (*moving closer*) Come down from the carriage.

Elizabeth I warn you, I'll shout the place down!

Abdullah (*slow, with heavy breathing*) Give me your hand – or I will cut it off!

Elizabeth Abdullah! Keep away… from me… (*shouts*) Abdullah!

Suddenly a commanding Arab voice echoing from other end of alley

Fuad Seeb ha! (*Leave her alone!*)

Heavy frightened breathing from Abdullah

Ya shaikh! Sami'mi? (*Old man! Do you hear me?*)

A panicked shout from Abdullah puts the horse into a bolt, and the carriage races off. In the middle of this, Fuad's footsteps running towards Elizabeth

Elizabeth! Elizabeth, are you all right?

Elizabeth (*recovering*) I wouldn't be if I was still in that carriage. (*suddenly aware that it is Fuad*) Fuad! What are *you* doing here?

Fuad I saw you get into the carriage at the Temple of Luxor. I followed you here in a car.

Elizabeth Well, that's very noble of you I must say! After ditching me in that tomb yesterday!

Fuad Elizabeth, I can explain about –

Elizabeth You'd better, because you've now proved to me you've already found another way into that place. And I'm warning you, I want to know…

The sound of people approaching

Fuad (*nervous about being seen*) I'll tell you, Elizabeth, I promise I'll tell you. Will you meet me later?

Elizabeth Well, I don't know…

Fuad Do you know Markaz Square?

Elizabeth I'll find it.

Fuad Find the small cinema in the street nearby. Buy a ticket and go to the last but one row from the back. I will wait for you there at nine o'clock. Will you come?

Elizabeth I tell you I don't… Fuad! (*calls*) Fuad!

An Arab gathering. Mix into this the soft singing of an Arab lullaby drifting across the Nile. It is on board Achmed Araby's small boat 'Horous', moored at the river's edge. Mr O'Hara approaches from alongside

O'Hara (*calling gently*) Achmed. Achmed Araby. Are you down there?

Achmed Mr O'Hara. Welcome to my boat! Welcome!

O'Hara Do you mind if I come aboard?

Achmed Come down – please! I am going to make us some mint tea.

O'Hara (*climbing aboard*) Ah! Your mint tea. I don't know anybody in Luxor who makes it like you.

He is now on board

Achmed Welcome!

O'Hara Thank you. She's a beautiful boat, Achmed. There's not another one like 'Horous' on the Nile.

Achmed is preparing the kettle in the background

I hope I haven't disturbed you. (*pause*) You've paid your respects to Mecca, have you?

Achmed Yes. Not again now until the morning.

O'Hara I must say I have the greatest respect for you, Achmed. You make your religion an important part of your life.

Achmed Mohammed *is* life for Achmed. But you too are religious, Mr O'Hara. You are good Christian – no?

O'Hara Well, I believe in one God if that's what you mean. That's what they teach you in the Koran, isn't it?

Achmed You? You have read the Koran?

O'Hara How would I know what goes on inside you people if I didn't? It's at this time of day, when those hills and the river disappear into the darkness, that I know I'm much more a part of this place than I'd ever realised. By the way, how are your two English friends? Er – Mr and Mrs Villiers, isn't it?

Achmed (*non-committal*) Friends?

O'Hara For the last two weeks your boat has rarely been out for hire to anyone else.

Pause

Achmed They have pay many piastres.

O'Hara They must think highly of you. Especially when they could have their pick of so many boatmen.

Achmed 'Horous' very good boat. None better in whole Upper Egypt.

O'Hara You can say that again, Achmed. And they won't find anyone who knows this river better than you. And those hills up there. I suppose that's why the Villiers chose you?

Achmed Ah! The kettle. Now we shall have the mint tea.

Movement from the cabin

O'Hara Hullo, who's that? Have you got somebody down below, Achmed?

Achmed No, no – is nothing! Just an old man.

O'Hara (*suspiciously*) Old man?

Achmed Abdullah. He is my friend. Very good friend.

O'Hara Abdullah. Does he always sleep on board?

Achmed No, no! Only tonight. He is old man and have no house. He is tired because work today have been very difficult for him.

Fade out

Pause. Fade in hotel reception

Wilder (*approaching*) Oh, Miss Warwick – there you are!

Elizabeth (*bored sigh*) Yes, Mr Wilder?

Wilder I tried to reach you on the telephone this afternoon. They said you were out.

Elizabeth Yes. I went for a little sightseeing drive. Why? Have I done something wrong again?

Wilder No, not at all. I really came to apologise. You must have thought me rather arrogant and stupid yesterday afternoon. I didn't mean to treat you like a schoolgirl.

Elizabeth I suppose you're only doing your job.

Wilder You're going out?

Elizabeth I have a dinner date with Doctor Fawzad. I was just on my way.

Wilder Oh, what a pity. I was going to ask if you'd care to join me. I know a little place where they do the most marvellous kebab.

Elizabeth Well, that's very kind of you. I'll take you up on that, perhaps another evening.

Wilder Before you go, Miss Warwick. Actually there was something else.

Elizabeth Yes?

Wilder There's another English couple staying at this hotel. A Mr and Mrs Villiers. I was wondering if you've come into contact with them at all?

Elizabeth Once or twice. We share the same table in the dining-room.

Wilder Do they ever talk much about their life – back home in England?

Elizabeth Of course. English tourists abroad never stop talking about life back home. What else can most of them talk about? Why?

Wilder Have they ever mentioned their family?

Pause

Elizabeth No. I can't say they have. (*on guard*)

Wilder Never? You mean, they've never told you about their son?

Elizabeth Son? I didn't know they had one.

Wilder He deserted from the British Army during the Suez landings in 1956.

Elizabeth Oh really? How sad.

Wilder You didn't know that?

Elizabeth Why should I? It's hardly a thing you'd expect the Villiers to boast about, now is it?

Pause

Wilder No. No, of course not. (*pause*) Well, if you do happen to hear anything, I'd be very grateful if you'd let me know. If this person is in Luxor, we're going to find him.

Elizabeth And if you do?

Wilder He'll be sent back to England for court martial.

Elizabeth Regardless of the reasons he did it?

Wilder I'm afraid that's quite immaterial. I mean you don't just desert the flat you're fighting for – do you? Anyway, don't you give it another thought, Miss Warwick. I hope you and Doctor Fawzad will have a most enjoyable evening.

Elizabeth (*coldly*) Thank you.

Wilder Forget all about antiquities for a while. Go out and have a jolly good laugh!

Very sharp cut to the shrieks and laughter of the Arab cinema audience. In the middle of this, in background, soundtrack of the Arabic film

Elizabeth (*voice lowered*) You're late!

Fuad I came as soon as I could. I didn't want to be seen.

Elizabeth What *is* all this cloak and dagger stuff? Why have we got to meet in this filthy bug-hutch of a place?

Fuad Elizabeth. Listen to me. There is something you have got to know.

Elizabeth Yes! How did you get out of that tomb? There *is* another entrance, isn't there?

Fuad (*reluctantly*) Yes.

Elizabeth Then why didn't you tell me, instead of leaving me alone in the dark like that?

Fuad I wanted to tell you, but I heard someone moving around outside. I just couldn't take the risk.

Elizabeth All right. Where is it?

Fuad I can't tell you. Not yet.

Elizabeth What do you mean, you can't tell me? You *will* tell me!

Fuad Listen to me carefully. The second entrance was found two years ago.

Elizabeth Two years!

Fuad It leads directly to another chamber – a much bigger one. Before we could get there we had to –

Elizabeth *We*? You're working with somebody else. Who?

Fuad I can't tell you. I dare not!

Elizabeth It's the Villiers' son isn't it? Brian Berkeley.

Fuad (*trying to quieten her*) Elizabeth… please!

Elizabeth He was in the same regiment as my brother Michael. He knew what my father was trying to do down here. That's why he deserted.

Fuad No!

Elizabeth Don't lie to me! I don't believe a word you say. In fact I don't even think you *are* Fuad Yassif.

Fuad Please keep your voice down! We can be heard…

Elizabeth Now you listen to me, my friend. You've found something in that tomb, and I want to know what it is. Do you hear me, Fuad? I want to know!

Uproar of laughter from the Arab audience as the film continues. Cut this sharply as Wilder opens the door of Mahmoud's office at the Police Station

Mahmoud (*in jovial mood*) Ah! Mr Wilder, my friend! Come in. (*door is closed*) I think maybe you have smelt the bottle. Come and have a glass of Arak.

Wilder (*approaching*) What is this? Some kind of celebration?

Mahmoud But of course! Have you not heard? In two weeks I am to be married.

Wilder Married? But I thought you already had a wife?

Mahmoud I have. Two wives – or is it three? Oh dear – these days I can never remember.

Wilder One of the joys of being Muslim.

Mahmoud (*pouring drink*) I can tell by the look on your face that you are going to depress me with more news? Am I right?

Wilder I spoke to London on the telephone this afternoon. About the Villiers – or I should say Berkeleys.

Mahmoud Yes?

Wilder Their son is a Lieutenant Brian Berkeley. He's a deserter from the British Army.

Mahmoud During the landings at Suez. Correct?

Wilder You know?

Mahmoud Of course! I am very efficient Police Inspector you know. Here! Drink some Arak. It will make you as beautiful as me!

Wilder (*taking glass*) Thank you. (*takes a gulp and squirms*) What the heck is this stuff? Sulphuric acid?

Mahmoud Also I can tell you that this Lieutenant Berkeley was in the same regiment as the brother of Miss Elizabeth Warwick.

Wilder Michael Warwick.

Mahmoud Correct!

Wilder And you think there's some sort of connection?

Mahmoud Who knows?

Wilder Well, I must say Miss Warwick herself was a bit evasive about the Villiers. She says she's never heard of the son.

Mahmoud You asked her?

Wilder Yes, why not? Though I must say I find it hard to believe she didn't know the two men were in the same regiment. They were supposed to have been close friends.

Mahmoud But Lieutenant Michael Warwick was killed in action soon after the landings?

Wilder Yes. Poor devil.

Mahmoud And this Michael Warwick – he never had the chance to come to Luxor.

Wilder Apparently not.

Mahmoud But even that does not mean he didn't know what was happening up at Harshak.

Wilder Even if he did it wouldn't make much difference. That tomb is worthless.

Mahmoud (*takes a gulp of Arak*) I wonder.

Sharp knock on the door

Come in!

Captain Aziz enters. He is very excited

Yes, Captain? What is it?

Aziz The English woman.

Mahmoud Yes?

Aziz My men followed her from the hotel. She went to Markaz Square. But they lost her in the crowd.

Wilder She'll be all right. She's with Doctor Fawzad.

Mahmoud Doctor Fawzad?

Wilder I met Miss Warwick at the hotel just before she left. She has a dinner date with the Doctor.

Aziz She was with no one. She was quite alone.

Wilder But she can't be.

Mahmoud Oh yes, Mr Wilder, she can. Doctor Fawzad left Luxor early this morning. He has gone to inspect an excavation at Abu Simbel near Aswan.

Wilder Oh my – !

Mahmoud (*to Aziz*) Captain. I want as many of your men as you can spare. Please be good enough to surround the Markaz Square without further delay.

Aziz (*leaving*) Yes!

Door shuts

Wilder She's in danger, isn't she?

Mahmoud Yes, my friend. I'm afraid she is.

Cut back to hysterical laughter of the Arab audience watching the film. Fuad is more and more edgy

Fuad No, Elizabeth! The only thing you can do is to go. Get out of the country as soon as you can – before it's too late.

Elizabeth To leave you sitting on top of a million pound fortune? Oh no!

Fuad I'll help you. I promise I'll help you. But you can't stay here. Whatever there was in that tomb can only bring you disaster.

Elizabeth I'm not superstitious. (*pause, defiantly*) All right, Fuad. If you won't show me how to get into that chamber – I'll find my own way.

Fuad No! Listen. I will take you there, but you've got to promise me something. You got to promise me that –

Elizabeth Promise what? (*pause*) Well, go on!

Fuad suddenly adopts a completely different tone, changing the conversation as someone is nearby

Fuad (*shaking with fear*) What a great pity that you cannot understand the Arabic language, Elizabeth. This film is really very funny.

Elizabeth What? To hell with the film!

Fuad Do you know, the man on the screen is one of our most famous actors… (*nervous laugh, to join in with audience*)

Elizabeth What are you trying to do? What's the matter with you?

Fuad Watch the film, Elizabeth. *Please…* watch the film!

Elizabeth You're – up to something. I don't like this. I'm getting out of here…

Man (*soft voice, last heard with Fuad in cafe in Episode 3*) No. Don't go Elizabeth. Don't miss the film.

Elizabeth Who's that? Who… are you…?

Man No – don't turn around. I can see you quite well from behind. (*pause*) I've missed you, Elizabeth. I've missed you… an awful lot…

Elizabeth That voice. I know… that voice!

Man But now we're together again, Elizabeth. Just like we used to be. Just like old times.

Elizabeth You…!

Man No, Elizabeth! (*grinding his teeth angrily*) I said – don't turn around!

He has put a gag over Elizabeth's mouth. She tries desperately to break loose, but is gradually overcome by ether sprinkled onto a handkerchief

That's better, Elizabeth. Much, much better.

Another uproar of hysterical laughter from the Arab audience into which we cut the penetrating shrill call of the muezzin, held under announcement

END OF EPISODE FOUR

Kill the Pharaoh!
by Victor Pemberton

Episode 5: A Face in the Crowd

Produced by John Tydeman

REHEARSALS:	Tuesday 22 August 1967	1030–1730
RECORD:	Tuesday 22 August 1967	1730–1830
STUDIO:	B.10	
R.P. No.	TLN34/DA851H	

CAST:

Elizabeth	Sheila Grant
Mahmoud	James Thomason
Mr Wilder	John Humphry
Fuad	David Spenser
Charles	Rolf Lefebvre
Margaret	Marion Mathie
Abdullah	Antony Viccars
Bertie	Barry Lowe
Captain Aziz	John Justin
Michael	Christopher Bidmead
Blind Arab	Douglas Hankin
Arab Woman	Rosalind Shanks
O'Hara	Denis McCarthy

S.M.s: Panel: Amna Smith; Grams: Keith Salmon; Spot: Enyd Williams

SECRETARY: Judy Munk, PABX 2168

The call of the muezzin is broken by the shrill call of police whistles, car sirens, running feet etc. We are in Markaz Square in Luxor, where pandemonium has broken out amongst the street traders as police and troops search for Elizabeth Warwick

Wilder (*tired, irritated*) It's no use Inspector – we might as well just face it. Your men have been searching these streets all through the night. Elizabeth Warwick has disappeared, and there's absolutely nothing we can do about it.

Mahmoud On the contrary, Mr Wilder. I can assure you we are going to find this lady if we have to pull down each one of these buildings in Markaz Square.

Wilder (*bitterly*) And what happens if we're too late? If we find her lying in some back alley with her throat slit?

232

Mahmoud (*a deep sigh*) Then, my friend, there is nothing we can do. It can only be the will of Allah.

Captain Aziz approaches

Aziz Inspector Mahmoud.

Mahmoud Yes, Captain – what news?

Aziz We have found a man who may be able to help us. He thinks the English woman stopped to speak to him last night.

Mahmoud Who is he?

Aziz A blind street beggar. He sits outside the cinema in Marguf Street. But I warn you, it may be a lie.

Mahmoud I'll speak to the man. Will you bring him here please?

Aziz (*shouts to his men*) Gib ir-razil al-agouz hina bi sur'a! (*Bring the old man here – quickly!*)

Wilder If the man is blind, how can he possibly know if the woman was Elizabeth Warwick. There must be thousands of tourists passing through here night and day.

Mahmoud That is true. But I think we must not forget that sometimes the blind can see more than we who have eyes.

The blind beggar is brought forward. He is very old, and nervous

Aziz Here you are Inspector. This is the man.

Mahmoud Good! (*to old man, in Arabic*) Ai ba'a ya Shaikh. Ana aizak la'oolli – (*Now old man. I want you to tell me –*)

The old man interrupts him in a clear and precise broken English accent

Old man You have no need of to speak to me in Arabic, Inspector. The effendi here is English. (*proudly*) I speak the English language so good.

Wilder (*taken aback*) Good Lord! How on earth did you – ? (*flattered*) That's very kind of you. (*to Mahmoud*) Inspector. Do you mind?

Mahmoud (*rather amused*) No, no, no, I don't mind. Go right ahead!

Wilder (*a soft tone*) Old man. You talk of an English lady who spoke to you.

Old man Yes. Last night… er – tissa…

Mahmoud Nine o'clock.

Wilder Where was this?

Old man At the same place I have been for the last five and four years. Never do my eyes permit me to go inside the picture house, so I listen to the laughter from outside – on the pavement.

Wilder What did this lady say to you?

Old man (*with affection*) She said: "Old man. Why do you sit on the pavement? You are too old." (*a contented sigh*) She take hold of my hand, and into the palm she put – twenty-five piastres. (*with delight*) Twenty-five! (*pause*) It was a good voice. Strong – but good.

Aziz The man is a fool! How does he know she was English? She could have been an American…

Old man (*defiantly*) No! For many years I have live in Cairo. English very good. They give me work. (*sneeringly at Aziz*) I too know the English, effendi. They have given me great happiness!

A scornful dismissal from Aziz

Mahmoud Old man. Do you know in which direction the lady go?

Old man Into the picture house.

Wilder The cinema!

Mahmoud How do you know that?

Old man The sweet smell of oleander…

Wilder Of course – her perfume! She was wearing it when I met her, just before she left the hotel. It was terribly strong.

Old man (*with urgency*) But effendi, listen to me! Although I wait many hours, the sweet oleander stay in the picture house.

Wilder You mean the lady didn't come out of the cinema?

Old man No.

Mahmoud (*to Aziz*) Captain, please to get your men to the cinema. Do not allow anyone to enter or leave.

Aziz leaves

Maybe we are still not too late.

General activity in the background

Wilder (*gently*) Old man. Take this. (*offers money*)

Old man (*firmly*) No! I will not take your money, effendi. All I ask of you is that you let no harm come to the oleander.

Fade out

Pause

Fade up the sound of flies buzzing mercilessly in the morning heat. In the middle of this, Elizabeth struggles to recover from the deep sleep into which she had been forced the previous evening

Elizabeth (*groaning*) Oh… my head! (*breathing heavily*) Where am I…? The heat…

There is a sudden movement across the other side of the room, and a peasant woman approaches. As the woman does not speak English, her only means of communication is by agreeing to everything Elizabeth says, and this is achieved by an irritating, almost mad-like chuckle

Who are you!

Woman (*an agreeing chuckle*)

Elizabeth What am I doing here?

Woman (*an agreeing chuckle*)

Elizabeth What is this place? Where are we? (*irritation to boiling point*) Damn you woman! Can't you understand anything I say? No! Keep away… from me…

Elizabeth becomes desperate

Water. (*slow, precise*) Do you understand me? I – want – some – water. Er… Mayya.

Woman (*delighted*) Ah! Mayya, mayya!

Elizabeth (*angrily*) Well don't just stand there woman! Go and get me s–…

She is interrupted by the souond of water being poured into a tumbler behind her

It is the man who had spoken to her in the cinema

234

Man There you are Elizabeth. I'm sure that'll make you feel better.

Pause. Elizabeth is staring hard, unable to believe what she can see

Elizabeth You! It… can't be!

Man It's good to see my little sister again after all these years. (*pause*) I've missed you… honest.

Elizabeth Michael… you're dead. You were killed in action… at Suez…

Michael (*negative*) You mustn't believe everything the War Office tell you. (*enjoying the joke*) And anyway, I can assure you – I don't feel in the slightest bit dead. (*pause*) Drink your water.

Elizabeth (*drinking water straight down*) Why? In Heaven's name why? What happened?

Michael That's rather a long story Liz, old girl. (*stops*) 'Liz'. It's been a few years since I was able to call you that. 'Liz'.

Starts to walk around

I apologise for the rather unconventional way of bringing you here Liz. I must say I do agree with you about that cinema. It really is rather a bug-hutch, isn't it? (*pause*) But then it wouldn't have been necessary if that mutual friend of ours Fuad Yassif hadn't…

Elizabeth (*still shaken*) What do you want of me?

Michael (*walking back*) I wanted to see my sister. There's no crime in that – is there Liz? (*pause*) D'you know something? The last time I saw you, you had freckles and pig-tails.

Elizabeth And the last time I saw you, you were a soldier. (*bitterly*) Or supposed to have been.

Pause

Michael (*half cynically*) Then we've both changed – haven't we Liz?

A sharp cut to the sound of Mahmoud's steps echoing on the stone floor of the cinema, as he paces anxiously up and down. The Arab cinema manager is very upset

Manager Please, please Inspector – you've got to believe me. This is respectable cinema. I am an honest man. I would not allow no trouble.

Mahmoud Good! I am pleased to hear it. That means you have given up selling drugs to American tourists?

Manager (*hurt*) Inspector! That was long time ago. I tell you I am an honest man. Always I will help police.

Mahmoud There was an English woman in your cinema last night. She was seen coming in – but she did not come out.

Manager Dear sir! I do not permit people to sleep in my cinema.

Mahmoud Then you do not remember such a lady?

Manager I did not say that.

Wilder (*eagerly*) You mean, you saw her?

Manager Yes, of course. We show only Arabic-speaking films here. We do not have many Europeans to visit us.

Mahmoud What did she look like, this lady?

Manager Not so tall, blue eyes, hair was coloured light…

Wilder That's her all right! It must be.

Mahmoud You have good memory, my friend. Perhaps then you also remember where in the cinema she was sitting?

Manager Of course! The last row but one. Both she and her two friends.

Wilder } Friends?

Mahmoud } What friends?

Manager The two gentlemen she left with. One was Arab, the other European.

Wilder Yassif! He's kidnapped her…

Mahmoud They left together. By which door?

Manager (*indicating*) Over there. The one just below the screen. I do not think they like the film very much. They only stay for quarter of an hour. And I think maybe the lady was not so well.

Wilder Not so well? What d'you mean by that?

Manager Because the two men have to hold her up. Maybe she was feeling a little sick. (*pleading*) Inspector. If there is anything I can –

Mahmoud That will be all, thank you.

Manager But –

Mahmoud (*snaps*) Il faddal! (*That is all I say!*)

The manager nervously obeys and withdraws

Manager Yes, sir. Yes… (*leaves*)

Aziz The man should be punished. He is a liar and a thief.

Mahmoud No Captain. He is a rogue, but I think he is telling the truth.

Wilder She's been drugged. Anybody can see that. But what do they want with her? What?

Aziz If you will allow me to interrogate the cinema manager, I think you will find he will tell me far more than he has told you, Inspector.

Mahmoud (*wryly*) No doubt, Captain. But that will not be necessary, thank you.

Aziz (*losing temper*) What's wrong with you? Don't you intend to take any disciplinary action against this man? What has happened, has happened in his cinema. For all we know he may even have arranged it.

Mahmoud If we are to take discipline at all Captain, it will be against those who are responsible for Miss Warwick's abduction. Not against fools who know no better.

Aziz (*an outburst*) He is an enemy of the state!

Mahmoud Nonsense!

Aziz And so too are you Inspector Mahmoud!

Pause

Mahmoud (*withholding real anger*) Will you please now leave us, Captain Aziz.

Pause. Aziz moves off at an angry pace

Aziz (*calls back*) And don't think Cairo will not hear about this!

As he leaves he slams the door which echoes throughout the hall

Wilder (*sadly*) I know how he feels. All this is so frustrating. She may even be dead by now.

Mahmoud Yes, my friend – maybe she is. (*thoughtfully*) But somehow… I do not think so…

As he speaks last line, mix in the buzzing of flies in the shack where Elizabeth is virtually her brother's prisoner

Elizabeth Berkeley. Brian Berkeley. Of course – that's the Villiers' son. (*pause*) So it is true what they said. The two of you were in the same regiment. And you both deserted at the same time.

Michael No Liz. I'm afraid it's not quite like that. He didn't desert. He stayed behind.

Pause

Elizabeth (*unbelievingly*) But –

Michael Brian Berkeley was killed in action. (*cynically*) Fighting for his country. (*pause*) I took his place.

Elizabeth (*distraught*) Oh my – ! How could you be so cruel!

Michael All I had to do was change identification papers. After all his body was so mutilated it couldn't be recognised. (*quite casual*) He stepped on a land-mine, you know.

Elizabeth (*scornfully*) And Michael Warwick?

Michael Lies a-mouderin' in his grave. In the British War Cemetery near Cairo. (*pause. Pleased with himself*) Come on Liz. You and father knew that. *You* got the telegram from the War Office, didn't you?

Pause. Elizabeth is almost too shocked to speak

Elizabeth It's almost one of the most despicable things I've ever heard in my – . You let that boy's parents think their son is a criminal. And worse than that, you give them hope that he's still alive. (*attacking*) What sort of a person are you? Don't you have any feelings?

Michael (*uncomprehendingly*) Feelings?

Elizabeth That boy was supposed to have been your best friend!

Michael And so he was. None better.

Elizabeth And yet you let a dead man take the blame for something he didn't do. Why?

Pause

Michael (*calculating*) I needed a name. A different one. (*pause*) And Berkeley obliged by giving me his. It's as simple as that. (*pause*) Oh, not that I bother to use it now. There are plenty of other ways to exist.

Elizabeth Rotten ways!

Michael I was hoping you were going to be a little more understanding. After all, I *am* your brother Liz.

Elizabeth (*bitterly*) Don't remind me! I'm only grateful father's not alive. To see you like this.

Michael Would it really have made so much difference to him?

Elizabeth He was your father.

Michael More yours than mine.

Elizabeth That's nonsense, and you know it! Don't blame him for your own inefficiencies!

Michael (*angrily*) I blame him for the sort of man he was! Arrogant, self-contained, confident of his own genius.

Elizabeth He loved *you*.

Michael Me? (*bursts out laughing*) Oh no, Liz. No. He loathed me as much as I loathed him. Even now – after he's dead – after all these years. (*pause*) He never wanted his son to be his equal. That was beyond him. All I was ever allowed to be was second best.

Elizabeth You never gave him a chance. He was a sad and lonely man, and he tried hard to make it up to you. But you never gave him a chance!

Michael (*sarcastically*) And you did, of course. Well let me tell you this, my girl. You needn't be so smug. You may think he loved you, but if he did – it was only because you reminded him of our dear mother – that is when she was sober...

Elizabeth springs up to make for the door. Michael grabs hold of her

No, no, no! Don't go Liz.

Elizabeth Let go of me! I don't want to stay with you another minute!

Michael Well, you're at liberty to go if you want. But I warn you, you may find it rather a long walk. We've got five miles of desert around this shack.

Pause

Elizabeth (*still in his grip*) It was you who got Fuad Yassif to write to me, wasn't it? It was you who wanted me out here.

Michael But of course. (*tauntingly*) You're my little sister. My father's daughter. It's only natural that I should want to see you again – now isn't it?

Elizabeth Don't try and fool me Michael. I *know* why you've brought me here. But do you really think I know more about that tomb than anyone else?

Pause

Michael (*amused, but serious*) I don't know, Liz. But we shall find out – won't we?

A sharp cut

Pause

Fade in Wilder and O'Hara walking through Markaz Square, now back to normal

O'Hara (*distressed*) It's no use, Mr Wilder. I blame myself for all this. We should never have let a young girl like that come to a place like Markaz Square all on her own. And after dark.

Wilder (*sighs*) I know Mr O'Hara. I feel exactly the same way myself. But there's not much the Consulate can do. The police were supposed to have been watching her day and night. But you know Miss Warwick. She's quite a determined young lady.

O'Hara Just like her father. Though Lord knows why anybody should want to kidnap her.

They come to a halt

Wilder Actually, Mr O'Hara. There is something I've been meaning to ask you. (*pause*) You spent quite a bit of time yourself up at the Harshak Tomb, didn't you? During the excavations?

O'Hara Yes, I did.

Wilder Tell me honestly. If Sir Richard hadn't been forced to leave the country, would any further work up there have proved important?

Pause

O'Hara To be frank – I don't think so. It was fascinating to find something above, instead of actually in the Valley of the Kings, but –

Wilder But in your opinion, it was not Pharaonic?

O'Hara No. If it was, I think the people from the Cairo Museum would have found something. They spent nearly six months up there after Sir Richard left.

Wilder Yes. That's what I thought. (*pause*) Oh well, we'll just have to sit tight and hope no harm comes to her. Can I give you a lift somewhere? My car's parked just on the other side of the Square.

O'Hara No, thanks all the same. I'm going to hang around for a bit – just in case they get any news of Elizabeth.

Wilder Right. (*as he leaves*) Let me know if they do, won't you?

O'Hara I will. (*calls*) Goodbye!

Wilder (*calls back*) Goodbye!

O'Hara (*anxious*) Be careful of the traffic, Mr Wilder. It's a bit mad round here today.

Wilder (*calling*) I will! Goodb–…

Before he has had a chance to finish what he is saying, a car approaches at full speed, horn blazing away. There is a screech of brakes as Wilder shouts out as though he has been hit

O'Hara Mr Wilder! Merciful Heavens – Mr Wilder!

The car, without stopping, disappears into the distance. Bring up panicked Arab crowd running to help. Mix in hotel dining-room effects

Pringle (*approaching*) Ah! There you are Mr Villiers. I've been looking all over for you.

Villiers (*a bored sigh*) Yes, Mr Pringle?

Pringle (*squirms*) Don't know how you can eat that muck! You wouldn't catch me eating at the hotel. I'm sure they make their tea with water from the river.

Margaret (*sarcastically*) Then we won't ask you to join us for breakfast, Mr Pringle.

Villiers Is there something I can do for you, Mr Pringle?

Pringle Oh no. It's what I can do for you, Mr Villiers. I've got an idea I've seen that bloke you've been looking for.

Villiers } What!

Margaret } Oh Charlie!

Pringle Round about thirty, brown eyes, bit taller than me…

Margaret (*very excited*) Yes, yes! That's him!

Villiers Mr Pringle. Where was this?

Pringle Well that's just it you see. It's quite a coincidence really. He was in that cafe I met you in the other day. The one in Markaz Square. As a matter of fact, I had a drink with him.

Villiers You – didn't mention us, by any chance?

Pringle Oh no. I thought I'd better check with you first. Just in case it wasn't him.

Margaret (*overpoweringly eager*) His name. Did he tell you his name?

Pringle Well, yes he did, Mrs Villiers. The only trouble is, I can't quite remember...

Margaret (*as quick as a flash*) Berkeley...

Villiers (*trying to stop her*) No Maggie!

Margaret (*disregarding*) Brian Berkeley.

Pringle Why yeah! That's it! So it is the same bloke.

Villiers Mr Pringle. Please listen. How long ago was this?

Pringle Oh – no more than half an hour.

Villiers Was he still there when you left?

Pringle No, I'm afraid not. He was going back to his own place. He doesn't live in Luxor. Apparently he's got a small villa up in the hills – few miles the other side of Harshak.

Villiers Do you know how to get there?

Pringle Well – yes...

Villiers Would you come with me?

Margaret But Charlie, it's nearly all sand and desert out there. It's miles.

Pringle That is true Mr Villiers. I warn you it's pretty tough going. This bloke told me the last part of the journey he has to go by camel.

Villiers We could hire a couple of camels, couldn't we?

Pringle Well, yes. I suppose...

Villiers With a bit of luck, we could be there and back by nightfall. (*pause. A quiet desperation*) Mr Pringle. You've no idea how important this is to us. (*pause*) Will you come with me... *please*?

Cut back to Arab crowd gathered around the groaning Wilder in Markaz Square

O'Hara (*rushing in to approach*) Mr Wilder! Mr Wilder, are you all right?

Wilder (*aching*) Yes, thank the Lord – but only just. What the hell that maniac thought he was doing, tearing through the Square at that speed. Another half inch and I'd have been killed.

O'Hara Did you manage to get a look at his face?

Wilder No. But he threw something out of the window at me.

O'Hara (*puzzled*) Threw something?

Wilder Yes – a piece of stone or metal... can you see it around anywhere?

O'Hara (*looking around*) No, I don't think... no, wait a minute! What's this? (*picks up something*) You're right. It's a bit of stone wrapped up in... (*deadly serious as he unravels a piece of paper*) Mr Wilder. You'd better take a look.

Wilder Why?

O'Hara It's a note.

Wilder (*grabbing note*) Let me see! (*shocked at what he reads*) Oh no! I knew it!

O'Hara What? Is it Elizabeth?

Wilder (*reading*) "If you want to see English woman live, go to the New Mosque at half-day."

O'Hara You're not going?

Wilder Of course I'm going. What else can I do?

O'Hara (*with concern*) Mr Wilder, it's too dangerous. They're obviously holding Elizabeth for ransom. You can't go wandering into a Mosque on your own. You're not even a Muslim.

Wilder I've got to try. If it's money they want, we must give it to them. But I just can't leave that girl in the hands of a gang of cut-throats. (*pause*) Half-day. That's twelve noon isn't it?

O'Hara Yes. But Mr Wilder, I beg of you. Leave it to the police.

Wilder No! Now listen to me Mr O'Hara. Whatever you do, please say nothing to the police. If they go anywhere near the place, we don't stand a chance. Now will you promise?

Pause

O'Hara Well, if I have to. But I don't like this. Will you at least let me come with you?

Wilder (*emphatic*) No! I must go to that Mosque on my own. If Elizabeth Warwick is still alive, I've got to save her... somehow...

Mix into crowd effects, the buzzing of flies in the desert shack where Elizabeth is being held against her will

Michael (*angrily*) Don't lie to me, sister dear! Do you really expect me to believe that my father worked all that time up at Harshak without finding out anything at all about the place?

Elizabeth (*also angry*) The Harshak Tomb is worthless. It's nothing more than a mirage in the middle of a stinking hot desert. The sooner you realise that the better.

Pause

Michael (*calm, disbelieving*) Really?

Pause. He walks around

Tell me Liz. What made you want to come to Egypt?

Elizabeth I accepted an invitation...

Michael From a man you'd never met, or had any contact with? Isn't that a bit – adventurous?

Elizabeth Fuad Yassif was a friend of my father's.

Michael I'm told father had a lot of friends in Luxor. Why Yassif? (*pause*) No, Liz. Let *me* tell you why you came here. You came because one day you knew you had to come. You were expecting that letter from Yassif...

Elizabeth (*dismissingly*) What *are* you talking ab...

Michael He had his instructions. Immediately father died, he was to write to you, make contact, and arrange for you to share a king's fortune.

A slight pause, and then Elizabeth bursts out laughing. Michael is adamant

Elizabeth A king's fortune? You surely don't mean that broken down shack in the middle of nowhere...?

Michael The Pharaoh's tomb, Liz. The Pharaoh you're going to identify for me.

Elizabeth You must be out of your mind!

Michael I've already found one other chamber, but there's not much there I'm afraid. However, I'm sure you'll help me to find the rest.

Elizabeth How many more times do I have to tell you. Father knew nothing about that tomb. All he ever had were theories. (*pleading*) Michael. Please – for your own sake – give up all this nonsense. If anybody catches you out at that tomb, you'll be shot.

Michael (*amused*) Don't be silly, Liz. I'm already dead – you know that.

The door opens. Fuad Yassif enters

Fuad There's a storm coming. If you want to get back to Luxor you'll have to hurry.

Michael Come in Yassif! (*an edged politeness to him*) We've just been having a little chat about you.

Yassif closes door

My sister here tells me you were a friend of my father.

Elizabeth I'm not interested –

Michael Yes. You two must have got on well together. It's what my father always wanted. A son who loved him.

Elizabeth Don't play games any more, please Michael. I know very well this man is not the real Fuad Yassif, so don't try and pretend that he is.

Michael (*play-acting*) Did you hear that Fuad? My sister's calling you a liar! *You* of all people! (*to Elizabeth*) Really Liz, you shouldn't talk to Fuad like that. He's a very sensitive person. Someone you can trust. Someone you can look up to. A true Arab. (*pause. Cynically to Fuad*) Isn't that so Fuad?

Fuad (*calm, unfaltering*) The others are waiting for you outside.

Michael (*tauntingly*) Fuad. Tell my sister that she's wrong. (*pause*) Go on. Show her you're not scared of her.

Elizabeth Michael!

Michael Or are you going to stand there like you always do, until you crack like the shell of an egg! (*attacking*) Go on! Tell her how you weep if you have to look at the face of a dead man!

Elizabeth (*angrily*) Stop this!

Michael (*shouts, out of control*) You're not Fuad Yassif! Why don't you tell her – you're a fake!

Elizabeth (*trying to restrain him*) Michael! What's wrong with you? Why are you doing this?

Pause. Michael attempts to control himself

Michael He's weak. There's nothing I despise more in a man than weakness. (*as though nothing has happened*) Well, I must be off. I don't want to get caught in that sandstorm. It's such a strain on the eyes. (*making his way to door*) Anyway, when I get back we can have another little chat, can't we Liz?

Opens door

Don't worry. You won't be lonely. I'll leave your friend Mr Yassif here to keep you company. I'm sure you two have a lot to talk about. (*about to go, then stops*) Oh, and Liz. Do have a think about what I said. If you *do* feel you have something I ought to know about, *I* don't mind waiting – if *you* don't.

He goes. Slams the door. Cut

Pause

The impatient groans of two camels, already mounted by Pringle and Villiers

Pringle Aw shut up, will yer! I never could bear camels you know. They remind me of too many bods I know. Reckon they're so superior!

Another loud groan from a camel

    Shut up!

Margaret Oh Charlie, do be careful! The tracks up in those hills are very dangerous.

Villiers I shall be quite all right. Just stay at the hotel, and don't go out until I get back.

Margaret But you've never ridden a camel before.

Pringle It's not the camel you have to worry about, Mrs Villiers. It's what they carry about with them…

A slapping sound

    …fleas!

Villiers Right! Shall we go?

Pringle gives his camel a dig. Another objection from the camel

Pringle Come on! Get up will you!

Villiers Which way?

Pringle Up there. Left fork.

Villiers Left? But that doesn't lead up to Harshak, does it?

Pringle (*awkwardly*) Er – no. (*a quick excuse*) We have to bypass Harshak. We've got to get to the hills on the other side. But don't worry. It's a lot quicker this way.

Villiers You've got plenty of water?

Pringle Yes! Enough to sink a battleship.

Villiers Right! Let's go.

Pringle starts to move off on his camel

Margaret (*stopping Villiers*) Charlie – please!

Villiers What's the matter?

Margaret (*an impassioned plea*) If you see him. If you see Brian… tell him I still love him…

Pause

Villiers (*refusing to show emotion*) I'll be back as soon as I can.

His camel starts to move off. Pringle calls back

Pringle For goodness' sake cover up your head, Mr Villiers! This sun's hotter than ever!

The camels trek off, groaning as they go. Mix into this the sandstorm raging outside the desert shack. It is shut into the background as Fuad closes a window

Fuad Another twenty minutes, I think it will be over.

Elizabeth Does it matter? We're stuck here anyway.

Fuad It's no use blaming me, Elizabeth. It was not my idea to bring you here.

Elizabeth What sort of a person are you anyway? To let him speak to you like that?

Fuad You heard what your brother said. I'm weak.

Elizabeth And that's enough to allow yourself to be humiliated? To have your face ground into the dust by a bully?

Fuad I have no choice.

Elizabeth (*bitterly*) What do you mean, you have no choice?

Fuad I mean, if I don't do what he says, your brother will kill me.

Elizabeth (*puzzled*) Kill?

Fuad And he would have no hesitation in doing the same to you, I can assure you. (*pause*) Did you know he was unbalanced?

Elizabeth (*reluctantly*) It isn't very hard to guess. But that doesn't make him a killer.

Fuad It did once. I see no reason why it should not again.

Elizabeth (*angrily*) What are you talking about? Why should my brother want to kill anyb... (*stops dead. She remembers with horror*) Oh no! Not that boy? Not the Villiers' son?

Fuad (*solemnly*) Lieutenant Berkeley was not killed in action, Elizabeth.

Pause

Elizabeth (*distressed*) I don't believe you!

Fuad You don't have to. But it happens to be the truth.

Elizabeth But why?

Fuad For the same reason that he would kill you, or me, or anyone else who got in his way. (*pause*) That is why you have got to tell him what you know about the Harshak Tomb.

Pause

Elizabeth Who are you? (*pause*) If you hate my brother so much, why don't you get out? Why d'you keep on working for him?

Fuad I didn't say I hate him. I am afraid of him.

Elizabeth You see. He *was* right. You *are* weak. Weaker than any man I've ever known.

Fuad Is it such a disgrace? Have you never been afraid of anything Elizabeth?

She does not answer, but goes to window

Elizabeth It's almost stopped. I can see the sky again. (*turns around to plead with him*) Fuad! Or whoever you are – if you really mean what you say, help me to get out of here. We could both be back in Luxor before Michael returns...

Fuad No. I'm sorry, I couldn't do that.

Elizabeth (*snapping*) Why not!

Fuad Because I'm weak.

Pause

Elizabeth (*angrily*) Hypocrite! (*She suddenly produces a knife which she has been hiding*)

Fuad Elizabeth! What are you doing? Where did you get that knife from?

Elizabeth You see! Now it's my turn. You shouldn't allow your old lady to leave things lying around. (*pause. Moving backwards*) Now. Get away from that door!

Pause

Fuad (*quite unmoved*) No.

Elizabeth I warn you I shall use this thing if I have to!

Fuad Very well. (*pause*) Well, go on. What are you waiting for? (*shouts across room to her*) Look! I've opened my arms out wide. All you have to do is to press the knife into my ribs. (*pause*) What's the matter Elizabeth? What are you waiting for?

Pause. Elizabeth, with a dejected sigh, drops the knife on the floor

You see, Elizabeth. It's not easy to be strong, is it? (*pause*) Or weak.

A marked pause, before fading up the chanted midday prayers at the New Mosque in Luxor. (NB for authenticity: prayers relayed by tannoy is the modern method used in most mosques in Egypt.) Wilder mingles with the vast Muslim gathering, until he is at last approached by the old Arab, Abdullah

Abdullah (*an asthmatic whisper*) Do not move, English man.

Wilder jumps, as he is taken by surprise

No! Do not turn around. You will keep the face turned towards Mecca.

Wilder (*sceptically*) Who are you?

Abdullah It does not matter who am I. Why do you come here?

Wilder I was told if I wanted information about – about an English woman – I should come here to the New Mosque at midday. Is it you I'm supposed to meet?

Pause

Abdullah You are alone?

Wilder Of course.

Abdullah Then listen to me English man... no! Do not turn around! (*He moves closer*) Do you want to see your English woman alive?

Wilder Naturally.

Abdullah How do you know is not already with death?

Wilder I don't. Isn't that why I came here? Do you know where she is?

Abdullah Yes.

Pause

Wilder (*nervously*) Well, for Heaven's sake man, aren't you going to tell me where?

Abdullah What will you do for me?

Wilder If it's money you want...

Abdullah (*scornfully*) Money! I do not want your money. (*anger raised*) Only from you do I want that you take this woman away from Luxor – from Egypt. Will you do that for me, English man?

Wilder Why should I do that?

Abdullah It is not for you to ask the questions. Will you do it, or shall the woman die?

Pause

Wilder I'll do my best. But I warn you, if I find she's been molested in any...

Abdullah Do you know the Village of the White Scorpion?

Wilder Hasia? Yes.

Abdullah Soon you will go there.

Wilder Soon?

Abdullah When the dervish begins to dance – not before.

Wilder (*immediate concern*) The dervishes? You mean they're going to take her there? But – they'll kill her. You've got to tell me when… how do I find her?

Abdullah When the dervish begins to dance, you will go to the village of Hasia, and there you will…

He stops what he is saying abruptly, as Wilder suddenly realises he has been scared off

Wilder There I will what? (*turns around*) Hey! Where've you gone? (*calls*) Hey! Don't go! Please…

Mahmoud approaches

Mahmoud Ah! There you are Mr Wilder.

Wilder (*angrily*) Inspector Mahmoud! What the hell d'you think you're… how long have you been here?

Mahmoud For several minutes. But you need not worry, my men have surrounded Mosque.

Wilder You fools! You damned fools! Now how the hell d'you think we're going to find Elizabeth Warwick? How did you know I was here?

Mahmoud Mr O'Hara have great concern for you. He tell me about the note you have received.

Wilder Mr O'Hara promised me…

Mahmoud Is too dangerous for you here, my friend. The Mosque is holy ground. (*pause*) But you have met this man?

Wilder (*bitterly*) Yes. I've met him. And, thanks to you, have now lost him. *And* probably our only chance of saving Elizabeth Warwick.

Mahmoud No, no! This man cannot leave the Mosque without passing my men. All you have to do my friend is show me who the man is.

Pause

Wilder Show you – ? (*pause*) Take a look around you Inspector. How many worshippers would *you* say there are here? Five, six hundred? Well, there they are. All of them wearing identical white, all of them bowing towards Mecca. (*pause*) So. Take a good look Inspector. Tell me if *you* can see the man we're looking for?

Bring up to full the mass prayer chanting, until we suddenly cut in the closing call of the muezzin, over which we read our announcements

END OF EPISODE FIVE

Kill the Pharaoh!

by Victor Pemberton

Episode 6: At the Point of a Triangle

Produced by John Tydeman

REHEARSALS:	Wednesday 23 August 1967	1030–1730
RECORD:	Wednesday 23 August 1967	1730–1830
STUDIO:	B.10	
R.P. No.	TLN34/DA852H	

CAST:
Elizabeth ....Sheila Grant
Mahmoud..................................James Thomason
Mr Wilder ....John Humphry
Fuad ....David Spenser
Charles......................................Rolf Lefebvre
Margaret....................................Marion Mathie
Achmed.....................................Haydn Jones
Bertie ....Barry Lowe
Michael ....Christopher Bidmead

S.M.s: Panel: Amna Smith; Grams: Keith Salmon;
             Spot: Enyd Williams

SECRETARY: Judy Munk, PABX 2168

The call of the muezzin is broken by the sound of Wilder slamming his office window

Wilder Madness! Absolute madness! What possible chance d'you think we have of finding Elizabeth Warwick now. She might even be dead.

Mahmoud Mr Wilder. You should not have gone to the Mosque alone. It is too dangerous for one who is not Muslim.

Wilder If you and your men hadn't followed me there, we'd have found out a lot more.

Mahmoud But this man who have spoken to you in the Mosque – you do not recognise?

Wilder Oh don't talk nonsense man! How am I expected to recognise someone who has his face covered? And in the middle of five or six hundred other worshippers.

Mahmoud And the voice? Do you think you could recognise his voice?

Wilder (*dejected*) I don't know. I just don't know. This whole thing has now got out of hand. (*pause*) But I tell you this. If and when we do get that girl back, she's going to be put on the first plane to England.

247

Mahmoud (*authoritative*) No, my friend. I do not think I could permit.

Pause

Wilder (*injured pride*) I – beg your pardon? Aren't you forgetting something Inspector? Miss Warwick happens to be a British subject.

Mahmoud Who must now be considered a security risk.

Wilder What!

Mahmoud (*apologetically*) With regret, of course. At first opportunity she will be placed in our protective custody.

Wilder You mean, you're going to arrest her?

Mahmoud We wish only for Miss Warwick, her safety.

Wilder (*sneeringly*) Safety! A fat lot *you* can do to save her once the dervishes get…

Mahmoud (*with sharp concern*) Dervish? What do you know of this?

Wilder I know that they're a bunch of religious maniacs who'd stop at nothing to kill.

Mahmoud But what has this to do with Miss Warwick?

Wilder The old man who talked to me at the Mosque. He warned me that if I wanted to see the English woman alive again, I would have to wait until the dervish begins to dance. And this is going to take place in –

Mahmoud The Village of the White Scorpion. Hasia.

Wilder You know?

Mahmoud There are still many who practise the dervish rites in this village.

Wilder But I thought it was illegal?

Mahmoud It is. And very dangerous for those who try to watch. You see, when the dervish begins to dance, his mind his no longer his own. He becomes immune to anything around him. He can feel no physical pain. It is like a state of hypnotism – or if you like – a trance.

Wilder Yes. But what happens if someone tries to break the trance?

Pause

Mahmoud Mr Wilder. The trance must *not* be broken.

A sharp cut. Pause. Water being poured into a glass

Fuad Here. Drink some water. You'll feel better.

Elizabeth (*proudly*) No thank you.

Fuad Don't be foolish. It's very hot in here. (*no reply. Impatient*) What good do you think it will do to stare out of the windo…

She angrily knocks the glass to the floor

Elizabeth I've told you I don't want any water! Now leave me alone will you!

Pause. Fuad controls anger

Fuad You know you can't escape from here, don't you?

Elizabeth All you have to do is open that door.

Fuad And then what? Will you walk alone – across miles of open desert?

Elizabeth I'd sooner take my chances out there.

Fuad How many more times do I have to tell you? Your brother has no intention of letting you go until you have told him what he wants to know.

Elizabeth (*scornfully*) My brother? I have no brother, didn't you know? They buried him in the sand out there.

Fuad Elizabeth – please. All you have to do is to tell him what information your father passed on to you. How to reach the other chambers of that tomb.

Elizabeth My father had no such information, and as far as I am concerned, the Harshak Tomb is nothing more than a mirage.

The door is flung open. Michael Warwick enters. Neighing donkeys outside

Michael Ah! There you are. (*approaching*) Sorry to keep you waiting so long Liz. I had one or two things to attend to.

Elizabeth Would you mind telling me how much longer you intend keeping me locked up in this filthy hole?

Michael Keeping you here? Whatever gave you that idea. You're free to walk out of here any time you like.

Elizabeth (*taken aback*) You're – letting me go?

Michael The donkeys are waiting for you outside right now.

Fuad No! You can't! She'll go straight to the police.

Michael I don't think so. (*to Elizabeth*) You wouldn't – would you Liz?

Fuad Of course she will!

Elizabeth I make no promises.

Fuad You see!

Michael And what would you tell them Liz? That your loving brother has come back from the dead – after all these years?

Elizabeth I'd tell them that you're a thief, a bully, and a murderer.

Michael (*pointedly*) And also the son of that eminent, respected, and much-loved English gentleman – Sir Richard Warwick. (*pause*) Would you really tell them that Liz?

A tense pause

Elizabeth What's happened to you, Michael?

Michael Good! Are we all ready to go then? No Liz! Come back. (*holding her*) Not that way.

Elizabeth You just told me the donkeys are…

Michael The scenery between here and Luxor is very dull, Liz. You really wouldn't enjoy it.

Elizabeth (*panicking*) W–what are you doing?

Michael (*to Fuad*) Hold her!

Elizabeth Oh no please Michael – not that again! No…!

He smothers her mouth with a handkerchief. During this:

Michael Get the boat ready.

Fuad (*bewildered*) Why are you doing this?

Michael I said get the boat ready, and don't ask questions!

Fuad about to leave, stops

Fuad Is there a change of plan?

Michael Yes.

Fuad But she hasn't told us anything?

Michael No. But she will. And *before* the dervish begins to dance.

Elizabeth flops into unconsciousness as we cut immediately to the sound of an irritated camel. Villiers and Pringle are making their way along the rocky tracks of the Theban Hills

Villiers (*weary and hot*) How much further Mr Pringle? I don't think I can stand this heat much more.

Pringle Just at the top now Mr Villiers. Once we reach that track we'll stop for a breather. Then I'm afraid we'll have to ditch the camels.

Villiers You mean we have to go the rest of the way on foot?

Pringle 'Fraid so. It's a sheer drop on the other side of that Peak. The camels couldn't make it.

Villiers Well then how far?

Pringle Well, if this bloke's villa is where I think it is, we've got about another couple of miles.

Villiers Miles!

Pringle And I warn you, it's much worse than this. Nearly all sand and open desert. Think you can make it?

Villiers (*a parched swallow*) Of course.

Pringle Well, all I can say is let's hope you think it's all worth it. 'Cos if this bloke ain't the one you're lookin' f… (*stops abruptly*) Hallo.

Villiers What's wrong?

The camels have stopped

Pringle There's someone down there. D'you see – behind you. Coming up the track.

Villiers (*looking*) Where? Oh yes. Looks like an old Arab. D'you think he's following us?

Pringle I don't know. But we'll wait here and see.

Villiers Why? He looks harmless enough.

Pringle Maybe. That is, provided he's on his own.

Quick fade out

Pause

Fade in to an excitable Arab crowd on the Luxor quayside. Mahmoud and Wilder push their way through

Mahmoud (*calls in Arabic: Get out of the way! Get out of the way!*)
Wilder Is it her?
Mahmoud Yes. Quick Mr Wilder! Help me into the boat.

Wilder helps Mahmoud into boat

Miss Warwick. Dear lady. Can you hear me?
Wilder (*background*) Is she dead?
Mahmoud No, I don't think so. She has been drugged. Dear lady!

Elizabeth begins to move

Ah!

Wilder climbs into boat

Wilder Here! Use my hat as a shade. Miss Warwick. Are you all right!

Elizabeth groaning

There are no oars in the boat. That means she could have been drifting for miles.

Mahmoud We are lucky boat have not turned over. The water have strong current. It was only the fishermen who have save her.

Elizabeth (*slowly coming out of sleep*) Oh… it's so hot…

Wilder We've got to get her out of this heat.

Mahmoud We shall take her to my office at Police Station.

Wilder Police Station? What for?

Mahmoud To recover, Mr Wilder. What else?

Wilder Recover? In other words – she's under arrest?

Bring up background Arab crowd effects. Mix into this the buzzing of flies – otherwise a marked silence

Villiers (*low voice*) Can you still see him?

Pringle No. I've got a feeling he's hiding behind those rocks somewhere.

Villiers But why is he following us? (*pause*) We just can't sit out here all day. There's no shade.

Pause

Pringle I'm going down there.

Villiers I'll come with you.

Pringle No. Better leave this to me, Mr Villiers. I know these people. If there's any trouble, I shall know how to deal with him.

Villiers But if we're going to get to that villa before dark, we can't hold up for much longer.

Pause

Pringle Tell you what you do. Make your way up to that rock. (*indicating*) D'you see? On the left there.

Villiers (*looking*) Yes.

Pringle Sit down and have a bit of a breather until I get back. If I come across any trouble, at least I know where to find you.

Villiers (*reluctantly*) Very well.

Pringle shouts and digs at the camels, who immediately bolt

Why are you doing that? Why are you getting rid of them?

Pringle 'Cos we've got no more use for them.

Villiers But –

Pringle From now on it's up to us. (*moving off*)

He stops, calls back

From now on, we're on our own, Mr Villiers. Just the two of us. You – and me. See you!

He disappears into the distance

Villiers (*a worried loud whisper*) Mr Pringle! Mr Pringle…

A sharp cut to the whirring of an electric fan in Mahmoud's office

Elizabeth Frankly, I don't care *what* you think, Inspector. I've told you the truth about what happened to me last night.

Mahmoud So you do not deny that you went to a cinema in the Markaz Square?

Elizabeth No.

Mahmoud Why? Do you speak Arabic?

Elizabeth Am I supposed to inform Police Headquarters every time I visit a cinema? (*pause*) As it so happens, I wanted to see what an Arab cinema was like.

Mahmoud And, no doubt, you have found out? You were kidnapped.

Elizabeth A bunch of thugs who thought they were on to a good thing. They found out I had no money, so they let me go. It's as simple as that.

Mahmoud But they keep you for nearly twenty-four hours. You can explain that?

Elizabeth I presume they thought they could hold me up for ransom. They got cold feet, that's all.

Mahmoud No, Miss Warwick! Not satisfied.

Elizabeth What do you mean, you're not satisfied!

Wilder Really Inspector. This has gone far enough. Miss Warwick has been under the most tremendous strain. You have no right to subject her to such an interrogation…

Mahmoud Miss Warwick. Now has come the time to tell me the reason you have come to Luxor.

Elizabeth I've told you why I came. For a holiday.

Mahmoud No. Is not the truth.

Wilder Inspector!

Mahmoud You have come to see the tomb at Harshak…

Elizabeth I really don't know what you're…

Mahmoud To try to find out what your father could not.

A tense pause

(*closer to her*) Miss Warwick. Your father knew that the tomb at Harshak – was that of a Pharaoh. Am I correct?

Wilder Inspector Mahmoud. I really think all this has gone far…

Elizabeth Yes.

Wilder stops dead

Wilder (*stunned*) What?

Elizabeth He had no definite proof. Just a series of circumstances which led him to a theory.

Mahmoud What kind of theory?

Elizabeth That one day it would be proved the Harshak Tomb is one of the most important archaeological discoveries of the twentieth century. Maybe even more so than Tutankhamen.

Wilder What!

Elizabeth My father was convinced that somewhere in that tomb lies the sarcophagus of the King. If we can find that, we shall know the Pharaoh's identity.

Mahmoud Such a sarcophagus would be priceless.

Elizabeth Precisely. And so would all the other treasures.

Wilder All this is beyond me. Why on earth didn't you tell us this was the real reason you were coming here?

Elizabeth Because I had to find that sarcophagus before anybody else. I want nothing from this other than to prove my father's theories. (*to Mahmoud*) You've got to believe me, Inspector. I can assure you, I'm neither a spy nor a propagandist. (*pause*) I happen to have loved my father very much. His work out here meant to him – well, it meant an awful lot. All I want is the chance to prove that he was right.

A moment of silence

Mahmoud (*who has listened intently*) Very well, dear lady. I will believe. But you will not forget that you still do not know how to reach such a sarcophagus, even if it does exist

Elizabeth I'm sorry Inspector, you're wrong. You see – I *do* know.

A sharp cut to a door opening at the desert shack. Pringle enters

Michael Pringle! What are you doing here?

Pringle (*approaching*) I've got someone waiting to see you.

Michael Who?

Pringle Villiers.

Michael Villiers! You mean you've brought him here?

Pringle That's right.

Michael Why?

Pringle He wanted to see his son. I thought I'd better find out if his 'son' wanted to see him.

Pause

Michael Where is he now?

Pringle The other side of the Peak. (*with relish*) He doesn't know he's only a stone's throw away from the place.

Pause

Michael Good. You know what to do.

Pringle Right! Oh, by the way. Did you put a tail on me?

Michael Tail?

Pringle There was a chap followin' me up the track. I didn't touch him just in case he was somethin' to do with you.

Michael No, he's not. (*pause*) Is he still there?

Pringle Far as I know.

Michael Leave it to me.

Pringle Right! (*starts to leave*)

Michael And Pringle.

Pringle stops

You're sure you know what to do about Mr Villiers?

Pringle (*very confident*) 'Course!

Leaves. Door

Michael Fuad. I want this place cleared by the morning. We're moving out.

Fuad Moving? But how can we? You haven't done anything about –

Michael Elizabeth? You needn't worry. That's been taken care of. (*pause*) And I must say, you do seem to have taken quite an interest in my little sister. (*close to Fuad*) Perhaps I'd better warn you, my friend. I'd sooner you didn't.

Pause

Fuad (*unfaltering*) Where are we going?

Michael That's no concern of yours, Fuad. You just obey instructions.

Fuad Maybe I won't go.

Michael Maybe it won't be necessary.

Pause

Fuad You won't kill me.

Michael No?

Fuad (*confidently*) No. I am too useful. To you – *and* the police.

Michael (*amused*) Dead men tell no tales, you know.

Fuad They don't have to. All they have to do is to write a letter – and then ask a good friend to post it – at an appropriate time of course.

Pause

Michael (*an admiring laugh*) Good for you Fuad! D'you know something? You're really beginning to improve!

Fade out

Pause

Back to the whirring of an electric fan in Mahmoud's office

Mahmoud Fantastic! Absolutely fantastic! But of *course* it is possible.

Wilder Well I can't believe it. I just can't. You mean to tell us that the Harshak Tomb was built to hold the remains of a Pharaoh who was assassinated?

Elizabeth Why not? Don't you see Mr Wilder, it all adds up. That fresco in the Temple of Luxor. The arrow of the man behind, pointing directly at the shoulders of the Pharaoh. The scene obviously depicts a royal murder. That's why the tomb was never completed. There wasn't time.

Mahmoud And the remains of the King were hidden? In a secret chamber?

Elizabeth Of course! To prevent his enemies from desecrating them.

Mahmoud Remarkable!

Wilder But even supposing there is a sarcophagus, how do we reach it?

Pause

Elizabeth Let me go there, and work it out for myself.

Wilder You?

Elizabeth My father firmly believed that if there was another entrance, it would have to be worked out mathematically. We can only do that by going to the tomb itself. And the sooner the better. Tonight in fact.

Wilder No, that's out of the question.

Elizabeth Why?

Wilder Because, Miss Warwick, this whole thing has gone far enough. We cannot afford to jeopardise your life any more.

Elizabeth Rubbish!

Mahmoud Dear lady, I would like to know why you have need of such urgency to find this sarcophagus.

Wilder Precisely! After all the damned thing has been lying there a couple of thousand years. It can wait a bit longer.

Elizabeth That's just it. It can't.

Mahmoud Why not?

Pause

Elizabeth Because if you want that sarcophagus to remain in Egypt Inspector, we have to find it as soon as possible.

Wilder You mean, there are others after it as well?

Elizabeth (*awkwardly*) I – don't know.

Mahmoud Fuad Yassif?

An unexpected pause

Elizabeth I beg your pardon?

Mahmoud The man who have invite you to come to Luxor. Does he also look for sarcophagus?

Elizabeth (*covering up*) No, no of course not. He's got nothing to do with it. Why d'you ask?

Mahmoud (*evasively*) No reason, dear lady.

Pause

Elizabeth Well? Who's coming out to that tomb with me?

Wilder I'm dead against it.

Mahmoud Then we shall go alone Miss Warwick.

Elizabeth No police, no soldiers. What we find – we find alone.

Mahmoud All alone, dear lady.

Elizabeth Then you agree to tell no one?

Mahmoud No one at all. Not even my dear mother – rest her soul.

A sharp cut. Pause

The quayside. In the extreme background, the call of the muezzin

Margaret (*approaching, anxious*) Achmed! Achmed, I've been looking all over for you.

Achmed Dear lady. Do you not hear? It is time for prayer. I must turn to Mecca.

Margaret My husband and Mr Pringle have gone up into the hills. They should have been back long ago. You've got to go and look for them.

Achmed (*nervously*) No, Mrs Villiers! Not possible for Achmed.

Margaret But if they get lost in that desert…

Achmed (*sudden interest*) Desert?

Margaret Mr Pringle has made contact with my son. They went to look for him at a villa – the other side of Harshak.

Achmed In the desert?

Margaret Yes.

Achmed I do not know such a villa.

Margaret But you must. Mr Pringle says…

Achmed In the desert near Harshak there are only the tribesmen. Not good to go there. They do not like many people. Very dangerous.

Margaret (*horrified*) Achmed! We've got to do something. I knew we couldn't trust Pringle. (*bitterly*) If he's let any harm come to... Achmed. You've got to go after them.

Achmed (*defensively*) No lady! Achmed not go to desert.

Margaret But you've got to! You're the only one that knows the way. (*almost pleading*) Oh please, Achmed. I know something's happened to him. (*pause*) We can't leave Charlie all alone up there to fend for himself. He's not a young man any more. He wouldn't know what to do in that type of... It's almost dark!

Achmed (*a cool defiance*) I will not go to the desert.

Pause

Margaret (*proudly*) Very well. (*starts to leave*) I'm sorry to have disturbed your prayers.

She stops, turns back

Oh, by the way, Achmed. Whilst you're at it, you might say one for my husband. Because, wherever he is right now, he's going to need a few prayers!

A sharp cut to the screeching wail of a jackal. For a moment we hold on to the chorus of jackals, hyenas, owls, bats, and barking dogs from the valley, as the night air is penetrated unnervingly

Villiers, alone in the Theban Hills, trudges his way blindly through the darkness

Villiers (*shouting nervously*) Pringle! (*stops walking*) Pringle! Where are you?

He jumps with a start as his only reply comes from the screech of a nearby hyena

Oh God! What am I going to do? I'm lost. I can't see a thing... (*shouts almost hysterically*) Pringle! Don't leave me here! (*his voice echoing throughout the valley*) Please...!

Suddenly, in the middle of this, the sound of approaching footsteps nearby

Pringle! Is that you? (*with relief*) Thank God! (*calls*) I'm up here!

The footsteps stop

(*puzzled*) Pringle! What are you doing? (*no reply. Angrily*) Why don't you come up... (*still no reply. An angry determination comes over Villiers*) All right! If you won't come up here, I'll come down to... you...

He takes no more than one or two steps before shouting out in horror, as he falls down a rock face

(*shouting*) Pringle! Help me! I've been stung by a snake! (*desperately*) My leg! Oh... my leg... (*shouts louder, hysterically*) Pringle! Please... help me...!

Yet another wail of a hyena, taken up by the night chorus which we bring up to an almost deafening pitch until it is cut out abruptly by the sound of Mahmoud swatting a mosquito on his face. He and Elizabeth have reached the entrance to the Harshak Tomb

Mahmoud (*disgruntled*) Mosquitos! They are the curse of my life!

He pushes open the iron doors of the tomb. This brings Elizabeth rushing forward

Elizabeth (*approaching*) Inspector! What are you doing?

Mahmoud I am going into the tomb.

Elizabeth Not that way. This is where everybody has been going wrong. This is not the main entrance.

Mahmoud (*puzzled*) Not?

Elizabeth Just stand still and think about it for a moment. Why do you think the ancient tomb robbers were never able to find the treasures of Tutankhamen?

Mahmoud I have heard it was because they found the much larger tomb of Ramses the Sixth.

Elizabeth Which partially obscured the bigger prize. Precisely! Then why shouldn't the same thing have happened here?

Mahmoud You mean that this tomb is some kind of a hoax?

Elizabeth Why not? You know as well as I do that the construction of a Pharaoh's tomb often used to start shortly after his birth. Some of those tombs in the Valley of the Kings took a whole lifetime to complete.

Mahmoud But you say that this Pharaoh, whoever he was, was killed by an assassin?

Elizabeth Yes.

Mahmoud Then his tomb was never completed?

Elizabeth That's what his enemies were made to believe. (*pause*) I think differently. I think the Pharaoh's body is in there right now.

Mahmoud But I still cannot see how –

Elizabeth Look. If the King's family didn't want his remains to be desecrated, surely the last place they'd dare risk would be his own tomb? (*pause*) No. The tomb has somehow been divided.

Mahmoud So when the Pharaoh's enemies broke in, they desecrated the chamber because there was no sarcophagus. (*pause*) Then, dear lady, what you say must be right. Somewhere in the tomb lies the mummy of the Pharaoh?

Elizabeth Yes.

Mahmoud But if the Pharaoh's enemies could not find him – how can we?

Pause

Elizabeth By mathematics, Inspector. The ancient art of mathematics.

A sharp cut to impatient banging on the door of Wilder's flat. He is irritated at being woken up

Wilder (*calls*) Wait a minute, can't you? Give me a chance!

Opens the door

Don't you know what time it… oh. It's you.

It is Margaret Villiers, nervous and strained

Margaret I'm terribly sorry to disturb you. It is Mr Wilder, isn't it?

Wilder Why yes, Mrs Villiers.

Margaret My name's not Villiers. It's Berkeley. Margaret Berkeley.

A tense pause

Wilder I think you'd better come in.

She enters. Wilder closes door

Now then. What's the matter?

Margaret (*in desperation*) I need your help, Mr Wilder. I must have your help.

Mix into the night chorus in the Theban Hills. Villiers, groaning in agony, is sprawled out on the ground. Footsteps approach and stop

Pringle (*now sinister and tormenting*) Oh, there you are, Mr Villiers. I've been lookin' all over for you...

Villiers (*in great pain*) Pringle... you've got to help me... my leg... I think it's broken...

Pringle Oh dear, oh dear. You are in pain aren't you. Didn't I tell you not to go wanderin' around on your own – and in the dark too.

Villiers I fell... down the slope... (*suddenly very angry*) Don't just stand there man! I've got to get to a doctor.

Pringle (*with surprise*) Doctor?

Villiers D'you want me to die?

Pause

Pringle (*pointed amusement*) To tell you the truth, Mr Villiers – I'm easy.

Pause. Villiers cannot believe what he has heard. He is stunned

Villiers What! Pringle – what are you saying...?

Pringle Now just you lie still, Mr Villiers. You're only makin' yourself uncomfortable.

Villiers You planned this didn't you? You left me without water – all alone. (*anger building to hysteria*) You wanted me to die. Why?

Pringle (*ignoring him*) D'you know something, Mr Villiers? There must be millions and millions of stars up in that sky. I've always wished I could have the time and patience to sit back and count them. (*pause*) Reckon that's something you'll be able to do – between now and the morning.

The screech of a jackal in distance

That is, if *he* lets you...

Pringle starts to move off

Villiers (*in panic*) Pringle. Where are you going? Pringle! (*calls*) Don't leave me...!

Pringle's footsteps disappearing

(*his voice echoing*) No! Please... don't... leave me...!

His voice is drowned by the screech of a jackal, which is taken up by the night chorus of animals

Mix into the sound of buzzing mosquitos and cicadas outside the Harshak Tomb

Mahmoud Mathematics? Dear lady, I still do not know what this has to do with the tomb.

Elizabeth Look up there at the stars, Inspector. A whole universe of mathematical equation. (*pause*) Isn't that the way the ancient astronomers used to work? And the architects?

Mahmoud Architects?

Elizabeth Wasn't it the ambition of every Egyptian architect to create the perfect single shape? The triangle? Surely you only have to look at the great Pyramids at Giza?

Mahmoud Of course! The triangle.

Elizabeth My father believed that the large passage inside this tomb was only one side of a triangle. And if we could just find the supreme point of that triangle…

Mahmoud The King's Chamber!

Elizabeth (*with great deliberation*) Yes. There's no doubt that the architects who were commissioned to design this tomb had one major problem to face. And that was how to mislead an enemy who tried to break in and reach the King's sarcophagus.

Mahmoud And so – they have done it mathematically.

Elizabeth Right. So let's say that the passage inside leading from this main entrance – is one side of a triangle. What we've got to do is to find the other side… either to the left – or to the right.

Mahmoud Nothing. Miles of desert over there to the right. Sand – only sand.

Elizabeth What about over there – to the left?

Mahmoud (*sighs*) Again – nothing. Except… could it be as far as the caves?

Elizabeth Caves? What caves?

Mahmoud The Harshak Caves. No one ever goes there. It is old Coptic burial ground.

Elizabeth How far?

Mahmoud One, maybe two miles. But I do not think it is the place. The people of the village do not enter because of fear. They talk of evil spirits…

Elizabeth (*excitedly*) Then that's the place to go! (*dashing off*) Come on!

Mahmoud (*apprehensively*) But Miss Warwick – suppose is true? Suppose there *are* evil spirits?

Cut. Pause. Footsteps approaching inside the Coptic caves.

(*approaching in a whisper*) Be careful how you go, dear lady. It is not easy to see.

Elizabeth There's no need to whisper, Inspector. I don't think there's any fear of waking the dead. (*pause*) Could you shine the torch ahead of you please? (*pause*) Is that a path?

Mahmoud No. I am afraid we shall find nothing. The catacombs have not been used for years.

Elizabeth (*looking around*) Extraordinary how still death can be. (*pause*) It needs no effort just to lie there – weighed down by a huge piece of stone.

Mahmoud The Copts were very remarkable people. Like the Christians in ancient Rome, they also had to die for their faith.

Elizabeth Strange there are no wall paintings here either. The Coptic graves I saw in Cairo were much more decorated.

Mahmoud Dear lady, I think we must turn back. We shall find no entrance to the Harshak Tomb here.

Elizabeth But if there is another side to the triangle, I'm positive this is just the sort of place we'd find it. You see…

She jumps with fright as a dog suddenly springs out snarling at her

Inspector!

Mahmoud Don't move dear lady! Don't move!

The dog continues to snarl for a moment, then disappears into the distance. His barks are heard on echo

Are you all right?

Elizabeth Yes. But look! D'you see where that dog came from? Quick! The torch.

Mahmoud (*looking*) It's a passage. A small passage.

Elizabeth (*excitedly*) Quick! Help me through.

Mahmoud (*with concern*) Now be careful Miss Warwick! Be careful!

They climb into the passage

Elizabeth Look Inspector! This is not Coptic. There have been hieroglyphics on these walls.

Mahmoud Yes!

Elizabeth And they've been scratched out. D'you see?

Mahmoud Extraordinary!

Elizabeth (*almost a delirium*) This *is* the other side of the triangle, I know it is! (*running off ahead*)

Mahmoud Then if there is a chamber it must be…

Elizabeth (*calling from beyond*) Inspector! Quick! Come over here!

Mahmoud rushes forward to join her

Mahmoud What is it?

Elizabeth All these rocks. It looks as though there's been a landslide or something. Please! Help me to get up. The passage can't stop here. There must be something on the other side.

Mahmoud Very well. But I am coming with you.

They climb up the rocks

Elizabeth Give me the torch.

From now on, as they speak their voices are on a much more open echo, as they have entered without realising it a large chamber, almost a vast hall

It's so dark up here. Whatever you do, don't slip down onto…

Mahmoud (*with dramatic intensity*) Miss Warwick! Be quiet.

Elizabeth What is it?

Dead silence after echo

Mahmoud Our voices. Don't you hear? They are different. We are no longer in a passage…

Elizabeth (*seeing what is before her, aghast*) Oh my…! Inspector! Look! Down there!

Mahmoud (*stunned*) The Chamber! It *is* the King's Burial Chamber!

Elizabeth (*unable to contain her exhilaration*) And there's the sarcophagus!

She is already scrambling down the rocks

Mahmoud Miss Warwick! Come back! (*calls*) Be careful!

Both are now in the Chamber, having rushed up to the sarcophagus

260

Elizabeth (*breathless in the silence*) I can't bear it. We've found it! We've actually found it.

Mahmoud (*with shrewd observation*) Yes. But we are not the first. Someone has been here before us.

Elizabeth And the walls. Everything's exactly the same as in the other Chamber. No hieroglyphics or paintings…

Mahmoud I am going to climb up to look into the sarcophagus.

Elizabeth Oh no – please Inspector! Let me. What happens after tonight is up to you. But at least let me do this – for my father.

Pause

Mahmoud Take my hand. (*helping her to climb up*) Now!

She is standing alongside the sarcophagus

Elizabeth Give me the torch.

Mahmoud Can you see anything?

Elizabeth The top has been removed. This is extraordinary… How on earth could they… (*She lets out a horrified gasp as she sees something which shocks her*) Inspector!

Mahmoud What's the matter? What is it?

Elizabeth There is a body in here. (*shaking with horror*) But – it's not the body of the Pharaoh!

A sharp cut to the shrill call of the muezzin as we superimpose closing announcements

END OF EPISODE SIX

Kill the Pharaoh!

by Victor Pemberton

Episode 7: When the Dervish Begins to Dance

Produced by John Tydeman

REHEARSALS:	Thursday 24 August 1967	1030–1730
RECORD:	Thursday 24 August 1967	1730–1830
STUDIO:	B.10	
R.P. No.	TLN34/DA853H	

CAST:

Elizabeth	Sheila Grant
Mahmoud	James Thomason
Mr Wilder	John Humphry
Fuad	David Spenser
Charles	Rolf Lefebvre
Margaret	Marion Mathie
Achmed	Haydn Jones
O'Hara	Denis McCarthy
Michael	Christopher Bidmead
Dr Fawzad	Nigel Anthony
1st Reporter	Anthony Jackson
2nd Reporter	LeRoy Lingwood
3rd Reporter	Alexander John

S.M.s: Panel: Amna Smith; Grams: Keith Salmon; Spot: Enyd Williams

SECRETARY: Judy Munk, PABX 2168

The call of the muezzin is broken by the deathly hushed and grim voice of Inspector Mahmoud. He and Elizabeth Warwick are still staring into the sarcophagus of the newly discovered chamber of the Harshak Tomb

Mahmoud Do you know this man, Miss Warwick?

Elizabeth Yes. (*with difficulty*) It's Abdullah. It was his house I went to in the village of Hasia – soon after I came to Luxor.

Mahmoud Abdullah?

Elizabeth Why should anybody want to do a – dreadful thing like this? And then to just leave him here in the sarcophagus… it's horrible!

Mahmoud Can you tell for how long he has been dead?

Elizabeth I should say for no more than an hour. The blood's still quite warm. He has two knife wounds in the back. One must have pierced the heart.

(*pause*) But how did he get down here. The same way as us? Through the Coptic caves?

Mahmoud (*moving around*) I think we are not the first to reach this chamber, dear lady. And nor was Abdullah.

Elizabeth You mean – someone was waiting down here for him?

Mahmoud Perhaps. But now we have found one body, we must look for another.

Elizabeth The Pharaoh. (*pause*) You think it's been stolen – the mummy?

Mahmoud Look around you dear lady. Do you think at one time this was the chamber of a great King?

Pause

Elizabeth I don't know.

Mahmoud Why not?

Elizabeth Everything's so bare. Oh, it's big enough all right, but the walls look exactly the same as the main entrance hall. You know as well as I do that there's hardly a tomb in the Valley of the Kings that wasn't found to be heavily decorated – and full of royal treasures.

Mahmoud (*pointedly*) Yes.

Elizabeth (*looking around*) And again this extraordinary thing – no hieroglyphics. On the walls, the ceilings, even on the sarcophagus. (*stops suddenly as she discovers something*) Inspector! Quick! Come and look at this.

Mahmoud (*joining her*) What is it?

Elizabeth Shine the torch a little lower… yes!

Mahmoud A cartouche!

Elizabeth (*excitedly*) I thought so!

Mahmoud Do you recognise it?

Elizabeth Yes. I recognise it all right.

Mahmoud Then you know the dynasty? Which Pharaoh?

Elizabeth Not a Pharaoh, Inspector. This is the ancient mark of the assassin.

Mahmoud What!

Elizabeth Don't you see? This proves what I said was right. That fresco in the Temple of Luxor… 'The Hunter'… the arrow pointing at the Pharaoh's back. (*pause*) This Pharaoh, Inspector – whoever he was – was assassinated.

Mahmoud (*triumphantly*) Of course! That is why the tomb is not complete.

Elizabeth Why his family had to find a way of keeping his enemies from desecrating the sarcophagus. (*pause. Working it out*) Which means – if the passage leading from the Coptic caves is one side of a triangle, and this chamber is the point of that triangle, somewhere there must be a connecting door which leads to…

Mahmoud The main entrance hall…

Elizabeth A door which can only be opened from this side of the chamber.

Mahmoud As soon as possible we must call the Department of Antiquities. I think Doctor Fawzad is going to have some shock. (*walks slowly back to join her*) So now – all we have to do is find a Pharaoh – and his treasures. Where do we look, Miss Warwick. Where do we look?

Elizabeth I wish I knew, Inspector. You've got to believe me.

Mahmoud *You* are the one who have discovered the Harshak Tomb, dear lady. You, and your father. Now, you must accept what is to follow.

Elizabeth Follow? What are you talking about?

Mahmoud A Pharaoh sleeps for two, maybe three thousand years. Now he is awake – and the world must know.

A sharp cut to the rowdy scenes outside Elizabeth's hotel bedroom. A crowd of excited reporters and journalists jam the corridor, besieging Elizabeth with questions after hearing the news of the Harshak discoveries

1st Reporter Miss Warwick! Is it true your father knew how to reach the King's Chamber…?

2nd Reporter Miss Warwick! Are you going to co-operate with the Egyptian authorities…?

Elizabeth Please gentlemen…! Let me get to my room…

3rd Reporter Can you tell us the name of the Pharaoh…?

2nd Reporter Are you going to be allowed to leave the country…?

Elizabeth (*desperation*) Please!

Crowd surging forward

(*above the din*) Let me pass…!

Wilder (*pushing through, above the din*) Miss Warwick! Over here!

Elizabeth Mr Wilder!

Struggles to reach him

Wilder Another little mess you seem to have got yourself into. Give me your hand.

Elizabeth Where are we going?

Wilder Don't ask questions. Just follow. (*pushing through crowd*) Right you are gentlemen! Make way please… thank you…

Resentful jeers from the reporters until Wilder reaches a bedroom door, opens it, pushes Elizabeth into the room and slams the door and noise behind her

Elizabeth (*relief*) Thank goodness! I thought I was going to be lynched.

Wilder Think yourself lucky you weren't… they're out for your blood.

Elizabeth If you're going to start nagging…

Wilder A man's body was found in that chamber, and *you* had to be the one to lead the police straight to it.

Elizabeth So what's that supposed to mean? That *I* was the one who murdered him? I think you're forgetting, Mr Wilder, that I'm a doctor. I don't take lives. I save them.

Wilder But you can't deny you knew exactly how to get into that tomb?

Elizabeth Oh don't be absurd! My father had a theory, and *I* made it work. What's so wrong about that?

Wilder Well, I'm warning you Miss Warwick, this has gone far enough. You're going to have quite a few answers to give, and not only to the authorities here in Luxor. Don't forget it would be quite easy for the Consulate to…

Elizabeth Confiscate my passport? You can have it – you're welcome.

Wilder For Heaven's sake don't be so facetious!

Elizabeth Then stop treating me like a two-year-old.

Wilder I don't think you appreciate just how serious a matter this is. Once the State Security people hear about those reporters out there, we're in for trouble.

Elizabeth International relations are your problem, Mr Wilder, not mine. I'm no diplomat.

Wilder Don't be proud of that, Miss Warwick. Just be grateful.

Pause

Elizabeth (*exhausted, but relenting*) Look Mr Wilder, I've been up half the night wandering in and out of that tomb. Just tell me what you want me to do.

Pause

Wilder You can start by telling me what has happened to Lieutenant Brian Berkeley.

Elizabeth (*sharp interest*) Who?

Wilder A few hours ago, Mrs Villiers came to see me. She told me that she and her husband are the parents of a Lieutenant Brian Berkeley – a deserter from the British Army. (*pause*) He was in the same regiment as your brother.

Elizabeth So?

Wilder Yesterday afternoon, Mr Villiers – together with a man called Pringle – went up into the Theban Hills to look for his son. They have not returned.

Elizabeth I'm sorry. I don't know anything about it.

Wilder Then you've not made any contact with this Lieutenant Berkeley?

Elizabeth Absolutely not. Why should I?

Wilder (*pointedly*) I don't know. (*pause*) All I'm saying is that *if* you have, you'd be well advised to tell me about it. You see, it's no longer just a question of a court martial. The Harshak Tomb has been robbed of Pharaonic treasures. And I don't think I have to remind you that in this country, an offence like that is punishable by a firing squad. (*pause*) Do I make myself clear, Miss Warwick?

A sharp cut to the sound of water splashing in a bowl. Fuad Yassif is washing himself. Michael Warwick calls from background

Michael Yassif! (*no reply*) Yassif, is that you?

Fuad (*resentfully*) Yes.

Michael (*approaching*) What are you doing?

Fuad Getting ready to go.

Michael What time is it?

Fuad Five thirty. The lorry is waiting outside.

Michael Good. Have you cleared anything?

Fuad Yes. All except the coffin.

Michael Leave that until last. I don't want our royal guest exposed to this heat longer than he has to. He has a long journey ahead of him. (*pause*) What's the matter?

Fuad (*wiping himself*) Nothing.

Michael You're very edgy this morning. Scared?

Fuad No.

Michael You don't think we'll get that coffin as far as Cairo, do you?

Fuad It doesn't matter what I think.

Pause

Michael (*a warped teasing*) What are you going to do when this is all over, Yassif. I'm afraid your countrymen won't be in a very charitable mood after we've gone. (*no reply*) Why not go abroad? Jordan, the Lebanon, even Israel...

Fuad I don't know.

Michael You could come with us if you –

Fuad (*emphatically*) No.

Pause

Michael You're not very patriotic, are you Fuad Yassif? I mean, considering that coffin contains part of your national heritage.

Fuad That mummy is useless until the Pharaoh has been identified.

Michael True. But I think we can rely on my sister to take care of that for us, don't you?

Fuad You have no right to do this to her. You *know* what happens when the dervish begins to...

Michael No right?

Fuad You're a murderer!

A tense pause

Michael Start loading the trucks.

Fuad Your own sister!

Michael I said start loading the trucks! (*menacing*) Before I take you at your word!

Sharp cut to early morning call of various muezzins in distance, mingled with street effect. All this is cut into background as Mahmoud lowers his blinds

Mahmoud So dear lady. Now you tell us your name is Mrs Berkeley – not Villiers. Is that correct?

Margaret Yes.

Mahmoud But for why have you kept this secret?

Margaret I was scared. If you'd caught up with my son he'd have been sent straight back to a court martial in England. I love my boy, Inspector. I'd do anything to try and persuade him to give himself up.

Mahmoud Of course. (*to Achmed*) And you. You are the boatman, Achmed Araby?

Achmed Yes, Inspector.

Mahmoud And you have been helping this lady and her husband to look for their son?

Achmed Yes.

Mahmoud Do you know this is illegal? I could take away your licence?

Margaret Oh please Inspector. He was only trying to help. We paid him very little.

Mahmoud (*a scornful grunt. Pause*) Mrs Berkeley. This man who calls himself Pringle. What do you know of him?

Margaret I've never met him before we came to Luxor. But he seems to have been here for quite a long time.

Mahmoud He is English?

Margaret Oh yes.

Mahmoud From London?

Margaret Couldn't be anywhere else. Why?

Pause

Mahmoud Did you know that this 'Pringle' was also in the British Army. In the same regiment as your son.

Margaret (*shocked*) What!

Mahmoud A corporal I believe.

Margaret But – he never told us.

Mahmoud You are sure?

Margaret Of course! He must have known all along. All this time he let me suffer…

Mahmoud Achmed Araby. You took Miss Elizabeth Warwick in your boat to the village of Hasia on the first day she was in Luxor?

Achmed Yes, Inspector.

Mahmoud Did you know that this man Pringle was also in the same village that day?

Margaret Achmed!

Achmed (*defiantly*) No! I did not see this man.

Mahmoud (*on the attack*) But you did know that the village was in flood…?

Achmed Yes, but…

Mahmoud And that the people had gone because of the typhoid sickness.

Achmed Miss Warwick made me go. I did not want…

Mahmoud begins his attack

Mahmoud Mr Pringle was not the only person to wait for this lady in the village of Hasia. (*pause. To Achmed*) Achmed Araby. I am going to ask you a question, and I want for you to give me a correct answer. (*pause*) Do you know the man who have call himself Abdullah?

A tense pause

Achmed (*with effort*) Yes. (*sadly*) He was my friend. He did not wish to harm the English lady. He was the only man in the village who want to protect her. (*pause*) And now – he is dead.

Mahmoud Two people have died in the fire at the house of Abdullah.

Achmed Yes.

Mahmoud Name them.

Achmed One was the brother of Abdullah.

Mahmoud (*moving in closer*) And the other.

Silence. Snaps

Ana awiz a'raf! (*I want to know!*)

Still no reply from Achmed

Very well Achmed Araby. I will tell you. The other man in the fire was the son of Abdullah who was killed in car crash in the Valley – one month before!

A sharp cut to the ringing of the village school bell at Harshak. Bring up children playing, until we fade them into the background, cut bell, and join Mr O'Hara and Elizabeth

267

O'Hara Alive? My dear young lady. D'you realise what you're saying?

Elizabeth I tell you my brother Michael is alive. I've seen him with my own eyes. And I only wish I hadn't. Because he's changed. He's become nothing more than a sadistic bully, an animal.

O'Hara But if he changed identity with this other young officer, what made him come down to Luxor?

Elizabeth The Harshak Tomb. He knew there was money to be made out there, but he dare not come down as Sir Richard Warwick's son.

O'Hara You mean he's been working out at that tomb all this time, completely unnoticed?

Elizabeth Well, it was quite easy, wasn't it? After all, the Egyptian authorities just left the place to rot. And now he's got hold of the Pharaoh's mummy, and probably all the treasures with it.

O'Hara Yes, but even if he does have the mummy, surely it's no good to him until it's been identified? You said yourself all the hieroglyphics have been defaced.

Elizabeth All except for one small cartouche on the side of the sarcophagus.

O'Hara Cartouche?

Elizabeth Inscribed with the ancient mark of the assassin. This Pharaoh was murdered, Mr O'Hara. There's no doubt about that. (*sighs*) But if I could just get a glimpse of that coffin – or even of the bindings – I know I could work out which dynasty it came from.

O'Hara (*sharp interest*) *You* could do that?

Elizabeth I'm sure I could.

Pause

O'Hara All right Elizabeth. What d'you want to do?

Elizabeth First of all, tell me what you know about the dervishes.

O'Hara Dervishes?

Elizabeth Just before I was forced into another of my pleasant little dreams, I overheard Michael talking about some plan to smuggle the coffin out during the dance of the dervishes. Now if I could only find out where and when all this was going to take place…

O'Hara The Village of the White Scorpion – Hasia.

Elizabeth Hasia?

O'Hara They've been practising the dervish rites up in that village for years. The police have never been able to do anything about it.

Elizabeth Do you know anything about this dance? When the next one is going to take place?

O'Hara Yes. Tonight.

Elizabeth Tonight! That means we'll have to go up there.

O'Hara (*horrified*) Go there! My dear child, are you out of your mind? Have you any idea what these devils are like? They're religious fanatics – they'd cut you to pieces.

Elizabeth We've got to take the chance. We can't let Michael get away with that fortune.

O'Hara Leave it to the police, Elizabeth. For Heaven's sake – don't get involved.

Elizabeth It's no use, Mr O'Hara, I have no choice. Whatever I like to think, Michael *is* still my brother. I've got to try and save what little there is left of his conscience.

O'Hara Yes, I know but –

Elizabeth Mr O'Hara. At this moment I feel as though you're the only one I can really trust. Because *you* respected my father. (*pause*) So, if you feel you're not able to do this for me – then will you do it for him?

Pause

O'Hara I'll pick you up at your hotel at sunset.

Fade out

Pause

At the Department of Antiquities, Dr Fawzad pulls down a wall diagram. A slight echo in the room

Fawzad Mathematics? Yes gentlemen. That is an interesting conclusion. As you can see by this diagram, the Harshak Tomb has been designed geometrically.

Wilder But if this is true, I still can't understand how your own Department of Antiquities couldn't have realised this years ago.

Fawzad Mr Wilder. We have many tombs in the Valley of Kings, many of them awaiting answers to questions which have yet to be asked. But, unlike the European archaeologists, we in this country do not have a government who can put at our disposal the necessary facilities for us to concentrate all our efforts on one small tomb in the middle of a desert.

Wilder Doctor Fawzad, you can't allow a bunch of thieves to walk off with an archaeological fortune like that. The Harshak Tomb has been robbed.

Fawzad (*wryly*) We are used to the tomb robber, Mr Wilder. He is as much a part of Egyptology as the Pharaoh himself.

Mahmoud Doctor Fawzad. Now that you have seen this new chamber, can you estimate the period of the tomb.

Fawzad Very difficult. But to judge from the method of construction, the materials used – one can only assume that it is somewhere around maybe twelfth dynasty.

Wilder As early as that?

Mahmoud But in your opinion, the tomb *was* built to hold the remains of a Pharaoh?

Fawzad A Pharaoh, his queen, a nobleman – who can tell? The only thing that is now clear is that the tomb itself was never completed.

Wilder Except that there *is* a sarcophagus, and there must be a Pharaoh's coffin. Surely all you've got to do now Inspector is to find the brute who planned all this.

Mahmoud Lieutenant Berkeley? The deserter?

Wilder Isn't it obvious?

Mahmoud (*evasively*) Perhaps. (*pause*) But maybe we will know more after we have been to speak with Miss Warwick.

Wilder Miss Warwick? What's she got to do with it?

Mahmoud My friend. Even a thief knows that in order to find a fortune, you must first have someone who can recognise it. (*with due concern*) I think we must go quickly to the hotel.

Wilder Doctor Fawzad. If these people – whoever they are – if they did get away with that coffin – what would be its worth?

Pause

Fawzad Mr Wilder. On a quiet day, twenty-fifth November, nineteen hundred twenty two, the heart of the world stopped beating when two of your countrymen, Lord Carnarvon and Mr Howard Carter, looked for the first time onto the golden face of a young Pharaoh. Today, Tutankhamen is at peace in the Museum of Cairo. There, the world can only come to look and to stare. (*pause*) No, Mr Wilder, there is no money that would *buy* a Pharaoh.

A sharp cut to the sound of coins being dropped into the hands of Fuad Yassif. We are outside the desert shack, the purring of a lorry engine in background

Michael All right. Pay them off! Each man two hundred piastres – not a penny more!

Fuad It's not enough.

Michael What d'you mean it's not enough?

Fuad You are not only paying these men for their work. You are paying them for their silence.

Michael I've never bought anyone's silence.

Fuad Perhaps you have never stolen a Pharaoh's coffin before.

Pause

Michael throws the remaining coins to the ground. Three or four excited Arab workers scramble after them

Michael There! I hope it chokes you! (*to Fuad*) Now get them out of here. We're leaving.

Fuad Leaving? But it is not sunset for another hour.

Michael Precisely.

Fuad But, what about the people waiting for us in Hasia? All the arrangements?

Michael It's not our problem to worry about the arrangements Yassif. We go to Cairo – not Hasia.

Fuad (*angrily*) What sort of game are you playing? (*gradually realising*) You're going to leave Elizabeth alone with the dervishes, aren't you? (*near shouts*) Your own sister!

Michael (*turns on him angrily*) Stop preaching at me, will you! You've got a job to do Yassif, and if you don't want to do it you can stay behind and rot with your ancestors in the Valley!

Fuad (*trying to reason*) Listen to me Michael, please… You haven't a hope of getting to Cairo with that coffin. If the police follow Elizabeth to that village…

Michael Can't you get it into your thick head that it doesn't matter if they *do*? (*pause*) By that time we'll *all* be in Cairo… you, me, Pringle, and one Pharaoh. D'you understand?

Fuad I only understand that if anything goes wrong, we're going to be put up against a wall and shot down like animals.

Michael Then that's where you're wrong, my friend. Because we're not going to get caught. And d'you know why? Because it's not our job to worry *how* something is going to be done; that's been taken care of. We don't give orders Yassif – we obey them. (*pause*) So, it's up to you. You'd better make up your mind once and for all. Are you coming with us – or aren't you?

Sharp cut to background chatter in hotel foyer

Wilder Not in her room? Well, don't they know where she's gone?

Mahmoud At the desk they think Miss Warwick have not been in hotel for over one hour.

Wilder Perhaps she's gone into the town to do some shopping.

Mahmoud Perhaps. But now we must be quick. As soon as possible Miss Warwick must be put under arrest.

Wilder Arrest! What the devil for?

Mahmoud For her own protection Mr Wilder. I believe she is now in more danger than before.

Wilder But why?

Mahmoud Because she is unfortunate enough to be the only expert the tomb robbers can trust.

Wilder You mean she's deliberately working for them?

Mahmoud No. But in her efforts to prove her father's theories, she is unconsciously helping someone to earn a fortune.

Wilder The Pharaoh's identity!

Mahmoud Precisely, my friend. That is why we have to stop her before she is able to do this.

Wilder Yes, but tell me how? Apart from Berkeley and Pringle, we don't even know how many people are mixed up in all this.

Mahmoud How many? I think it would be more useful to know the name of just one person. Someone who has been working out such a plan for years. Someone we could trust – a person who we would not think twice about. Perhaps even a respected member of our community.

Margaret Villiers comes rushing forward, in a very distressed state

Margaret Inspector! Inspector Mahmoud! What's happened? Please – tell me what's happened? My husband has been gone for over twenty-four hours now. I can't bear this any longer!

Mahmoud I am sorry Mrs Berkeley. My men have been searching the hills for many hours. They can find nothing.

Margaret But they must! Charlie's up there somewhere!

Mahmoud I can assure you we do everything possible.

Margaret Oh yes, I'm sure you do! But you let that woman get away, don't you?

Wilder Woman?

Margaret Don't try and fool me! I know very well Elizabeth Warwick is mixed up in all this. *She* knows what's happened to my son.

Wilder (*with urgency*) Mrs Berkeley. Have you seen Miss Warwick in the last hour?

Margaret Yes, I've seen her.

Wilder Where?

Margaret I can't remember. Anyway, who cares?

Mahmoud Mrs Berkeley, I think I should warn you. If you want to see your son again, you had best to tell us what have happened to Miss Warwick.

Pause

Margaret She's gone out to that village.

Wilder Village? What village?

Mahmoud Hasia?

Margaret That's the place. I saw her just before her friend came to pick her up.

Mahmoud Friend?

Wilder What was his name?

Margaret I don't remember.

Wilder (*forcefully*) Then for Heaven's sake – try!

Margaret I tell you I... (*thinks better of it*) Some schoolteacher. Name of O'Hara.

Wilder (*shocked*) O'Hara?

Mahmoud Quick Mr Wilder! We must go.

Wilder Go where?

Mahmoud To the village of Hasia. Before it is too late.

Wilder For what?

Mahmoud To save the life of Miss Warwick. You have forgotten my friend. Tonight the dervish begins to dance.

A sharp cut to the strange, wailing music which accompanies the whirling dervishes. Elizabeth and O'Hara are hiding in the thicket watching the dance. Both speak in a hushed whisper

O'Hara Keep your head down Elizabeth. For Heaven's sake don't let them see us! All these villagers are members of the whirling dervishes. They're a law only to themselves. Much more dangerous than the people who try to imitate them back home in London. They'd kill us if they knew we were here.

Elizabeth They look so strange, just standing there in a circle. Are they the ones who actually perform the dance?

O'Hara Yes. Do you see? There are twelve of them. The idea is that each represents a different world. For a few minutes they'll just stand there – they won't even move a muscle. And then gradually they sink into a kind of unconsciousness.

Elizabeth The beginning of the trance.

O'Hara Yes. From then on they surrender their minds completely to the will of Allah. One man will start the chant – and that's the signal for the dance to begin.

Hold music for a moment

Elizabeth The music – it's so weird.

O'Hara You've heard nothing yet. Once it gets going you'll think it'll never end. (*intensely*) Each dancer will start to scream, to yell... spinning on his feet like a top.

Elizabeth (*a sense of strangulation*) I hate this village! I feel as though I'm going to stifle. Mr O'Hara, can't we move back a little further?

O'Hara No!

272

Elizabeth But there's no sign of Michael…

O'Hara (*hushing her*) Keep still! We're too late!

Pause

Elizabeth (*not daring to move*) What is it?

O'Hara Can't you see. Over there. The man on the left. (*slowly, descriptively*) He's… raising his head… This is it Elizabeth! This is it! The dervishes are beginning to move!

The night air is pierced with the nasal sound of one man chanting the ritual. Mix into this the sound of a modern Arab female singer on car radio. We are in the driver's cabin of a lorry with Michael and Fuad

Michael (*irritated*) Turn that thing off!

Fuad turns off radio

Fuad Why do we have to go the long way around? We should follow the river.

Michael All the way to Cairo? No. That's precisely what a lot of people would like us to do. Then we'd be a sitting target for every soldier in the country. At least this way we can do most of the journey under cover of dark…

Fuad Maybe. But I still don't think we should… (*stops abruptly. In panic*) Police!

Michael What? Where?

Fuad Dead ahead! Look! Can't you see? He's just stepping onto the road… into the light.

Michael Pull up.

Fuad I told you! I told you!

Michael (*angrily*) I said pull up!

Fuad brings the lorry to a halt. Now dead silence

Fuad (*voice lowered*) He's coming towards us.

Michael Keep your mouth shut.

Fuad But if he looks in the back of the lorry…

Michael Shut!

Silence. Gradually the sound of footsteps approaching

Fuad Where are you going? What are you going to do?

Michael Just stay where you are.

Michael gets out of the lorry. Door. Silence except for the nervous breathing of Fuad. Suddenly a revolver shot rings out. A yell from the policeman, suitable horrified reaction from Fuad. Michael climbs back into the lorry

Fuad You fool! Do you know what you have done?

Michael Let's go.

Fuad You'll have every policeman and soldier on our trail within the next hour. We don't stand a chance now of…

Michael (*quite restrained*) It's quite all right Yassif. I have three bullets left. If necessary, I'm quite prepared to use every one of them. (*menacingly*) Now – let's go!

Fuad starts up the lorry. It drives away as mix back into the combined chanting of the dervish dancers

Elizabeth (*very tense*) What are they doing?

O'Hara Whatever you do Elizabeth don't say a word. One false move from us and we're both dead.

Elizabeth But there's no sign of Michael – or Fuad.

Music becoming fast and furious.

O'Hara This is the heart of the ceremony, Elizabeth. The sacred rites.

Elizabeth What's happened to them? Why aren't they here?

O'Hara Look at them. They're peering into a life after death…

Elizabeth I want to go…

O'Hara A life where there is no death…

Elizabeth (*pleading*) Mr O'Hara, please!

O'Hara (*voice raising*) A life where there is only glory and splendour…

Elizabeth They'll hear us!

O'Hara A Pharaoh's life, Elizabeth…

Elizabeth (*shocked*) W–what are you saying?

O'Hara (*voice lowered again*) Didn't you hear what I said? I said… (*shouts at the top of his voice*) A Pharaoh!

At this precise moment the chanting and music comes to a complete stop. There is silence

Elizabeth (*hardly able to speak for fear*) Mr O'Hara! They've seen us! They're coming towards us…

The silence is broken by the combined high-pitched warbling of the dervishes as they rush forward. Mix into this the sound of the police car motor horn racing along the road towards Hasia

Wilder But is O'Hara mad or something? Taking Elizabeth out to that village – on the night the dervishes dance?

Mahmoud Mad? No, I don't think so my friend. Mr O'Hara have live in this country for many years. He know the people maybe even better than me.

Wilder But why take her out there?

Mahmoud Who knows? Perhaps to look for a Pharaoh.

Wilder You mean, you think Elizabeth is being helped by O'Hara?

Mahmoud He was a friend of Sir Richard.

Wilder So was Fuad Yassif. And we know what happened to him.

Mahmoud No my friend. That is the point. I am afraid we do *not* know. But what we *do* know is that Miss Warwick have something as valuable as perhaps the Pharaoh itself.

Wilder Such as?

Mahmoud Knowledge, my friend. Knowledge.

Wilder Which somebody's trying to buy?

Mahmoud Or take.

Wilder But who? Who'd be willing to sacrifice somebody's life for the sake of a coffin full of old bones?

Mahmoud All of us, Mr Wilder – believe me. Soldier, policeman, archaeologist, diplomat. (*pointedly*) Yes. And even a schoolteacher…

Another blast from the car siren. Mix in the heavy breathing and strange mumbling of a dervish dancer – a sound resembling a deaf and dumb mute. He and Elizabeth are now face to face

Elizabeth (*tense*) What does he want? Why is he staring at me like that?

O'Hara Don't move an inch Elizabeth. If you break the trance…

Elizabeth He can't be in a trance. His eyes are wide open.

O'Hara He can't see you, I promise. But he knows you're there. (*voice very soft*) He's in a different world, Elizabeth… a different life. And you are on the outside – looking in.

The dervish makes indistinguishable mumbles

Elizabeth What's he trying to say?

O'Hara (*firmly*) Perfectly still now!

Elizabeth But he's going to touch my face… please don't let him…!

O'Hara Don't bring him back to life Elizabeth! Don't do it!

The mumbling becomes more furious

Elizabeth I can't bear this!

O'Hara We're in the middle of the circle. We have to ober the will of Allah. We must!

Elizabeth No I won't. (*breathlessly*) I won't! I won't!

She lets out a piercing scream. Almost simultaneously the terrifying squawk of a crow, together with bats who screech and flutter their way out of the trees. Fade out

Pause

Fade in with Mahmoud, Wilder and soldiers searching the deserted village of Hasia

Wilder Where have they all gone? I thought you said the dervishes were dancing here.

Mahmoud (*dejected*) I think not. There will be no more dervish dancing in this village tonight.

Wilder (*walking around*) Everything's so quiet… so still. Where have they gone…

The air echoes with the sound of a rifle shot

What the…?

Mahmoud Quickly! Over here…! My men have found something.

They move to the river's edge. The sound of a man's groan. He is lying in a boat

Wilder Good Lord! It's Mr Villiers. Look at the state of him!

Villiers, in great pain, tries to speak

Mr Villiers, Mr Villiers, can you hear me? (*to Mahmoud*) How did he get in this boat?

Achmed (*approaching*) It was me. *I* bring him here.

Mahmoud Achmed Araby, you!

Wilder Are you responsible for this?

Achmed (*defensively*) No, Mister! No! I went to look for Mr Villiers in the Valley. He was near some rocks. Very sick!

Mahmoud The soldiers have been looking for this man all day.

Wilder But you knew exactly where to go, didn't you?

Achmed No Mister, no! At first I was not happy to go into hills alone. These people have bring Achmed much trouble. But then Abdullah – he was killed. (*sadly*) Abdullah was my friend.

Villiers struggles to speak

Villiers Wilder – listen to me – I – I went there.

Wilder (*leaning in closely*) Yes, Mr Villiers. *Where* did you go?

Villiers (*with difficulty*) They tried to kill me... they left me to die. But I managed to follow Pringle to the hut... I heard them talking.

Wilder Who? Who did you hear?

Villiers Pringle... and... and... the schoolteacher.

Wilder (*shocked*) Schoolteacher!

Mahmoud Mr O'Hara! Is not possible?

Wilder Then he's the one who's responsible for...

Villiers Miss Warwick... she's in great danger. They're taking her to...

Wilder (*impatiently*) Yes...?

Mahmoud (*urgently*) Where, my friend? To where are they taking Miss Warwick?

Villiers The... the City. The City of the Dead.

Wilder City of the Dead? What does that mean?

Mahmoud It means, my friend, that the Pharaoh has gone to Cairo.

Wilder (*staggered*) Cairo! But we must stop them.

Mahmoud I am afraid it is too late, my friend. You see, Mr O'Hara have disappeared from the village. And with him he have taken Miss Elizabeth Warwick.

The call of the muezzin over which are our closing announcements

END OF EPISODE SEVEN

Kill the Pharaoh!

by Victor Pemberton

Episode 8: ~~The Muezzin~~ [Call of the Muezzin]

Produced by John Tydeman

REHEARSALS:	Friday 25 August 1967	1030–1730
RECORD:	Friday 25 August 1967	1730–1830
STUDIO:	B.10	
R.P. No.	TLN34/DA854H	

CAST:	Elizabeth ....Sheila Grant	
	Mahmoud..................................James Thomason	
	Mr Wilder ....John Humphry	
	Fuad ....David Spenser	
	Bertie ....Barry Lowe	
	O'Hara ....Denis McCarthy	
	Michael ....Christopher Bidmead	
	Colonel Riza ....Anthony Jackson	
	Arab Hostess............................Barbara Mitchell	
S.M.s:	Panel: Amna Smith; Grams: Keith Salmon; Spot: Enyd Williams	
SECRETARY:	Judy Munk, PABX 2168	

The call of the muezzin is broken by the whine of a turbo prop airliner on its way from Luxor to Cairo

Wilder It's no use Inspector. I still find it incredible to believe that O'Hara [on his own] was able to carry out his own excavations in that tomb for all those years, and without anybody knowing about it.

Mahmoud He was schoolteacher, Mr Wilder. A position of great trust. Also you forget he himself have work with Sir Richard Warwick.

Wilder I don't think Sir Richard would have passed on information to anybody.

Mahmoud Not even to his daughter?

Wilder If Elizabeth Warwick was mixed up with O'Hara he certainly wouldn't have kidnapped her. No. I think someone else has been helping O'Hara – someone who was close enough to Sir Richard during his lifetime to know about his work up at that tomb.

Mahmoud (*considerable interest*) Someone else?

Wilder There was one other child in the Warwick family[, remember]. Elizabeth's brother, Michael.

Mahmoud But you have told me yourself he was killed in action with the British Army at Suez.

Wilder My information is that the features of the body were so badly mutilated that he could only be identified by the disc around his neck. But I say Michael Warwick is very much alive. That he swapped identification papers with the body of someone who is now listed as an army deserter.

Mahmoud Lieutenant Berkely, the son of Mr and Mrs Villiers. Of course!

Wilder But what did Villiers mean about the City of the Dead in Cairo? Why use a Muslim Cemetery to smuggle a Pharaoh out of the country? Can they get away with it?

Mahmoud Yes, my friend I think they can – if we allow them to. Only if we allow them…

Air hostess (*on tannoy*) Ladies and gentlemen[, your attention please]. In a few moments we shall be landing at Cairo International Airport. Will you please fasten your seat belts and extinguish the cigarettes.

From the whine of the aircraft engines, we mix to the sound of Michael Warwick climbing the stone steps of a minaret. After passing through a door, he reaches the muezzin's parapet

Michael Pringle! Yassif! What the hell d'you think you're doing up here? I thought I told you not to come up the minaret?

Pringle (*defensively*) Sorry Michael. We only came up to have a look at the view.

Michael What's the matter with you? You've been in a cemetery before, haven't you?

Pringle (*apprehensively*) Not one like this. Look at all those tombs and graves – they stretch for miles. And the people, wanderin' in and out like a lot of zombies. It's unnatural – gives me the creeps.

Fuad There is nothing unnatural about the City of the Dead. It is no different to any other. Streets, houses, mosques, traffic signals, people…

Pringle They're all dead, aren't they? Don't you call that different!

Fuad No Pringle, I don't. There is as much life in this City as in the streets of Cairo itself. Those who sleep here are never forgotten. And those who are left behind are quite happy to spend a Feast Day in the tomb in the company of all members of the family – past and present, rich and poor. Even the great Caliph who lies in the mausoleum beneath us.

Pringle Well, I think the whole thing's disgusting!

Fuad That is only because you have come to look upon death as the end of life – and not the beginning.

A loud blast from a motor horn below

Michael That's them! Yassif. Get down there and give them a hand.

Fuad goes. Parapet door

Pringle! Get away from that edge will you! D'you want to be seen?

Pringle (*leaning over, amazed*) Hey, come and have a look at this. O'Hara's brought that girl up from Luxor all the way in that thing – a hearse!

A sharp cut to the control room at Police Headquarters in Cairo. Background effects of telephones, radio transmitters etc. Mahmoud and Wilder confer with Chief of Police, Colonel Riza

Riza No gentlemen, is not possible! Every road and track from Luxor to Cairo has been watched by soldiers and police. These people you are looking for cannot have reached the city limits.

Wilder Well, if this is so, Colonel Riza, why haven't your men picked up O'Hara and Miss Warwick? They left Luxor soon after sunset last night.

Riza (*a rising irritation*) Mr Wilder. Between Luxor and Cairo are many hundreds of miles. Miles of desert and difficult country. Under such conditions you can hardly expect us to find two people – and under the cover of dark.

Mahmoud Then we must now assume they have reached the City of the Dead.

Wilder So what does that mean?

Mahmoud It means my friend, that we have a very great problem to face. The City of the Dead is a vast cemetery – over five square miles.

Wilder Five square miles!

Riza It will take my men days, maybe weeks, to search each one of those tombs and mausoleums. And you do not ask a Muslim to leave the tomb of his family at the point of a gun.

Wilder ~~Five square miles!~~

Mahmoud So we must presume that the plan of these people is to smuggle the Pharaoh's casket out of the country. ~~Perhaps to Saudi Arabia or even Jordan.~~

Riza ~~I would suspect to Palestine.~~

Mahmoud But even more important, now that they have got the casket into the City of the Dead, how do they propose to get it out again.

Wilder (*unconsciously*) I would have thought that obvious.

Mahmoud You think so?

Wilder Well, yes. You said the City of the Dead is a cemetery, didn't you?

Mahmoud Correct.

Wilder Well, surely a funeral procession is quite a common sight inside a cemetery. (*pause*) Isn't it?

Mahmoud (*with excitement*) A funeral!

Wilder I don't know how you people do it out here, but all you need is a hearse, a carriage, a few mourners…

Riza Sanruddin!

Wilder What?

Riza Raoul Sanruddin, the Nationalist leader. His body is being removed from the cemetery today.

Mahmoud Where do they take it?

Riza To the family shrine in Alexandria.

Mahmoud (*very excited*) The Port of Alexandria! So! That's how they're going to do it!

Wilder Do it? Do what? Would somebody mind explaining?

Mahmoud Colonel Riza. At what time is the start of the funeral procession?

Riza At the call of the muezzin.

Mahmoud Sunset. Good! Then we still have time.

Wilder Time for what?

Mahmoud To stop the procession...

Riza (*horrified*) Stop the procession! Inspector, do you know what you are doing? You cannot stop the funeral procession of a Nationalist leader [hero].

Mahmoud (*adamant*) We must stop it before it is too late.

Wilder Late for what?

Mahmoud Because, my friend, in order to save a hero – we may lose a King. (*dashing off*) Come on.

Bring up background control room effects. This is cut out immediately as we hear the echo of the great doors of the mausoleum being pushed open. Elizabeth is being held in the open doorway by O'Hara

Elizabeth (*a gasp, background*) You fools!

Running in to mic

You crazy fools! What have you done?

O'Hara (*joining her*) Done? I'll tell you what we've done Elizabeth my dear. We have resurrected Egypt, you and I. Bow your head, Elizabeth. You are standing before the golden casket of a Pharaoh. You're very privileged to be received in royal audience.

Elizabeth You maniac! How dare you blaspheme!

O'Hara (*puzzled*) Blaspheme? When I offer a Pharaoh eternity?

Elizabeth (*dismissingly, scathingly*) Eternity!

O'Hara What's the matter with you Elizabeth? Don't you trust me any more? You did when we were in Luxor.

Elizabeth Before I knew what sort of person you really are. All those years you've been up at that tomb trying to disgrace my father's name and you ask me to trust you!

O'Hara Your father was a fool my dear. And it's a pity, because he had the chance to be a very rich man — as you can see for yourself. (*to Fuad*) Yassif. Open the casket!!

[**Fuad** Very good.]

Elizabeth (*turning away*) No! I don't want to see it.

Michael (*background, rushing forward*) Elizabeth!

Elizabeth I tell you I want no part of it!

Michael Don't be a fool! What difference do you think it makes to our precious father now?

Elizabeth You're mad! All of you – mad! There isn't a museum in the world that would touch this casket.

O'Hara Take a closer look my dear, I'm sure you recognise pure gold when you see it.

Michael Its value on the bullion market alone is enough to –

Elizabeth (*horrified*) Bullion market! You wouldn't dare...

O'Hara In two hours' time the casket will be on its way to a private dealer. For obvious reasons he'd be far more interested in the identity of the Pharaoh than its worth in bullion. But, if it should be necessary to –

Michael (*beggingly*) Listen to me Liz. This is why I brought you to Egypt. I know very well father had his own ideas about which dynasty that tomb came from and the only person in the world he'd pass those ideas on to would be you. (*moving closer to her, confidingly*) I beg of you [Liz] – if you want to save that casket, name the Pharaoh – don't kill him.

Pause

(*to Fuad*) Open the casket.

The lid of the casket is opened. Pause

All right [Liz]. Now, who is he?

Elizabeth takes a few steps forward to peer into the casket. Silence. Gradually, Elizabeth starts to laugh

O'Hara (*above this*) What's she laughing at?

Elizabeth's laughter now almost hysterical

(*shouting angrily*) Did you hear what I said! What is she laughing at...!

Mix from Elizabeth's hysterical laughter echoing throughout the mausoleum, to the soft murmur of a small family crowd and friends gathering outside the gates of the tomb of Raoul Sanruddin

Wilder (*voice hushed*) Is this the tomb of Sanruddin?

Mahmoud (*voice hushed*) Yes. We have to get inside the court yard [there] before the start of the funeral procession.

Wilder (*anxiously*) Look Mahmoud, you can't open up somebody's coffin in full view. These people will lynch you.

Mahmoud We shall be quite protected. I have given instructions for the gates to be kept locked until after we have left the cortege.

The crowd is gradually moving to silence

Wilder What's happening? Why are they going so quiet?

Mahmoud (*with reverence*) It is the last moments before sunset. For the Muslim they are sacred moments – between only himself and Allah. Soon we shall hear the call of the muezzin.

Wilder (*sympathetically*) This is agony for you, isn't it? How can you bear to interrupt such a moment of dedication when you yourself are a Muslim?

Pause

Mahmoud (*with great dignity*) I will tell you my friend. Yes, it is true. I am a Muslim. But like the great Pharaoh himself, not only am I a Muslim, I also am an Egyptian.

Bring up faint crowd murmur, then slowly mix in the angry scene at the mausoleum

Elizabeth No! No! No! What's the matter with all of you? Are you too scared to face the facts?

Michael (*trying desperately to convince*) She's lying I tell you! She must be. This is a Pharaoh!

Elizabeth And I tell you you're wrong. If you don't believe me, look at the bindings on the mummy [yourself]. Look at the [this] necklace.

O'Hara (*trying to remain calm*) What's wrong with the necklace?

Elizabeth The same as the casket itself. (*firmly*) It is not pure gold!

281

THE SLIDE AND OTHER RADIO DRAMAS

A gasp from O'Hara, Fuad

Michael Don't listen to her! It's a trick!

Elizabeth Can't you see the metal is inferior. No *royal* house would have used anything like it. And look – here. Each plate of the necklace contains an identical image. The goddess Sekhmet. The symbol of vengeance. This man's life – whoever he was – I was taken in revenge. He's probably [just] a commoner.

O'Hara ~~So what~~ are you trying to tell us…?

Elizabeth (*cautiously*) I'm trying to tell you that you've been wasting your time. Neither the casket nor the mummy inside are worth more than a few hundred pounds at the most.

Michael It's a trick I tell you!

Pringle, panic stricken, rushes in

Pringle Mr O'Hara, Police!

O'Hara What?

Pringle They're all over the place. Mahmoud is in the crowd near Sanruddin's tomb. He's got that bloke ~~from the consulate~~ [Wilder] with him.

Michael I told you we should never have come here! We're trapped.

O'Hara (*urgently*) Get the casket into the hearse. Quick! (*amidst activity*) Everything stays the same. We'll use the south gate of the cemetery. If necessary, we can blast our way through.

Pringle What about – her?

A sharp halt from O'Hara. Pause

O'Hara Oh yes. Elizabeth. Well, Mr Pringle, I'm sure I can rely upon you to make the young lady your special responsibility. (*dashing off*) Come on! Let's get the hell out of here!

Pringle (*ultra polite*) Right Miss Warwick. Shall we go?

Elizabeth Go where?

Pringle I thought we might go up [to the top of] the minaret. We don't want to miss the signal do we?

Elizabeth Signal?

Pringle The muezzin, Miss Warwick. It's almost time for the muezzin…

Bring up crowd murmurs outside the tomb of Sanruddin

Wilder It's gone. [The sun –] D'you see – over there? The sun has almost completely disappeared behind the tombs.

Mahmoud (*complete stillness*) Yes.

Wilder Everything's turning a deep red. (*with feeling*) It's beautiful. (*pause*) What happens now?

Mahmoud Now we must wait.

Wilder What for?

Mahmoud Shh! Listen.

Pause

Wilder I can't hear anything.

Mahmoud (*voice very hushed*) Listen…!

But for the buzzing of flies, there is a very market silence. Suddenly the air is pierced by the first distant call of the muezzin. This is followed by a collective murmure of recognition from the crowd

Wilder (*excitedly, dramatically*) The [call of the] muezzin!

Mahmoud (*urgently*) Kneel down, my friend! Kneel down. We must turn the face towards Mecca. Look! They are opening the doors of the tomb. The funeral is going to begin…!

We mix the opening of the tomb doors into the call of the first muezzin, a call which is taken up by another, and then another. Gradually, we hear many calls drifting in from different areas of the cemetery. During this we cut back to the top of the minaret, retaining the muezzin calls in the background

Pringle (*looking around*) One thing about these minaret things. You get a marvellous view from up here. (*turns to Elizabeth*) Come on Miss Warwick. Come and look over the edge. You can't see anything from back there. (*pause. No reply*) Well, come on. You're not scared of *me*, are you?

Pause. Elizabeth's footsteps slowly approaching. She stops

Elizabeth (*unfaltering, firm and strong*) No Mr Pringle. I am *not* scared of you.

Pringle (*amused*) No. Course you're not. (*moves in closer*) You're pretty tough, aren't you? Just like your old man, so they say.

Elizabeth Would you mind telling me how long we're expected to stay up here? ~~I'm getting hot.~~

Pringle What? Bored already, Miss Warwick? With all that racket goin' on out there. Just listen to it. (*listens to muezzins*) ~~Must be dozens of 'em.~~ That's how they call 'em all to prayer. Did you know that?

Pause. No reply

~~Suckers!~~ That's not the only thing they're calling them to – if only they knew it!

Elizabeth Where are they taking the casket, Pringle? ~~Jordan? Israel…?~~

Pringle (*innocently*) Casket? What casket's that, Miss Warwick…?

Elizabeth Don't be a fool man! You could be a very rich man without stealing a Pharaoh.

Pringle Do I smell a bribe when I hear one?

Elizabeth I merely think you have more intelligence than the others.

Pringle That's true. (*pause*) All right Miss Warwick. (*moving in even closer*) Let's talk this over.

Elizabeth I'm warning you Pringle. You put your hands on me and I'll tear you to pieces.

Pringle (*confidently amused*) It's a long way down to the bottom, Miss Warwick. We don't want you havin' no accidents, now do we? Come on. Let's see how really tough you are…

He squirms as she strikes out at him

You little…! My face! You've scratched my face…! (*angrily*) All right! I'll show you just how I can…!

He is about to lunge forward when right beside him we hear the penetrating call of the muezzin. Pringle, terrified, turns around, taken completely off guard

What the…! You! What you are doing up… no! Get away from me! Did you hear what I…no! (*shouting out hysterically*) Get away from me…

A terrifying scream as he is pushed from the parapet, falling below. Mix into the solitary funeral lament of a mourner at the Sanruddin tomb. Mahmoud and Wilder are hiding in the courtyard

Wilder You can't do it, Mahmoud. You just can't do it! You can't open that coffin in full view.

Mahmoud (*calmly defiant*) I will not exchange the Pharaoh for the body of a dead hero.

Wilder But we can't even be sure they *have* swapped the Pharaoh's body. Please believe me Mahmoud. This is madness! If the crowd get through that gate…

Mahmoud The gates are locked…

Wilder You *hope* they're locked!

A commotion in the crowd

What is it? What's happening?

Mahmoud Keep still! Don't let them see us. Here comes the coffin… now.

A wail of lament from the crowd at the gates

(*quietly, to himself*) Let them come [go]… just a little… further…

Wilder No Mahmoud! For Heaven's sake – no!

Mahmoud steps out, shouts in Arabic

Mahmoud Ma titkharig, ya has, ma titkharig (*Stay where you are! Everyone, stay where you are!*)

An immediate outburst of protest from the crowd at the gates

(*in background calls*) Mr Wilder! Over here – quickly! I am going to open the coffin!

Bring up crowd protests. Gradually fade this as we cross-cut back to the minaret. Hold crowd effects in distance

Elizabeth Fuad Yassif. *You!* *You* killed Pringle to save me.

Fuad [I had to.] O'Hara left instructions for Pringle to kill us both. You first and then me. I had to stop him.

Elizabeth (*scathingly*) I don't believe you. Why should you kill one of your own men to save me? Why don't you give up this pretence and tell me who you really are?

Pause

Fuad (*solemnly*) I am Fuad Yassif.

Elizabeth Did you hear what I said? I said give up the pretence. Fuad Yassif loved my father. He'd never have agreed to work for two criminals like my brother and O'Hara.

Fuad I had no choice. They came out to my village many times to try to get me to work for them. Each time I refused. I *did* love your father. He was the only real friend I ever had.

Elizabeth And that's why you agreed to help discredit his name?

Fuad I told you. I had no choice. It was only because of the accident.

Elizabeth Accident?

Fuad (*with difficulty*) There were two of us in the car – in the Valley of the Kings. We had been drinking. I was driving but I was not to blame for his death. Someone had interfered with the engine of the car. (*pleads*) You've got to believe me, Elizabeth.

Elizabeth Go on.

Fuad There was a crash. My friend was killed. When your brother found out he [blackmailed me. He] threatened to go to the police unless I agreed to work for him and Mr O'Hara. I had no idea they had been working up at that tomb. That they had found the Pharaoh.

Elizabeth What work were you expected to do?

Fuad I was to write to you – bring you to Luxor. But to everyone else, Fuad Yassif was the one who died in the crash.

Pause

Elizabeth Who was the other person in the car?

Fuad His name was Ali. The son of Abdullah.

Elizabeth Abdullah! But he tried to kill me!

Fuad (*adamantly*) No, Elizabeth, no! That's not true. He didn't know what he was doing. Abdullah hated anyone who was my friend. To him, I was responsible for his son's death. He could never understand that my grief was as much as his – and always will be.

Pause

Elizabeth You say you loved my father.

Fuad Always! Yes!

Elizabeth Then tell me where they're taking the Pharaoh.

Fuad Across the border – to Palestine.

Elizabeth Israel! I thought as much. Then we've got to stop them – before they reach the cemetery gates.

Fuad Stop them? No, Elizabeth, we are too late. The funeral procession has already begun. There is nothing we can do to save the Pharaoh now. Nothing.

Crossfade to the background angry crowds battering on the gates of Sanruddin's tomb. Mahmoud and Wilder are opening the hero's coffin

Wilder (*frenzied anxiety*) For Heaven's sake – hurry up man! In a few moments they're going to tear down those gates, and us with them!

Mahmoud (*struggling with the lid*) Nearly... the lid of the coffin... is nearly...

The lid comes off with a thud

    ...open!

A loud protest from the crowd nearby

Wilder (*horrified*) Oh my – ! It isn't the Pharaoh!

Mahmoud (*thoroughly dejected*) We were wrong. This is Sanruddin, the hero.

Wilder Now we're really in trouble. Where do we go from here?

A shout from Elizabeth in the middle of the crowd at the gates

Elizabeth (*background*) Inspector! Inspector Mahmoud! Over here...!

Mahmoud (*turning, surprised*) Miss Warwick!

Wilder (*calls*) Elizabeth!

Mahmoud and Wilder join Elizabeth at gate

    Elizabeth! Where the hell have you been?

Elizabeth It doesn't matter about me. You've got to hurry. You've been tricked. This whole funeral has been used as a decoy!

Mahmoud Dear lady, how do you know this?

Elizabeth I've got Fuad Yassif with me.

Wilder Yassif!

Elizabeth You've only got half an hour to stop them. They're making their way across the border ~~into Israel~~.

Mahmoud ~~Israel.~~ Of course!

More commotion from crowd

    Dear lady! (*calls*) Make your way to police car at the East Gate. We shall meet you there in a few moments. (*calls*) But be careful! [Be careful!]

Mix from angry crowd to the interior of the funeral hearse in which O'Hara and Michael Warwick are crawling along

Michael (*irritated*) Can't you make this thing go any faster?

O'Hara You don't break the speed limit in a funeral hearse.

Michael We'll never make that air strip in time. It's after half past now.

O'Hara (*calm confidence*) Don't worry. We'll make it.

Michael This crank who wants the Pharaoh. Suppose he doesn't turn up. How d'you know you can trust him?

O'Hara When you talk about a hundred thousand pounds you don't have to trust people. Either they want it – or they don't.

The hearse is slowing down

Michael (*edgy*) What's up? Why're you slowing down?

O'Hara (*unruffled*) Police.

Michael Police…!

O'Hara Don't be a fool! Put your gun away. He's not stopping us. He's waving us on. Don't you understand when someone's paying their last respects to the dead? Even the law…

The sound of a traffic gong. Bring up and then fade out traffic effects

Pause

The City of the Dead. Fade up crowd in extreme background. Alternative to this would be a mix from the last scene

Wilder (*studying a map*) Abu Gariz. Yes, here it is on the map. Looks quite a way.

Mahmoud The other side of the step pyramid at Sakkara. I don't know this place.

Elizabeth It's apparently an old RAF air strip. (*to Fuad*) You've been out there, haven't you Fuad?

Fuad Yes. Your brother and O'Hara are going to be picked up by helicopter.

Mahmoud ~~Who?~~ Who is going to pick them up?

Fuad He is a dealer – from America. He is willing to pay one hundred thousand pounds for the Pharaoh's mummy and casket – but only if ~~the~~ Pharaoh can be identified.

Mahmoud And what happens if he can't?

Fuad (*solemnly*) Even the gold alone would be of much value ~~on the bullion market~~.

A solemn pause

Mahmoud (*great urgency*) At what time is this meeting with the helicopter?

Fuad ~~At one hour after~~ The [early] call of the muezzin [in the morning].

Mahmoud ~~Seven o'clock!~~ [Then] we must ~~hurry~~ [not delay]. [It will take some time to reach Abu Gariz. The roads are no so good out there.]

~~**Wilder** Seven o'clock! That only gives us less than half an hour. We'll never make it   especially in the dark.~~

Mahmoud Miss Warwick. Before we go, one question please.

Elizabeth Yes?

Mahmoud You yourself have now seen the mummy of the Pharaoh. (*with great expectation*) Now. Now can you tell us his name?

Pause

Elizabeth Yes. Yes, Inspector – I think I can.

~~*A sharp cut to the screech of brakes. The funeral hearse comes to an abrupt halt on*~~ *The air strip of Abu Gariz. O'Hara and Michael get out. There is a gentle but eerie night breeze*

Michael (*a cold shiver*) It's cold. Why the hell do we have to rendezvous in the middle of ~~the~~ [a] desert?

O'Hara (*also cold*) It's the night air. It's to be expected ~~after sunset~~ this time of year.

Michael At least let's turn on the headlights – I can't see a damn thing.

O'Hara (*stopping him*) ~~Don't be a fool!~~ D'you want to lead the police straight to us? In a few minutes we'll be on our way.

Michael (*looking up*) It's almost on the hour. Where's this helicopter then?

O'Hara It'll be here – don't worry.

Michael And what about the others? Where are they?

O'Hara (*evasively*) Others?

Michael Pringle, Yassif, Elizabeth… you said they'd be here before us…

O'Hara Does it matter *when* they get here?

Michael What d'you mean, does it matter?

O'Hara We've got what we set out for, haven't we? We've got the Pharaoh.

Michael (*catching on*) What's happened to Elizabeth? What have you done ~~with~~ [to] her?

O'Hara (*irritated*) Your sister won't be joining us…

Michael (*mounting anger*) What? What did you way?

O'Hara She's no more use to us. You said so yourself. She tricked us.

Michael (*grabbing hold of O'Hara*) You…!

O'Hara (*struggling*) Take your hands off me…!

Michael What have you done to her! Tell me what you've done to her!

O'Hara Don't be a fool man! Remember what you told me. She's like your father – just like your father. She tricked us!

Michael No! It was you who tricked me. All those years up at that tomb… you made me believe I could trust you!

O'Hara You can, Michael! I promise you – you can! Think what we've achieved together, you and me. Something that no man has done since Howard Carter first set light on the face of Tutenkhamen. We discovered a Pharaoh, Michael – a golden Pharaoh!

Michael (*disregardingly*) I'm going… to kill you, O'Hara. I'm going to kill you…

The distant approach of the helicopter

O'Hara (*stops dead*) Michael – listen!

Michael It's no use…don't try and…

O'Hara (*shouts*) I said – listen…!

Hold approach of helicopter

They're here! Michael! Listen – they're here! Go and put on the car headlights! (*shouting triumphantly*) Hey! Here we are! Hey…!

Hold approach of helicopter as we mix to the police car screeching to a halt on the edge of the airstrip nearby. Car doors slamming

Wilder (*running in*) Over there!

Elizabeth Where? I can't see…

Wilder Standing in the middle of the airstrip. D'you see? O'Hara's getting the coffin out of the hearse…

Mahmoud And the helicopter. Right on time!

Wilder The damn fools! They'll get themselves shot to pieces!

Elizabeth (*shouts*) Michael! Michael…!

Wilder Can't somebody do something? Let them know we're here?

Mahmoud (*gravely*) That will not be necessary. We are too late. [Do you see?] The soldiers have [already] arrived.

Approach of soldiers running in. Mix back to helicopter hovering above the near hysterical O'Hara and a dazed Michael

O'Hara (*struggling with the casket*) Come on man – don't just stand there! Help me with the casket!

Michael No. Leave it alone.

O'Hara Leave it… what are you talking ab…?

Michael The Pharaoh stays ~~behind~~ [in Egypt].

O'Hara ~~Behind?~~ Are you out of your mind or something? After all we've worked for?

Michael (*almost trancelike*) Worked?

O'Hara (*impatient irritation*) What's the matter with you man? Don't you want the money?

Michael You did this to spite my father didn't you? That's why you had Elizabeth killed…

O'Hara (*completely muddled*) Your father! You hate your father. You always hated him… you told me! (*beggingly*) Michael. Listen to me. You never wanted to be second best – remember? Well, now's your chance. You don't have to be. They'll always remember that you're the one who found the Pharaoh, not your father.

The helicopter hovering above, starts to move off

They're going! The helicopter…they're going…!

O'Hara shouts up angrily at the pilot

(*shouts*) Come back! You fools…come back…!

The helicopter disappears into the distance. O'Hara is completely shattered

Gone. (*uncomprehendingly*) They've gone. (*a nervous disbelief*) You fool. Do you see what you've done? (*shouts angrily*) They've gone.

Michael Yes.

O'Hara We're stuck here. You, me, and the Pharaoh. Don't you realise what you've done?

Michael [Oh] Yes. (*quite unmoved*) I trusted everyone else except those who trusted me.

The sound of soldiers running in to approach

O'Hara (*suddenly turning*) What's that? ~~Oh my…!~~ Soldiers! We're trapped…!

Michael Stand out of the way.

O'Hara (*panicking*) What are you doing? Don't be a fool, man! Put that gun away! You fire one shot and they'll mow us down…!

~~Michael fires one shot from his revolver~~

An immediate response of bullets from the approaching soldiers. O'Hara shouts out in agony as we fade out on a hail of rifle and machine gun fire

Pause

Complete silence but for a gentle breeze. The sound of Elizabeth's footsteps approaching to a halt

Elizabeth (*still, unemotionallly*) Are they dead?

Wilder (*solemnly*) I'm sorry.

Elizabeth It's all right. That's how it *should* be. (*pause*) The only thing is, I just wish I could have spoken to Michael once more. It's quite ironic really. I didn't really have the chance to tell him that he'd grown to look exactly like father.

Wilder I'm sorry it had to be someone so close to you.

Elizabeth Don't pity my brother, Mr Wilder. Save ~~it~~ [your pity] for Mr and Mrs Villiers. They're the ones that have had to suffer a dream all these years. A dream that one day they'd see their son again – alive.

Wilder At least he wasn't the deserter your brother made him out to be.

Elizabeth [That's true.] ~~Yes. But I'd hate to be the one to have to tell his parents that it's no use dreaming unless you're wide awake.~~

Mahmoud approaches

Mahmoud The helicopter has been intercepted. [And] We have the pilot under arrest. (*a change in tone*) Dear lady, what can I say? I have deep distress for you.

Elizabeth (*without emotion*) Then, please don't. Remember Inspector, you have your Pharaoh.

Mahmoud Ah yes! The Pharaoh! I think maybe now he will go to the museum in Cairo – to lie in state in the Chamber of the Royal Mummies.

Elizabeth Do you think that's wise? I mean considering this is not the ~~mummy~~ [body] of a Pharaoh...

Mahmoud & Wilder (*shocked*) What!

Mahmoud Dear lady! What is this you say?

Elizabeth The Harshak Tomb was a Pharaoh's hoax, ~~I'm absolutely convinced~~. My guess is that it was built to convince the Pharaoh's enemies that he was dead.

Wilder You're very sure of yourself. How d'you know all this?

Elizabeth You remember – just inside the coffin there's a cartouche – inscribed at the head of the mummy. This is identical to the one we found scrawled on the side of the sarcophagus in the Harshak Tomb.

Mahmoud The mark of the assassin.

Elizabeth Precisely. Now then. This matched up quite naturally with the fresco of the 'Hunter' in the Temple of Luxor. The unknown figure pointing an arrow at the Pharaoh's back. So the only possible conclusion we could draw was that the Pharaoh – whoever he was – had been assassinated and placed in the sarcophagus at Harshak. (*pause*) Or at least, that's what I thought until I saw the necklace around his neck.

Mahmoud Necklace?

Elizabeth Each piece contains the inscription of the Goddess Sekhmet. The Goddess of Revenge. (*pause*) I don't believe it was the Pharaoh who was put into that sarcophagus. It was the body of the assassin himself.

Wilder The assassin!

~~**Mahmoud** Yes!~~

Elizabeth Of course, I can't be sure. After all what archaeologist can [be]? But the whole thing is like a vast jigsaw puzzle. A tomb without wall decorations, hieroglyphics, treasures. In other words – everything defaced by the very person who was going to lie there himself. No gentlemen, this is a man I would love to have known. A practical joker – a sense of humour.

Wilder You mean a sense of the macabre.

Elizabeth Perhaps. But at least he achieved something that most of us would love to be able to do. He gave up life without actually 'dying'. (*pause*) With or without a name, I think the world is going to remember this Pharaoh.

Wilder And to think – your brother and O'Hara digging up at that tomb all these years – just for this. (*sighs*) Oh well. I suppose even the mummy of an assassin would have brought in a hundred pounds or so.

Mahmoud Dear lady. ~~We Egyptians~~ [Our country] owe you much gratitude. I hope maybe you will come back one day to Luxor. To finish your father's work.

Elizabeth Thank you Inspector, but my work is in London. I must go home. Mr Wilder. Will you take me back to the car please? [It's almost dawn]

Wilder Of course. [What about you] Inspector?

Mahmoud No. I will follow later. I want first to take another look at the mummy.

Elizabeth Then I'll say goodbye.

Mahmoud Dear lady. You are most remarkable person. [Mahmoud] I will not forget you.

Elizabeth And I won't forget you [Mr Mahmoud]. Goodbye.

She and Wilder walk off. Silence but for the gentle breeze

Mahmoud opens the lid of the casket

Mahmoud Well now, my friend [sleeping in your coffin]. Let me look at you. Ah yes. You know I think maybe you have forgotten one thing. You may take away the body of the Pharaoh – but not the soul. And do you know why, my friend. Because the Pharaoh was – and *is* – Egypt. (*a sigh*) And may the Lord Allah always let it be so.

The sudden call of the muezzin to close the episode

THE END

The Fall of Mr Humpty

ave you ever taken the last suburban train home and found it to be a rather unnerving experience, particularly if you are the only passenger in the carriage? Dim lighting, draughty, the deafening rattle of train wheels, making it difficult to concentrate on reading your book or newspaper, suspiciously watching those reflections in the windows against the passing dark of the countryside outside? Well, that's how it used to be when I first wrote this 45-minute play. That, of course, was at a time when trains weren't as sleek as they are today; where carriages were split up into compartments, with 'No Smoking' and 'Ladies Only' signs. It was also at a time when, if you missed the last train, then it could be a long wait for the next one. That's what nearly happened to Richard Penfold. Unfortunately, though, he *did* catch that last train; and his encounter with his only fellow passenger was to lead him into what I called 'A Nightmare for Radio'.

I have to admit that I have a sneaking affection for this play, mainly because it gave me the chance to explore my own nightmares, the images of travelling on trains late at night. But *The Fall of Mr Humpty* is not all it seems. Yes, it is a supernatural horror story, but it also deal with a sombre analysis of children's nursery rhymes. Mr Humpty himself is, of course, an image of what I describe in my script notes as 'A well-spoken, rotund, middle-aged man', but it was the egg-shaped character of the children's rhyme I took as my inspiration. To achieve that certainly needed an actor who could suggest in sound not only physical size, but a portrait of a man on the edge of a mental breakdown. Fortunately, the role was filled by Timothy West, an actor of immense stature, dramatic strength, and versatility. In his eerie encounters with his fellow passenger, Jimmy, a 12-year-old boy, Timothy projected perfectly the true terror of a man caught up in a living nightmare: a man who was trapped in his own mundane world, an egg just waiting to fall off a wall.

I have always thought that many nursery rhymes are not as charming as we remember. As when Penfold asks the boy, 'Aren't you a little old to be reading a book of nursery rhymes, young man? They're for children much younger than you.'

Jimmy replies, 'Oh no, sir – you're wrong. Nursery rhymes are for grown-ups too – not just children.'

He could be right. Just think of, 'Jack and Jill went up the hill to fetch a pail of water, Jack fell down and broke his crown and Jill came tumbling after.' Then how about:

'Three blind mice, three blind mice
See how they run, see how they run
They all run after the farmer's wife
Who cut off their tails with a carving-knife,
Did you ever see such a thing in your life
As three blind mice?'

Pretty chilling stuff, don't you think? Well, it was pretty chilling for Mr Humpty in that dark old farmhouse, with a wind-up gramophone that starts up all on its own, and the sound of *Rock of Ages* Mr Humpty plays on that old harmonium much to the hysteria of the mysterious young Jimmy.

For as many years as I can remember, I have always liked to read ghost stories, and to see creepy films. As a child I had a vivid imagination; and, during the nights I shared a bed with my brother, I would stare up at the ceiling, my mind's eye turning the plaster casts around the dangling electric light on the ceiling into gargoyles, spooks that would go bump in the night and drop down to kidnap me. All this whilst my brother snored loudly at the side of me. Of course, Mr Humpty was written during a time when there were also real-life nightmares. This was 1975 and, although the IRA had declared a ceasefire in Northern Ireland, the bombs and the hatred were still going on. In London that same year 43 people were killed in a tragic accident on a London Underground train at Moorgate Station, whilst across the world inVietnam, the bloody civil war raged on. So reality was just as frightening as those dark dreams of the night.

Since my foray into the world of radio soaps back in 1967, I had written two 90-minute full-length radio plays for the *Saturday Night Theatre* slot. One was called *Eyes of the Buddha*, a psychological adventure thriller set on the island of Sri Lanka, which, of course, was once known as Ceylon; and the other was *Escape to Lhasa*, an adventure spy thriller which followed the extraordinary alliance to help regain a valuable ancient Buddhist document in the remains of a crashed airliner in the mountains of Tibet. You will not be surprised to know that both plays were vehicles for David Spenser, for he was actually born in Sri Lanka, and in the Tibetan drama he ended his career as an actor to take up the reins as a radio and television director. During that time, we also collaborated on the two children's radio serials about the Pharaohs; and, during the same year as Mr Humpty, I also managed to fit in an autobiographical play about my father called *Looking Back*, starring that wonderful cockney comedian, Arthur English, from television's *Are You Being Served?*

Oddly enough, I first had the idea for *Mr Humpty* in a cold BBC rehearsal room in West London, where, as I already mentioned, I had been bludgeoned into taking a role as a Turkish corporal in Cedric Messina's Lawrence of Arabia television film. Maybe it had something to do with the terrible cups of tea one used to get during rehearsals, usually made by a harassed assistant floor manager, and which reminded me so much of the same weak brew that British Railways used to serve up at their stations; but whatever it was, the idea soon took a back burner when I was called to the telephone by a lady script editor called Ruth Boswell.

Ruth, a highly talented and intelligent lady, asked if I would be interested in helping out with a new science fiction serial she was preparing at ATV called *Timeslip*. It appeared that although Ruth had devised the series, the scriptwriter, Bruce Stewart, was finding it a bit of a strain to find a solution for the final episodes. That's where I was asked to come in. It was a tall order. To find a solution to something that another writer had set up was, for me at least, pushing it a bit – especially as Bruce was such a fine, experienced writer, and Ruth very definite in what she wanted for the story. However, I was very flattered to be asked and, after reading the scripts written so far, accepted the commission before heading off to Cedric's location in the Sahara desert to mull it all over.

The only trouble was, there was a very tight deadline (isn't there always?). In fact, as I remember, they had already started to tape the first episodes, so I didn't really have much time to think about my oily Turkish corporal character, nor indeed poor old Mr Humpty, who was just left squatting on that wall. Well, as I'm sure you all know, thanks to Ruth and Bruce, *Timeslip* became a huge success, and the cult it is today, and I'm very glad to have been even a part of it. Oh, by the way, when David Spenser and I formed our company Saffron Productions Limited some years later, it was suggested that we buy an option on *Timeslip*, but after the usual lot of talks and discussions, the idea fizzled out.

Oddly enough, between *Timeslip* and my Oscar-winning performance as the oily Turkish corporal, I was kept quite busy contributing to other television series. Every time I tried to turn to those notes about poor old Mr Humpty, I was invited by London Weekend Television to write for a detective series called *New Scotland Yard*, and then by the same company to write an hour-long episode for the women's prison drama series, *Within These Walls*, which during my time starred the great Googie Withers as the prison governor. Oh yes, there are plenty of stories about *those* shows, but they will have to wait for the next twenty volumes of my memoirs!

So back to 1975, and finally I returned to Mr Humpty sitting on that wall. But it wasn't easy to get him to fall off, because at that time I was having what is popularly known as a 'writer's block.' Now, despite the fact that by this time I had been writing for some years, this experience had not really hit me before; but when it came it was wretched. Night after night I lay awake in bed, mumbling to myself, 'Go away Block!' Then I would get up and stare out at the cold rural landscape, a full moon turning the fields into a glistening plethora of white. 'Damn you Block!' I would splutter, as quietly as possible for fear of waking the entire household. But Egbert our Labrador dog knew; so did Suki and Yaki, our Siamese twin cats. Why is it that animals know so much more than us? Why is it they sense danger and tension, when their routine is threatened? Could it have something to do with the fear of not getting their fair share of nosh?

Anyway, one night – four o'clock in the morning to be exact – off I went to my study, turned on the light, turned on the electric fire, wrapped my far too big woollen dressing gown well around me, and sat in front of my beloved old typewriter. Well it wasn't so beloved on that occasion I can assure you, because I snarled at it: 'Well don't just sit there – *do* something!' Answer came there none. The stupid, shiny black Everest machine just sat there on my desk, snoring away, unwilling to budge an inch. And even when I fed it a blank page of typing paper, it seemed to smirk back at me and say – 'So what?'

But then an extraordinary thing happened. I heard a panting at my side, and when I looked down, Egbert was there, and so were the Oriental ones, eyes blurred, yawning, begging to be given a midnight snack – persistent as hell! Needless to say, I relented, got up, went into the freezing cold farmhouse kitchen and opened the fridge door. As I did so, an egg came tumbling out, and smashed on the floor. The Labrador and the Orientals were lapping it up, but they had also fed *me*. In a flash I was back at the typewriter, writing the first voice of the play that had been lounging in my mind for so many years:

'Humpty Dumpty sat on a wall

Humpty Dumpty had a great fall

All the King's horses and all the King's men

Couldn't put Humpty together again.'

It's strange how, at that time, the supernatural was beginning to interest me more and more. Oh, it had always been there as a listener and cinemagoer – I had loved the chilling atmosphere of W.W. Jacobs's *The Monkey's Paw* and the renowned *Appointment with Fear* series on the BBC Home Service; but somehow I had never really thought seriously about writing in this area myself. But *Mr Humpty* was different. Somehow, he had an effect on me; and as I watched and listened, from the control room at Broadcasting House, to Timothy West and the young schoolboy Nicholas Dillane interacting with enormous tension and passion at the microphone, I realised that there was something inside me that wanted to experiment with not just things that go bump in the night, but the effect of the dead on the living. Of course, I continued this theme with a later radio play, *Dark*, which you can also hear in a new CD version with this book; and even later in *The Night of the Wolf*, a tale of lycanthropy in Victorian England, also presented in a new CD version with this book. But I like to think that *Mr Humpty* started it all.

Because of modern over-sensitivities, the relationship between Mr Humpty and young Jimmy would be somewhat difficult to project today. The egg-shaped Richard Penfold doesn't really like this boy – this brat; he is just fascinated by him. Who is this mysterious boy from the farmhouse? Is he real? Where are his parents? Who *is* this dark and disembodied voice singing *Rock of Ages* in the loft upstairs? Why is it that Mr Humpty never gets the chance to meet the boy's sinister old guardian, Uncle John? And Penfold hates the way the boy keeps calling him 'Mr Humpty'.

'I like the name,' insists Jimmy, with a smirk in his voice.

'Why do you like it?' barks the very irritated Penfold.

'Because you're like an egg,' replies the deadpan boy, adding with a hysterical unnatural laugh, 'I hope you don't fall down the well. You might crack!'

In one sense, this mysterious youngster is a reflection of what lay dormant in Penfold's own mind. In his own unnerving way, the boy is merely opening the door of that mind, an intruder to what lies within. When Jimmy shows Penfold his 'castle' and talks about what he would do if he saw people coming up the hill, Penfold objects when the boy sings: 'Jack and Jill come up the hill…' Penfold thinks that it is a horrible story, but something inside tells him that that isn't what he *really* thinks.

When the play was originally broadcast, I remember one listener who wrote to me saying that, after listening to this play, she would never ever be able to catch the last train home – but that, if the play were ever repeated, she would certainly listen to it again. *Mr Humpty* brings out a lot of hidden feelings inside us all, a lot of fear, a lot of anxieties. Isn't it amazing how children have featured so much in ghost stories from the past, such as Henry James's *The Turn of the Screw*, which became a stage play and film called *The Innocents* – the dead possessing the young to convey messages to the living – and in so many other short stories. Remember the trilogy of films, *The Omen*? What is it about a child like Jimmy, who can manipulate an arrogant, vulnerable, lost soul like poor Mr Humpty? Is *this* a story about satanic manipulation? If so – why does he do it? What *has* Mr Humpty to learn from this strange encounter?

If I were writing *The Fall of Mr Humpty* today, I would still keep the story in the same framework. During my long lifetime I have learnt a lot about things that don't seem real at the time, don't have any real significance, only to discover in retrospect that there *is* always something behind the mask, that what seems absurd is not as absurd as we think. In the case of Richard Penfold, his latter years have crashed around him, leaving him floundering in a sea of suspicion, bitterness and uncertainty. In the climax of this play you will read how the past and the present are mixed together in a time warp. Is this madness? Or an attempt by someone from Penfold's past to use a child to change him – maybe either to destroy him, or to bring him back to a real life again?

Well, there it is. Thanks to Egbert the Labrador and those inscrutable Orientals, Suki and Yaki, I finally whipped my beloved old typewriter into active service again. One thing it did do, of course, was to make my regular working wake-up call four o'clock every morning, which I still do every day. For me, writing is best done at that time – no cars ploughing past on the road outside, no telephone calls, no dogs barking (except at the fridge in the kitchen downstairs). But most of all, it is the silence, that golden time that all writers crave – well *nearly* all writers. Mind you, the silence can at times be quite noisy, especially when the adrenalin gets going, and you want to get on and on, you want Mr Humpty to have that fall. How I miss the tap, tap, tap of my beloved old typewriter. Computer keyboards and laptops are all very well, but they don't talk to you like typewriters. They are automatons, waiting for you to push a button. But a typewriter – at least *my* typewriter – was like a friend: temperamental at times, but in the end finally willing to co-operate. In fact, even as I typed those final few words…

(BRING IN ENGINE HOOTER TO FULL.
TRAIN SPEEDS OFF)

'THE FALL OF MR HUMPTY'

THE END.

…I knew that it wouldn't be long before the Labrador, the two Orientals, and one black shining typewriter would be getting together again. But what I didn't know was that, like Mr Humpty, my instinct would once again soon want to explore the *Dark* of another haunted mind…

The Fall of Mr Humpty
A nightmare for radio
by Victor Pemberton

Produced by John Tydeman

STUDIO: 6A STEREO

REH/REC: Saturday 11 January 1975   1030–1800
          Sunday 12 January 1975   1030–1830

EDIT: Tuesday 14 January 1975   H54 1000–1800

R.P. REF: SLN03/DL296H

TX: Wednesday 22 January 1975   Radio 4: 2015–2100
RPT: 14 April, 1976   Radio 4

CAST:
Mr Humpty ....Timothy West (OA)
Old Man ....Haydn Jones (OA)
Jimmy......................................Nicholas Dillane (OA)
Vicar..Siôn Probert (REP)
Stranger ....David Ericsson (REP)
1st Woman..............................Carole Boyd (REP)
2nd Woman ....Eva Haddon (REP)

Announcer ....Edward Cole 10 Jan 1430–1445

SMs: Jock Farrell, Marsail McCuish, Penny Leicester

SECRETARY: Linda Wood   Ext. 2168

Announcer "Midweek Theatre".
Child's voice (Jimmy) (*singing*) "Humpty Dumpty sat on a wall,
    Humpty Dumpty had a great fall.
    All the king's horses,
    And all the king's men,
    Couldn't put Humpty together again."
Announcer "The Fall of Mr Humpty"

Stark cut to the screeching of a train through tunnel

In one of the compartments, the voice of a well-spoken, rotund, middle-aged man – Richard Penfold

Penfold Blast!

Hold train F/X briefly, until it finally emerges from the tunnel

    (*irritation*) And about time too! (*startled*) Where the devil did *you* come from? You shouldn't have sneaked in like that in the dark. It gave me quite a shock.

297

No reply from fellow passenger

It's these damned lights in the compartments! Every time we go through that blasted tunnel, they go off! I say it's just not necessary. A person could be murdered sitting alone in here in the dark without lights. (*pause*) Crass inefficiency, I call it! Always the same – night after night. Nothing ever works on this line.

Slight pause

(*to fellow passenger*) I didn't see you come in…

Penfold's only fellow passenger is Jimmy who could be about twelve or thirteen. But from the book he's reciting from, we can only assume that he's backward for his age

Jimmy (*reciting*) "Goosey, goosey gander,
Where shall I wander?
Upstairs, downstairs,
In my lady's chamber…"

Penfold Aren't you a little old to be reading a book of nursery rhymes, young man?

Jimmy (*sweetly*) But I like them, sir. I like the stories.

Penfold The stories? But they're for children much younger than you.

Jimmy Oh no, sir – you're wrong. Nursery rhymes are for grown-ups too. Not just children. I've got lots of books like this one, I know some of the stories off by heart. (*recites*) "There was an old woman who lived in a shoe,
She had so many children she didn't know what to do…"

Penfold When I was your age, I was reading Emily Brontë and Charles Dickens.

Jimmy Who, sir?

Penfold (*double-take*) Who? D'you mean to tell me you've never heard of one of the greatest novelists in the English language? *Charles Dickens*?

Jimmy (*awkwardly*) I don't know him, sir.

Slight pause

Penfold Which school do you go to, young man?

Jimmy I don't know.

Penfold Don't know?

Jimmy I – can't remember.

Penfold Can't remember the name of your own school?

Jimmy It's in the village.

Penfold Which village?

Jimmy Near where I live.

Penfold And where's that?

No reply from Jimmy

I said – where *do* you live?

The boy is saved from answering by the shrill hoot of the train's horn. Hold train travelling at speed, to suggest the passing of time

Then mix to Penfold sleeping, waking up rubbing his eyes

Penfold Where are we? (*stretching*) It's long past my bedtime. (*slight pause*) Finished your book, have you?

Jimmy (*staring out of window*) So many lights out there. It hurts your eyes.

Penfold Then draw the blinds... (*starts to do so*)

Jimmy (*stopping him*) No! Don't do that! I like to look at them. I wonder if they're looking at us?

Penfold Who?

Jimmy People.

Penfold Well, they can hardly ignore us, can they? The train practically ploughs through their back gardens!

Jimmy I wish *I* could live where the trains go by. I'd watch them all the time! Every single day!

Penfold So you like the trains, do you?

Jimmy Oh yes, sir!

Penfold Well you wouldn't – if you had to travel on them as much as I do. Back and forth – day after day. Same old routine. Just like one, long, never-ending journey. (*slight pause*) Why do you like trains so much then?

Jimmy I like the sound they make.

Penfold The sound?

Jimmy Yes. I keep waiting for it to stop. But it never does. (*pause*) Sir? What would happen if we pulled the communication cord?

Penfold (*a start*) If we what?!

Jimmy Would it cause a crash?

Penfold The communication cord is only for use in the event of an emergency...

Jimmy (*unselfconsciousness*) How many people would die, sir? Would it be thousands?

A chilling pause

Penfold Young man. (*looking at watch*) It is now... ten minutes after midnight. Do your mother and father know you're out at such a late hour?

Jimmy I don't have a mother and father sir. Uncle John looks after me.

Penfold Well – does Uncle John know?

Jimmy I promised him I'd be home before dark.

Penfold Yes? Then you're not being very fair to him, are you? It's been dark for hours.

Jimmy Yes, sir. I know.

Penfold What have you been doing all this time?

Jimmy I've been on the trains, sir.

Penfold On the trains?

Jimmy I told you. I like to ride on them.

Penfold You've been riding back and forth on the trains? For how long?

Jimmy I don't remember, sir. Since this morning, I think. Not all the way to London though.

Penfold By now your poor Uncle has probably called in the police to search the whole county for you.

Penfold Oh no, sir. Uncle John would never do that.

Slight pause. Penfold is astonished by the boy's complete vagueness

Penfold Which station are you getting off at?

Jimmy At Stamfield.

Penfold Stamfield? But this is the last train of the day. It never stops at Stamfield.

The boy does not react

Penfold Do you understand what I'm saying, lad? This train doesn't stop until we get to Yaxford. That's almost twenty miles past your station.

Jimmy Yes, sir.

Penfold Well, what are you going to do about it? How are you going to get home? Walk?

Jimmy Don't know, sir.

Penfold Don't know?! (*frustration*) You really are a very vague young man. You know that don't you? (*pause*) What's your name?

Jimmy Jimmy, sir.

Penfold Well, Jimmy – the only thing I can suggest is that you telephone your Uncle the moment we get off at Yaxford.

Jimmy We don't have a telephone at the Farm, sir.

Penfold No telephone? (*sighs*) Well, do you have any money on you for a taxi?

Jimmy No, sir.

Penfold No, well you wouldn't have, would you? If you've been riding about on trains all day. (*pause*) Whereabouts is this Farm you live?

Jimmy The other side of Stamfield, sir. Just off the old by-road.

Penfold Stamfield eh? Oh well, my car's parked at the station. (*with a sigh*) I suppose the only decent thing I can offer to do, is to drive you home…

Bring up train travelling at speed, then crossfade into car interior, as it comes to a halt, but engine still ticking over

Penfold Is this the place?

Jimmy Yes, sir.

Penfold Can't see a thing in the dark. Where's the Farmhouse?

Jimmy (*indicating*) It's over that way – on the other side of those trees.

Penfold (*trying to look*) I don't see any lights?

Jimmy I expect Uncle John has gone to bed.

Penfold Bed! And you're not even home yet?

Jimmy "Early to bed, early to rise," he always says. Uncle John likes to get plenty of sleep.

Penfold (*sourly*) He's not the only one! How do we get to this house?

Jimmy The road stops here. We have to go the rest of the way on foot.

Penfold What!

Jimmy It's not a very good road, you see. We keep meaning to have it done, but Uncle John says repairing roads costs money.

Penfold sighs in frustration, turns off the car engine

Penfold Come on then. Let's get going – or I'll never get home tonight.

They get out of the car. Car doors slamming

Penfold How does anyone ever get out to a place like this?

Jimmy Oh, there are ways, sir – once you know how. But we don't get many visitors. You don't have to come with me if you don't want to.

Penfold (*slightly off*) I can't see a thing! It's pitch-black... There's not even a moon up tonight. Don't we need a torch or something?

Jimmy No, sir. We don't need a torch. I can find my way anywhere in the dark. (*moving off*) But keep close behind me. It gets quite muddy after a while...

They start to walk

Penfold This is absurd! Why do country people always insist on burying themselves in the middle of nowhere? It must be an inferiority complex or something.

Jimmy I told you, sir. We don't have company very often. Uncle John doesn't like it.

Penfold Why not?

Jimmy Because we like to keep ourselves to ourselves. (*pointedly*) We don't like snoopers...

Penfold Even so. It's ridiculous to have to trudge all this way, in and out of the trees every night. And in the pitch dark...

Jimmy (*stops walking*) You could turn back – if you're scared, sir?

Penfold Scared?

He comes to a halt

What am I supposed to be scared of?

Jimmy Lots of things. (*pause*) Being alone in the dark.

Penfold The only reason most people feel nervous in the dark, is because they feel so – helpless. But *I* don't scare easily...

Jimmy Listen!

Penfold What is it?

Jimmy Listen!

Absolute silence. No breeze, not even bird life

Penfold Can't hear a thing.

Jimmy That's because you don't want to. But they're there all right, sir. All around us. In the trees, the bushes... they're watching us from everywhere...

Penfold (*looking around apprehensively*) Watching us? Who's watching us? What are you talking about?

Jimmy When it's quiet like this, you can almost feel them – stretching out their hands to touch you... (*pause*) Whenever I walk in the dark, it's the only time when I know I'm not alone.

An uncomfortable pause

Penfold (*with a shrug*) I'm surprised we could ever feel alone, knowing these trees are bulging with bird life. That's what I loathe about the countryside. It's such a threat...

An owl hoots

For goodness' sake, let's get a move on...

He starts to walk on, but stops almost immediately

Which way now?

No reply from Jimmy

    Jimmy. Are you there?

Still no reply

    Jimmy! (*calling from side to side*) Jimmy! Where the devil are you…!

The rustle of twigs nearby

    (*swings with a start*) Don't play stupid games with me, boy! Or I'll go straight back to the car.

No reply from Jimmy

    (*angrily*) Did you hear what I said…!

From side to side now, we hear Jimmy's voice, bleating like a lamb

Jimmy Baaaa-aa…!
Penfold (*with a start*) What the – !
Jimmy (*from another position, off*) Baaaa-aa…!
Penfold (*nervously, calls back angrily*) Stop that! Stop it, I say!

The rustle of twigs again

Jimmy (*approaching, singing*) "Baa, baa, black sheep,
    Have you any wool
    Yes, sir, yes, sir,
    Three bags full…"
Penfold (*intense*) Don't ever play games like that with me again, boy! D'you understand?
Jimmy (*sweetly*) But you were scared, sir! You were scared to be alone.

Sharp cut into the creaking of the front door of the farmhouse

Jimmy (*slightly off, calling*) Uncle John! Uncle John, are you there?

No reply

    (*at the foot of the stairs, off*) Uncle John! Are you upstairs? It's me. I'm home.

No reply

    (*approaching*) It's no good. He must have gone out.
Penfold Gone out! At this time of night?
Jimmy Oh yes, sir. He often goes out in the evenings. (*proudly*) Uncle John has a lot of friends in the village.
Penfold D'you mean to tell me that your Uncle stays out, knowing that you're in this place all on your own?
Jimmy But I don't mind, sir. After all, I'm not a child, am I? I'll light the lamp.
Penfold Is there no electricity?
Jimmy (*getting the lamp*) Oh no, sir! Uncle John would never have that.
Penfold Why not?
Jimmy (*quoting Uncle*) "These new-fangled ideas are a menace." Everyone knows that, don't they, sir? Now where did Uncle John put the matches? (*finds them*) Ah! Got them!
Penfold It smells damp in here. As though the place has never been lived in.
Jimmy (*having lit the lamp*) There! Now we can see.

As the room is lit, Penfold is taken aback with admiration by what he can see

Penfold Good Lord! It's incredible!

Jimmy We spend most of our evenings in this room. Uncle John reads to me sometimes. But only from the Bible.

Penfold is wandering around. Studying, observing everything with tremendous admiration and enthusiasm

Penfold Why, this house must be at least four or five hundred years old. Earlier! Just look at these beams!

He taps them

Solid oak! They knew how to build houses in those days. Except they must have built them for dwarfs! I can hardly stand up in here, the ceilings are so low. (*wandering around in background, off*) Is it like this throughout the house?

Jimmy Oh yes. Uncle John would never change anything.

Penfold I'd do anything to own a place like this. Far better than the dingy hole I live in. (*pause*) And yet – something makes me feel that I've seen it all before. This room – it has an immediate identity.

He goes to the mantlepiece in background, studies photographs there

Penfold Who are the photographs? This one on the beach… the small boy. Is it you?

Jimmy Yes – it's me. When I was little.

Penfold Great Yarmouth, isn't it?

Jimmy How did you know?

Penfold I recognised it at once. My parents used to take me there a lot when I was your age. They were good holidays.

Slight pause. He picks up another photograph

Are these your parents, Jimmy?

Jimmy Yes, sir.

Penfold It's a very nice photograph. They look very happy. (*pause*) You have your mother's looks. The same eyes.

He puts the photograph back

What happened to your parents. Jimmy? Did they die?

Jimmy I don't know.

Penfold Don't know?

Jimmy Well, I've never seen them – at least I don't think I have – so I don't know what happened to them. I suppose they must have died. (*pause*) Uncle John looks after me now.

Penfold again wandering around the room. He stops to look at some water-colours on the wall

Penfold Well. I'll say one thing for your Uncle. He has taste. These watercolours are quite superb. (*looking*) All seascapes. Strange, for someone who spends so much of his time on the land.

Jimmy Uncle John doesn't work on the land anymore.

Penfold Oh? Why not?

Jimmy He can't get around like he used to. He lost a leg in the war. His new one is made of wood.

Penfold Oh dear. What rotten luck.

He suddenly notices something he admires on the other side of the room

Good Lord! I haven't seen one of those for years!

He rushes across to a harmonium in background off

(*excited*) It's in beautiful condition!

He fingers the notes of the harmonium

In good tune too!

Jimmy (*nervously*) Please sir. Don't do that…!

Penfold ignores him, continues to finger the harmonium

Jimmy Don't touch the harmonium, sir… please! Uncle John wouldn't like it…

Penfold Don't worry. I'm a great one for music – it happens to be a passion of my life. I've played one of these things before. Now then, what have we got here? What's the music he's left open…?

He turns the pages of the music sheet

Oh yes! This is an old favourite!

He sits down at the harmonium, starts to play the hymn: "Rock of Ages"

(*singing the words as he plays*) "Rock of ages, cleft for me,
Let me hide myself in thee…"

Jimmy (*on mic, upset*) Please sir! I asked you not to…!

Penfold (*continues to sing*) "Let the water and the blood
From the riven side which flowed,
Be of sin the double cure,
Cleanse me from its guilt and power…"

Jimmy No, sir! No…!

Penfold (*starting second verse*) "Not the labours of thy hands…"

Jimmy (*with a great shout*) I said – no…!

Go with him as he rushes across, slams down the harmonium cover, to Penfold's intense shock

Penfold What the devil…!

Jimmy (*upset*) I told you not to do it! I told you! No one's allowed to play the harmonium but Uncle John! No one…!

Penfold (*angry*) Is that any reason to try and crush my fingers, you young idiot!

A tense pause

Jimmy (*awkwardly*) I'm sorry sir. Truly I am. It's just that Uncle John is very particular about who plays the harmonium. He's very attached to it.

Penfold So it seems.

Jimmy "Rock of Ages" is his favourite hymn. He never sings anything else.

Penfold (*relieving the tension*) What you're really trying to say is, you can't bear the sound of *my* singing. Isn't that it?

A brief pause, until gradually both see the joke and begin to laugh. Nevertheless, the tension has been evident, and their laughter soon fades to another awkward pause

Jimmy You'd better go now, sir.

Penfold Very well. If you're sure you'll be all right?

Jimmy Oh yes. Uncle John should be home soon.

Penfold I hope so. (*pause, going*) Then I'll say goodnight…

Jimmy Will you come back and see us again?

Slight pause

Penfold (*hesitant*) I – don't know. Would you like me to?

Jimmy Oh yes, sir! And Uncle John would love to meet you. I know he would. (*eagerly*) Why don't you come back and have tea with us tomorrow afternoon?

Penfold I can't make any promises, Jimmy. I usually work at home on Saturday afternoons…

Jimmy Oh *please*, Mr Humpty – please! I'd like you to come.

Penfold What did you call me?

Jimmy Mr Humpty.

Penfold My name is Penfold. Richard Penfold.

Jimmy I prefer Mr Humpty. It's one of my favourite stories. Will you come tomorrow? Will you?

Slight pause

Penfold Very well. Jimmy, I'd be glad to. Something tells me I shall have quite a lot to talk to your Uncle about…

They are suddenly interrupted by a sharp thumping sound, coming from a room above them

What was that? Where did that sound come from? There's someone upstairs! I thought you said…

Jimmy There's no one sir.

Penfold But I distinctly heard…

Jimmy It's only the mice, sir. They're my friends. They always wait to come out and talk to me at night. It's the only time they feel safe. I shall be angry with them for making you scared.

Penfold I must be going. (*going to door*) Don't bother to come with me. I can find my own way back to the car.

Jimmy (*with Penfold at door, off*) You will come tomorrow, won't you?

Penfold (*at door*) Yes, Jimmy, I'll come.

Jimmy Promise?

Penfold I promise! Goodnight.

Jimmy Goodnight – Mr Humpty.

Penfold's footsteps are heard moving away from the house off. Jimmy closes the door. Pause

Jimmy (*calls*) All right. You can come out now. He's gone.

Silence

I'm waiting.

After a moment, we hear the sound of two or three mice squeaking their way out from their hiding places

(*app*) You're not to do it, d'you hear? You're not to scare our Mr Humpty like that. Because the next time you do – you know what will happen… (*sings*)
"Three Blind Mice
Three Blind Mice
See how they run!
See how they run.
They all run after the Farmer's wife
Who cut off their tails with a carving-knife,
Did ever you see such a thing in your life,
As Three Blind Mice?"

Crossfade the squeaking mice to the background. Twitter of birds in the farmyard outside. It is the following afternoon. Jimmy's voice echoes down to the bottom of the dried-up farmhouse well

Jimmy (*on echo*) Hallo Mr Humpty! Hallo Mr Humpty…

Penfold For heaven's sake be careful, Jimmy! I don't want to have to hoist you up from the bottom of that well!

Jimmy But it can't hurt. It's dried up.

Penfold Even so. Your Uncle should know better than to leave the well open like this. It's extremely dangerous.

Jimmy (*peering down well*) I wonder what would happen if somebody fell down there? I wonder if they'd die?

Penfold Well I have no intention of finding out, thank you very much. So for goodness' sake — be careful, will you.

Slight pause

Jimmy I mean – there's no water down there, so they wouldn't drown. But it's so deep, they'd never be able to get out of there again alive. Would they?

Penfold You know Jimmy – you're an odd boy. I don't think I've ever met anyone with such a bizarre curiosity. I can't imagine why you asked me to come back here.

Jimmy I'm glad you did, Mr Humpty.

Penfold Did you think I wouldn't?

Jimmy I wasn't sure. But I hoped you would.

Penfold I thought the whole point of my coming was to meet Uncle John?

Jimmy I told you. He had to go to London on business.

Penfold Business? On a Saturday afternoon?

Jimmy He said I was to thank you for bringing me home last night.

Penfold And what time did he get home himself?

Jimmy Quite late I think. He'd been drinking.

Penfold Lucky man!

Jimmy It makes him lose his temper. I get frightened. I hate him when he loses his temper. It makes me wish he was dead.

Slight pause

Penfold Did you tell your Uncle where you'd been all day? Riding up and down on trains?

Jimmy No.

Penfold Why not?

Jimmy Because he never tells me *his* secrets. So why should I tell him mine? (*pause*) Come on, Mr Humpty! I'll race you to the windmill…

Penfold I wish you'd stop calling me by that ridiculous name! You only do it because I happen to be a little large around the waistline…

Jimmy I like the name!

Penfold Why do you like it?

Jimmy Because you're like an egg. I hope you don't fall down the well. You might crack!

Jimmy roars with laughter at his joke. After a moment, Penfold too joins in

Penfold I must say, this is just the sort of place I'd like for my own. (*looking around*) Quiet. Peaceful. Far from the madding crowd. (*pause*) People who have all this don't know how lucky they are. They don't know what it's like to be shut up in a flat all day, with no one to talk to but a telephone operator.

Slight pause

Do you ever find it lonely – cut off from the outside world like this?

Jimmy Lonely?

Penfold Do you ever see any friends?

Jimmy I see Uncle John.

Penfold I mean, young people of your own age?

Jimmy I prefer to be on my own. Then I can do what I want.

Penfold And what's that, Jimmy? What *do* you do with yourself all day? Climb trees or something?

Jimmy (*snapping*) No! I hate trees!

Penfold Hate trees? A boy of your age? But why?

Jimmy Because… because sometimes – when I lie down and look up at the trees, it's as though they're going to fall down on top of me. If I had *my* way I'd have all the trees all over the world cut down – everywhere! *Then* I'd feel safe… (*with a start*) Ssh…!

Penfold What is it?

Jimmy (*voice lowered*) Keep still! Don't move. Over there – in the bushes. There's a rabbit. Quick! Help me find a stone.

Penfold (*horrified*) A stone! What for?

Jimmy To throw, of course! I'm going to kill him!

Penfold (*shocked*) Jimmy!

Jimmy searches around, finds a stone

Jimmy I've found one! Now keep still… (*slowly*) He's just coming out of the bushes… now!

But Penfold suddenly grabs the stone from Jimmy's hand

Penfold No, Jimmy…!

Jimmy (*struggling*) What are you doing? Give me back my stone! Let me go! Let me go!

Penfold You are not – going to throw – that stone…

Finally the stone drops with a thud to the ground

Jimmy He's gone! The rabbit's got away! I hate you! I hate you!

Penfold Why kill for the sake of killing, Jimmy? What harm has that poor creature ever done to you?

Jimmy He was *my* rabbit! And *you* let him get away! (*close and menacing*) I won't forgive you for that, Mr Humpty. I won't forgive you…

Behind this, bring up windmill flaps in a gentle breeze. Hold briefly, then fade into background. We hear the huge cog wheel grinding slowly in the upstairs grain room

Penfold Well? Am I forgiven?

Pause: no reply

> I'm sorry I had to upset you, Jimmy. But what you were going to do seemed to be so wrong. I never could bear the thought of killing poor, defenceless animals. We have no right to take advantage of our superiority!

Pause: still no reply

> If you're going to sulk for the rest of the afternoon, I might as well go home…

Jimmy This room is where we used to keep the grain. We can't use the windmill any more.

Penfold I'm not surprised. It all looks rather worn out to me.

Jimmy This is my Castle. I can see everyone from here. I can watch them if they try to come up the hill.

Penfold What would you do if they did?

Jimmy Pour boiling water over them.
> (*recites at speed*) "Jack and Jill
> Went up the hill
> To fetch a pail of water
> Jack fell down,
> And broke his crown,
> And Jill came tumbling after…"

Penfold That's a horrible story. I don't like it.

Jimmy Why not?

Penfold Because human life is precious. We should treat it with respect.

Jimmy (*so direct*) Are you afraid to die, Mr Humpty?

Penfold (*taken aback*) That's an odd question, from someone of your age?

Jimmy Are you?

Pause

Penfold Nobody *wants* to die. But it's something none of us can avoid.

Jimmy I saw a dead man once. His eyes were wide open. (*pause*) I wasn't scared.

Penfold Those are things you shouldn't dwell on, Jimmy. You should think about life – not death.

Jimmy (*pause*) I wonder what it's like to die?

An uncomfortable pause

Penfold Tell me about Uncle John.

Jimmy Why?

Penfold Well, since I'm obviously not going to be allowed to meet him, I'd like to know that's all.

Slight pause

Jimmy He's quite old.

Penfold Are you good friends?

Jimmy Sometimes.

Penfold Only sometimes?

Jimmy We argue a lot.

Penfold Oh? Why's that?

Jimmy He's very strict.

Penfold Strict?

Jimmy He doesn't like me telling lies.

Penfold Nothing wrong in that.

Jimmy Not even small ones.

Penfold Small lies often grow into large ones.

Jimmy That's what Uncle John always says. He says that if I read the Bible every night before I go to bed, I'll never want to tell another lie.

Penfold Hmn. I'm not sure I go along with that.

Jimmy We go to Church every Sunday.

Penfold *Every* Sunday?

Jimmy In the morning *and* in the evening.

Penfold Do you like going to Church?

Jimmy (*dourly*) Sometimes. (*pause*) I prefer coming to the windmill. I've got people I can talk to up here.

Penfold (*puzzled*) People? What people?

Jimmy Well. You can't actually see them. But they're here all right. They're here now. Watching us…

Penfold Now we're not going to to start all that old nonsense again…

Jimmy They tell me stories. Just like Uncle John.

Penfold I don't believe in ghosts, Jimmy. I only believe in things I *know* exist.

Jimmy They won't talk to just anyone, Mr Humpty. They won't let you hurt me.

We are very aware here of sounds:windmill flaps in breeze; slow grinding of cog wheel. All this is to intensify Penfold's growing feeling of being pressurised

Penfold Why do you think that I should want to hurt you, Jimmy?

Jimmy I don't know. But you might.

Slight pause

Penfold (*showing signs of irritation*) A boy like you shouldn't lock yourself up in a place like this. There are too many pressures…

He moves around

Jimmy You should go out and meet *real* people… instead of riding up and down on trains all day!

Jimmy But *you* ride on trains— don't you, Mr Humpty?

Penfold That's different. I *have* to. But it's no fun, I can tell you. Back and forth to London day after day – lights going off in the compartment every time we go into that blasted tunnel…

Jimmy Do *you* have any friends, Mr Humpty?

Pause

Penfold Friends? Me?

Pause

No. I don't have friends. I don't need them any more. (*pause. Inwardly*) And I don't have a wife any more either. (*as though thinking aloud*) She thinks I can't live without her. But she's wrong! I don't need her any more.

Slight pause. Penfold is trying to work something out of his system. But it just won't work

What am I saying! Of course I need her! I *hate* being alone! I hate it! Oh God! How did I let my life get into such a hell of a mess?

Jimmy (*again so direct*) *I* won't leave you, Mr Humpty.

Slight pause

Penfold Huh? What did you say?

Jimmy I said – *I* won't leave you. After all, *we're* friends, aren't we, Mr Humpty? In fact I'm never going to leave you. Not ever again…

Sharp cut to an old, scratched 78rpm record, almost sinister in timing and context

Man's voice on record (*singing*) "Hickory, dickory, dock
The mouse ran up the clock,
The clock struck one,
The mouse ran down,
Hickory, dickory, dock."

Jimmy takes off the record

Jimmy I've had that record a long time. Uncle John bought it for me when I was little. It's getting a little worn out now.

Penfold (*approaching, in disbelief*) Are you telling me that this really is your bedroom? That you actually sleep in here?

Jimmy (*hurt*) Don't you like it, sir?

Penfold (*pause, awkwardly*) I – I don't know what to say to you. Jimmy. This type of room is usually only for – for tiny children. It's a Nursery.

Jimmy Uncle John wanted to change it. But I told him not to. I like it this way. I don't want it ever to change. Would you like to see some of my toys? I've got lots of them.

He rushes around the room, picking up various toys to show Penfold

This is a brick set; I can build things with that. (*moving*) I've got cars, a fire-engine… d'you like this, Mr Humpty?

He taps on a toy typewriter

It's a typewriter! Not a real one though. (*moving proudly*) I've got my own train set!

310

He turns on the train engine. We hear it winding around the toy track

(*excited*) What do you think of it, Mr Humpty? Isn't it smashing! It's just like the one you go on. Look! *I've* got a tunnel…!

As the toy train engine passes into the tunnel, Jimmy makes engine hooter sounds

Penfold Turn it off, Jimmy.

Jimmy makes more hooter sounds

Jimmy! I said turn it off!

Jimmy turns off the engine, which immediately comes to a halt

Jimmy (*sad*) Don't you like my train set, Mr Humpty?
Penfold I just don't like trains, that's all.

Slight pause

Jimmy D'you know what my favourite toy is, Mr Humpty? It's over there. In the corner. I'll show you!
Penfold A rocking-horse!

Jimmy, in background rolling to and fro on the rocking-horse

(*wildly*) It's my favourite toy in the whole wide world…! I'm going to ride all the way to London…!

He moves the rocking-horse faster

Penfold Jimmy, you're far too old for a thing like that. A rocking-horse is for small children…
Jimmy (*rocking wildly*) Faster! Faster…!
Penfold For goodness' sake, stop behaving like a child, Jimmy! You're old enough to know better…!
Jimmy (*over this, reciting; rocking at speed*)
    "Ride a cock-horse to Banbury Cross,
    To buy little Johnny a galloping horse,
    It trots behind and it ambles before,
    And Johnny shall ride till he can ride no more."
Penfold (*shouts*) Jimmy!

Jimmy brings the rocking-horse to a halt. Pause

Jimmy (*approaching*) You'd like a ride on my horse, wouldn't you, Mr Humpty? Only you can't – because you're too fat!
Penfold (*snaps*) That's not a nice thing to say, Jimmy! Not even to a friend.

Pause. He moves to a table, where there are some cardboard boxes

What are in all these boxes…,?
Jimmy (*snatching one from him*) Leave them alone! They're mine!
Penfold Aha! Secrets! What's inside them?
Jimmy (*aggressively*) I'm not going to tell you!
Penfold Oh? But I thought we were supposed to be friends?

Slight pause

Jimmy You really want to know?
Penfold Of course.

Slight pause

Jimmy All right, Mr Humpty. I'll show you. This is my collection.

He open the box

Penfold (*with horror*) Jimmy…!

Jimmy Don't you like it? It's a rabbit. (*proudly*) I killed it.

Penfold (*distaste*) How could you do such a thing?

Jimmy But it's ever so easy. I do it with this. (*picks up razor*) It used to belong to Uncle John.

Penfold An open razor?

Jimmy He let me have it – for my experiments. (*opening other boxes*) I've got lots of them in the other boxes. Spiders, moths, cockroaches, a blackbird… I've got some mice too… (*with menace*) It's their own fault. I told them not to upset you, Mr Humpty.

Penfold But *why* Jimmy? Why must you kill? Why must you do things like this?

Slight pause

Jimmy But I only want to see what makes them work, Mr Humpty – that's all.

Tense pause

Penfold I'm going home now, Jimmy…

Jimmy No! Not yet – please…!

Jimmy rushes forward to prevent Penfold from leaving the room

I haven't shown you the rest of the house.

Penfold (*firmly at door*) I've told you – I've got work to do. I've been here too long as it is…

Jimmy (*now quietly aggressive, sinister and menacing*) But I want you to stay, Mr Humpty! Do you understand?

He has a razor in his hand poised towards Penfold

Uncle John and I *want* you to stay.

Tense pause

Penfold Give me the razor, Jimmy.

No reply

Did you hear what I said…?

Jimmy (*moving close on mic*) I could cut you up into little pieces if I wanted to, Mr Humpty. Just like my experiments…

Penfold (*nervously*) Put down the razor. Jimmy. Before one of us gets hurt.

Jimmy Are you scared, Mr, Humpty? Are you?

Tense pause. Jimmy drops the razor to the floor

There you are… You're safe now…

Penfold (*angrily*) You – idiotic child! How dare you threaten me like that! You're no friend of mine! You could never be! I never want to see you again as long as I live…!

He tries to leave. But the door is locked

The door. It's locked!

Jimmy (*across the room, off*) You're never going to leave me, Mr Humpty! Never! Never! Never!

Penfold (*angrily*) Give me the key, Jimmy! At once!

Jimmy You'll never run away from me, Mr Humpty! Because I'll always be with you! Always…!

Penfold (*shouts*) Jimmy…!

Jimmy is back on the rocking-horse again. He begins to rock to and fro at a furious pace, reciting wildly at speed, and in rhythm with the rocking motion

Jimmy "Ride a cock-horse to Banbury Cross,
   To buy little Johnny a galloping horse;
   It trots behind and it ambles before,
   And Johnny shall ride till he can ride no more."

Penfold (*pressurised, shouts back*) Jimmy, stop that! Nursery rhymes are unhealthy! They're evil…!

The rocking continues

   (*the pressure mounting*) Open this door, will you…!

Jimmy (*ignoring him, again reciting at speed*)
   "Ride a cock-horse to Banbury Cross
   To see a fine lady upon a white horse;
   Rings on her fingers and bells on her toes,
   And she shall have music wherever she goes…"

Penfold (*shouting, bordering hysteria*) If you don't open this door at once… I shall go to Uncle John!

Jimmy brings the rocking-horse to an immediate halt. Followed by a tense pause. Then, Jimmy's footsteps, as he approaches on the bare floorboards

Jimmy (*quiet and sinister*) All right, Mr Humpty. I'll open the door for you.

Goes to the door, unlocks it, stands there

   But if you want to go to Uncle John – then just see if you can find him!

Jimmy dashes out, slamming the door behind him. His footsteps hurrying down stairs etc.

Penfold (*calls*) Jimmy!

He rushes to the door, opens it, shouts down the stairs

   Jimmy! Come back…! Come back…!

Sharp cut to the gentle peel of church bells. Crossfade this with footsteps and voices approaching on gravel through the churchyard. Penfold is talking with the parish vicar

Vicar I'm sorry, Mr Penfold. But I've only been Vicar of this Parish for the past eighteen months or so. I'm afraid I know very little about the Farmhouse you're referring to. Other than what one hears in the village, of course.

Penfold But you must know the old man and his nephew? The people who live there.

Vicar Who – live there?

Penfold Well aren't they regulars in your Church every Sunday? At least, that's what the boy told me.

Vicar Mr Penfold. I think it's possible that you've made some kind of mistake.

Penfold Mistake?

Vicar To my knowledge, the Farmhouse we're talking about hasn't been lived in for years. It's been up for sale for some considerable time.

Penfold (*shock, disbelief*) What!

Vicar In fact, the last I heard was that the place is just falling apart with rot and decay. If somebody doesn't buy it soon, it will just fall down...

Penfold But there *are* people living there, Vicar! I was out at the Farm only yesterday afternoon. The house is full of furniture – and everything else...

Vicar (*firmly*) The Farmhouse is derelict, Mr Penfold. In its present condition, it would be impossible for anyone to live there.

They stop walking

Penfold What are you trying to keep from me, Vicar?

Vicar (*indignantly*) I beg your pardon, Mr –

Penfold Oh, don't worry. You're not the first.

Slight pause

Vicar Mr Penfold. If you'd just tell me what it is you're trying to find out...

Penfold I want to know about Uncle John. I want to know why he's been kept away from me.

Slight pause

And the boy... he's ill... irrational. He's not responsible for what he's doing.

Slight pause

Something has happened out at that house. And I'm too scared to think what it might be...

Vicar Mr Penfold. My advice to you is that you go home and forget all this. Think of it as a bad nightmare. When you wake up, it will all be over.

Slight pause

Mr Penfold? Is anything wrong? (*pause*) What are you staring at?

Penfold (*a strained, distant voice*) This Churchyard. I – I've been here before.

Vicar Is that so unusual?

Penfold I don't know what's happening... (*strained*) Everything's so – blurred...

Vicar Would you like to sit down and rest for a minute, my dear fellow?

Penfold That smell... what is it? Something's burning...

Vicar Yes. There are always plenty of bonfires around at this time of year.

Penfold (*sharply*) I – hate it! It – reminds me of something... (*fast breathing*) I... I've got to get away from here... I've got to get away... (*rushing off*)

Vicar Mr Penfold! What is it? (*calls*) Where are you going?

Penfold (*rushing off, calling back*) I'm going back to the farm! I'm going to find Jimmy! I *must* know what's happened to Uncle John...!

Crossfade Penfold's footsteps rushing off, with exterior night sounds at the farmhouse: an owl hoots, the squeal of bats, etc. After a moment we hear Penfold knocking at the front door

Penfold (*calls gently*) Jimmy? Jimmy, are you in there?

No reply. He knocks again. No reply. He tries the door handle. It is open. The door creaks open

Cut to interior, as Penfold comes into the sitting-room of the house

(*calls again*) Jimmy? Jimmy, it's me – Mr Humpty. I only want to talk to you…

He stumbles over something in the dark

Blast! Can't see a thing in the dark…

Moving into room, off

Now what did he do with that oil-lamp… (*finds it*) Ah! Should have some matches here somewhere… (*finds a box of matches*) Yes!

He lights the lamp

(*sigh of relief*) Thank goodness. I can see what I'm doing now… (*looking around*) So many shadows…

He is suddenly startled by a loud thumping sound coming from upstairs

(*calls*) Hallo! Is anyone up there?

No reply

(*calls again*) Jimmy? Is that you?

Now the faint squeak of mice nearby

Mice! This place must be running alive with them. Probably hiding in every cupboard in the house…

Again the thumping sound from upstairs

(*calls*) Who's there?

He rushes slightly off mic. Calls up the stairs, in background

Jimmy? Is that you?

No reply

It's no use pretending! I know it's you. (*pause*) I'm coming there, Jimmy. (*louder*) Did you hear what I said? I'm coming upstairs to the Nursery…!

Sharp cut to Penfold's footsteps climbing the creaking stairs. He comes to a halt on the landing outside Jimmy's nursery room

(*calls*) Jimmy?

He taps on the door of the nursery

Jimmy, are you in there? I'm coming in!

He opens the door, and goes in. No one appears to be there. Only Penfold. Footsteps echo across the bare floorboards. He stops. Silence

It's silly to play games, Jimmy. I know you're here.

Silence

We've got a lot to talk about, you and I…

The door suddenly slams in background

(*with a start*) Jimmy…!

But Jimmy is not there. Silence again. Penfold is clearly becoming edgy, but is trying not to show it

What's the point of all this, Jimmy? We're friends, aren't we? You said so yourself. (*pause*) We don't have to lie to each other, you and I. And d'you know why? Because we're very alike.

Pause. He moves a few steps, stops

Jimmy. I want to tell you something. You were right when you said that I'm scared of the dark. I *am* scared. Sometimes I lie awake at night too scared to even go to sleep. I imagine there are eyes watching me from the shadows in every corner of the room. I hate the dark, Jimmy! I hate people! Nobody understands. They don't want to. I feel so helpless, Jimmy. *You* know that, don't you...

He swings with a horrified start, as he hears the sound of the rocking-horse squeaking back and forth in background

Oh my God! The rocking-horse...!

The rocking-horse squeaks on at a leisurely pace

It's only a stupid toy! It's for children! (*calls*) Where are you, Jimmy...!

The rocking-horse comes to a halt. Silence, but for the sound of Penfold's tense breathing

You think I don't know your secret, don't you, Jimmy? Well – I do!

Silence

Where is he, Jimmy? What have you done with Uncle John? Is *he* one of your experiments too...!

Now – a horrifying sound: a man with a wooden leg hobbling along the landing outside. Is this Uncle John?

There's someone outside...! (*with fear*) It's him...!

The hobbling sound continues

It's Uncle John!

But before he can reach the door, another sound takes over to distract him: it is the children's gramophone record

Man's voice on record (*singing*) "Hickory, dickory, dock,
The mouse ran up the clock.
The clock struck one,
The mouse ran down,
Hickory, dickory, dock..."
Penfold (*with a great shout*) No...!

As he rushes across to tear the record off the gramophone, this is quickly followed by Jimmy's child-like voice, on echo distort, challenging him from various corners of the room

Jimmy (*on distort echo*) "Three Blind Mice.
Three Blind Mice.
See how they run.

See how they run…"

Penfold (*shouting over*) No, Jimmy! No! Where are you? Where are you…?

Jimmy (*continued*) "They all ran after the Farmer's wife,

Who cut off their tails with a carving-knife,

Did you ever see such a thing in your life,

As Three Blind Mice?"

Penfold (*shouting*) Nursery rhymes are the work of the devil…!

A tense silence

(*louder*) Did you hear what I said?!

Now Jimmy's voice comes from another corner of the room, closer to mic. It is sweet and child-like

Jimmy (*reciting*) "Humpty Dumpty sat on a wall

Humpty Dumpty had a great fall

All the king's horses and all the king's men

Couldn't put Humpty together again."

Silence again, except for Penfold standing alone in the middle of the room, breathing hard and nervously

Penfold (*shouts*) Where is he, Jimmy? Where *is* Uncle John?

From the room below we hear a spine-chilling sound: Uncle John's shakey voice is singing "Rock of Ages", to his own accompaniment on the harmonium

(*sheer terror*) Uncle John! (*louder*) Uncle John…!

Slightly bring up the old man's voice and harmonium. Hold. Now Penfold's footsteps as he comes down the creaking stairs, stops at the door of the sitting-room

(*breathing hard*) That smell… from the Churchyard… burning…!

He bursts into the room. The harmonium and singing cuts out at once

Uncle John it's you…! It *is* you…!

But he is answered by another more rational man's voice

Old man (*angrily*) You talk to me like that boy, and I'll knock the livin' daylights out of yer…!

Psychiatrist (*in Magistrates' Court*) In my opinion, sir, the boy is mentally ill. He is a prisoner in his own world. After the terrible tragedy that has happened, he needs time to adjust…

1st Woman …a sensitive child…

Jimmy (*reciting*) "Goosey goosey gander

Where do you wander?

Upstairs, downstairs

In the lady's chamber…"

2nd Woman I love you, Richard. But I'm going to leave you. It seems the only logical thing I can do…

Vicar …the Farmhouse hasn't been lived in for years. It's been up for sale for some considerable time…

Jimmy After all, *we're* friends, aren't we, Mr Humpty? I'm never going to leave you. Not ever again…

Old man (*angrily*) You're just like your mother! Stubborn to the last...

1st Woman ...a sensitive child...

Psychiatrist (*in Court*) He needs a long period of rest. Time to forget...

Behind this now, bring in again the old man at the harmonium, holding it in background throughout the following

Jimmy (*sobbing, upset*) I don't want to go to Church tomorrow! I won't go...!

2nd Woman You're like a child, Richard! You're spoilt! Spoilt...

Jimmy (*sobbing*) I won't go! You can't make me...!

Vicar Think of it as a bad nightmare, Mr Penfold. When you wake up, it will all be over...

Jimmy (*sobbing, shouting hysterically*) I hate you! I hate you! I hate you...!

1st Woman ...a sensitive child...

The old man's hymn singing builds towards climax

Psychiatrist He's dead, Richard!

The harmonium, singing stops sharply

Your Uncle John died a long time ago. He's dead... dead... dead...

Jimmy (*a piercing scream*) No...!

Penfold (*a great shout*) No...!

Cross-fade Penfold's great shout, with the sound of the train horn screeching its way out of the tunnel

As we fade train F/X to end montage, we find Penfold in a high state of tension, having relived the whole thing

Penfold No... no... no... no... no...!

Stranger (Psychiatrist) It's all right, Richard. It's all right...

Penfold (*bewildered, half-sobbing*) He's *not* dead! Uncle John's not dead. I won't believe it! I won't...

Stranger Calm yourself, Richard. Just relax.

Penfold, breathing hard, calms

Penfold (*pause; with effort*) Who – are you?

Stranger It's Doctor Cooper. You're quite safe now.

Penfold (*confused*) Doctor Cooper? Then – you knew I was here?

Stranger Oh yes, Richard. I knew you were here. In fact, I've never been far away from you. Not since – not since you began to give in to all this. But I had to let you come back here.

Slight pause

Penfold (*looking around, bewildered*) This – this room. Everything's changed... I don't understand? There's nothing here. Everything's gone... the furniture... pictures... the harmonium! What... where's the harmonium? Everything...!

Stranger This room is the way it should be, Richard. Everything about this house, everything you thought you saw – was from the past. *Your* memory of the past.

Slight pause

Penfold I – don't believe you. It's not possible! I was here... I *saw* it all! (*agitated*) Where's the boy? He'll tell you! He was here with me. *He* knows... (*calls out*) Jimmy! Jimmy, where are you...?

Stranger You won't find him, Richard.

Penfold (*in background*) I *will* find him! I know he's here somewhere... (*calls*) Jimmy...!

Stranger You won't find him – because he's never left your side.

Slight pause

Penfold (*approaching*) What are you talking about?

Stranger He's been with you all the time, Richard. Jimmy – is you.

Pause

Penfold You're trying to tell me – I imagined him? Meeting him on the train, coming back here...?

Stranger It's all been in your subconscious for a very long time, Richard. Sooner or later it had to come to the surface.

Penfold hesitates, trying to take it all in

Penfold But – Uncle John... he's alive, I know he is! He feels such a part of me...

Stranger Uncle John is dead, Richard. It's a fact you've just got to accept.

Penfold I don't believe it. He's here... in this room... now...! If Uncle John is dead then you're going to have to prove it to me!

Stranger No one can do that for you, Richard. Only yourself.

Penfold How?

Stranger By telling me everything that happened, the night your Uncle died...

Penfold No!

Stranger Why not?

Penfold I don't remember –

Stranger (*pursuing*) You *do* remember, Richard. But you don't want to! Don't you understand? Jimmy has always been fascinated by the thought of death, but when it came to the reality – he couldn't face up to it...

Penfold No! It's not true...!

Stranger It *is* true, Richard! And until you face up to that reality, you will never rid yourself of your guilt. (*slight pause*) Now. What happened the night Uncle John died?

Pause

Penfold (*slowly at first and with great effort*) We'd had a quarrel. It – wasn't very much... he wanted me to go to Church the next day. I told him I didn't want to go... that he'd got no right to force me. He told me to go to bed. I lay in the dark a long time – crying, saying to myself over and over again how much I hated Uncle John! How I wished my mother and father hadn't been killed in that train crash when I was little.

Slight pause

Suddenly – I heard something. It was Uncle John singing at the harmonium downstairs...

Behind this now, the old man singing at the harmonium; "Rock of Ages"

It was the same old tune... the same old hymn that I'd heard over and over again...

Singing continues behind

I decided I'd tell him I didn't like his singing any more. That I wouldn't keep doing the things he wanted me to do. (*pause*) I got out of bed – and went down the stairs...

The stairs creak as Jimmy goes down the stairs

I stopped outside the door of this room – and listened to his voice...

The old man singing, playing

He sounded so – confident. So sure of himself! Every second I was hating him more and more...

Pause

Suddenly, I couldn't bear it any longer! I opened the door – and shouted at him...!

Jimmy I don't like your singing any more, Uncle John!

Singing, playing stops dead

Penfold The old man stopped playing the harmonium at once! He turned around, and took a long, slow look at me... The look in his eyes... like ice. Although I was scared, I came further into the room...

Jimmy And you can't make me go to Church tomorrow morning, if I don't want to...!

Penfold For a moment, he just stared at me... without saying one single word. Then he reached for his walking-stick, and slowly... came towards me... (*breathing hard*) I was cold with fright. I'd never seen that look in his eyes before... I felt as though he was going to kill me! (*pause*) But then – something happened. His face... all of a sudden it just crinkled up... he clutched his chest with his hand – and cried out in pain!

Old man (*shouts out in pain*)

Penfold Before I could even reach him, he'd fallen to the floor! His hand knocked against the oil lamp... it went smashing to the floor...!

Oil lamp smashes on floor

There were flames all over him...! I – I couldn't do anything...! He was burning...! I – I... the flames...!

Flames crackling

I rushed upstairs and pulled a blanket off one of the beds... I came down and threw it over Uncle John. It seemed to take ages before the flames went out...

Flames die out

(*slowly, with agony*) But it was too late. When I pulled the blanket away – Uncle John was... his face... it was black – and charred... And his eyes... they were wide open... just staring at me...

Tense pause. Close to tears

320

I shook him, and shook him, and shook him! But there was nothing I could do, but run away! I ran as fast as I could…I don't know where… I just had to get away…! (*sobbing now*) I… I… I didn't hate Uncle John… He was my friend… I *loved* him.

A delicate, highly charged moment as Penfold breaks down into tears

Stranger It's all right, Richard. All right. You've done it. You've done it on your own. You're 'together' again, Richard. 'All the king's horses and all the king's men' couldn't do it – but *you* have…

Bring up engine horn, as train speeds its way into tunnel

Penfold Blast!

Hold train F/X briefly, until it finally emerges from the tunnel

Penfold (*irritation*) And about time too! (*startled*) Where the devil did *you* come from? You shouldn't have sneaked in like that in the dark. It gave me quite a shock.

No reply from fellow passenger

It's these damned lights in the compartments! Every time we go through that blasted tunnel, they go off! I say it's just not necessary. A person could be murdered sitting alone here in the dark without lights. (*pause*) Crass inefficiency, I call it! Always the same – night after night. Nothing ever works on this line.

Slight pause

(*to fellow passenger*) I didn't see you come in… (*suddenly, with suspicion*) What's that book you're reading?

Penfold's only fellow passenger is a young boy, who could be about twelve or thirteen

Boy This sir? (*showing book*) It's Macaulay's 'History of England'.

Penfold Yes. Well when I was your age, I was reading… What did you say?

Boy Macaulay's 'History of England', sir.

Penfold (*clearly taken aback!*) Oh – really? Good reading, is it?

Boy Oh yes sir. First class. I hope to take English History for my 'A' levels.

Penfold Oh – really? Well I hope you do well,

Boy Thank you sir.

Penfold (*pause, awkwardly*) Then you don't read Nursery rhymes, then?

Boy (*horror*) Nursery rhymes, sir!

Penfold Just wondered that's all.

Boy Good heavens – no sir! Why would someone of my age want to read stuff like that? Nursery rhymes are only for children…

Bring in engine hooter to full. Train speeds off

THE END

Dark

I remember it well. It was one rainy afternoon in the Essex countryside, and I was crouched on the floor in front of the open log fire talking with David Spenser about an idea I had for a full-length supernatural ghost play set in London. By this time, David had had enough of his acting career, and had decided to go off in a new direction as a radio producer. He was very interested in my idea, mainly because it seemed that I wanted to explore another part of my writing potential. He also felt that because of the psychological and sexual nature of the story, I might find it difficult to sell to the Radio Drama Department.

A few days later, I talked it over with John Tydeman, who up until that time had produced virtually all my radio plays. Although a bit sceptical that the idea was very different to anything I had attempted before, he was intrigued enough to encourage me to work on it. After a lot of soul-searching, I sat down at my faithful old typewriter and sketched out a synopsis. Actually, the idea developed much faster than I'd ever imagined, and the only three characters in the story sprang to life as though I had always known them.

Eventually I submitted the idea to Richard Imison – the late, lamented, much loved Head of the BBC Radio Script Unit – whose initial reaction, like John's, was wary. But after the three of us had discussed what I had in mind for the play, they both showed enough confidence (and courage!) to commission the script. However, it was quite nerve-wracking, for the commission was for the *Monday Night Theatre* 90-minute slot, which was a bit more highbrow than the stuff I had been used to writing! So in the early winter of 1977 I sat down at my 'old faithful' typewriter, and again we went into battle.

By 1978, television in every form was now playing an increasingly greater role in the awareness of the British public. Whereas the big-screen version of *Superman* with Christopher Reeve was proving to be an enormous success at the cinema, the BBC was winding up the final episode of the long-running television police series, *Z Cars*. Another innovation that year was that the BBC were beginning to broadcast the first of the entire repertory of Shakespeare's plays, thanks to the skill and determination of Cedric Messina, who fought to bring the whole thing together, mainly with funds from the United States. Nonetheless, radio drama was still a force to reckoned with, with plays from well-known modern writers, some not so well known and new to the medium, and, of course, regular transmissions of the classics, especially on Radio 3 which was once known as the Third Programme. But my own time was now completely dominated by three people: Virginia Preston, a reckless, sexually frustrated American widow who was living under the hostile shadow of her dead former husband; her overpowering, all-knowing mother who was just as possessive as her daughter; and, in the middle of them both, Simon Elliott, the young English boy who carried around with him the burden of a troubled, sensitive, spiritualistic mind, a link between the dead and the living. In fact my inspiration for Simon came from seeing a young telepathic boy on television describing how he had been so possessed by spirits from the dead that he had innocently attracted aggressive poltergeist activity in the school dormitory where he slept amongst his schoolmates.

This play is not about turning off the light and finding yourself alone in a cloud of fear and uncertainty; it is about what psychiatrists call 'the dark side of the mind' – for what I did learn whilst writing this play is that there *is* one tiny area of the mind that none of us really knows about, a 'dark' area. Over the years, humankind has lost the ability to 'communicate' telepathically with the past – it has lost the ability even to 'communicate' with someone in the next room. Just think how animals can sense something which none of us can see or hear. Even our own domestic pets freeze when they hear a sound which is way beyond our own register. So *Dark* is about that tiny area of the mind which the experts still haven't been able to get at, an area that may be used for good – or for evil. In other words we just don't know. There is no doubt that, in this play, that tiny area in Simon Elliott's mind was being used by 'someone' – just who (or what?) you will discover when you read or listen to the play. The fact that Virginia's dead husband George was a sexually aggressive man is of real significance in this plot, especially as the young medium – if one can think of him as such – is gay. When the play was first broadcast, there were quite a few raised eyebrows at the extraordinary interplay between the three characters of the highly sex-charged woman, the dead husband and the gay young outsider, but at least it did provoke a lot of fascinating discussion amongst psychics!

For such a play as this, the casting was, of course, vital. When John first talked to me about who he wanted to play these three characters, he mentioned that the distinguished American film actress, Lee Remick, would be ideal for the part of Virginia, especially as she was living in England with her British husband at the time. But sadly Lee Remick went back to America where she died very young of cancer. Fortunately, John offered the part to a British actress of great renown, well known for her roles as Cathy Gale in the cult television series *The Avengers* and the irresistibly sexy Pussy Galore in the James Bond classic, *Goldfinger*. As expected, Honor Blackman was perfect for the role, for not only did she possess the dramatic passion and inventiveness for the part, but she also had a first-rate American accent! As for 'Mother', I was absolutely thrilled when John managed to secure the American screen legend, Bessie Love, to play the role. I had long been a fervent admirer of Bessie, right from the time when I first saw those twinkling toes dancing in her Oscar-nominated role in the musical *The Broadway Melody*, and in later life on the London stage in Arthur Miller's *Death of a Salesman*; but to have her in a play of my own was a real bonus for me. (Sorry to fawn like this, but Bessie was worth it!)

Playing Simon Elliott was a fine, highly experienced radio actor, Nigel Anthony, with whom I had worked several times. Nigel was – is – one of the most versatile radio actors I know, who has the rare distinction of being able to play anything from sixteen to ninety years old! He must have been in his forties when he played this part, but he brought all the passion of someone at least twenty years younger than himself. I remember watching him at the microphone as he was delivering his major speech about when he was a young lad living in a tiny farm labourer's cottage in Norfolk, and the sensitivity he showed both physically and through the spoken word was deeply moving. But although I was indeed fortunate to have such a cast, I hope you will look forward as eagerly as I will to hearing the new CD version with this book.

The year before had been memorable for world events, not least the deaths of Elvis Presley, Charlie Chaplin, Maria Callas and Bing Crosby: all, in one way or another, icons of the entertainment business. But that Christmas I was manically finishing off the last pages of *Dark*, whilst trying to embrace the festive season, putting the final glitter and tinsel to the Christmas tree whilst quickly rushing back to the high supernatural drama of *Dark*'s climax. The television channels were, of course, full of happy Christmas films and special shows based on the year's output of situation comedy; but tucked away in the festive schedules was that proverbial Charles Dickens' classic, *A Christmas Carol*, with Sir Michael Hordern as Ebenezer Scrooge – a gentle reminder that Christmas and Boxing Day would not be complete without that traditional dip into the supernatural, which *Dark* would continue early in the New Year.

Rehearsals for *Dark* began in Studio 6A of Broadcasting House on Thursday 9 February 1978. The schedule was for four days of rehearse/record, and they turned out to be four very hectic days for everyone. Naturally enough it was a very emotional time for the three artistes at the very heart of the play; and it was, for me, a lesson in how actors and actresses threw themselves into the characters they were playing, especially as I had never written characters like this before. It was very strange really, for although the studio was bright, and full of activity, watching from the Control Room with John and the Studio Managers I did feel an odd atmosphere had pervaded the proceedings. And I was soon to find out how much it had affected one particular member of the cast.

At the time of the rehearsals for *Dark*, David and I had rented an apartment in central London, thereby avoiding the necessity for getting up at crack of dawn every morning to travel in by train to London. After the first day of rehearsals, we had been invited to a friend's house for dinner, so I parked the car at the kerb whilst David went off to buy a bottle of wine for our host. Whilst waiting outside the driver's side of the vehicle, casually glancing through the evening newspaper, a rather ritzy-looking BMW sped to a halt, brakes screaming. I looked up to find the driver coming towards me. He was a massive guy, probably around six feet four or so, thick set, looking a bit like a rich thug. Anyway I smiled at the guy, thinking he was about to ask directions or something, but to my abject horror and surprise, he landed one hell of a punch on my face with a fist that was cocooned in a metal knuckle-duster. You can imagine how I immediately saw stars and sank to my knees, blood running down my face and chin, my eyes crossing like a short-sighted chicken. Then, without saying anything, the guy just turned around, got back into his car where a flashy-looking blonde was waiting for him, and, to the sound of David yelling at him from the door of the off-license, drove off as fast as he had arrived. Oh by the way, I had never seen the man before in my life! Now tell me what *that* was all about?

I spent an hour or so at the local hospital, and turned up at rehearsals the next morning sporting a heavily bruised face and several stitches in a wound. Needless to say, everyone was utterly shocked to hear my astonishing tale, and I was cosseted all day like I had just returned from the battlefield. The one person who remained totally quiet and withdrawn about it all was Bessie Love; but it was not until she had got me alone during the morning coffee break that she explained to me why.

It emerged that for the best part of her life, Bessie had been some kind of dedicated psychic, and deeply religious. In fact she told me how when she was a small child in a very rustic, bleak area of Texas, she had lived with her parents in a disused railway station, where at night she would feel the presence of an old man who came from a Red Indian reservation some miles away, but who had died long ago. Although she had never actually seen the old Indian watcher, she had been convinced that he was there to protect and warn her of any hidden dangers, and that he would pass on these 'gifts' to her.

With this in mind, Bessie had a message for me. I can still see her as she gently took my hand and, staring straight into my eyes, told me that she knew *something* was going to happen to me the previous evening, for all day during the rehearsals she had 'seen' a ring of light around me, which had thoroughly disturbed her. But when I asked her why she didn't give me some kind of warning so that I could have avoided the terrifying experience I had gone through, she replied that she had considered her options with deep inner convictions, and decided that to warn me would have sent waves of panic and alarm though my entire mind. At this point I really did think that Bessie might just be a bit of an old crank, but it wasn't until she asked me where this 'incident' took place that I felt shivers down my spine. The name of the street was George Street. The name of the aggressive dead man in the play was – George. Make of it what you will. Crank or just plain spooky? But it *did* happen. Was that dark side of the mind trying to tell me something that I didn't know?

Dark was broadcast on the evening of Monday 27 February 1978 and repeated the following Sunday 5 March. The response was what I had hoped – listeners were not only unnerved by the play but also drawn into a discussion about the psychological aspects of the subject. One chap in Gloucester wrote to tell me that it got him and his wife thinking about that proverbial old subject of whether there is life after death; and, surprisingly, it opened up a discussion amongst some people about the merits for and against a return of the death penalty. Others, of course, were scared out of their lives by the sheer terror of the situation, and a young schoolboy wrote to say that he would never sleep with his light off again! But there was no doubt about the praise heaped on the three actors who had brought the play off so powerfully. Honor's rather neurotic Virginia earned special praise from critics and listeners for her highly charged and emotional performance. Nigel also was admired for giving what was described as a 'powerful reading of a very chilling and complex' character. As for Bessie, well, those who remembered her as a musical star in her silent and early talkie films were astonished by the force and depth she brought to the part of Virginia's mother. John Tydeman's carefully worked out production was singled out for sustaining the suspense throughout, for making quite sure that the actors did not 'go over the top', and for working the plot up to that terrifying climax. There were of course critics, especially those who thought I hadn't gone far enough in exploring the psychology of that dark side of the mind. There were also those who thought the piece a bit of old hokum; but my feeling was that if you don't believe in the subject of the dead returning to life in whatever shape or form, then *Dark* is not for you. But I must say, I was very happy and content at the way the play was received. It had certainly whetted my appetite for what I wanted to do in the future – especially with Victorian werewolves!

I must say that I do think that, together with *The Slide, Dark was* a turning point in my life. I just felt that I was spreading my wings into new territory; and, although I had written more traditional radio plays between 1975 and 1987, *Dark* is one of the subjects that gave me a lot of insight into the unknown, into the drama and passion of people who lived their lives outside my own area of experience.

Dark

by Victor Pemberton

Directed by John Tydeman

STUDIO:	6A STEREO	
REH/REC:	Thursday 9 February 1978	1030–1800
	Friday 10 February 1978	1030–1800
	Saturday 11 February 1978	1030–1800
	Sunday 12 February 1978	1020–1900
TX:	Monday 27 February 1978	
RPT:	Sunday 5 March 1978	
R.P. No.	SLN06/DM724	
EDITING:	Monday 13 February 1978	H54
CAST:	Virginia Preston	Honor Blackman
	Virginia's mother	Bessie Love
	Simon Elliott	Nigel Anthony
SMs:	Jock Farrell, Janet Mitchell, Enyd Clowes	
Prod. Sec.:	Judy Footiff, 6104 B.H.	Ext. 2186

Announcer "The Monday Play".

A woman, sobbing quietly

Virginia It isn't fair, George. It just isn't fair! I mean, why can't it be like the old days? You and I used to have such good times together. We used to have fun. (*sadly*) So many laughs. (*nervously*) I… I don't like the way it is now, George. It – scares me. (*She gets up, moves around*) I don't get laughs now, George. Not any more. Not since you've been gone. But I think a lot. Oh yes. I do that all right. (*voice low*) George? George, can you hear me? I want to tell you something. (*quiet and intimate*) At night… I often lie awake thinking about you. Yes! Even after all these years. I think about the nights when it was just you – and me. It's as though I can almost feel your warm flesh pressing up against mine… (*voice to a whisper*) Oh God, George – how I miss you! No one ever made love like you. They wouldn't know how! (*pause*) But let me tell you. Despite what happened, despite everything that happened between us, I've never stopped loving you. Never!

She reacts nervously, as the lights go out

The lights! No, George! Please don't turn off the lights. You know how I hate the dark. Please don't leave me alone in the dark…

On the other side of the room, a window slams

(*trembling nervously, voice to a whisper*) George? Are you... here? Are you – *really* here?

A cold silence, broken only by Virginia's piercing scream

George...!

Echo, and out

Announcer "Dark", etc.

We are in 'The Chapel', an attic-room on the top floor of Number 13 Willow Drive, a large, detached house, in a quiet North London cul-de-sac.

"Dark".

Pause

Simon Jesus! Don't tell me anybody has ever actually slept here? Looks more like a church!

Mother We call it The Chapel. It was my daughter's idea. On account of the high ceiling and sloping walls. (*looking up*) What d'you think of the stained glass windows up there? Real creepy, huh?

Simon (*amused*) If you say so.

Mother I tell you. I can't bear this room. (*shivers*) It's ~~so hell~~ cold [as hell] up here at this time of year. George absolutely refused to install central heating. So typical of you English.

Simon (*mocking*) How right you are, madam!

Mother Mind you, I never come up here myself. Oh no. All those stairs would be the death of me. I have bad arthritis in my knees, you know.

Simon (*looking around*) Really? I'm sorry.

Mother Oh, not that I complain. No one can ever say I'm a burden on *my* daughter. I just go on in my own harmless way, waiting for the time when the good Lord calls me.

Simon Calls you? Calls you what?

Mother (*indignantly*) It's a figure of speech, young man.

Simon Oh, I see.

Mother And don't bother to ask me why the window's been bricked up, because I don't know. My daughter had it done soon after... well, soon after my son-in-law's death.

Simon (*at window, in background*) It's a pity. It makes the room so dark with only the one window in the ceiling. (*moving on*) Where does this lead to? Behind the curtain.

Mother That's an old Ironing Room.

Simon An Ironing Room? In the attic?

Mother In the old days, all this must have been the servant's quarters. (*calls*) It's full of junk back there, isn't it?

Simon (*calling from the Ironing Room*) Seems to be. ~~What's all this photographic equipment?~~

~~**Mother** My son-in-law used the place as a dark room.~~

~~**Simon** (*coming out of the Ironing Room*) Really? Bit of a camera enthusiast, was he?~~

~~**Mother** Something like that.~~

Simon Mrs Whitman. How long have you and your daughter lived in this house?

Mother Virginia came here soon after she married about ~~seventeen~~ [nineteen] years ago. I didn't join them until much later.

Simon Would that have been before, or after George Preston's execution?

A cold silence

Mother (*moving around*) I hate this house! I hate all it stands for. It's cold, and dark, and demanding. After the trial, I begged her to sell up and come back home with me to Vermont. She could have had it so good there, a chance to mix with her own kind. But no. She had to stick it out, to stay behind and face up to all the nasty little innuendoes. ~~God! People can be so cruel!~~ Even now, after all these years, they still stare at her in the street as though she's some kind of a freak.

Simon What's wrong with that? She should take it as a compliment.

Mother A compliment!

Simon It's a whole new scene now, Mrs Whitman. Nobody cares any more what you do, or how you do it.

Mother *I* care.

Simon Hey! Is that a wind-up gramophone over there? I haven't seen one of those since I was a kid. (*going to it*) Does it work?

Mother Unfortunately, yes. It was here when my son-in-law bought the house. He was very attached to it.

Simon (*eagerly*) I'm not surprised. (*opens lid*) There's a record on the turn-table. Doesn't anybody ever dust this thing? (*blows off dust. Reads label*) "See Me Dance the Polka". Great! Mind if I play it?

Mother I'd sooner you didn't.

~~Simon ignores her, winds up the old gramophone~~

Simon You know, I've never been able to understand why people get rid of old possessions.

Mother I *know* why you're here, young man.

Simon I mean, if somebody left me a work of art like this, I'd treasure it for the rest of my life.

Mother Did you hear what I said, Mr Elliot? I know why Virginia brought you here.

~~Simon puts on the scratchy old 78 rpm record~~

~~**Simon** (joining in with the dance tune)~~ Fantastic!

~~**Mother** (almost shouting)~~ [But,] It won't do any good, you know. She's not well. She hasn't been well for a long time. Poor child. She's suffered so much all these years… ~~Oh for God's sake!~~

~~She hurries across to the gramophone, takes off the record~~

~~**Simon** Hey! I was enjoying that.~~

~~**Mother** Mr Elliot.~~ Did you know that my daughter could die at any moment?

Simon I beg your pardon?

Mother (*approaching*) The doctors say that if she doesn't take things easy, she has a heart condition that could – well, do her a lot of harm. I just thank God she has enough money to take good care of her health. Not my money, you understand. Oh no. You see, when her father died, he left everything to her.

He did so love his darling little daughter. To be precise, he loved her to the tune of 500,000 dollars in a New York bank account. (*pause*) Have you ever been to the United States, Mr Elliot?

Simon Er – no. As a matter of fact, I haven't.

Mother You should go some time. America is a land of opportunity, you know.

Simon So I've been told.

Virginia enters

Virginia Sorry I'm late. (*closes door*) There's an awful lot of traffic, and it's beginning to snow. (*approaches, awkwardly*) It's Mr Elliot isn't it? Mr Simon Elliot?

Simon (*shaking hand*) Hallo, Mrs Preston.

Virginia I recognised you at once. You're much younger than your picture in the magazine.

Mother Much younger.

Virginia Mother. I'm sure Mr Elliot would like a cup of tea. Would you be a dear?

Mother (*a bored sigh*) Why not? That's about all mothers are good for, I suppose.

Virginia Thank you, darling. There are some ginger cookies in the kitchen.

Mother (*at door*) I know there are. I made them! (*goes*)

Virginia and Simon laugh

Virginia You mustn't pay too much attention to Mother. She –

Simon Suffers with arthritis. In the knees.

Virginia (*amused*) Oh, don't worry. She'll outlive the lot of us. Well, me anyway. They make them tough in Vermont, you know. (*pause*) I must say, I feel a little awkward. It was good of you to come. I don't know why, but I didn't think you would.

Simon Is that why you weren't here to meet me?

Virginia I guess you could say I was a little – nervous?

Simon Of me?

Virginia Naturally.

Simon Why naturally?

Virginia Oh, come now. It's not every day I go around inviting people like you to call on me.

Simon People like me?

Pause

Virginia (*moving around*) How old are you, Simon?

Simon You read the article in the Colour Supplement.

Virginia Yes. But it was a little flip, a little in awe of you, I thought. How much of it was true?

Simon Oh, about sixty per cent?

Virginia What about the other forty per cent?

Simon I have a vivid imagination.

Virginia You may need it, if you're going to help me.

Simon Who said I was going to help you. Mrs Preston?

Pause

Virginia I'm sorry I can't offer you a cigarette or anything. You see, I don't smoke.

Simon Neither do I.

Virginia Good boy, Simon! ~~You'll live to be a hundred.~~ (*pause*) Tell me. Why did you take so long to answer my letter?

Simon I needed time to think about it.

Virginia You thought I was some kind of a ~~nutter?~~ [freak? crank?]

Simon Could be.

Virginia You still think so? Sorry. That's not a fair question. Would you like some time to look over the room?

Simon No, thanks.

Virginia (*puzzled*) No? But –

Simon I don't need to look over the room, Mrs Preston. I'd just like to ask a few questions, that's all. Could we sit down, please? Here, at the table.

Virginia Why not? (*She comes back to him*) Sorry there's so much dust everywhere. (*blows dust from chair*) We haven't used The Chapel since... well, not in a long time.

They sit at the table

Pause

OK. So what d'you wanna know?

Simon Mrs Preston. Why did you write to me? You do know I'm not a professional medium?

Virginia I don't want a professional medium. I'm not interested in all that crap about poltergeists and ectoplasm and paranormal phenomena. All I need is someone I can talk to. Someone who's just as much an innocent victim of the things he can't understand, as myself. (*pause*) My mother thinks I'm ~~mad. Quite, quite mad.~~ [crazy, absolutely crazy.]

Simon Are you?

Virginia That's up to you to find out.

Pause

~~He takes out a notebook~~

~~**Simon** D'you mind if I make some notes?~~

~~**Virginia** Not at all. Go right ahead.~~

Simon (~~writing~~) [Well,] It would help... if you could tell me when it all first started.

Virginia The urge to come up to this room, you mean? ~~To tell you the truth, I don't remember.~~

~~**Simon** I'm afraid you'll have to. Was it something you heard?~~

~~**Virginia** No, not exactly.~~

~~*Pause*~~

~~**Simon** Mrs Preston. I have to know.~~

~~*Pause*~~

Virginia It was about two years ago. I was sleeping downstairs – the room below this.

Simon You heard something?

Virginia No. Not a thing. It was just a feeling, a sudden urge to get out of bed and come up here to The Chapel. God knows why. I hadn't dared come through that door since... since the night it happened.

Simon (*scribbling*) Can you remember what time of year it was?

Virginia Oh yes. It was October. Libra, the scales of justice. I remember it vividly, because there was a smell of burning leaves in the park outside. It must have been that that woke me up. I've always hated the autumn. It has such a smell of finality in the air.

Simon You got out of bed, and came up here – to this room?

Virginia I turned on the light, and for a moment just stood here, staring at the room. Everything was exactly as it had been left all those years ago. The big double bed, the [that] carpet rolled up against the wall, table, chairs, wind-up gramophone, china jug and wash-basin, even George's photographs pinned up on the board over there. (*rises*) But none of it made any sense. As though I'd never even seen the room before.

She crosses to the bed

I sat down on the edge of the bed. (*does so*) It was so quiet outside. I couldn't even hear the traffic on the other side of the park. (*pause*) Suddenly, a feeling of deep depression came over me. I began to cry, to talk out loud. It was as though there was someone else in the room, sitting right there beside me. I found myself shouting out questions. And expected answers. But... there was no one there to answer me. And yet, all the time, I knew I could hear George's voice – loud and clear. (*pause*) Then, I had an uncontrollable urge to sleep in this room. I can't explain why, only that I had to do it. So I got some sheets and blankets, and made up the bed. I went to the door, locked it, turned off the lights, and settled down for the night. When I woke up the next morning, the top sheet and blankets had been stripped off the bed, and folded neatly over my feet. (*pause*) Since then, I haven't been able to resist coming up to this room, night after night.

Pause

Simon Mrs Preston. Yes. Where did you first meet your husband?

Virginia Curiously enough, it was a day rather like today. It was in a snow-storm in New York city. We were both coming out of Grand Central Terminal at the same time, and he quite literally fell at my feet! We laughed so much, we just had to meet again.

Simon He worked in a government office or something didn't he?

Virginia In those days, he was visiting the United States with a British trade delegation. We married about a year after that, and I came with George to England, to live with him in this house.

Simon Was it a happy marriage?

Virginia For most of the time – yes.

Simon Most of the time?

Virginia We had our disagreements, just like anybody else.

Simon (*rising*) Did you share your husband's interest in religion?

Pause

Virginia That's an odd question.

Simon The crucifix on the wall over there. The stained glass window in the ceiling…

Virginia He wasn't a religious maniac, if that's what you're implying.

Simon But he *did* believe in God?

Virginia Of course. It was only the interpretation he quarrelled with.

Simon The interpretation?

Virginia He just never went to church, that's all. George hated hypocrisy! But he loved reading from the Bible. He could recite by memory practically anything from it.

Simon (*in background, at bricked up window*) ~~Tell me.~~ Why did you have the window bricked up like this?

Pause

Mrs Preston.

Virginia (*sharply*) ~~I had it done, because~~ I couldn't bear the way people used to gather in the street below ~~just gawping up at the window all day~~. [that's why. Just gaping up at the window all day.] ~~It was so… obscene!~~

Simon But we're three floors up. Surely nobody could see very much?

Virginia doesn't answer

~~Mrs Preston.~~ Did you and your husband ever make love in this room?

Silence

~~Answer the question, please.~~

Virginia (*coldly*) That's not the kind of question I care to answer, young man.

Simon OK. Then there's not much point in my being here.

Pause

Virginia Sure, we made love here! Why shouldn't we? George *was* my husband, you know.

Simon But he wasn't the only man you slept with in this room, was he?

[*Pause*]

Virginia [(*coldly*)] ~~Goddamn you! You've~~ [Boy, you have] done your homework well, haven't you? ~~Now I know why you took so long to answer my letter.~~

Simon When was the first time your husband found out about you and Jonathan Curtis? Was it on the night he murdered him, ~~up here in The Chapel?~~ [here in this room?]

Virginia (*flaring up*) He didn't have to find out about anything. Because I told him! And I'm glad I told him. Because I *wanted* him to know.

Simon Because you weren't in love with him any more?

Virginia It may interest you to know, that the only time I knew I really loved George Preston, was on the day they hanged him for murder!

Mother enters

Mother I've made the tea. It's downstairs in the sitting-room.

Virginia Thank you, Mother. We'll be down in a moment.

Simon Just a minute, please. (*approaching*) Before you go, Mrs Whitman, d'you mind if I ask you a few questions?

Mother What about?

Virginia My mother knows nothing about it. Nothing at all.

Simon [Mrs Whitman. In which part of] ~~Whereabouts in~~ the house do you sleep?

Mother On the floor below this. Next to Virginia's room. Why?

Simon D'you sleep well?

Mother Sleep?! Why I practically live on valium. ~~What d'you expect in this damned English climate!~~

Simon Have you ever heard sounds coming from this room in the middle of the night?

~~**Mother** Huh?~~

~~**Virginia** This is ridiculous!~~

Mother Why should I hear sounds, when there's nobody living up here?

Simon You've never heard anyone moving about?

Mother If I did, I'd be out of this house before you could say J. Edgar Hoover!

Virginia I've told you! Nobody but myself knows anything about what's been going on in this room.

Mother (*coldly, revealing a sharper edge to her character*) Now that's not quite true, my dear – is it? (*pause*) As a matter of fact, I did once hear a rather curious sound coming from this room in the middle of the night. It was the old phonograph. (*She sings, hums the first verse of the Polka dance tune*) That same monotonous tune! Just like it always used to be. (*pause*) Of course, I knew I wasn't alone in the house at the time. So I presumed my daughter was up here in The Chapel again. She does so love that old record…

Virginia (*irritated*) Oh, Mother, do stop this!

Mother (*going to her*) Oh, my poor baby! What hell it's been for you all these years. (*holding her*) But you can't bring back the past, Virginia. None of us can. No, don't turn away from me, honey. ~~Mother~~ [Mama] loves you. You know I do…

Simon Thanks for your help, Mrs Whitman. Now would you mind waiting downstairs, please.

Mother Oh yes, of course. You know, I like you, young man. I just know you're going to help my poor baby.

She goes to the door, opens it

Oh, by the way Mr Elliot. D'you like white rum by any chance?

Simon White rum?

Mother I always keep a spare bottle in my room downstairs. Maybe you'd care to take a glass with me some time?

Simon No thanks. I don't drink.

Mother What a pity. It's a taste you could easily acquire.

Goes, door

Virginia If you believe *her*, you'll believe anything.

Simon (*at the gramophone*) What's so special about an old dance-tune?

He puts the old record on ~~again~~: "See Me Dance the Polka"

Virginia (*in no time at all, she is swaying, singing to the music*) When I was a little girl, this was my favourite party piece!

She is singing, dancing around the room

My mother hated it. But not Papa. I used to dance for *him* all the time…

Simon watches her, as the dance becomes quicker, building to climax

(*shouting*) Look at me, papa! I'm dancing for you…!

Shouting, singing, dancing

The tune comes to an end

(*falls back onto the bed, breathless, but helpless with laughter*) I promise you, I'm not as crazy as you may think. That silly tune just brings back so many happy memories that's all.

Simon (*taking off the record*) It seems fairly crazy to go around playing a gramophone in the middle of the night.

Virginia (*snapping*) Look! If my mother lived to be a hundred, she couldn't accept anything that is even remotely beyond her own comprehension. I swear to you I've never once played that phonograph. Not since the day my husband was taken from this house.

Pause

Simon Mrs Preston. (*He walks slowly back towards her*) Do you believe in the supernatural?

Virginia ~~Do I~~? Well, of course I do!

Simon Why?

Virginia If there's a natural, why shouldn't there be a supernatural?

Simon But what is it you've actually seen, or heard, or experienced, that proves to you the existence of life after death?

Virginia ~~For Christ's sake!~~ D'you have to see something to know it's there?

Simon (*on the attack*) How do you know something is here, Mrs Preston? Why do you come up to this room, night after night?

Virginia I told you! I can't explain it. It's just a feeling, that's all.

Simon You're sure it's not a guilt complex?

Virginia (*shouting*) And just what ~~the hell~~ d'you mean by that?

Simon Oh, you know the sort of thing. Husband hanged for the murder of his wife's lover. Returns to take his revenge at the scene of the crime. Come to think of it, it's quite a jokey idea.

Virginia I can see we're wasting each other's time!

Simon (*shouting*) He's dead, Mrs Preston! Your husband is dead. And you haven't given me one shred of evidence to prove that his spirit is inhabiting this room.

Virginia Well what d'you want me to do? Take a movie of it or something!

She gets up from the bed, strides angily scross the room

What about the night I slept up here alone?

Simon The bed-clothes folded neatly across your ankles? You call that proof?

Virginia (*pacing the room*) There were other things. Objects.

Simon Objects?

Virginia Scattered all over the floor. Things I've never seen before in my life! Bits of stale bread, half-burnt candles, ~~tin cans,~~ an old shoe, ~~antique spoons,~~ and lumps of hard clay. ~~Newspapers dating back to the beginning of the century!~~ Then there was George's open razor. That suddenly turned up from nowhere. Even the police hadn't been able to find that for use at the trial. Then what about the diary? That's right. George's diary! One night I came up here, I found it lying on the small table at the side of the bed, where he always used to keep it. And yet, I distinctly remember burning that diary myself, ~~soon after George was taken into custody.~~ You call *that* imagination?

Pause

Simon Mrs Preston. Have you any idea how many people wrote to me after that article appeared in the Sunday Colour Supplement? All kinds of people, trying desperately to cling on to the past, to someone or something they can't have any more. There was a middle-aged man, begging me to make 'contact' with his sister who'd just been killed in a coach crash. A teenage girl, who's convinced she can hear the voice of her dead mother, whom she's never seen. Others just want to compare their experiences with my own. A premonition, a shadow they can't explain, a voice in the night, a phobia, a manifestation, or even just a feeling of loss. But what none of them can understand is – I can't help them. Nobody can. When someone you love dies, there's nothing you can do but accept it. Death is final, Mrs Preston. It's the closing of a door. The end. Over. Kapputt! We don't have the right to cling on to those who belong to the past.

Virginia Simon, I am not trying to cling on to the past. What I've experienced in this room is fact. Fact, not hallucination.

Simon Hallucination? Are you sure that's all?

Virginia And what's that supposed to mean?

Simon Well, you know what they say. Sex can be the root cause of many a frustration.

Virginia (*coldly*) It may interest you to know that sex has played absolutely no part in my life since my husband died.

Simon What about when he was alive?

Virginia Well, for God's sake. ~~I was married to him you know!~~

Simon Then why did you sleep around with guys nearly half your age?

Virginia (*this takes the wind out of Virginia*) You know, young man, if you're not careful, you may find me asking you one or two questions about your sex life.

Simon You could ask. But I don't guarantee you'll like the answers.

Virginia Why not? What have you got to hide?

Simon turns away

(*teasing him*) Oh, come on now, Simon! You don't have to be shy with me. I know how you kids like to get your hands on anything that's going. What is it? An affair with some cute little schoolgirl?

Simon (*awkward*) I make it a rule never to discuss my private life.

Virginia Or maybe you prefer – older women? Golly! Don't tell me you don't like girls at all?

Simon (*awkward*) You never can tell!

Virginia (*completely taken aback*) ~~Huh?~~ [Oh I see.]

Simon Mrs Preston. Why did you kill your husband?

Virginia (*turning with a start*) What? What did you say?

Simon (*going to her*) D'you know the first thing I did when I received your letter? I went through every newspaper report about your husband's trial that I could find. It was quite a read, I can tell you. Why couldn't you bring yourself to say anything in defence of the man you yourself were sending to the gallows?

Virginia That's not true!

Simon You wanted him dead, didn't you?

Virginia ~~No damn you.~~ No!

Simon You wanted him dead, because he was no good to you alive...

Virginia (*gradually breaking*) How many times do I have to tell you? I loved George!

Simon ... because the one thing your money could never buy from George Preston – was his love!

Virginia (*a great roar*) No...! I never wanted George to die. I hated that boy, I tell you! I hated him...! (*sobbing*)

Simon Why lie to yourself, Mrs Preston? You can lie to me, or to anyone else in the world. But not to yourself! (*He draws closer to her. Calm and gentle*) Now, tell me the truth, Mrs Preston. What are you really afraid of in this room?

Virginia (*sobbing quietly to herself*) He's... going to kill me. George killed that boy, and now... he's going to kill me. Oh God! Why can't anyone believe what I say? (*She breaks down*)

Simon (*quietly*) I believe you, Mrs Preston.

Virginia (*stops crying, slowly looks up. Puzzled*) What? What did you say?

Simon I said, I believe you. You see, from the first moment I came into this room, I knew George Preston was waiting for me.

Out

After a pause, gradually bring in a group laughing record, the kind of novelty piece that was popular in the 1920s and 30s

Simon is stretched out on the bed in background, listening to it

As laughter builds to pitch, Virginia suddenly takes off the record

Did you have to do that?

Virginia I don't like that record. I never did. There's nothing I hate worse than forced humour.

Simon My old Gran had a record like that. She always played it to me when I went to see her on Sunday morning. Same old thing, week after week. It seemed ridiculous, sitting there, laughing at absolutely nothing. But that's what I did. So did she. Tears used to run down her cheeks. She lived on her own, you see. There wasn't much else for her to laugh at.

Virginia Simon. Are you sure this is a good idea?

Simon What?

Virginia (*going to him*) Your moving into The Chapel like this. After what you said about George... I don't have the right to put your life at risk.

Simon Who said there's any risk?

Virginia Isn't there?

Pause

Simon Who knows? That window up there. Where does it lead to?

Virginia (*looking upwards*) It's sealed up. You can't get out that way.

Simon Why not?

Virginia It's a sloping roof, a sheer drop to the street below. Why? Does it worry you?

Simon I hate the idea of being sealed in, that's all. Isn't there a way of opening it?

Virginia Not unless you break the stained glass. Might be a little sacrilegious, don't you think?

Simon ~~Lying on this bed, I~~ [Makes me] feel I'm looking up towards Heaven.

Virginia My God! Don't tell me you think such a place exists?

Simon If it doesn't, then we've nothing to worry about.

Virginia sits on the edge of the bed

Virginia You're a strange boy. When I first met you yesterday, you made me feel ~~like the biggest whore in London! I felt quite repulsive~~ [somehow cheap].

Simon (*getting up, awkwardly*) You're an attractive woman, Mrs Preston. You don't need me to tell you that.

Virginia Oh, but I do! I need to be told all the time. That was the trouble with George. He always took me for granted.

Simon is combing his hair at the mirror

You know something? Basically, you're really quite vain.

Simon What makes you say that?

Virginia Oh, I don't know. It's the way you keep combing your hair like that. Simon. Is it true what you said about yourself yesterday afternoon?

Simon Is what true?

Virginia About being, well – you know. About not liking girls and all that.

Simon That's not what I said.

Virginia That's what you implied.

Simon All right, Mrs Preston. Since you have to know. Yes. I am homosexual. I just don't go around shouting it from the rooftops, that's all.

Virginia (*after a pause*) How sad. I mean, it's such a waste!

Simon Look. If it worries you.

Virginia Oh no, not at all.

Simon Then if you don't mind, I'd like to get on with some work. (*moving in background*) Will you help me move some furniture, please?

Virginia Move the furniture? Whatever for?

Simon I want to try an experiment. Just the two of us, that's all.

Virginia An experiment? D'you mean – a séance?

Simon I've told you, Mrs Preston. I'm not a medium. ~~Now look.~~ [Let me explain.] Whenever you come into this room, into any room, you have a set image in your mind as to how it all looks. Right?

Virginia Well, yes. I guess so.

Simon Well, I want to try and change that image. I want to try and provoke a 'contact' with whatever it is we're trying to make 'contact' with. But I can't do it on my own.

Virginia Why not?

Simon (*after a pause*) Because you're the direct link, Mrs Preston, not me. Let's have the table a bit more to the left, please.

They move the table

No, not too far. Just a few inches this way… yes… that's it.

Virginia Tell me. When are we going to try this 'experiment'? Now?

Simon (*in background, moving bed*) No. Not until some time this evening. We've got too much work to do first. (*He comes back to her*) Here. Take this piece of chalk. Make a circle around the leg of every piece of furniture in the room.

Virginia (*taking chalk*) Huh? What for?

Simon Because from now on, if there's any psychic activity in this room at all, we're going to know about it.

Virginia (*on hands and knees, scrawls the first circle*) You mean… like this?

Simon (*looking*) That'll do fine.

Virginia marks the circles, whilst Simon moves furniture in background

Virginia ~~(*to herself*) Oh boy! I hope you can see me, George.~~

~~**Simon** What was that?~~

Virginia ~~I said,~~ I feel weird doing all this. You know, I was just thinking. There must be a hell of a lot of people in this world who think they're psychic. People like me~~, who have a need for the past.~~ ~~Say!~~ Have you ever been to Atlantic City?

Simon Where?

Virginia Atlantic City. It's on the east coast of the United States. I remember once, when I was a kid at boarding school, they took us on a day's picnic there.

Bring up faint background of sea crashing on shore

It's a great big, brash, adorable seaside resort. ~~Miles and miles of white, sandy beaches, crazy hats, candy stores, ice-cream parlors, and roller-coasters. It was so vulgar. That's why~~ [And] I loved it! Anyway, I had this girlfriend, see. A Jewish kid named Sadie. Well, Sadie and I decided we wanted our fortune told, so we went to see this old bird named Madam Zorina, who spent most of the day just staring out to sea from this broken-down shack on the promenade. Sadie went in first, but within two or three minutes she was out again, insisting that the old bird was nothing but ~~a schmuck,~~ a fake, and how deeply offended she was that she'd been robbed of her nickel piece. (*laughs*) Poor Sadie. (*pause*) Even so, I was still curious enough to want to sample the experience for myself. So, into the shack I went.

Take sea F/X to a barely audible background

There was a smell of stale beer and salt beef on rye bread. It was dark, except for a thin shaft of light filtering through the roof ~~of the shack~~. Madam Zorina was sitting at the small table waiting for me. I can see her now. Her face was heavily lined, like an old Greek peasant woman, and she was wearing an enormous moth-eaten black shawl ~~round her shoulders~~. I parted with my hard-earnt nickel, and was told to sit down in the chair facing ~~the old bird~~ [her]. She asked to see the palm of my right hand, and, for a moment, didn't say one single word. She just – sat there, holding onto my hand, staring down at it. (*pause*) Eventually, she did speak. She said I wouldn't live long, because I had an interrupted lifeline, or something like that. But then suddenly, her eyes flicked up at me, and… I could see my own face reflected in them, they were large, dark, sad eyes, ~~but sharp and penetrating – like diamonds~~. So alive! I began to feel cold. Chilled. (*shivers*) I don't know how long we sat there like that. It seemed hours. You see, the old ~~bird~~ [lady] had fallen asleep. And yet… her eyes were wide open – staring straight at me. (*pause*) And then, she started to speak. Not in her own voice, ~~mind you,~~ but younger, more like a child. She asked if I knew 'Edward'? Because 'Edward' had a message for me. I said I didn't know anyone by that name, that there must be some mistake. And would she please stop squeezing my hand, because she was hurting it. But the old bird with the child's voice insisted: "Edward loves you, Ginnia", ~~she said~~. "He's always loved you, and he'll always be around to protect you." (*pause*) My heart started to beat faster and faster. You see, "Ginnia" was the name my own father used to call me when I was little.

Pause

~~Gradually~~ [Slowly], my ~~own~~ reflection disappeared from ~~the old bird's~~ [her] eyes. ~~But~~ [And] in its place, I could see him quite clearly. A long, thin face, greying moustache and ~~smoothed~~ [slicked]-down hair. He was – smiling at me, his hands ~~outstretched~~ [reaching out] as though begging me to go to him. I don't know why, but I started to cry. It was my own father I could see. Edward. That was *his* name.

Pause

All I remember is screaming out loud, and with tears streaming down my cheeks, I ran out of the shack as fast as I could. It wasn't until later that I felt sorry for what I'd done. Oh, I know Sadie was right. The old bird was a schmuck, a fake. But my father – he was for real. At least, to me he was. He must have come to me, because I wanted him there. I must have wanted him real badly. Or else – why would he have come?

Silence

Virginia turns to look back at Simon, who is again lying on the bed, now drawing a sketch

Simon? What are you doing back there?

Simon I'm trying to work out what your husband looked like.

Virginia But there's no need to draw a picture. I've got plenty of photographs of him downstairs.

Simon I'd sooner do it my way, if you don't mind.

Virginia (*going to him*) But how can you draw a picture of someone you've never even seen?

Simon doesn't answer

Just like Jonathan. Drawing dirty pictures of me was about the only pastime that ever amused him. [Jonathan was always drawing pictures in this room. Pictures of me.]

Simon (*whilst sketching*) Mrs Preston. What really happened in this room, the night your husband killed Jonathan Curtis?

Virginia (*stiffening*) You read the newspapers. There's nothing more to tell.

Simon Were you in love with him?

Virginia ~~Are you crazy?~~ Me in love with that ~~fatuous little shit~~!

Simon He was a good bit younger than you?

Virginia I never bothered to ask. (*a bored sigh*) He was about your age.

Simon Where did you first meet?

Virginia He worked in the same office as my husband. George thought the boy had a brilliant mind. Personally, I thought Jonathan Curtis was full of crap, up to here with political ideology.

Simon Really? In what way?

Virginia That boy resented every brass nickel I had! OK so I inherited a few bucks. But what was I supposed to do about it? Fly in a helicopter, and drop dollar bills on the poor and needy of the world!

Simon But you slept with him quite regularly after that?

Virginia (*after a pause*) I must have been out of my mind. I should have known he was only using me, as a way to get his own back on all the things he hated most...

A water jug smashes to the floor in background

Simon!

Simon Stay where you are! Don't move!

He goes to inspect the broken pieces of glass

Virginia (*nervously*) What is it? What's happened?

Simon (*stooping*) It's the water jug. It must have fallen off the table at the side of the bed.

Virginia But – how could it have done? There was no one over there. My God! Look at this chair! It's moved. It's moved outside the chalk marks...

Simon, in background, lets out stifled, anguished groan

Simon! (*She rushes across to him*) Simon, what is it? What's wrong?

Simon (*gripping the bed-rails, shivering, as if in a fever*) I'm... I'm all right. Just leave me alone.

Virginia But look at you. You're shivering from head to foot! You're ill. ~~Let me call a doctor...~~

She flinches, as he suddenly looks up at her, grabs hold of her hand

Simon (*a different voice, edged with a strange, bottled-up anger*) You're the one who's sick, Virginia – not me.

Virginia (*after a shocked pause*) What – did you say? Simon... Simon, let go... of my hand...!

A knock on the door, Mother walks straight in

Mother Sorry to barge in, but there's someone downstairs, who's brought you a rather weird-looking machine. I think it's a tape-recorder.

Without saying a word, Simon rushes out

Virginia Simon – wait...!

Mother (*at door, calls*) There's a £1.50 delivery charge!

Simon slams the door as he goes, charges down the stairs, off

I thought Englishmen were supposed to have perfect manners? (*approaches, her voice low and mischievous*) But I was right, wasn't I? That boy is like Jonathan…

Virginia (*turning away*) Mother, I've told you to keep out of this!

Mother (*following her*) The past is over, Virginia. Why can't you leave the dead alone?

Virginia Because I need George! To me, he's as much a part of the present as we are now.

Mother Then why try to get rid of him?

Virginia (*her eyes scanning the room nervously*) If I don't… if I don't get rid of him – he's going to kill me.

Mother No Virginia! The dead are dead. But you're alive! (*holding, patting her*) D'you remember the time when you were a little girl? How you were afraid of the dark and used to scream out in the middle of the night? I never let anyone harm you then, did I, my baby?

Virginia (*childlike*) No, Mama.

Mother No, of course I didn't. And I'm not going to let anyone harm you now, I promise you! Believe me. Mama knows best.

Pause

Virginia (*puzzled*) Mother? What is it? What are you looking at?

Mother (*coldly*) That sketch of George on the wall over there. Where did it come from?

Virginia It's one of Simon's. He drew it himself.

Mother (*going to sketch*) But how could he know? How could he possibly know? Did you show him a photograph or something?

Virginia Why would he need a photograph?

Mother (*looking at sketch*) It's uncanny! Quite unlike anything I've ever seen. The eyes. It's got something to do with the eyes. They're so real – so alive.

Virginia (*strangely*) He'll never forgive me. He'll never let me go…

The blocked up window suddenly slams

Mother ~~Jesus!~~ What was that? (*after a pause*) It sounded like a window slamming. (*She stops to listen*)

We gradually hear a very faint murmur of voices

(*voice to a hush*) What's that? Am I going mad or something? I can hear voices. (*clearing her head*) I can hear people talking!

Voices continue, barely audible

(*a nervous whisper*) Virginia, can't you hear it?

Voices stop, silence

It's stopped. Yes. (*a relieved sigh*) Oh, thank God! It's stopped.

Virginia (*a firm, resolute voice*) No, Mother. It's not stopped. It's just beginning.

Out

Pause

Fade up the ticking of a small clock. It strikes the hour: 10pm

Virginia and Simon are alone, seated, facing each other across the table

A tape-recorder is on the table, recording

Pause

Virginia Are we allowed to talk?

Simon If you want to. Why not?

Virginia With that tape-recorder listening to everything we say, I'm terrified to even open my mouth.

Simon I've told you. There's nothing to be nervous of. This is merely an experiment in paranormal contact.

Virginia D'you think it'll work?

Simon I've no idea.

Virginia What happens if you really do make contact with George?

Simon If I do, then we'll talk to him.

Virginia Talk to him? Just like that?

Simon Mrs Preston. I'm not a medium, this is not a séance. My only objective is to try and create an atmosphere, which will prompt either a manifestation, or, at the very least, a communication with whatever psychic force is trapped within these walls.

Virginia Is that how you received that picture of George over there? By psychic communication?

Simon (*guarded*) Something like that.

Virginia You know, you really are the most extraordinary person I've ever met.

Simon (*smiling*) Really?

Virginia No, I mean it. Basically, you're just an ordinary working-class boy like anyone else. And yet, you possess gifts that are well beyond the normal range of human understanding. Why, Simon? Why you? When did you first know?

Pause

Simon You really want to know?

Virginia Yes.

Simon (*after a pause*) My first experience was when I was out walking the dog.

Virginia Walking the dog!

Simon I was seven years old at the time, living with my granddad in this tiny farm labourer's cottage in Norfolk. It was beautiful. We were surrounded by miles and miles of rich agricultural land – just wind and sky. (*pause*) I had this dog. A white Labrador named 'Bouncer'. He was about the only real friend I had in those days. Every morning before breakfast, Bouncer and I used to take our run down to the woods at the far end of the fields…

Bring up faint sound of dog barking

I can see it now. It was late summer, and the corn was towering above me, just waiting to be cut. (*pause*). When we were half-way across the field, Bouncer suddenly got the sniff of something, and tailed off after it. I thought it might have been a fox or something, because the local Hunt had been charging in and out of those woods just the day before. But it wasn't the Hunt. (*pause*) For a few moments, I just stood there. I was all alone, in the middle of a vast field that stretched for as far as the eye could see. All around me were corn husks, rustling in the wind…

Gentle breeze in distant background

Suddenly, I don't know why, I turned to look back over my shoulder. Someone was calling my name. At least – I thought they were. But the funny thing is, I couldn't actually *hear* a voice. I started to walk back home. But although I had no reason to do so, I gradually felt the urge to stop. My foot… it touched something. Something lying quite still in between the rows of corn. Something quite small and helpless, no bigger than my own hand (*pause*) It was a rabbit. A baby rabbit. At first, I thought it was dead. But when I bent down to touch it, its tiny body quivered in my hand. I took a closer look. Its head was twice its normal size, inflated like a balloon. And its eyes – they were bulging out of their sockets like huge, blood-red marbles. Yes. It was the Myx all right. Myxomatosis. That marvellous invention the scientists came up with, to rid us of our wild rabbit population. Pests, they call them. Vermin. But as I looked down at that small, half-crazed bundle at my feet, I couldn't help wondering which one of us *was* the vermin?

From this moment on, we gradually become aware that Simon is being consumed by an alien personality. His voice becomes that of an older, matured man, which we slowly realise is in maked contrast to Simon's own youth and personality

I got up, and started to walk away. But again, I felt the urge to remain quite still. Somehow, I just couldn't bring myself to leave that ~~pathetic~~ creature lying there, to die slowly, in agony. I had to do something to put it out of its misery. But no! I couldn't do it! I wouldn't! I'd never killed anything in my whole life. But then, I heard my name being called again. I looked around. But there was no one there. The rabbit slowly raised its head. It seemed to be – watching me. I turned away. It was then that I noticed something else lying on the ground nearby. A stone. A large, heavy stone. I'm sure I hadn't seen it before. I shook my head (*shouts*) No! I won't do it. I *can't*! But then… my hands… I had no feeling in my hands. It was as though someone else was moving them for me. (*pause*) I stooped down. With both hands, I… picked up the stone, raised it high above my head, and hesitated. The rabbit's eyes were wide open, staring at me, begging me to do what I *had* to do. (*pause*). With one swift movement – it was all over.

The stone comes crashing down with a thud

Cut background breeze

Pause

I was seven years old. But from that time on, my life has never belonged to me.

Silence

Virginia (*shivers*) It's getting cold in here. D'you mind if I light the fire?

Simon doesn't reply

Simon?

Simon (*his 'other' voice*) Plato said: "He who desires to inflict rational punishment, does not retaliate for a past wrong which cannot be undone…"

Virginia (*puzzled*) What was that? What did you say?

Simon "He has regard to the future, and is desirous that whoever is punished, and he who sees him punished, may be deterred from doing wrong again"…

Virginia (*gasps*) The lights! ~~What's happening to the lights?~~ They're going on and off…

Simon "And when Jehu was come to Jezreel, Jezebel heard of it; and she painted her face, and tired her head, and looked out at a window. And as Jehu entered in at the gate, she said: Who slew his master?"

Virginia (*nervously*) ~~For Christ's sake!~~ [Simon!] Stop staring down at the table like that. Can't you see what's happening? (*pause*) Look at me, will you!

Pause. As Simon slowly raises his face to look at her, Virginia gasps

Simon (*eyes glazed and piercing, a whisper*) "And he lifted up his face to the window, and said: Who *is* on my side? Who?"

Virginia No! Don't touch me. Please don't touch me. Your hands, they're as cold as ice…

Simon "And he said: Throw her down. So they threw her down. And some of her blood was sprinkled on the wall…"

Virginia (*struggling to free herself*) Let… go… of me…!

Simon "And when he was come in, he did eat and drink, and said: Go, see now this cursed woman and bury her…"

Virginia breaks loose, rushes to the door. It is locked

Virginia The door. It's locked!

Simon (*rising*) "And they went to bury her…"

Virginia (*banging the door*) Somebody help me…!

Simon (*slowly approaching*) "But they found no more of her than the skull, and the feet, and the palms of her hands…"

Virginia (*banging on the door*) Open this door…!

Simon (*close, voice low*) "Wherefore they came again, and told him. And he said: This is the word of the Lord!"

Virginia (*shouting*) For Christ's Sake, Simon! What's wrong with you? What do you want of me?

Simon (*still in his 'other' voice*) What do I want?

He draws closer, pinning her back to the door

(*his voice soft and intimate*) I want you, Virginia. I want love. Your love…

Virginia I'm warning you. Keep away from me…!

Simon They say that when a man drowns, he can see his whole life laid out before him. That's how it is with me now. Everything is so clear. I can see you – and me, Virginia. I can see our whole life together. (*closer*) Just the two of us. You – and me…

Virginia I'm warning you! Touch me, and I'll tear your eyes out…

Simon smothers her with a forceful kiss. She resists, pulls away, spits in his face

(*shouting*) Bastard!

Simon Bitch!

Virginia Son of a bitch!

Simon You bit my lip! There's blood.

Virginia I'll do it again if you try to kiss me like that!

She flinches, as he grabs at her

Simon (*angrily*) Isn't it what you want, Virginia? Isn't it what you've always wanted?

Virginia ~~(spits at him again, shouting) Fag! Pervert!~~

Simon hits her across the face. Crying out in pain, Virginia reels across the room, knocking into furniture as she goes

Simon pursues her. There is a violent physical struggle between them

(*shouting*) Bastard! You dare to hit me…!

Simon (*grabbing her*) Love me, Virginia!

Virginia (*shouting*) Get away from me!

Simon (*holding her tightly, with menace*) I said – love me…!

Virginia (*shouting out*) No…!

Simon hits her again, knocking her against more furniture

(*half-sobbing*) My dress. Look what you've done to my dress. (*shouting*) You've torn it!

Simon (*a bland, deep-throated voice from the dead*) Love… me…

Virginia (*looking up at him, in terror*) Oh God! Oh God, Simon – look at you…

Tears streaming down her face, she flinches nervously as Simon closes in on her

No… No, Simon. Don't let me die. Please don't let me die…

Simon's breathing is close as he pulls her to him

No Simon! Can't you see what's happening to you? (*voice low*) It's this room, Simon. ~~It's The Chapel.~~ (*a whisper*) They're using you to kill me. They want to kill us both…

Simon (*voice from the dead*) Love me… (*He tightens his grip on her neck*)

Virginia (*sobbing*) Don't let them do this to us, Simon. In the name of God, don't let them…

Simon (*a whispered voice from the dead*) Love me… Vir-…ginia…

Virginia (*sobbing*) No…

Their lips meet

When they finally part again, Virginia finds herself staring at Simon. She is puzzled and confused

(*softly*) You? Is it – really you?

They kiss again

(*puzzled*) George? (*She suddenly throws her arms around him. A loud triumphant shout*) George…!

Blast in the old laughing record, gradually lose

Long pause

It is early the next morning

The room is in complete disorder: furniture has been toppled over, the bed has been toppled over, the bed pulled away from the wall, gramophone records are scattered around the floor, and the table has been moved to a different position, with tape spools spinning wildly

Most important of all, however, is Simon's sketched portrait of George Preston, still pinned to the wall in background, but torn right down the centre, leaving only one half of the charcoal sketch intact

Fade in Mother, on the landing outside, knocking furiously on the door

Mother (*off, calling*) Mr Elliot! Mr Elliot! (*banging on door*) Young man, are you in there?

Simon (*sitting up in bed, calls back*) What d'you want?

Mother Open the door, please. I want to talk to you.

Simon (*jumping out of bed*) You'll have to wait. I've got no clothes on. (*putting on jeans*) What d'you want?

Mother (*coldly*) My daughter didn't sleep in her room last night.

Simon (*going to door*) What d'you want me to do about it? (*talking through door*) Maybe she couldn't sleep?

Mother I should think not. With all that noise that was going on up here.

Simon Sorry about that. I was listening to a few tapes.

Mother Mr Elliot. *Where* is my daughter?

Simon Maybe she went for a walk in the park.

Mother The park! D'you know what time it is? It's only eight-thirty in the morning. That girl will drive me into an early grave.

Simon (*voice low*) Bit late for that.

Mother What was that?

Simon I said, try the park!

Silence

(*He puts his ear to the door*) Mrs Whitman? Are you there?

Mother I'm warning you, young man. If I don't find my daughter, I'll be back. (*She disappears down the stairs*)

Simon waits for her to go, then goes to the table, turns off the tape-recorder

Pause

Simon Doesn't miss a trick, does she?

Virginia (*rustle of bed sheets*) You'd better get some clothes on.

Simon Seen all you want, have you?

Virginia (*snapping*) Now look, sonny boy! It wasn't my idea to go to bed with a – [well,] with someone ~~who gets the big turn-off every time he's even touched by a woman!~~

Simon (*awkwardly*) I'm sorry. I'm sorry for what happened. What more can I say?

Virginia Oh, I'm not complaining. Actually, it was quite a pleasant surprise. I mean, I didn't even know you could... One thing you have to say for the dead. At least they have a sense of humour! (*She gets out of bed, goes to him*) Simon? Are you all right ~~now~~?

Simon (*awkwardly*) Yes. I'm all right.

Virginia Sure?

Simon Of course I'm bloody sure! What d'you expect me to say?

Virginia Well, how am I expected to know? It may not have occurred to you, but you very nearly killed me last night.

Simon The man you slept with was your own husband, not me. My ~~entire~~ personality was dominated by an alien force.

Virginia I know that.

Pause

Simon How do you know?

Virginia ~~Because George Preston was the most sexually aggressive man I ever knew. It was the only way he could reach satisfaction.~~ [I remember what George Preston was like as a lover.]

~~**Simon** Mrs Preston. I'm not interested in how you get your sexual kicks.~~

Virginia ~~No? Then take a look at this, bubby boy! Go on! Take a good look. Where d'you think I got these bruises from, huh? (showing him her arms, legs etc.) Here! And here! And here!~~ Last night, it was as though George himself had come back from the dead, and was lying right there beside me. It was his eyes that were staring at me with contempt, a feeling of complete domination. (*voice lowered*) Is it possible, Simon? Is it really possible?

Simon is staring at her

What are you staring at?

Simon (*strangely*) You have a beautiful body.

Pause

Virginia (*uneasily*) Pass me my ~~skirt~~ [dress], please. I'm getting cold.

He does so

Thanks. (*She nervously grabs the skirt, continues dressing. Whilst dressing*) You know, for a time last night, I really was convinced you were going to kill me.

Simon (*genuinely shocked*) Kill you?

Virginia You're lucky I didn't drop down dead at your feet. I have a heart condition, you know. The slightest shock and –

Simon Mrs Preston. What [exactly] happened in this room last night?

Virginia (*stops dressing*) Huh?

Simon I want you to tell me everything, exactly as you remember it.

Virginia You mean – you don't know?

Simon The last thing I remember is sitting at that table, with the two of us talking into the tape-recorder. From then on, my mind is a complete blank.

Pause

Virginia [Dear God!] I hardly know where to start. It was ~~so extraordinary~~ [such a nightmare].

~~**Simon** In what way?~~

Virginia Your voice and personality seemed to change. You became older. An older man. Just like George.

Simon Go on.

Virginia At first, I didn't realise what was happening. But when you started the Bible-punching…

Simon Bible-punching?

Virginia Reciting from the Bible was *George's* way of trying to save me from eternal damnation. (*amused*) He needn't have bothered. I sold myself to the devil a long time ago.

~~Pause~~

~~Simon D'you mind if I take a wash?~~

~~Virginia Go right ahead. There's hot water in the bathroom downstairs.~~

~~Simon (*background*) No, thanks. This'll do fine.~~

~~He pours water from jug into basin~~

~~Virginia Would you like some breakfast?~~

~~Simon (*washing*) I never eat breakfast.~~

~~Virginia Naughty boy. Breakfast is the most important meal of the day, you know. How about some coffee?~~

Simon Mrs Preston. Why didn't I kill you last night?

Virginia ~~Huh?~~ [What?]

Simon You said there was a moment when you were convinced I was going to kill you.

Virginia That's right.

Simon They why didn't I? What stopped me?

Virginia What stopped you? How should I know what stopped you! You just suddenly went all – ~~peculiar~~ [well – strange]. And then you kissed me.

Simon (*stops washing*) Kissed you?

Virginia Uh huh.

Simon Jesus!

Virginia Well, thanks a lot! (*going to him*) If I'd known it was going to be such an effort for you, ~~I'd have grown a moustache!~~

Simon ~~Don't be so bloody facetious!~~ [Oh shut up!]

Virginia (*shouting*) Well, what d'you expect, for ~~Christ's sake~~ [God's sake]! D'you think I enjoyed what you did to me last night?

Simon I wouldn't be at all surprised! [(*awkwardly*) I – I'm sorry. I shouldn't have said that!]

~~Virginia slaps his face~~

Pause

Virginia ~~(*awkwardly*) I – I'm sorry. I shouldn't have done that.~~ Oh, Simon. Why won't you tell me what you want me to do.

Pause

Simon I want the truth, Mrs Preston.

Virginia The truth?

Simon About what really happened in this room, on the night your husband murdered Jonathan Curtis.

Virginia gasps. She has suddenly noticed the torn sketch of George's face

What is it? What are you looking at?

Virginia The picture. That sketch you drew of George. Look at it! (*going to it*) It's torn in half, from top to bottom, right down the centre – right through the face. Just one eye, staring at us… (*shivers*)

No reaction from Simon

Simon, look at it! (*pause*) Why won't you look? (*pause*) Did – you do this? (*going to him*) Simon, answer me! Did you tear that picture?

Simon (*turning away*) I don't know!

Virginia What d'you mean, you don't know? You must know!

Simon (*drying himself*) I keep telling you! I don't remember a thing that happened to me last night. Every time I try to see what happened I find myself wandering in a desert, a bleak dark wilderness. I can't see – anything. I can only hear a voice. A voice urging me to do something. (*pause*) He won't forgive you, Mrs Preston. George will never forgive you.

Pause

Virginia ~~(*she flops down into a chair at the table*) I could do with a drink.~~

Simon ~~Sorry. I don't drink liquor.~~

Virginia ~~Neither do I. But I'd still like one.~~

Simon ~~I could offer you a Coke, if that's any use?~~

Virginia ~~Why not? If we have to be decadent, why not go the whole way!~~

Simon ~~(*collecting Coke, mugs, etc.*) I hope you don't mind drinking out of a mug. I have no glasses up here.~~

Virginia ~~Dreadful! You must complain to your landlady.~~

Simon ~~(*returning*) I'll do that.~~

~~*He opens the Coke can, pours two mugs, gives one to Virginia*~~

~~Here.~~

Virginia ~~(*taking mug*) Thanks.~~

Simon ~~Cheers.~~

Virginia ~~To ripe old age. (*calls out*) Did you hear that George?~~

~~*They drink*~~

~~Tell me something.~~ Is it likely to happen again? I mean, will George try to use you to kill me?

Simon If he wants to do that, he could have done it last night.

Virginia Then why didn't he?

Simon I don't know. Anyway, you've never told me why George Preston should *want* to kill you?

Virginia For ~~Christ's sake!~~ [God's sake!] I ~~sent~~ [did send] him to the gallows, ~~didn't I?~~

Simon You still have a conscience about that?

Virginia Of course I have a conscience about it! I loved that man. I never wanted him to die. If it hadn't been for Jonathan, for that boy… Oh, God! How I despised him!

Simon They why did you sleep with him? [Why?]

Virginia You really want to know?

Simon Yes.

Virginia (*gets up, moves to the blocked up window*) He made me feel young again. Pathetic, isn't it?

Simon But at the time, you couldn't have been much more than a young woman yourself.

Virginia I was thirty-two.

Simon Is that old?

Virginia For me it was. When a married woman is flattered by a boy younger than herself, there's no such thing as matrimonial fidelity.

Pause

Simon You know what I think? I think you should sell this house, and get the hell out of here.

Virginia ~~Sell this house?~~ Why?

Simon It might save your life.

Virginia ~~You think so? You really think so?~~ (*smiles*) ~~Then you are wrong.~~ [No.] There's not a place in the world I could run to. Wherever I went, George would always be waiting for me.

Simon Then why try to get rid of him?

Virginia I don't want to get rid of him! Can't you understand? I need George now more than I ever did when he was alive. I just want him to give me the chance to tell him so. (*She moves around*) You know, soon after George's execution, there were times when I was convinced I could actually see him up here in The Chapel. I tried desperately to remember all the little things he used to do, where he'd sit, how he'd be looking at me. I spent hours staring at his favourite chair over there, determined to prove to myself that I was psychic, and that I could actually see him sitting there. (*sighs*) But I never could. (*pause*) D'you suppose it's always like that when someone dies?

Simon Could be.

Virginia (*at the bedside table*) That's odd. (*She picks up a packet of cigarettes*) I thought you said you didn't smoke?

Simon I don't.

Virginia Then where did this packet of French cigarettes come from?

Simon (*looking*) I've no idea.

Virginia They're the same brand that Jonathan used to smoke.

Simon (*sits at the table*) Mrs Preston. On the night of the murder, how did your husband know you were up here in this room, making love ~~with~~ [to] Jonathan Curtis?

Virginia (*vaguely*) I don't know. I've never known.

~~**Simon** You mean, it never came out in evidence during the trial.~~

~~**Virginia** Perhaps it did, but I don't remember.~~

Simon Isn't it possible someone could have told him?

Virginia I don't see how. Nobody knew.

Simon You're quite sure about that?

Virginia Of course I'm sure!

Simon Why?

Virginia Why? Because Jonathan and I were always careful enough not to be seen together.

Simon Not once?

Virginia Not once.

Simon Not in all the time you'd known him? What was it, eighteen months or so?

Virginia The only time Jonathan Curtis ever came to this house was on Wednesday evening. That was when George always spent the night in Birmingham, on his weekly business trip.

Simon But he wasn't in Birmingham *that* night.

Virginia Oh, but he was. Or at least, he was for part of the time.

Simon What d'you mean?

Virginia I telephoned George at his hotel. Must have been about six-thirty that evening. It was one of those cosy little ~~matrimonial~~ rituals that husbands and wives can't do without. Anyway, as soon as I heard George's voice at the other end, I knew the coast was clear. (*pause*) Jonathan arrived soon after seven, and we had dinner together. (*She moves around*) It was a strange evening. Jonathan was never the easiest person to be with at the best of times. His head was always too full of politics, and nasty jibes about my rich American background. And he hated to be argued with. If I ever tried to answer back, he'd just turn away and sing that same ridiculous tune, over and over again:

(*sings*) "Ha! Ha! Ha! You and me,

Little Brown Jug don't I love thee;

Ha! Ha! Ha! You and me,

Little Brown Jug don't I love thee."

Oh God, how he irritated me! I only ever wanted him for one thing. And he knew it. (*pause*) But that night – it was different. The whole evening, he flattered me. For the first time. I felt like a woman any man would desire. Oh boy! My ego never had it so good! (*pause*) But then, I became suspicious. Jonathan asked if he could come up here to this room, to The Chapel. I wanted to know why. But he said he was just curious, because this was one room in the house that he'd never seen before. He was lying, of course. Coming up here to George's own private lair was a challenge. The idea excited him. (*She sits on the edge of the bed*)

Simon (*gets up, puts on his shirt*) Are you quite sure no one ever saw you and Jonathan alone together?

Virginia Never.

Simon What about your mother?

Virginia Oh, she'd seen us a couple of times. But only when George was around. Actually, my mother quite liked Jonathan. I once caught them having a little *tête-à-tête* together. White rum and Coke!

Simon (*in background*) What about the night of the murder? Surely your mother must have heard something going on up here?

Virginia ~~No, not at all.~~ She was in Cambridge. Mother always spends Wednesdays and Thursdays in Cambridge. She has an old school chum up there. They brew a witches' cauldron together.

Simon You and your mother are not really the best of friends, are you?

Virginia My mother hates me. She's always hated me. Ever since my father died and left everything to me, she's tried hard to make me believe that my mind is unbalanced. When I was a child, she used to stand outside my bedroom door at night, and make weird tapping sounds. I was terrified of the dark, and convinced it was the dead who'd come to carry me off to the graveyard. (*smiles*) You wonder I'm neurotic?

Simon has disappeared into the Ironing Room

Simon?

Simon (*calls, off*) I'm in the Ironing Room. Where does this door lead to?

Virginia The landing outside. At the top of the stairs. Why?

Simon It's locked. (*trying door, off*)

Virginia I know it is. It has been for years.

Simon Do you have the key?

Virginia As far as I know, there's never been a key. At least there hasn't been since George and I moved here.

Simon (*coming back*) But during the trial, it was stated that, on the night your husband found you and Jonathan Curtis together in this room, he entered through the Ironing Room door. (*approaching*) How could he have done that, Mrs Preston, if there was no key?

Virginia I don't know how he did it. He must have [Perhaps George] had a key without telling me anything about it.

Pause

Simon I see.

He goes to the table, starts to rewind the recorder tape

Virginia What are you doing?

Simon I'm rewinding the tape.

Virginia What for? Don't you believe anything I've told you?

Simon Yes, Mrs Preston. Unfortunately, I do. But there are too many things that don't add up.

Virginia What d'you mean?

Simon I mean that if George Preston wanted to use me to kill you last night, he could have done so without any trouble at all. So what stopped him?

Virginia How do you know he won't try again?

Simon I don't know. But maybe the tape does.

Tape is now rewound

What we hear now is part of a recording of Virginia and Simon's conversation from the night before

Virginia (*tape; shouting*) For Christ's sake, Simon! What's wrong with you? What do you want of me?

Simon (*tape; still in his 'other' voice*) What do I want?

He draws closer, pinning her back to the door

(*his voice soft and intimate*) I want you, Virginia. I want love. Your love…

Virginia (*tape*) I'm warning you. Keep away from me…!

In tape background, we hear the eerie sound of a man's laughter, deep and resonant, a slowed down tape speed

Simon, what's that? That voice [laugh] in the background!

Simon Listen!

Simon (*tape*) They say that when a man drowns, he can see his whole life laid out before him. That's how it is with me now. Everything is so clear. I can see you – and me, Virginia. I can see our whole life together. (*closer*) Just the two of us. You – and me…

Virginia (*tape*) I'm warning you! Touch me, and I'll tear your eyes out…

Simon smothers her with a forceful kiss

During which, we again hear the eerie slowed down laughter in tape background

Oh my God! There it is again…! (*tape*; *shouting*) Bastard!

Simon (*tape*) Bitch!

Virginia (*tape*) Son of a bitch!

Simon (*tape*) You bit my lip! There's blood.

Virginia (*tape*) I'll do it again if you try to kiss me like that!

Eerie tape laughter becoming louder

She flinches, as he grabs at her

Simon (*tape*; *angrily*) Isn't it what you want, Virginia? Isn't it what you've always wanted?

~~**Virginia** (*tape*; *spits at him again, shouting*) Fag! Pervert!~~

Eerie tape laughter builds to a crescendo

(*shouting out*) No, Simon! No…! Turn it off! For God's sake, turn it off…!

The tape seems to speed out of control

(*tape*; *shouting*) Bastard!

Simon (*tape*) Bitch!

Virginia (*tape*) Son of a bitch!

Eerie laughter

(*backing away, shouting out*) Turn it off…!

(*tape*; *shouting*) Bastard!

Simon (*tape*) Bitch!

Virginia (*tape*) Son of a bitch!

And so on, with distorted tape voices becoming faster and faster, eerie laughter to a pitch

Simon turns off the tape-recorder

Simon It's all right, Mrs Preston. There's nothing to worry about.

Virginia What d'you mean there's nothing to worry about! Didn't you hear that voice in the background laughing at us?

Simon I heard it.

Virginia There were only two people in this room last night. You – and me!

Simon I know that! In psychical research, it's not unusual for a tape-recorder to pick up the sound of an alien voice.

Virginia But this was the voice of someone we couldn't see [or hear at the time]. Someone who was right here in this room, watching [us], laughing at us!

Simon Did you recognise the voice?

Virginia ~~I don't know. The recording was too distorted. But~~ that was George's laugh all right. It must have been.

Simon is at the tape switch again

What are you doing?

Simon I want to hear the rest of the tape.

Virginia (*rushing back to him*) No, Simon! I couldn't take another minute of it!

Simon (*trying tape switch*) That's odd. The tape spools are jammed. (*switch not moving*) They won't move. Mrs Preston. Would you check the plug in the wall over there for me, please.

Virginia (*moving*) Where is it?

Simon Just by the door. Can you see it?

Virginia (*in background*) Got it!

Simon Is it plugged in?

Virginia Yes. It's plugged in all right. And it's switched on.

Simon I don't understand. There's no electronic power coming through…

Mother's voice calls from downstairs

Mother (*off*) Virginia? Are you up there?

Virginia (*voice lowered*) Mother! She's back.

Simon You'd better go.

Mother (*off*) Virginia?

Simon (*calls*) She's not here, Mrs Whitman.

Mother (*off*) I heard voices up there!

Simon (*calls*) It was the tape recorder, Mrs Whitman!

Virginia ~~(*trying door*) The door's locked. I don't have the key.~~

Simon ~~Here. (*unlocks door*)~~

Virginia ~~I'll see you later…~~

Simon Mrs Preston. ~~Before you go. Just one question.~~

Virginia Yes?

Simon Can you remember at what time of night the murder of Jonathan Curtis took place in this room?

Virginia What time? I don't know. I can't remember.

Simon (*with urgency*) Try hard, please!

Virginia (*flustered*) I don't know, I tell you. Soon after eleven p.m. I think it was.

Mother (*off, impatiently*) Virginia!

Simon The exact time, please. It's important.

Pause

Virginia It was ten minutes after eleven.

Simon Ten past eleven. And can you remember what clothes you were wearing at the time?

Virginia Huh?

Mother (*calls*) Virginia! Are you up there?

Simon (*with urgency*) What were you wearing, Mrs Preston?

Virginia I – I don't remember. An ordinary black cocktail dress I think…

Simon D'you still have it?

Virginia No. The police used it for evidence during the trial. There were blood stains…

Simon Could you wear something like it, and come back here tonight?

Virginia What! Are you kidding?

Simon (*close, and urgent*) Mrs Preston. The only way we're going to communicate with your husband, is to make that night happen all over again – exactly the same as it was at the time Jonathan Curtis was murdered!

Virginia No! I won't do it! I can't…!

Mother (*calls*) Virginia!

Simon Will you trust me, Mrs Preston? Will you?

Virginia After what happened here last night, I'll never [I don't think I can] trust anyone again!

Simon This is your only chance, Mrs Preston. The last chance! I could walk out of that door now, and keep away from you for the rest of your life. But believe me, it wouldn't solve anything. Sooner or later, George Preston would find someone else to kill you.

Mother (*calls off, losing patience*) I'm coming up there, Virginia!

Simon Eleven o'clock tonight, Mrs Preston. Will you do it?

Virginia I'll be here. [(*trying the door*) The door, it's locked. I don't have a key.]

Simon Here. (*unlocks door*)

She opens the door

Virginia Oh God. Can I really trust you? [Can I?]

She goes, door

Virginia rushes down the stairs off

Pause

Simon goes to the table, takes a cigarette, and lights it. He exhales

Simon (*reciting [talking] to himself*)
    "My wife and I lived all alone,
    In a little log hut we called our own.
    She loved beer, and I loved rum,
    And oh we had a lot of fun…"

He exhales smoke again

Bursts into song

    "Ha! Ha! Ha! You and me,
    Little Brown Jug don't I love thee?
    Ha! Ha! Ha! He! He! He!,
    Little Brown Jug don't I love thee…

Slow fade

Pause

Later that evening, eleven o'clock at night

Knocking on door, off

    (*calls*) Just a minute!

After a pause, Simon goes to the door, unlocks, opens it

356

Virginia is there, wearing the black cocktail dress. She's been drinking

Thank you for coming.

Virginia enters. Simon closes the door

I wasn't at all sure you would. (*pause*) You look great. (*awkwardly*) The dress I mean.

Virginia (*ignoring him, looking around*) What's all this for? The white adhesive tape.

Simon I went out and bought a reel of it this afternoon— at your little shop just around the corner. I charged it to your account. I hope you don't mind?

Virginia (*moving around*) Chalk marks all over the walls... arrows on the floor... You've taped everything down. Even the ash-trays?

Simon Just a precaution, that's all.

Virginia Precaution?

Simon In case the action gets a little too lively! (*moving away*) Will you excuse me for a minute, please? I want to tape up the sides of the door.

Virginia watches him as he goes to the door, locks it, tapes up the edges

Virginia Tell me. Is all this to prevent something from getting in, or to stop it from getting out?

Simon (*turning, with a smile*) You never can tell. [Who knows. Oh,] There's a pair of scissors on the table over there. Could you pass them to me, please?

Virginia finds the scissors, takes them to him

Thanks.

He cuts the tape

Virginia Simon. What were you and my mother talking about this afternoon?

Simon Your mother?

Virginia Oh come on! I know she came up to this room, because I saw her. What was the price of admission? A white rum and Coke? That's usually her style.

Simon As a matter of fact, we had afternoon tea and cakes.

Virginia (*coldly*) Really? What did she make the tea with? Sulphuric acid?

Simon She wanted to talk about you.

Virginia (*laughs*) I bet!

Simon You know, I think you've got your mother all wrong. She just wants to help you, that's all.

Virginia My oh my! I have a sweet little grey-haired old lady for a mother, and nobody told me. Well, I'm warning you buddy boy. My mother eats [people] pretty young things like you for dessert. It was like that with Jonathan, and she'll do the same to you. So beware!

Pause

Simon I thought you said you didn't drink? [You've been drinking, haven't you?]

Virginia I don't. But if I'm to spend the rest of the night locked up in here with Jack the Ripper I need fortification!

Simon What are you so afraid of, Mrs Preston?

Virginia Afraid! Me? (*roars with laughter*)

Simon Why are you so jealous of your mother?

Virginia Am I?

Simon She knows it. It hurts.

Virginia Oh boy! Has she done a good job on you! And what exactly am I supposed to be jealous of?

Simon I don't know.

Virginia Maybe she's better in bed than I am. You should try her some time. I'm sure Mama has one or two quaint variations on a theme!

Simon (*he would like to answer her, but thinks better of it*) What time is it, please?

Virginia (*holding out her wrist*) Here's my watch. Help yourself.

Simon (*looking at watch*) It's just after eleven. We'd better get started.

He starts to busy himself

Virginia Haven't you forgotten something?

Simon What's that?

Virginia The stained glass window up there in the ceiling. Aren't you going to seal that up too?

Simon It won't be necessary.

Virginia (*looking upwards*) I can see the new moon. Just my luck to see it through glass…

Simon (*briskly*) Mrs Preston. We haven't much time. Would you come over here to the table please?

Virginia (*she goes to him obediently, saluting*) Present and correct, sir! What d'you want me to do?

Simon Take this piece of cord, and tie my wrists behind my back.

Virginia Huh! You're kidding?

Simon I know what I'm doing, Mrs Preston! Believe me, this is for your protection, just as much as my own. Now, do as I say, please.

Virginia (*specially*) OK. If that's the way you want it.

She ties his wrists behind his back

Simon Make the knot as tight as you can. No… more than that… it's too loose… (*He flinches, as she makes the knot really tight*) …That's it!

Virginia If you ask me, this whole idea is absolutely crazy! What are you trying to do anyway?

Simon Whatever energy has been retained in this room has to be fought on its own ground.

Virginia Energy? D'you mean – a poltergeist?

Simon I mean a violent psychic force, [(*scared*)] which can manifest itself in a living form. And if that form should happen to be me…

Virginia (*panicking*) Jesus Christ! [Then,] I was right, wasn't I? George is going to try again. He's going to use you to kill me.

Simon You're perfectly safe, Mrs Preston.

Virginia Safe!

Simon As long as you obey my instructions, no harm will come to you. There's another piece of cord on the table. Now, I'm going to sit down, and I want you to bind my hands to the back of the chair. But hurry, please! We don't have much time left.

He sits at the table. Virginia quickly binds his hands to the back of the chair

Virginia It's crazy! Absolutely crazy! I must have been out of my mind bringing you to this house… There! (*ties knot*) Get out of that if you can!

Simon What time is it now?

Virginia What again?

Simon The time, please!

Virginia OK! OK! It's, er… (*straining to look at her watch*) …five minutes after eleven. At least, I think it is…

Simon Right! Take your position, please.

Virginia Huh? What?

Simon Mrs Preston. On the night your husband murdered Jonathan Curtis, at the precise moment that murder took place, where in this room were you positioned?

Virginia You mean – where exactly?

Simon Exactly!

Virginia (*after a pause*) It was… (*pointing*) over there. I was standing just in front of the window that's been blocked up.

Simon Could you go over there, please.

Virginia Why?

Simon Mrs Preston. If you want to make contact with your husband, then you've got to help me reconstruct those last few minutes. Now stop asking questions, and do as I say, please!

Virginia OK! OK! Keep your hair on!

She goes to the blocked up window

(*in background*) It was just about – here.

Simon Were the curtains drawn at the time?

Virginia At the window – yes.

Simon And what about Jonathan? Where was he?

Virginia [(*nervously*)] He was standing… there. Just there. With his back to the Ironing Room curtains. ~~Goddamn you!~~ You're not even looking!

Simon What did you talk about, Mrs Preston? You and Jonathan.

Virginia Talk? Are you joking? (*She moves around, circling the bed*) He wanted to make love. I told him it was a sick idea, that we should go back downstairs to my room. But he wouldn't listen. You see, he'd already made up his mind to humiliate us, both of us – me, and George. Anyway, I tried to get out of the room. But the door was locked. Jonathan had the key. I told him, if he didn't open that door right away, I'd scream the place down! But that just made him laugh even more, and he slammed the window and bolted it! Poor Jonathan. It was such a pathetic, childish humour. He never grew up. Always playing games. (*moving around*) From then on, I got really mad at him. I picked up an ash-tray – and threw it at him! This made him come right on at me. He grabbed hold of my arm, twisted it behind my back, ripped off my dress, and… and practically threw me across the other side of the room. (*She sits on the edge of the bed. Shivers*) For a moment, I was too scared to do anything. I just crouched here on the bed, hardly daring to move. Jonathan didn't say a word. He just glared at me, with a look of absolute hate in his eyes. Oh God, how that boy resented me! Then he started all over again, tried to ridicule everything I said. He accused me of trying to buy my way into bed with him. He taunted me, made me feel cheap and dirty. Son of a bitch! He thought he knew it all. But he knew nothing! (*pause*) It was then that I saw those curtains move. Someone had come in quietly through the Ironing Room entrance. (*pause*) It was George. He was holding a razor in his hand. The open razor he always used to shave with up here in The Chapel. Jonathan didn't see him. I don't think he ever did. Oh God! I should have warned him. But – I couldn't! I just couldn't! (*pause*) It was over so quickly, I hardly realised it had happened at all. All I remember is Jonathan lying there, his eyes ~~bulging out of their sockets~~ staring up at me in agony and disbelief. And that long, silent gash in his throat. Like a river of blood, flooding its banks… (*pause*) What's that smell? (*sniffing*) Something's burning. (*goes to ash-tray*) Simon! There's a cigarette burning in the ash-tray. Simon? Are you listening to me?

Simon doesn't speak, he is sitting on his chair at the table, head drooped forward

~~For Christ's sake!~~ [God almighty!] (*going to him*) ~~This is a fine~~ [What a] time to go to sleep! (*shaking him*) Wake up, will you! Wake up!

She swings with a start, as we hear a gentle tapping on the door, off

What's that? (*rushing to door, calls*) Who is it? Who's there?

Silence

(*listening*) Mother? Is that you?

More tapping sounds

(*shouting angrily*) Answer me, goddamn you!

Silence

(*voice to a whisper*) Suppose… suppose it isn't Mother. Oh my God…! (*She rushes back to Simon, shouting at him angrily*) This is all your fault, you little bastard! (*punching, shaking, pulling him*) Wake up, will you! Wake up! (*Simon doesn't stir*)

Beginning to fear the worst, she bends down to take a closer look at him, gently

Simon? What is it? What's wrong with you…

She leaps with a start, as the window slams in background

~~Jesus!~~

Silence

(*looking around nervously*) George? Is it you? Is it? Oh darling! If you're there, please listen to me. I'm weak, George. I've always been weak. But you're strong. How many times have I tried to tell you that? How many times have I tried to tell you that you're the only one who ever meant anything to me. (*calling out*) Oh, George! Where are you, darling? Why can't I *see* you? When someone you love dies, why can't you *see* them through the dark?

Silence

~~No! (*to herself*) You've got to stop this, Virginia, d'you hear? You've got to stop talking - to yourself. Be practical. Yes! That's the thing to do. What time is it? If only my head was clear... (*straining to look at watch*) Ten afer eleven? It can't be! Bloody watch - stopped again! (*rips the watch off her wrist, shouts out*) Crummy Swiss precision!~~

~~She hurls the watch across the room~~

I've got to find a way out of here. (*moving around*) But how? He's locked the goddamn door!

She goes back to Simon, slaps his face, shakes him

Simon! Wake up, Fairy Queen! Wake up!

Simon doesn't stir

(*shouting out*) For Christ's sake! What am I going to do? (*stumbling around*) There must be another way out somehow! (*pause*) The Ironing Room!

She staggers her way towards the Ironing Room, knocking against furniture as she goes; after she goes in, there is a brief pause

(*piercing screams*) No...!

In his chair, Simon's head jolts with a start. His eyes spring open, and he is staring dead ahead

(*in a state of shock, comes rushing out of the Ironing Room*) No! No! No! No! No! No...!

Simon speaks, but again, he has become possessed of an alien personality

This time, it is the spirit of Jonathan Curtis, a young man, roughly the same age as Simon himself

Simon Virginia? Is that you?

Virginia (*staggering towards him*) You've killed her. You've killed my mother. (*shouts*) Bastard! (*revulsion*) Blood! Look at my hands! (*She shows him her blood-stained hands*)

Simon (*turning away, timidly*) Don't do that, Virginia. You know how I hate the sight of blood.

Virginia Why? Why!

Simon Why did I kill her? Because she talked too much. That's the trouble with old people. They never know when to stop. (*pause*) I warned her so many times, you know.

Virginia (*she circles him, risks a close look into his face*) George? (*a whisper*) Is it you? Is it – really you?

~~**Simon** Cut me loose, Virginia.~~

~~**Virginia** How much did she tell you, George?~~

~~**Simon** Enough.~~

Virginia How much! (*smiles*) Did she talk about money by any chance? My money?

Pause

Simon What's it like to be rich, Virginia?

Virginia silent

Come on now. You were never the one to be so shy about your wealth.

Virginia (*terror*) There's nothing wrong in being rich, George. Capitalism is the foundation of democracy.

~~**Simon** Capitalism? You mean, all for one, and to hell with everyone else!~~

~~**Virginia** (*angrily*) In this world, we all get what we work for!~~

~~**Simon** And how much have you worked for what you've got, Virginia?~~

~~**Virginia** George! Why are you talking to me like this? You know as well as I do, I never had a brass nickel in my pocket until I was eighteen years old. And anyway, since when has it been a sin to inherit wealth?~~

Simon Wealth! The great American Dream!

Virginia (*staring at him, puzzled*) George?

Simon (*rambling on*) The ice-box, the Cadillac, the jumbo-jet, Empire State Building, and the Hollywood bowl. If it's bigger, it must be best. Isn't that right, Virginia?

Virginia This isn't you, George. It can't be…! (*backing nervously*) Who… are you?

Simon Why did you bring him back from Birmingham that night, Virginia? Why did you bring George Preston back here to this very room?

Virginia Jonathan!

Simon You brought him back, because it was your last desperate hope that only his jealously would get him back into bed with you!

Virginia (*shouts*) No…!

Simon He couldn't bear to touch you, could he, Virginia? It was only anger hat ever gave George Preston the courage to make love to you.

Virginia No…!

Simon That's why you telephoned him in Birmingham that night. Yes – *you,* Virginia! That night I was to be the pawn in your neat little game!

Virginia (*at the door*) Let me out of this room! Let me out…!

Simon *You* killed me, Virginia! You killed us both: George – *and* me. And d'you know why? Because the one thing you could never buy – was our love!

Virginia (*shouting*) No…!

She stifles her cry, as once again, we hear the same gentle tapping on the door

(*voice to a whisper*) There's someone on the landing outside. (*calls*) Who is it? Help me. Please help me…!

Simon (*taunting her*) He's come to collect you, Virginia. Why don't you let him in?

Virginia (*nervously*) Come to collect me? What are you talking about?

Simon He's been waiting a long time, Virginia. We *both* have…

More tapping on door

Virginia (*quite suddenly, she bursts into laughter*) You fool! You poor, stupid, misguided fool! (*helpless laughter*) Did you really think you could scare me with your pathetic little tricks? (*approaching*) Did you really think that by killing my mother, you could actually hurt *me*? (*drawing close*) Don't you understand, darling? I wanted her dead. I'd have done it myself years ago if it hadn't been for George, if he hadn't been around to protect her. You see, George and my mother had so much in common, so much to gain by joining forces against me. But it didn't work then, and it won't work now. Poor Mother! I always tried to warn her about the company she keeps. There's no such thing as honour amongst thieves, you know. I remember once, when I was little, Mother told me that she was going to live forever. But she was wrong. Nobody lives forever, Jonathan. Even when they're dead.

Simon (*angrily*) Cut me loose, Virginia!

Virginia Cut me loose? Oh dear, how thoughtless of me. I was forgetting how painful it must be for you, sitting there with your hands tied behind your back. Now what shall I use? (*looking around*) Ah! What shall I use? (*approaching*) Recognise this, darling? (*smiling, brandishing the open razor*) You remember it, don't you, Jonathan? (*close*) It's George's old cut-throat razor…

Simon turns his face from her

(*standing behind him*) Shall I tell you something, darling? There was a reason why I brought you up here to The Chapel that night. It was all a game, Jonathan. Just a game. Only the stakes we were playing for – were your life!

Simon struggling to free himself

No. Don't try to move, darling. I wouldn't want you to hurt those delicate white wrists of yours… (*She bends down, to whisper into his ear*) You see, just before you arrived at the house that night, I telephoned George at his hotel, and told him everything. I told him how I'd been intimidated by this two-bit punk of a kid, who'd gotten into the habit of calling on me every time my husband left the house. I wouldn't be responsible for what might happen. (*pause*) George didn't say a thing. (*smiles*) But I knew he'd taken the bait. Unfortunately, when he did get here, he lost his nerve. Oh, I knew he would. You see, I always had to do everything for him.

Simon You mean, he refused to commit murder for someone he didn't love?

Virginia That's a lie! George *did* love me. He always loved me!

Simon And I tell you he didn't! With that half a million dollars of your tucked away in a New York bank account, all you ever meant to George Preston was a passport to a very secure future…

Virginia slaps his face

(*laughs out loud*) Don't you understand. (*after a pause*) You can't hurt me any more, Virginia. No man can die more than once.

Virginia You're no more use to me, 'Jonathan'. Or George, or Simon – or whoever you are! You're no more use to me now, alive – or dead. (*She is talking to him over his shoulder from behind, holding the razor close to his face*) You know, the last time I used this razor, was on you, 'Jonathan'. Yes, darling. I'm afraid it was me that killed you. It wasn't George. How could it be? ~~It's odd, isn't it? I mean, here we are, back here in The Chapel, just like it was before, just like it was that night.~~ But why didn't he stop me from killing you? I mean, in a sense, that makes George just as guilty as me, doesn't it, Jonathan? Doesn't it? And yet… when they sentenced him to death for a murder he didn't actually commit, he didn't even look at me – not once! He just let them take him to those gallows, and… and…

Tapping sounds on the door again

Simon Open the door, Virginia.

More tapping sounds

   Go on! Open it, if you dare!

Now the tape-recorder turns itself on, groaning voices at low speed

Virginia The tape-recorder! (*for a moment, she listens to the distorted voice, then suddenly breaks in laughter*) Oh, very good, Jonathan! Very good! No one can play like you. No one!

A glass decanter smashes to the floor in background

   (*She shakes with laughter*) Bravo!

Now the knocking on door is repeated, but is heavier, impatient

Simon Let him in, Virginia. Why don't you let him in?

Virginia Because there's no one there! There never has been! (*She leans forward again, to whisper into Simon's ear*) There's no one to see me... now, 'Jonathan'. No one. Not even George...

Simon flinches, as she grabs hold of his hair, holds the razor at his throat

Simon You're wrong! He can see you! George... can see you... (*shouting out*) No...!

But before Virginia can use the razor on Simon, Mother's voice booms out from the other side of the room

Mother Virginia!

Cut all F/X

Virginia swings with a look of horror, to find Mother standing in the curtained entrance to the Ironing Room

Virginia (*in a state of deep shock*) George...!

Mother (*approaching*) Give me the razor, Virginia.

Virginia (*backing*) No...!

Mother (*firmly*) Give it to me!

Pause

Virginia (*she hands over the razor. Rambling*) Don't do it, George, I beg you! Don't kill him. He's not worth it!

Mother Virginia...

Virginia [(*rambling*)] Oh, I know I shouldn't have telephoned you like that. But I couldn't help myself, George. I *wanted* you to love me. I wanted you to love me so much...

Mother Virginia, listen to me. George is dead. Dead, d'you hear?! And you're alive...

Virginia We'll send him away. Yes! That's what we'll do. We'll send him away, and we won't ever have to see him again...

Mother (*taking Virginia in her arms*) Virginia. My poor baby...

Virginia But don't kill him, George. If you kill him, we'll both die. You – and me...

Mother George is dead, Virginia! It's all over, d'you understand. All over.

Long pause

Virginia (*puzzled*) All – over? (*staring at her*) Mother? You're alive!

Mother [Yes, no thanks to this maniac here.] ~~I was the one who telephoned George that night, not you. I knew what was going on between you and that boy, and I had to do something about it!~~

Virginia (*confused*) *You* telephoned George?

Mother Jonathan Curtis wanted everything he could get out of you, but I was determined not to let him get away with! Oh, not because I wanted your money, Virginia. The money your father left you is yours. (*wistfully*) You see, I was never a real wife to him. I never did anything to earn his love, so why should he care what the hell happened to me after he was gone? He must have hated me so much. But you know, he never actually told me so. It's odd, isn't it? How people can't actually tell you what they think of you until after they're dead. (*She turns to glare at Simon*) But I was not prepared to allow that boy to get away with anything! I'd have killed him with my own hands first! (*the razor pointing towards Simon*) It would have been so easy…

Virginia But it's not true. It can't be! Don't you understand, Mother? I killed Jonathan. When George came through that curtain, like you did just now, I… I took the razor from him, and I… I killed Jonathan with my own hands…

Simon (*returning to his normal voice*) No!

Virginia [What?] ~~Jonathan!~~

~~**Mother** Keep away from him!~~

~~**Virginia** Tell her Jonathan! Tell her the truth about that night! Tell her…!~~

Simon (*breathless*) Jonathan Curtis is dead, Mrs Preston. But you didn't kill him.

Virginia Lies!

Simon When George Preston found you in this room with Jonathan that night, he realised for the first time in his life that he couldn't bear to live without you. He took hold of that ~~very~~ razor…

Virginia No!

Simon He took hold of it, and tore into Jonathan's throat, with all the violence that he could only find during the act of love itself!

Virginia No…!

Simon He killed – for you, Mrs Preston. Because he loved you. He still loves you.

Virginia is sobbing

(*puzzled*) It was a feeling of guilt that brought you up to this room night after night. Guilt that made you believe you'd committed a murder you were not responsible for. That's why you brought me to this house. When you saw my photograph in the Colour Supplement magazine, I immediately became your one hope for a link with the past. I even look a bit like Jonathan, don't I? That made it even more likely that I was the one person who could help rid you of your guilt. (*pause*) Mrs Preston. There's a dark side of the mind in every one of us. The trouble is, we none of us know how to use it.

Pause

Virginia (*she is composed again, slowly looks up*) The razor. Give me the razor, Mother.

Mother Virginia? No!

Virginia (*firmly*) Do as I say, Mother. Please. (*pause. Smiling*) I want to cut Simon loose.

Simon (*relief*) That won't be necessary. (*He releases his hands, holds them out in front of him*)

Virginia Simon! Your hands! How did you free them?

Mother (*backing*) Keep away from him, Virginia! He tried to kill me in this room this afternoon.

Simon What happened in this room this afternoon, had nothing to do with me, Mrs Whitman. The spirit of Jonathan Curtis dominated my sub-conscious whenever he chose to do so. He was determined to take his revenge.

Virginia But how do we know he's gone? I mean really gone.

Simon (*moving around*) If you had taken my life with that razor a few minutes ago, Jonathan Curtis would have lived forever. But now, he's gone. And he'll never come back again. George won't let him.

Mother (*moving to door*) I need a drink! If anyone cares to join me, I'll be in my room.

Goes to door, but finds it locked

The door's locked.

Simon (*going to her*) Oh, just a minute, please.

He goes to door, unlocks it

We shan't be needing all this adhesive tape any more. (*rips it off*)

He opens the door for her

There!

Mother Thank you. You know, young man, if I had a son like you, I wouldn't sleep at night. At least I can't say it hasn't been an interesting experience. (*goes*)

Pause

Virginia (*awkwardly*) Well, I guess that's about it.

Simon (*approaching*) If I was you, I'd go and get a good night's sleep. You're going to need it.

Virginia (*looking around*) You know something? I think I'm going to get this room decorated. A coat of paint would make all the difference. Yes, and I'll have that window unblocked again. It needs some light in here! I – I don't suppose you've made any plans yet? I mean, your own personal plans?

Simon If it's all right with you, I'll move out first thing in the morning.

Virginia Oh, there's no rush! I mean, as far as I'm concerned you can stay as long as you want. I mean, nobody ever uses this room. What I'm trying to say is, I – I owe you an awful lot.

Simon I'll be going in the morning, if you don't mind.

Pause

Virginia Oh well… (*moving to door*) I'd better go and see how poor Mother is. That was a nasty gash on her arm, you know. I hope she doesn't have to go to hospital. (*She reaches the door, stops, turns*) Simon. Is it true? I mean, what you said about George? Did he love me? Did he really love me?

Simon I told you, Mrs Preston. He still loves you.

Pause

Virginia And Jonathan? Will he leave me alone from now on?

Simon (*after a pause, smile*) Jonathan's gone, Mrs Preston. You'll never see him again.

Virginia Thank you – Simon.

She opens the door, but to her surprise, it is locked again

That's funny. The door's locked. (*pause*) Did you lock the door again?

Simon doesn't reply

Simon?

Simon gently begins to whistle: "Little Brown Jug"

Simon?

The blocked up window slams in background

Simon?

Simon whistles the tune

(*her voice a whisper, almost too scared to speak*) Simon. No…!

Simon whistles on, behind which we read closing announcements

THE END

Postscript

A nd so there you have them. Three early radio plays of mine, and two serials; all of them seem to have come from a lifetime away. I don't think I have to tell you that these were not the only part of my writing output over the years. Between 1975 and *Dark* in 1978, I wrote two one-hour plays: *Looking Back*, a semi-autobiographical story about an old soldier who kept a traumatic secret from his wife and family about his time spent in the trenches up front during the First World War; and *Jubilee*, a 60-minute play specially commissioned to celebrate the twenty-fifth anniversary of the Coronation of Queen Elizabeth II, starring the late Jack Warner in his last play for radio.

But in 1978 I embarked on what has turned out to be one of the most important assignments of my career. As a tribute to my parents, who were by this time quite elderly, I wrote a full-length 90-minute play for *Saturday Night Theatre* called *The Trains Don't Stop Here Any More*. I presented it as 'a love story for radio', for it was about two people who had never stopped loving each other over more than fifty years of marriage, and who had suffered many heartaches and tribulations during their time together. I received a sackful of the most wonderful letters from listeners, including the actor Rowan Atkinson who wrote a most touching letter of admiration to the then Head of Radio 4, and a letter to John Tydeman from the eminent playwright Tom Stoppard. I had intended to go on with the story, to write a trilogy; but in 1977 my father died and my energy to continue the series ran out.

Therefore, in 1979, in between television writing commitments, I wrote a radio adaptation of H. Rider Haggard's stirring adventure story, *She*, which was the first of my plays to be produced by David Spenser. After that came another highlight in my career when Richard Imison, Head of the BBC Radio Script Unit, asked me to come up with an idea for a gothic thriller for the American film legend, James Stewart, who wanted to play either Frankenstein or Dracula. The BBC had to point out to him that both those dramatisations had already been broadcast, but promised they would try to come up with something else. That's where *Night of the Wolf* came in, my tale of lycanthropy in the fens of Victorian Lincolnshire. Stewart apparently loved the idea, but when the script was finished and the studio booked at Broadcasting House, he became ill and had to leave the cast of the stage play *Harvey*, which he was playing in London at that time. Fortunately, two other well-known film names were also starring on the London stage at the same time and so, with John's quick decisiveness, he managed to acquire the services of Vincent Price and his wife Coral Browne. I will not talk too much here about *Night of the Wolf* as you will have the opportunity to listen to Fantom Films' new CD version of the play with this book. All I will say, however, is that it was an experience I shall not forget in a hurry!

In 1987, with David Spenser's encouragement, I plucked up enough courage to return to the trilogy of plays about my parents and family. The next two full-length 90-minute plays were called *Don't Talk to Me About Kids* and *Down By the Sea*, and both of these were produced with the utmost sensitivity by my friend, David. I think it would be immodest of me to tell you that, when broadcast, both plays received massively high ratings, and once again my postbag was full. Eventually the plays were transmitted as a trilogy on three consecutive Saturday evenings with repeats on the following Monday afternoons. They were then repeated again at a later date. Their overwhelming success prompted a publisher to ask me to write a novelisation of the trilogy, which I did, and once again the response from readers was astonishing. After that, well, I'm sure you know that there have been lots more; but that's for another day, another book!

Before I complete what I have been telling you in between your reading my scripts, and at the risk of sounding too much like an Oscar winner thanking everyone from his agent to his cleaning lady, I would just like to say that I have many people to thank for whatever it is that I have achieved in my writing career – especially during my time writing for radio drama. It would be churlish of me not to mention supporters off-microphone such as Peter Bryant, John Tydeman, Richard Imison, Keith Williams, David Spenser and, from television, Cedric Messina. But I also do not forget the Studio Managers, Production Secretaries, 'Knob Twiddlers', and Sound F/X technicians, all of whom contribute so much to the hard work of getting anything on the air. And I also thank all those artists – famous names, not so famous names, and past members of the BBC Drama Repertory Company – who gave radio drama the dedication and fine reputation it has maintained over the years.

Afterword

Few members of the general public will be aware that, before the mass means of distribution by television, radio or film, dramatists chiefly made their money by the publication of their scripts in print form – through the *printed* rather than the spoken word. In this way they reached out to a much wider audience than could have witnessed their work by a limited run in a theatre. The same applied to composers, whose income largely came from the publication of sheet music.

Of such writers, one thinks especially of George Bernard Shaw, Ibsen, Pinero, Galsworthy and so on; and even of Shakespeare, whose plays were first published in collected form in 1623, though he, alas, received no financial benefit since he had died seven years beforehand! But think back to our schooldays and remember that most of us first encountered Shakespeare's plays on the printed page. Maybe we read his fictions as tales told in story format by such as Charles and Mary Lamb.

Even in the present day a play can be developed in many different forms – it can start life as a radio play which, along with the television play, is generally the most ephemeral form of drama. It is transmitted but once in most cases, though sometimes repeated a few times if it proved popular with the audience – which has been the instance with most of Victor Pemberton's plays published here. Publication gives once ephemeral works a kind of eternal life – for which we are extremely grateful to Fantom Publishing as preservationists.

Among the many radio dramas that have survived in other forms one thinks, for example, of Bill Naughton's *Alfie*, which started life as a radio play and subsequently became a TV play, a stage play, a novel and then a film starring Michael Caine (and there has been a recent remake). Even the long-running *The Mousetrap* by Agatha Christie started out as a radio play – and there are a host of others from *A Voyage Round My Father* to *A Man For All Seasons*.

But here in these pages you have been able to read the fictions as originally written. You, the reader, can become both director and audience. The script is a blueprint for you to work upon. You do your own casting and you design your own scenery. ("The scenery is always better on radio," said the small child!) In any case a radio play on the page can be considered as a novel or short story with the narration omitted – just the dialogue and a few helpful audio hints as to where, when and who.

I hope you have found as much pleasure in living out these stories in your own head as I did in directing them in a Sound Studio. In experiencing a written play you become an active participant rather than a passive member of an audience – and *activity* is always more rewarding in terms of pleasure received. Be entertained, and above all – enjoy!

John Tydeman
March 2010

Also available from

fantom publishing

MARY TAMM

First Generation

THE AUTOBIOGRAPHY

In the 1970s, she travelled the universe aboard the TARDIS... 30 years on, actress Mary Tamm now recounts the story of her own, earthbound, adventures.

Born to Estonian parents in 1950s Bradford, her rise to fame took her from a Northern childhood to life in the fast lane: via TV appearances in *Coronation Street* and *The Girls of Slender Means* to leading roles in feature films – including the cult *Tales that Witness Madness*, and *The Odessa File* which pitched her career into the international arena.

In 1978, Mary became part of essential Saturday night television as she joined the cast of *Doctor Who* alongside Tom Baker, as the superlative Time Lady, Romana!

Packed with recollections and exclusive photographs, this autobiography follows Mary on a journey of self-discovery to her parents' homeland of Estonia, where she finally comes to terms with her true identity...

ISBN 978-1-906263-39-3

Available in paperback and audio from

www.fantomfilms.co.uk

Also available from

fantom publishing

The memoir of *Doctor Who* producer

Barry Letts
1925 – 2009

Foreword by Terrance Dicks • Afterword by Katy Manning

Barry Letts began his screen career as an actor, starring in the Ealing film *Scott of the Antarctic* and TV dramas such as *The Avengers, The Moonstone* and *Gunpowder Guy* in which future *Doctor Who* actor Patrick Troughton took the lead role. In the 1960s he switched to directing, taking the helm of classic shows such as *The Newcomers* and *Z Cars*.

Barry got his first taste of *Doctor Who* in 1967 when he directed the six-part serial *The Enemy of the World*. In 1969, he took over as the show's producer. This was an exciting time for *Doctor Who* – the show had a new lead actor, and was being broadcast in colour for the first time. Barry reveals his memories of this era, talking about his relationship with script editor Terrance Dicks and the show's cast, Jon Pertwee, Katy Manning and Roger Delgado.

Packed with behind-the-scenes gossip, fascinating production detail and witty anecdotes, *Who and Me* recounts Barry Letts' journey from struggling actor to successful producer, and the ups and downs of working on *Doctor Who* during the Jon Pertwee years.

Includes extra material not featured in the audio book

ISBN 978-1-906263-44-7

Available in paperback from

www.fantomfilms.co.uk

DEBORAH WATLING

Daddy's Girl

THE AUTOBIOGRAPHY
written with Paul W.T. Ballard

Daughter of renowned star of stage and screen Jack Watling, Deborah has entertained millions in a career which spans over fifty years.

From her early successes in series such as *The Invisible Man*, *The Power Game* and *Out Of The Unknown*, through to her iconic role as the scream queen Victoria Waterfield in *Doctor Who*, film roles opposite Cliff Richard and David Essex, and as the notorious 'Naughty' Norma in *Danger UXB*, Deborah has endeared herself to a broad spectrum of fans.

For the first time, in her own words, Deborah recalls the highs and lows of working on stage and in front of the camera as well as the behind-the-scenes personal struggles, and reminisces about working with a whole variety of famous acting names, including the late great Patrick Troughton.

Published mid 2010, the autobiography will be released in a standard paperback edition and a special hardback edition limited to only 200 copies. The special edition will be individually numbered and signed by Deborah herself and features an extra photo section featuring over a dozen never before published colour photos from the filming of the 1967 Doctor Who *story* The Abominable Snowmen.

Also contained in the limited edition hardback will be a treatment for a series entitled House of Watling. *This comedy was due to be launched by ITV in the early 1980s and would have seen the whole family playing themselves in a variety of real life situations. This is the first time the full premise will be made available to the public.*

Available from
www.fantomfilms.co.uk